Panic!

UNIX® SYSTEM CRASH DUMP ANALYSIS

CHRIS DRAKE ■ KIMBERLEY BROWN

SunSoft Press
A Prentice Hall Title

The publisher offers discounts on this book when ordered in bulk quantities. For more information, contact: Corporate Sales Department, Prentice Hall PTR, One Lake Street, Upper Saddle River, NJ 07458, Phone: 800-382-3419 or 201-236-7156, Fax 201-236-7141, e-mail: corpsales@prenhall.com

Editorial/production supervision: *Lisa Iarkowski*
Cover designer: *Kimberley Brown*
Cover illustration: *John Churchman*
Buyer: *Alexis R. Heydt*
Acquisitions editors: *Gregory G. Doench / Phyllis Eve Bregman*

10 9 8 7 6 5 4 3 2

ISBN: 0-13-149386-8

SunSoft Press
A Prentice Hall Title

Contents

≡

Part 2 — Advanced Studies

Panic! UNIX System Crash Dump Analysis

Figures

≡

Tables

≡

Code Examples

Acknowledgments

To Nasty Mac (finally).

— Chris Drake

To Mom, Dad, Nanny & Pa, who taught me to explore life and, of course, to Mogli.

— Kimberley Brown

We wish to give special thanks to the following SunService UK engineers for their support, technical input, and abuse: Steve Cumming, Chris Gerhard, Matthew Finch, Bede Seymour, Peter Davies, Steve White, Paul Humphreys, Nick Todd, Jon Bowman, Alex King, Paul Harvey-Smith, Kevin Unthank, Chris Beal, Terry Heatlie, and Gavin Thomas.

Special thanks to Carol Wilhelmy of SunSoft and Clive King from the Department of Computer Science at the University of Wales at Aberystwyth, for extensive proofreading.

We owe thanks to several folks who helped us with facilities and network support, including Gerard Krajenka, Bob Beaudette, Tom Young, Ginger Spory and Scott Woods, all from the SunService Solution Center based in Chelmsford, Massachusetts.

A big thanks goes to Glenn Wickboldt. When we first came up with the idea for *Panic!*, Glenn was the manager who approved the project and kept us going throughout *Panic!*'s infancy.

This book would not have been finished without support — technical, managerial, and emotional — from John Ryan, OS Product Support Manager of the UK Answer Centre, John Sanders, Adrian Cockcroft, Peter van der Linden, Dr. Stragenholm, Keith Bierman, Hal Stern, Tim Marsland, Marty Stewart, and especially Karin Ellison of SunSoft Press. Thank you all!

Finally, a very special thanks to Charles LaBrec and Ken Erickson for writing and customizing **kas**, and allowing us to include **kas** on the *Panic!* CD-ROM.

— Chris and Kimberley

Introduction

You've spent hours pouring over UNIX® vendor specifications and benchmarks. Managers, system administrators and accountants have gone over the various vendors' specs and weighed them against your company's needs and the costs. Finally, everyone agreed and selected the right computer for the right price.

You attended System Administration training courses prior to the system's delivery, giving you time to brush up on your skills, possibly learning some of the intricacies of a newer release of the operating system.

The vendor delivered the system, provided installation assistance, and gave you some additional hints on how to get the most from your system.

Since going online, you have been monitoring the system's performance and following advice from a good performance tuning book. You have fine-tuned your system for optimum performance during the periods of heaviest use and have even found some wins during lighter use.

Combining your programming skills and your system administration experience, you have utilized the **cron** daemon well. Backups are fully automated, system log files are regularly rotated and trimmed, and **/etc/syslog.conf** has been modified to suit your needs. You've programmed your system to nearly maintain itself, while letting you know when it needs your help, thus limiting the amount of time you have to babysit it.

The system has become a well-oiled machine, thanks to all of your time and effort. You've done well and the machine has been running like a champ for quite some time now. The users are happy and management is happy. You can put your feet up on the desk and rest now or move onto your next major project.

The phone rings and you answer. A user says his terminal is dead. As soon as you hang up, you receive another call and another complaint about no response from the computer. Ignoring the next call, you get to the computer console just in time to see the word "Panic" scroll off the top of the screen. Another message says something about "dumping," and now the system appears to be rebooting itself.

What happened?

Computers crash. It's just a fact of life. Depending on the hardware and software involved, some computer systems crash rather frequently, some once in a blue moon, some never. When the computer system in question is running the UNIX operating system, we often refer to the crash as a "panic."

What causes panics? What is happening when you see the "dumping" messages? How can you find the source of these and get the system back online and into working condition? This book answers those questions and many, many more.

What will Panic! teach you?

Ever since UNIX existed, there have been a slowly growing number of people who specialize in the black art of UNIX system crash dump analysis. These folks are able to analyze the postmortem files created when a UNIX system crashes and glean some idea of the cause.

System crash dump analysis is normally something only the gurus handle. Analysis of dumps is usually a trade secret passed on from the senior gurus to the juniors. Few, if any, courses or books exist on the topic. However, as UNIX continues to make its way deeper and deeper into the commercial world, we believe it's time to share some of the tricks of the trade.

Some UNIX gurus will tell you that a book can't be written about this subject. UNIX system crash dump analysis is simply too technical and requires access to the highly coveted and rather expensive UNIX source code. Another argument against a book on this topic is that the kernel, the heart of the UNIX operating system, continues to evolve. How can someone write a book that aims at a moving target?

While we understand these valid points of view, we also see the necessity and desire for general knowledge in this subject area in the UNIX user world as well as in UNIX service and support organizations. True, due to licensing agreements, we cannot show you yesterday's or today's UNIX source code in a compilable format; however, we certainly can get you started in the right direction when it comes to figuring out why your computer decided to suddenly keel over.

How will we do this? Well, for starters, together we will explore some of the files in the **/usr/include** directories. These files, known as "header files," provide great insights into UNIX and are actually the only part of the source tree that is normally provided to users on UNIX systems. We will show you how to interpret the valuable information tucked away in these files and how to use the data there.

In some cases, the demonstrations in this book will quite clearly point you to your system's problem and a solution. When a solution is not immediately obvious, usually due to a need to dive into the source code itself, we show you how to collect the most useful information available, which in turn you can forward to your system vendor. The more detail of the problem you can provide up front, the sooner your vendor can find a solution for you.

In the case of some vendors, once you've collected some system crash dump information, you may find your problem and the solution provided in a customer service newsletter, technical bulletins, or other post-sales support media provided by your vendor. For example, Sun customers may arrange to receive SunSolve™, the SunService™ information databases provided on CD-ROM, which provides this type of problem-and-resolution information along with much more technical data.

So many flavors of UNIX

Since both of us work for Sun Microsystems, this book is based on Sun's Solaris™ 1 and Solaris 2 operating environments. Solaris 1 is based on the implementation of UNIX known as BSD, which was done by the University of California at Berkeley (aka UCB). Solaris 2 is based on AT&T's SVR4 (System V Release 4) implementation. Both of the Solaris operating environments contain much more than just different flavors of the UNIX operating system. They also include OpenWindows™ and many other useful tools.

Even though Solaris is our working base, we both have experience with other flavors of UNIX, and we know that our audience is also working with a wide mix of UNIX, XENIX®, and other UNIX-like operating systems. So, with that in mind, as well as our limitations about not disclosing source, we endeavor to keep this book as generalized as possible while guiding you toward the goal of problem resolution.

The audience

If you are already a UNIX guru, this book might show you a few things you didn't already know, but not much more. Conversely, if you have never heard of UNIX before, you'll probably run into trouble beyond the first few chapters. However, if you have a good working knowledge of UNIX, maybe a couple years as a system administrator or support engineer, this book is for you.

Since we'll be working with SPARC® assembly language and the C programming language, any programming skills you have will be useful while you read this book. However, we understand that not every system administrator is an experienced programmer. We have done our best to help those of you who have yet to gain those skills.

Conventions used

Purely for simplicity, we use the male gender throughout this book. We know that the UNIX world includes people from more than one sex, so please don't take this limitation personally.

When discussing UNIX commands, we use boldface type, for example, when talking about the **adb** command or the **vi** editor.

When discussing kernel variables or symbols, such as *msgbuf* or *panicstr*, or other program variables, we use italics.

When referring to routines by name, we use *()* (parenthesis) after their name and italics again. As an example, we will talk a lot about the *panic()* routine.

When we refer to a directory, filename, or macro filename, such as **/usr/include/sys/vnode.h**, we again use the boldface. It will be quite obvious when we are discussing file names or commands, so we expect you won't get confused.

When referring to assembly instructions such as `sethi` or SPARC processor register such as `%g0`, we use `courier` font.

When demonstrating commands, we show them in a box, using `courier` font. User input is shown in bold. For example:

```
Hiya...   date
Sun Jan  8 19:12:30 GMT 1995
Hiya...   last | head
root      pts/4     s4c-ods       Fri Jan  6 16:29 - 16:31  (00:02)
peterd    pts/4     s4c-ods       Fri Jan  6 16:06 - 16:29  (00:23)
peterd    pts/7     greener       Thu Jan  5 14:36 - 14:36  (00:00)
peterd    pts/4     greener       Thu Jan  5 10:23 - 10:25  (00:02)
kbrown    ftp       zatch.Corp    Wed Jan  4 22:24 - 22:24  (00:00)
kbrown    ftp       zatch.Corp    Wed Jan  4 21:42 - 21:58  (00:15)
kbrown    pts/1     ulysses.East  Mon Jan  2 21:51 - 22:07  (00:15)
kbrown    pts/1     sunryse.East  Sat Dec 31 23:01 - 21:51  (1+22:49)
kbrown    ftp       pasta.UK      Sat Dec 31 22:49 - 22:58  (00:08)
kbrown    ftp       sunryse.East  Sat Dec 31 22:43 - 22:47  (00:04)
Hiya...
```

Also, since we include actual screen dialogs, as shown above, you will see a couple of different shell prompts being used. In the above example, "Hiya..." is the shell prompt.

Occasionally, to make things a bit more obvious, we underline <u>key data</u> in screen output. When we to do this, we point it out to you.

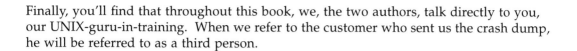

Finally, you'll find that throughout this book, we, the two authors, talk directly to you, our UNIX-guru-in-training. When we refer to the customer who sent us the crash dump, he will be referred to as a third person.

Contacting the authors

If you wish to contact the authors (good news is always welcome!) for any reason, feel free to email:

chris.drake@sun.com

kimberley.brown@sun.com

Welcome to Panic!

This is the first book of its kind that we know of. While we would love to see every system administrator, software engineer, and support specialist who reads it become a system crash dump hacker, we also sincerely hope, and expect, that you'll rarely make practical use of this book and that it will collect dust on your bookshelf. After all, system crashes, no matter how much you know about them, can ruin a perfectly good day!

Ready? Let's get started!

Part 1 — Getting Started

My System Has Crashed!

What is a system crash?

Since the beginning of time, midnight January 1st, 1970 according to UNIX, computer systems have crashed. A system crash often refers to several different conditions where the system has suddenly become useless. These include:

- System panics & bad traps
- Watchdog resets
- Dropping out (to boot PROM or bootstrap level)

In this chapter, we will limit our discussion to panics and bad traps.

What conditions cause panics?

While some folks see panics as horrible things, they really should be seen as system and data integrity safeguards. A good operating system programmer will embed calls to the *panic()* routine throughout his code when checking the integrity of the system resources he is referencing and manipulating.

For example, if the system programmer's section of code is about to free up a block of disk that is known to be in use, he might have his program first verify that the disk is *still* marked as in use. If the block is suddenly found to be marked as free *before* he freed it, then his code should not be freeing it. But how did the block magically become free? Somehow, somewhere, something went terribly wrong. By calling *panic()*, the system programmer can bring the system to a sudden stop, thus safeguarding the system and its data from additional corruption until the problem is found.

panic() can only be called by the operating system while in kernel mode. No user, not even the super-user, whom we will often refer to simply as "root" throughout this book, can actually write an application program that calls *panic()*. However, any program that exercises a bug in the operating system might trigger a panic. For example, if the user's program uses a new device driver that is still being debugged, program execution moves into kernel mode whenever the driver is needed. Once in kernel mode, panics are possible. It may appear to the user that his program panic'ed the system, but in reality, his program only triggered the chain of events that led to the panic.

Simply put, if a system panics, it is really because the operating system detected a condition where the integrity of the data was suspect or the data was in danger of being corrupted.

Let's try this data integrity concept again from a user level programming point of view. If you write a program that opens a file by using the *open()* system call, you will presumably check the return status of *open()* to make sure the desired file was indeed opened successfully before going on to the next step. If the *open()* status shows that an open failure occurred, you will probably have your program report this condition and either exit, prompt the end user for a new filename, or simply take a different course of action. If you open the file and ignore the status returned from the *open()* system call, you are asking for potential problems further down the line. The integrity of your data is at risk.

Does the automobile that you drive have something similar to the *panic()* routine? If it is equipped with air bags, then the answer is yes. When your car senses that something is very wrong, such as the front bumper suddenly being involved in a high-speed collision, chances are good that the air bag will inflate, thus (hopefully) preserving its driver.

As another example, this time from a chef's point of view, how many times does he want to add one pinch of salt to the dish he is preparing? If a chef could use *panic()*, he might use it to prevent someone from adding a second, third, or hundredth pinch of salt that would most certainly ruin the dish. The integrity of his epicurean masterpiece would be protected.

Given a choice, it is better to have more data integrity checks throughout the system code rather than less. Your data is safer in an operating environment that has built in safeguards throughout the code.

Note – Technically speaking, a Solaris 2 system programmer may call *panic()* or he may choose to call the *cmn_err()* routine giving a severity error condition code of *CE_PANIC*. *Cmn_err()* acts as a common, multipurpose, error-handling routine, whereas *panic()* is designed specifically for panic scenarios. In Sun's Solaris 2, both *cmn_err()*, when called with a code of *CE_PANIC*, and *panic()* call *do_panic()*, which in turn calls *setup_panic()* and finally, *complete_panic()*. From this point on, for purposes of simplicity, when we refer to *panic()* we also are talking about *cmn_err()* and other vendors' routines that help to eventually panic the system.

A word about bad traps

A computer system will also crash if it detects a condition in the hardware that should not happen. On UNIX systems, this type of crash is referred to as a "bad trap." From the system administrators' point of view, bad traps and software panics are handled in the same way.

UNIX systems perform millions of traps each day, so please don't panic when you hear the word trap. However, on rare occasion, you may encounter a bad trap. When your UNIX system sees that, it will invoke *panic()*.

Later on, in great detail, we will explore traps; both the expected good traps that occur on your system all day long and the unexpected, unwelcome bad traps.

The panic() routine

Let's talk about how *panic()* actually works. The *panic()* routine abruptly interrupts all normal scheduling of processes. From the user's point of view, the system is suddenly dead.

panic() copies the contents of the memory in use to a dump device. By default, the dump device is usually the primary swap device. It is rare to see a system that specifically has a separate chunk of disk set aside solely for dumps; however, it can be set up that way. On most UNIX systems, the dump device must be a disk partition. On some, a tape drive may be specified.

The dump image is written to the back end or high end of the dump device, unless a tape drive is in use. The beginning and end of this image contain a duplicated header record that includes a special code, called a magic number. The magic number simply identifies the current contents of the dump device as a system crash dump image. The duplication of the header record is used to identify whether the dump image has been partially overwritten by swap activity.

panic() records critical information about the current state of the Central Processing Unit, or CPU, that called *panic()*. This information includes the CPU registers, the stack pointer, and various state registers. We will be looking at these in greater detail later on.

We will talk about how to retrieve the system crash dump image of memory in Chapter 3, when we discuss using the **savecore** command. For now, it is important to note that unless you set aside a special dump device, if for no other reason than being prepared for a panic, your ***primary*** swap device should be large enough to hold a complete image of memory.

Once *panic()* has completed its task of dumping memory to the dump device, it initiates a reboot of the system.

How do you know if your system has panic'ed?

If your system panic'ed and rebooted while no one was witness to it, for example at 4 a.m. on Sunday morning, you may notice that the uptime of the system is not what you

expect it to be. Also, using the **last** command on some UNIX systems, you might see
entries such as:

```
kbrown      console        Thu Jan 20 20:03 - crash
root        /dev/ttya      Wed Jan 19 16:40 - crash
```

These entries are a fairly reliable indication that the system crashed while folks were
logged in.

If you were logged in when the crash occurred, you will find that you are no longer
logged in. If you suspect that the system panic'ed and you have set up your system to
capture system crash dumps, you'll find new entries in the **savecore** directory, assuming
everything went well. If disk space was full, you will not find new dump files. Again,
we will talk about **savecore** in greater detail in Chapter 3.

During a panic, the system no longer functions as expected. Those logged in will get no
response from the system. Those utilizing data via NFS and other network-based data
retrieval systems will no longer have access to that data. Only the person sitting at the
system console will see actual evidence as it happens that the system is panic'ing.

During the panic, the system console displays some information about why the system is
panic'ing. This information alone, however, is only partially useful. The contents of
memory, now being safely stored onto the dump device by the *panic()* routine, will later
be a critical piece of the overall puzzle as to why the panic occurred.

While sitting at the system console during a system panic caused by a bad trap condition,
you will see something like the following.

Figure 1-1   Example of console messages seen during a panic triggered by a bad trap

```
BAD TRAP
sh: Data fault
kernel read fault at addr=0x0, pme=0x0
Sync Error Reg 80<INVALID>
pid=556, pc=0xf000aaa8, sp=0xf0331670, psr=0x4000c4, context=3
g1-g7: 0, 0, ffffff80, 0, f03319e0, 1, ff467800
Begin traceback... sp = f0331670
Called from f0050668, fp=f03317e0, args=f0331844 0 f033184c 0 0 ff35be08
Called from f0093b68, fp=f0331850, args=0 0 1 0 f03318b4 f00c5b70
Called from f00245e4, fp=f03318b8, args=f0331e94 f0331920 0 0 4f074 f00b5218
Called from f0005acc, fp=f0331938, args=f00bc334 f0331eb4 0 f0331e90 fffffffc ffffffff
Called from 13c24, fp=effff678, args=4f074 effff6d8 3a 2f 1 4dc00
End traceback...
panic: Data fault
syncing file systems... done
```

Figure 1-1   Example of console messages seen during a panic triggered by a bad trap

```
1617 static and sysmap kernel pages
  56 dynamic kernel data pages
 168 kernel-pageable pages
   0 segkmap kernel pages
   0 segvn kernel pages
  51 current user process pages
1892 total pages (1892 chunks)
dumping to vp ff1e9d84, offset 116888
rebooting...
```

The panic sequence consists of:

- The actual panic message
- A stack traceback if a bad trap occurred
- Dump messages
- Reboot or reboot attempt

Let's talk about each of these.

Panic messages

Again, depending on the system programmer and the current operation, some panic messages are quite brief, whereas others provide great detail. Sometimes you will see messages that include the name of the calling program, the variables in use, as well as the line number of the source! Others might simply be a cryptic word that only the programmer will easily recognize.

The example above shows that the program **sh**, the Bourne shell, which was running as process ID#556, generated a bad trap. Specifically, the trap was a data fault, in this case an illegal attempt by the kernel to read memory address 0x0. This illegal action triggered the bad trap and panic.

This is an easy panic to force by altering a critical value in the kernel, *rootdir*, while the system is running. Later on, we will cause a similar panic and use it as a practice system crash dump for analysis.

Stack traceback

panic() shows the current stack traceback if a bad trap occurred. This is a history of sorts, showing the hexadecimal addresses of the routines that were called by other routines, working from the most recent kernel routine down to the least recently called, usually a system call or an interrupt handler. Shown along with the addresses of the routines will be the calling parameters used, again in hexadecimal. It won't be until we look at the crash's **savecore** files that we will know which routines were at those addresses and thus in use at the time of the crash.

The stack traceback only goes back to the point where the kernel was most recently entered. A stack traceback will not show the routines in use by the application that made the system call. To find out what application was actually in use, we will examine the user area, executing threads, and process structures.

Dumping messages

When *panic()* writes the contents of memory to the dump device, you will see several messages that describe how the pages of memory were in use, followed by the total number of pages.

This will be followed by a message telling us where the image of memory is being dumped, giving us the pointer to the *vnode* structure, which in turn points us to the device. Later on, we will look at the *vnode* structure in greater detail.

Reboot

Once an image of memory is saved to the dump device, the system will attempt to reboot. Depending on the nature of the panic, the system may reboot without incident and not panic again for hours, months, or years. However, again depending on the problem that initiated the first panic, the system may get in a loop of panic'ing and rebooting until the system administrator intervenes.

Capturing system crash information

It is very important to find out why your system crashed. After all, a system panic means that somewhere something in the system went wrong. There are usually only three ways you can collect system panic or crash information.

First, sometimes you will find information in the **/var/adm/messages*** log files. Second, if you were sitting at the console at the time of the crash, you can try to record as much of the data as you can on paper. However, to capture the best, most complete system crash data, you have to use the **savecore** program, which we will cover shortly.

What is a program crash in comparison?

When running a user program, you might see a message that alerts you to a condition and then announces "core dumped." A program that contains a bug in it might never fail, might stomp on good data, might generate faulty results, or might result in a core dump. It all depends on the nature of the bug in the program.

When the message "core dumped" is displayed, you will usually find a file called **core** in the directory from which the program was executed. This file contains information about the program, allowing the programmer to debug the program and locate the source of trouble. To anyone but the programmer, **core** files are generally not of interest and just eat up disk space. C shell users can use the **limit** command to prevent **core** files from being left behind, as shown below.

Figure 1-2   Limiting the core dump file size in the C shell

```
Hiya 3: limit
cputime          unlimited
filesize         unlimited
datasize         2097148 kbytes
stacksize        8192 kbytes
coredumpsize     unlimited
descriptors      64
memorysize       unlimited
Hiya 4: limit coredumpsize 1 megabyte
Hiya 5: limit
cputime          unlimited
filesize         unlimited
datasize         2097148 kbytes
stacksize        8192 kbytes
coredumpsize     1024 kbytes
descriptors      64
memorysize       unlimited
Hiya 6:
```

In this example, the user has limited the size of program core dumps to one megabyte.

Program core dumps and their **core** files are not to be confused with system crash dumps and their **savecore** files. A thousand users can all be crashing their own programs and the system will still be running like a champ and your data will still be safe... well, unless you are running one of the buggy programs!

≡ *1*

Panic! UNIX System Crash Dump Analysis

My System Is Hung!

System hangs can be a great source of frustration for system administrators. At some time or another, every system administrator has looked at a system and wondered if it was alive, dead, or just incredibly slow. After a few long moments, the admin begins to realize that he has been staring at a "hung" system.

What is a system hang?

System hangs come in all sorts of varieties, but they exhibit one common symptom: the system is no longer completely usable. Unlike panics, which instantly render the system completely unusable, a system hang might slowly eat the system resources, finally resulting in a completely useless system.

What conditions cause hangs?

One common source of system hangs is a deadlock, or a situation wherein one process is waiting for something that is locked up by another process, which is itself waiting for something that the first process owns. Deadlocks can be caused by what is referred to as "race conditions." Put more simply, a race condition occurs when more than one program tries to use a given resource without agreeing on some sort of locking or control mechanisms. For example, if two routines both try to manipulate the same data structure in memory without locking mechanisms, who can predict the results?

Race conditions exist outside of computers. Imagine sharing a bank checking account with ten other people. If you don't agree ahead of time on some sort of rules on how to manage the account, you could soon find yourself with a financial mess on your hands.

System hangs can also occur when resources dry up and the system has to sit around waiting for more resources before it can continue doing what was asked of it. In this case, it would make more sense for the software to report the resource problem to the system administrator, but in some cases this may not have been a predicted scenario, so the code may not have been designed to handle it well, if at all.

Occasionally, system hangs can be caused by hardware problems. For example, if a problem develops with the data transfer cable attached to a disk drive (part of the "bus"), the communication between the system and the disk drive could become so unreliable that the two would no longer be able to work together. The result might be a hung bus, or a system so confused that it gets stuck in a loop trying to do nothing else but communicate with the dysfunctional drive.

How do you know if your system is hung?

Depending on the cause of the hang, some users on the system might be able to continue working while others see the system as dead. On some occasions, you might not be able to remotely log in, with **rlogin**, from another system, but will be able to log in to the system at the console. Some hung systems will respond to low-level network commands such as **ping**, while others will not. Finally, some systems will slow down, creeping toward the hang, giving you, the observant system administrator, a hint of what is to come, while other hangs will appear to be instantaneous.

If the system is hung, you will *not* see panic messages on the console. However, if you are lucky, again depending on the reason for the hang, you might see output on the console that will point you to the source of troubles. The problem could simply be that someone powered down the disks or that an Ethernet cable became disconnected.

Unfortunately, system hangs can also be caused by programming problems or bugs at the system or kernel level.

Unless you immediately locate a simple hardware problem or a rather embarrassed programmer who just discovered the side effects of running his simulation program in real time on a heavily used DBMS server, you will need to attempt to force a system panic in order to get an image of memory for analysis.

What is a program hang in comparison?

Let's say you write a tiny C program that simply loops forever, as this program does.

Code Example 2-1   loop.c

```
main ()
{
  while (1)
  {
  }
}
```

This program will run, happily circling in a while loop, until interrupted by the user or terminated via the UNIX **kill** command.

Now, convert the loop program into a subroutine or function. Write thousands of lines of complex application code and have the new code jump into the little loop subroutine at noon on Thursdays.

You've now created a program that will hang at noon on Thursdays. The application will have to be **kill**'ed. Normal execution is now impossible because you are stuck in that simple little loop.

While the application is hung up in a loop, the rest of the users on the system are doing just fine. A hung program doesn't affect the rest of the system unless it happens to be eating a disk or two or other kernel resources in the process. So, it is very important to remember that if one user calls you and reports that the system is hung, it may not be true. Dig a bit deeper before you force a system panic!

Capturing system hang information

In most cases, a system crash dump of a hung system can be forced. However, this is not guaranteed to work for all system hang conditions.

To force a dump, you need to drop down to the boot PROM monitor, suspending all current program execution. On Sun systems using Sun monitors for the console, this suspension is done via what is referred to as "L1-A." L1 was the label on the earlier Sun keyboards for the top left key on the console keyboard. On the newer keyboards, this key is labelled "Stop." Some keyboards are labelled both ways. While holding down the L1 key, you press the A key. On systems using ASCII terminals for the console, usually the Break key can be used to get to the boot PROM monitor.

Depending on the boot PROM that you have, the boot PROM monitor will respond with:

```
Type b (boot), c (continue), or n (new command mode)
>
```

or:

```
Type 'go' to resume
ok
```

or simply:

```
>
```

If you don't see one these messages, you were probably not successful in stopping the system.

If you find you are at the > prompt, enter **n** to get into the new command mode which will give you the ok prompt. Once at the ok prompt, enter **sync**. The system will immediately panic. Now the hang condition has been converted into a panic, so an image of memory can be collected for later analysis. The system will attempt to reboot after the dump is complete.

If you have an older Sun that doesn't have the new command mode, enter **g0** at the > prompt.

Both the **sync** and the **g0** commands force the computer to illegally use location 0, thus forcing a panic: zero.

Not all hang situations can be interrupted. If L1-A or Break doesn't work, sometimes a series of the same will do the trick. Some hangs are even more stubborn and can only be interrupted by physically disconnecting the console keyboard or terminal from the system for a minute.

If all these attempts fail, you will have to power down the system, thus sadly losing the contents of memory. With luck, a subsequent hang will be interruptible.

Let's move on now to the next step, using the **savecore** program.

The savecore Program   3 ≡

We've already mentioned the **savecore** command and the **savecore** files quite a few times. Now we will talk about them in much greater detail.

What is savecore?

savecore is the command we use to transfer the system crash dump image, generated for us by the *panic()* routine, from the dump device to a file system where we can later access it for analysis.

How does savecore work?

During a system panic, whether forced by the system administrator in response to a system hang or caused by the system, the contents of memory in use at that time are written out to the dump device. When the system is rebooted, **savecore** can be run to retrieve the image from the dump device and archive it to a disk file. Let's examine this process in more detail.

When *panic()* executes, it looks into the kernel for the name of the preselected dump device. By default, the dump device is the primary swap device. However, in certain system configurations, such as when the primary swap partition is smaller than memory, a separate, more adequately sized dump device may be chosen.

panic() places the contents of memory in use at the time of the panic *toward the back end of the dump device*. This little-known fact works to the well-read system administrator's advantage should **savecore** need to be run manually shortly after booting, assuming that swapping hasn't already overwritten any of the image.

During the next boot up of the system, **savecore** may be called. **savecore** is invoked with the name of a preexisting directory where the copy of the image currently held on the dump device is to be saved. We'll refer to that directory as the "**savecore** directory."

Note – Should the **savecore** directory not already exist, **savecore** *will not* create it automatically. Therefore, it must be created prior to calling **savecore**.

---

savecore examines the image stored on the dumpfile device, testing for two conditions.

- The two magic numbers stored in the image on the dumpfile device (one at the beginning of the image, the other at the end) must both match the *DUMP_MAGIC* value defined in **/usr/include/sys/dumphdr.h**, 0x8fac0102 on Sun systems. This dual, magic-number test is used to verify that any swapping activity hasn't yet damaged the dump image.

- The dump must be from the same revision of the operating system that is currently executing.

If these conditions are met, the image of memory (core) will be placed in the **savecore** directory as a file called **vmcore.X**, where *X* is simply a sequence number. A copy of the kernel namelist will be built and also placed in the **savecore** directory. It will be named **unix.X** or **vmunix.X**, depending on the operating system in use.

The sequence number will start with zero. Once **savecore** has been run, a file called **bounds** will exist in the **savecore** directory along with the **savecore** files. The **bounds** file simply contains the sequence number to use for the *next* execution of **savecore**.

If you are interested in learning more about the details of the actual dump file layout on your system, refer to **/usr/include/sys/dumphdr.h**.

Disk space requirement & locations

At boot time, not all of a system's file systems may be **mount**'ed at first. Some system administrators may choose to **mount** certain file systems by hand after the system comes up. When selecting a file system for use with **savecore**, be sure to select a file system that will be **mount**'ed when **savecore** is run.

Depending on the usage of the system, specifically memory, at the time of a panic, the resulting **vmcore.X** file may be quite large. At most, it will be the size of memory. Therefore, the system administrator of a system experiencing frequent panics will need to keep an eye on the disk usage on the file system where the **savecore** files are being stored. If a large server with 512 megabytes of memory panics four times under full usage and load, you could easily find yourself with 2 gigabytes of postmortem files! Archiving the **savecore** files to tape or another disk may be wise. Remember also that the UNIX **compress** command can be very helpful in managing the disk space.

If maintaining a certain availability of disk space on the file system where the **savecore** directory resides is a concern, a file called **minfree** can be placed in the **savecore** directory. This file can be used to specify how much space, in kilobytes, must remain available on the file system once the **savecore** operation is complete.

Note – Early releases of Solaris 1 (SunOS™ 4.X) and Solaris 2 (SunOS 5.X) contained a bug in that the minimum free value was interpreted as being the amount of space, in kilobytes, required to be free *before* **savecore** was run instead of *after*.

Security issues

By default, **savecore** creates the **savecore** files with rather open permissions. This allows any knowledgeable user on the system to read and analyze the files. As you'll soon learn, even a user with few skills will be able to glean some information from the files.

Since the **vmcore.X** file provides the contents of memory at the time of the crash, the data contained in the file may include data that was not intended to be viewed by a wide audience. For example, if, at the time of a panic, someone was manipulating classified data, that data will probably be tucked away somewhere within the **vmcore.X** file. If security is a concern, the system administrator might want to check and tighten the access rights of the **savecore** directory and files.

Generally speaking, the system administrator is the person on the system who has access to most, if not all, of the data on the system. This includes the system crash dump files. However, if he is not trained in system crash dump analysis and needs to rely on the skills of another, less trusted person, it would be wise for him to closely monitor the analysis work performed by that person.

Note – If the system administrator is not trustworthy, security is already at great risk.

Solaris 1: How to set up savecore

Let's talk about how to enable the **savecore** command so that we can capture the image of a system crash. Although the concept is basically the same for both Solaris 1 and 2, there are some subtle differences. Here is the procedure for Solaris 1 systems.

Customizing /etc/rc.local

In Solaris 1, using the BSD-based SunOS 4.X, the **savecore** command is called from the boot-time, run-command script **/etc/rc.local**. By default, the **savecore** commands are commented out, as shown in this partial view of **/etc/rc.local**.

Code Example 3-1   Savecore commented out in /etc/rc.local

```
#
# Default is to not do a savecore
#
# mkdir -p /var/crash/`hostname`
# echo -n 'checking for crash dump... '
# intr savecore /var/crash/`hostname`
# echo ''
```

To enable **savecore** at boot time, the **/etc/rc.local** file needs to be modified so that the **savecore** command is enabled. Be careful not to uncomment the actual comment, which reads "# Default is to not do a savecore". Once modified, this portion of **/etc/rc.local** should read:

Code Example 3-2   Savecore enabled in /etc/rc.local

```
#
# Default is to not do a savecore
#
mkdir -p /var/crash/`hostname`
echo -n 'checking for crash dump... '
intr savecore /var/crash/`hostname`
echo ''
```

This sequence of commands will create a directory in **/var/crash** named after your system's hostname. The "hostname" portion of the command is interpreted to mean: First, run the UNIX **hostname** command, then use the output of that command as part of the **mkdir** command. For example, if your system's name is "maugrim", the resulting command will be:

```
mkdir -p /var/crash/maugrim
```

The **-p** option of **mkdir** says to create the parent directories if they don't already exist.

If you want to use a different **savecore** directory, modify both the **mkdir** command and the **savecore** commands. As an example:

Code Example 3-3   Savecore and the verbose option enabled in /etc/rc.local

```
#
# Default is to not do a savecore
#
mkdir -p /opt/spare/crashes
echo -n 'checking for crash dump... '
intr savecore -v /opt/spare/crashes
echo ''
```

In this example, the **hostname** command is not used at all, as we've specified the full directory name instead. Also, here we've called the **savecore** command with its only option, **-v**, which generates more verbose output when it runs. By default, **savecore** is called without options. You'll notice that we are also calling **savecore** via the **intr** command. Commands run within the **/etc/rc*** scripts are not normally interruptible; however, when called with the **intr** command, they are.

Finally, the two **echo** commands are there simply to print useful information to the console during the boot-up process.

Configuring a special dump device

We've already talked about the dump device and know that the primary swap device is usually used as the dump device. On Solaris 1 systems, it is very easy to specify a dump device other than the swap device. This is done through the system configuration file, on the config line, which describes where your root file system and swap partition exist. For complete details, refer to the man page on **config**(8).

As an example, here are config lines from two system configuration files. The first, shown here, will result in system crash dumps being stored on the swap device,

```
config vmunix swap on sd1b
```

whereas the second, shown below, specifies a dump device different from the swap device.

```
config vmunix swap on sd1b dumps on sd2f
```

If you want to specify a separate dump device, you will need to modify a kernel configuration file, **config** and **make** a new kernel, and boot up the new kernel. Please refer to the appropriate System Administrator's manual for guidance if you aren't already familiar with the procedure to build a new kernel.

Beware! Beware! Beware! Beware!

When specifying a special dump device on any UNIX system, *do not under any circumstances* specify a device that has a file system on it, nor a partition used in raw mode by a database application. Like a swap partition, the dump device knows *nothing* about file systems, superblocks, inodes, and data. During the panic, the contents of memory are written to the dump device without regard for what is being overwritten. Please choose your system crash dump device carefully!

We hope you understand and appreciate the importance of this.

Solaris 2: How to set up savecore

Here is the method for enabling **savecore** in Solaris 2 systems. Note the differences from Solaris 1 as we point them out.

Customizing /etc/rc2.d/S20sysetup

On Solaris 2 systems, the **savecore** command is called by the run-level-2 script **/etc/rc2.d/S20sysetup**, which is hardlinked to **/etc/init.d/sysetup**. By default, **savecore** is commented out, thus disabling it when transitioning to run level 2, as shown in this portion of the script.

Code Example 3-4   Savecore commented out in /etc/rc2.d/S20sysetup

```
##
## Default is to not do a savecore
##
#if [ ! -d /var/crash/`uname -n` ]
```

Code Example 3-4   Savecore commented out in /etc/rc2.d/S20sysetup

```
##
#then mkdir -p /var/crash/`uname -n`
#fi
#                      echo 'checking for crash dump...\c '
#savecore /var/crash/`uname -n`
#                      echo ''
```

To enable the **savecore** command, uncomment this area of the script, as shown.

Code Example 3-5   Savecore enabled in /etc/rc2.d/S20sysetup

```
#
# Default is to not do a savecore
#
if [ ! -d /var/crash/`uname -n` ]
then mkdir -p /var/crash/`uname -n`
fi
                      echo 'checking for crash dump...\c '
savecore /var/crash/`uname -n`
                      echo ''
```

Unlike the Solaris 1 **/etc/rc.local** script, this script first tests for the existence of the **savecore** directory and if the directory is not found, calls **mkdir** to create it. This is done by an **if...then...fi** Bourne shell command sequence. Be careful to uncomment or recomment all portions of this sequence or the script will fail.

Another difference you may note is that the UNIX command **uname -n** is being used. This command is the Solaris 2 equivalent of the Solaris 1 **hostname** command.

Again, if you want to use a different directory for your **savecore** files, change the **if**, **mkdir**, and **savecore** lines accordingly.

Configuring a special dump device

Solaris 2 supports much larger systems than does Solaris 1, allowing for up to 20 CPU modules and massive amounts of memory. In Solaris 2, we also have newer, more advanced swapping techniques. You'll read more about this in the advanced chapters later on.

The Solaris 1 informal and rather crude rule of thumb of having twice as much swap as memory doesn't apply to Solaris 2 systems. Indeed, some of the larger Solaris 2 systems run well with nearly no swap space defined at all!

Solaris 2 systems that have a minimal amount of swap space will need to have some sort of dump device at hand when system crashes occur. As with Solaris 1, you can specify a dump device other than your primary swap device. On the releases of Solaris 2 up to and including Solaris 2.4, this is not quite as easy to do as it was in Solaris 1, however, we will tackle this tricky subject anyway!

Both the *panic()* routine and the **savecore** program need to know where the dump device is located. Therefore, we need to define this before either executes. We cannot predict when *panic()* will run; however, we do know when **savecore** is executed. We need to redefine the name of the *dumpfile*, which is how the kernel refers to the dump device in Solaris 2, before */etc/rc2.d/S20sysetup* is run. To do this, we will create our own script, */etc/rc2.d/S19dumpfile*. The "S" or "Start" run-command scripts are executed in alphabetical order by **init** during run level transitions. Because this is so, we know our **S19dumpfile** script will be run before the **S20sysetup** script, as S19 comes before S20 alphabetically.

Before we can write this script, we need to know where to locate the current *dumpfile* name in the running kernel. Jumping ahead of ourselves, we are going to take a quick peek at the kernel by using the UNIX **adb** command. By the end of this book, you'll be a wizard when it comes to using **adb**, so don't get too worried if this seems a bit scary at first.

You need to be the super-user, root, to view and modify the kernel by using **adb**.

Code Example 3-6   Displaying the dumpfile kernel variable via adb

```
# adb -k /dev/ksyms /dev/mem
physmem  1b24
dumpfile/20X
dumpfile:
dumpfile:   0           0           0           0
            2f646576    2f64736b    2f633074    33643073
            31000000    0           0           0
            0           0           0           0
            0           0           0           0
dumpfile+10/X
dumpfile+0x10:   2f646576
dumpfile+10/s
dumpfile+0x10:   /dev/dsk/c0t3d0s1
$q
#
```

A full 32-bit word of memory can store 4 characters of a string, as a character only requires one byte, 8 bits, of storage. There are 4 bytes per full 32-bit word. Each byte has a unique address in memory; however, using **adb** we write to memory in full and half-words. Throughout this book, we usually reference full-word, hexadecimal addresses, which end in 0, 4, 8, and c.

In the above **adb** session, we start at the kernel symbol or variable name *dumpfile* and display 20 full words of memory in hexadecimal. The first 4 words contain zero. The fifth word contains 2f646576. This is actually the first 4 bytes or characters of the null-terminated string "/dev/dsk/c0t3d0s1."

The *dumpfile* string starts at address *dumpfile+0x10*. The kernel string that we need to modify is actually stored in memory this way:

```
Full word
  address        Characters
-----------------------------
dumpfile+10 = "/dev"
dumpfile+14 = "/dsk"
dumpfile+18 = "/c0t"
dumpfile+1c = "3d0s"
dumpfile+20 = "1"          (The last character is followed by three nulls or zeros)
```

Of these addresses, only the last three might require changing. The first two, representing the /dev/dsk portion of the device name, will not need to be changed.

Note – We do *not* specify a raw disk partition name; however, please remember that, in effect, the dump device is treated as such!

The next important thing for you to know is the hexadecimal values for the ASCII characters you might need to use to identify which dump device you want. You can refer to the **ascii**(5) man page to view the complete ASCII chart.

```
Character    0    1    2    3    4    5    6    7    8    9
Hex value    30   31   32   33   34   35   36   37   38   39

Character    a    b    c    d    e    f    k    s    t    v    /
Hex value    61   62   63   64   65   66   6b   73   74   76   2f
```

Let's have our **S19dumpfile** script change the dump device to **/dev/dsk/c1t2d3s4**. As you learn more about **adb** in later chapters, this will all become clear. Here's our script:

Code Example 3-7   S19dumpfile script

```
:   Automatically executed by the Bourne shell
#
#   S19dumpfile - Change dumpfile name
#
#
echo
echo "Changing dumpfile name to /dev/dsk/c1t2d3s4"
adb -k -w /dev/ksyms /dev/mem << END
dumpfile+18/W 2f633174
dumpfile+1c/W 32643373
dumpfile+20/W 34000000
END
echo "Done changing dumpfile name."
echo
#
#   end of S19dumpfile
#
```

When transitioning into run level 2, **/etc/rc2.d/S19dumpfile** will generate output similar to the following. Your *physmem* size may differ.

```
Changing dumpfile name to /dev/dsk/c1t2d3s7.
physmem 1b24
dumpfile+0x18: 0x2f633174 = 0x2f633174
dumpfile+0x1c: 0x32643373 = 0x32643373
dumpfile+0x20: 0x37000000 = 0x37000000
dumpfile+0x10: /dev/dsk/c1t2d3s7
Done changing dumpfile name.
```

Alternatively, you may have your **S19dumpfile** script write to locations *dumpfile+18* and *dumpfile+1c* by using commands such as the following.

```
dumpfile+18/W  '/c1t'
dumpfile+1c/W  '2d3s'
```

However, take care not to use this method for location *dumpfile+20*, since a null is required at the end of the string. Replace *dumpfile+20* with a hexadecimal value instead, as shown in the earlier example.

In future releases of Solaris 2 and other UNIX systems, the starting location of the *dumpfile* string may differ. Always check before you modify the string. Also, in future releases of Solaris 2, it may become possible to simply set the *dumpfile* string or something similar via the **/etc/system** configuration and tuning file, by specifying, for example:

```
set dumpfilename = "/dev/dsk/c1t2d3s4"
```

and then rebooting the system. However, as of Solaris 2.4, this is not possible.

Shouldn't I copy the kernel first?

This is a good question! However, as you'll come to understand later when we talk about **adb** in greater detail, the **S19dumpfile** script modifies only the contents of **/dev/mem**.

The kernel variable *dumpfile* is initially set to all zeros. During the booting process, the name of the dump device is stored in *dumpfile* in memory, **/dev/mem**. Therefore, we use **adb** to modify **/dev/mem** after *dumpfile* is set.

Swapless systems

Finally, here's one last note for those of you who are administering swapless systems running Solaris 2.0 up through 2.3. Due to a bug, **savecore** will not work unless you have at least a minimal swap space set up. Create a swap partition of at least 8K in size and a custom dumpfile, make the swap space available to the system so that it is accessible to savecore, and all will work!

Our system is now ready to capture a system crash dump image. Let's move on.

≡ *3*

Panic! UNIX System Crash Dump Analysis

Hey! We Got One! 4 ≣

Whether you were expecting it or not, you've discovered that your system has panic'ed. If all went well, **savecore** did its job and there are now system crash dump files in the **savecore** directory for you to analyze. However, not every crash goes so well.

Before we move on to analyzing postmortem files, let's discuss a few other issues regarding system crashes.

What to do when your system has crashed

Depending on the cause of the system crash, the system may not have been able to reboot itself successfully. Cases where this would be true include:

- Catastrophic hardware failure, such as faulty memory or a crashed disk

- Major kernel configuration faults, such as a buggy device driver

- Major kernel tuning errors, such as *maxusers* being much too big

- Data corruption including corruption of the operating system files

- Manual intervention is needed, for example, **fsck** needing answers to its queries

Was the system recently tuned?

If you just tuned your system and tried to reboot under the new kernel and the system panic'ed, you already have a good idea where to start your search for the cause of the panic. If you named your new, untested kernel **/vmunix** on your Solaris 1 system or if you directly edited **/etc/system** on your Solaris 2 system, you will most likely find the system in an endless boot and panic loop. Rebooting the "generic" kernel for Solaris 1 will get the system back up. For a Solaris 2 system in this scenario, you can use **boot -a** and choose **/dev/null** as your **/etc/system** file to return to a generic kernel.

When tuning systems and testing the new kernel changes, it's a good idea not to use **/vmunix** or **/etc/system** until you know the changes are good. Instead, use **/vmunix.test** or **/etc/system.test**, for example. That way, should the system panic, at least the system will have a better chance of coming back up under a known good kernel. This is particularly sound advice if you are planning on going on vacation right after tuning a new kernel and booting it up.

Has anything else changed recently?

If the system had been running beautifully for the past year, suddenly died, and now won't come back up, you will need to read the messages that appear during the boot attempts. Look for messages that might point to hardware trouble. It would be a good idea to check all of the cables for proper connections. Also, make sure all the disk drives and other peripherals are still getting power. If everything seems to be in order, attempt to run diagnostics on the hardware.

On occasion, systems demonstrate sensitivity to their environment. With a workstation sitting on your desk next to your plants and your coffee mug, it's sometimes easy to forget that computers are ultrasensitive electronic devices. Always remember:

- Proper air flow is required for cooling the electronic components.

- If the environment is much too hot for you, it is probably also too hot for your computer. Power down your computer equipment if you expect the air-cooling systems in your area to be shut down.

- Unless protected by an Uninterruptible Power Supply (UPS), your system can suffer damage during electrical storms and interruptions of power.

- Dirt and dust inside some computers can lead to problems over time. Discuss with your vendor whether Preventative Maintenance visits are recommended.

- Unless a system is designed to ruggedized standards, it can be damaged by high vibration and excessive movement.

- Power down all components of the system whenever you need to do hardware repairs, replacements, or rearrangements. Don't, for example, change SCSI devices while the system is running.

- Electrostatic discharge will easily damage your computer. **Never** *touch or let anyone else touch the internal workings of your system without proper ESD protection.*

Is the system still usable?

If the system reboots itself after a panic, chances are good that the system will be usable, if only for a short while. Some panics and crashes will show up once in a blue moon, whereas others, once encountered, will increase in frequency. It all depends on the nature of the crash.

Assuming that the system is usable for now, you can use the system to analyze the **savecore** files that are awaiting you in the **savecore** directory.

If your system is one that serves several users, whether directly or indirectly as a data server, you may want to notify your user base that the system may be going down unexpectedly in the near future. Although not the best of news, it does give the users the option of backing up their work more frequently. For the moment, though, assume that the system is usable.

If you have not backed up your file systems recently, now would be a good time! However, just to be extra safe, use a different set of tapes, in case damage has already been done and you need to revert to the prior set of backups.

Turn off savecore? (How many dumps will you need?)

Once an image of a system crash has been captured, you need to again assess how you are doing on disk space. Do you have room for a subsequent set of **savecore** files should the system crash again? If not, you might want to move the files to another file system for analysis, clearing up space for the next crash. If you don't plan to analyze the files yourself, archive them to tape as soon as possible and free up the disk space.

At this time, the second question you need to ask yourself is whether you really *need* another set of postmortem files? To answer this, you need to consider the recent history of the system's performance. Has it been crashing a lot lately and you've just enabled **savecore** to capture one crash? Have the symptoms of the past crashes been reliably predictable?

For example, if your system crashes only when you boot a certain kernel, you probably only need the one set of savecore files and can disable **savecore** for the time being. If, however, your system has never crashed before, it would be wise to keep **savecore** enabled for now. It is often a good idea to have at least two or more sets of crashes for comparison.

Generally speaking, we feel **savecore** should *always* be enabled and ready to go in case the worst happens and your system decides to panic.

If you choose to maintain the **savecore** files on disk, use the UNIX **compress** command to squeeze them down to a smaller size. This will gain you some disk space. If you've never used **compress** before, here's an example that might convince you of its worth. The following **savecore** files are from a large Sun SPARCcenter 2000 server.

Figure 4-1   Compress your savecore files to save disk space

```
Hiya...  ls -l
total 268154
-rw-rw-rw-   1 kbrown    15          1272308 Sep  1 12:28 unix.0
-rw-rw-rw-   1 kbrown    15        135077888 Sep  1 12:29 vmcore.0
Hiya...  compress unix.0 vmcore.0
Hiya...  ls -l
total 51082
-rw-rw-rw-   1 kbrown    15           669336 Sep  1 12:28 unix.0.Z
-rw-rw-rw-   1 kbrown    15         24592643 Sep  1 12:29 vmcore.0.Z
Hiya...
```

The 135-megabyte **vmcore.0** file compressed to less than 25 megabytes — a huge saving!

Saving the crash to tape for shipment or archives

When archiving a set of crash dumps to tape, you may wish to first **compress** the (**vm)unix.X** and **vmcore.X** files, again, to use less media space. This also makes life a bit easier for the person who will later read the tape onto his own system to analyze the files, initially allowing him to use less disk space until he is ready to **uncompress** the files and start the analysis work.

When compressing the files, please use the standard UNIX **compress** command instead of your favorite public domain or third-party compression utilities. Don't assume that the person to whom you are sending the tapes uses nonstandard programs.

After writing the files to tape, *write-protect the tape* and, only then, verify that you can read the tape successfully. Too many potentially valuable system crash files have been lost due to faulty tapes!

Finally, label the tape!

Once the **savecore** files are safely archived, you can remove them from the disk. In general, it is a good idea to maintain the **bounds** file, which contains the next sequence number to use. Not only does it help provide a history of how many crashes have been captured, but it helps prevent you from ending up with a dozen **vmcore.0** files on tapes over time. It also, again, makes life just a bit easier for the person you send your crashes to for analysis. He won't have to keep shuffling things around to avoid overwriting the previous crash that had the same sequence number and thus the same file names.

If you plan to send the tape to another person for analysis, it is best to provide the following information:

- System activity as best known at the time of the crash.

- A brief description of the crash history for this system from the system administrator's point of view.

- The system configuration and tuning files. From a Solaris 1 system, provide the kernel configuration file and the **param.c** file. From Solaris 2 systems, provide the **/etc/system** file.

- List of software modifications and patches installed, **showrev -p** output if Solaris 2.

- General system and network information, including:
  - Hardware configuration. From a Solaris 1 system, **devinfo -vp** output is helpful. From a Solaris 2 system, provide **prtconf -vp** output.
  - List of third-party drivers and applications.
  - Network-based server and client relationships.

- The **/var/adm/messages*** files.

The more information you can provide to the person who will analyze the crash files, the better idea he will have of where to start his search for the cause of the problem.

≡ *4*

Crashing Your Own System 5 ≡

We've talked about what a system crash is. We've discussed how to use the UNIX **savecore** program to capture an image of memory when the system crashes. Shortly, we will discuss how to analyze the system crash dump **savecore** files.

At this point, it is only fair to show you a fun and educational way to quickly crash your own system on purpose. If you have **savecore** set up properly, you'll have a set of files to experiment with during the following chapters.

Needless to say, crashing a system is not something you should do lightly. If your system happens to be a big database server or is being used by half of your department, forcing an unannounced crash will not make you very popular. Even if you are the only user on the system, you would be wise to save your mail, close any edit sessions, and exit as many tools as you can before proceeding. It would also be prudent to unmount any NFS file systems your system is using. Finally, just before you crash the system, run a few **sync** commands to make sure any lingering local disk data still in memory is flushed out to the disks.

Back up your system! If you cannot afford to lose even a single bit of data from your system disks, *back up all of them before proceeding any further.* Any crash, whether forced or not, can result in data loss.

Crash your Solaris 2 system

We'll start by crashing a Solaris 2 system. Is **savecore** ready? Okay, then, let's panic your system!

Figure 5-1   How to crash a Solaris 2 system

```
Hiya... su
Password:
# adb -k -w /dev/ksyms /dev/mem
physmem 1e05
rootdir/X
rootdir:
```

Figure 5-1   How to crash a Solaris 2 system

```
    rootdir:            fc109408
    rootdir/W 0
    rootdir:            0xfc109408       =          0x0
    $q
    #
```

How does this procedure crash your system? Solaris keeps track of the address of the root *vnode* structure in a symbol called *rootdir*. If this *vnode* pointer is zero, the next time the system tries to do anything that would require walking down a directory path, it will fall over trying to read location zero looking for the root directory's *vnode*. Reading memory location zero is an illegal operation which results in a bad trap, data fault.

Using **adb** we will write a zero into *rootdir* and the system will quickly panic.

If your system doesn't panic immediately, just use the UNIX **ls** command to get a directory listing of the root directory, */*. That will surely do the trick!

Crash your Solaris 1 system

Let's crash a Solaris 1 system now. (Isn't this fun!?)

Figure 5-2   How to crash a Solaris 1 system

```
    # adb -k -w /vmunix /dev/mem
    physmem ff4
    rootdir/X
    rootdir:
    rootdir:            ff00d5e0
    rootdir/W 0
    rootdir:            0xff00d5e0       =          0x0
    $q
    #
```

As your system crashes and reboots, watch the messages that appear on the system console. Once the system is up and running again, log in and take a look at your **savecore** directory. You should see a new set of system crash dump **savecore** files. If not, go back to Chapter 3 and read about **savecore** to see what steps you may have missed.

If you now have system crash dump savecore files, *Congratulations!*

Let's move on now to the next chapter where we start the analysis.

Initial Analysis Without adb 6 ≣

We are now ready to start analyzing a set of system crash dump files provided by the **savecore** command. While **adb** is currently the most heavily used tool for system crash dump analysis, there are some other UNIX commands that may be used to collect information from the crash files. Let's talk about some of them before we move on to analysis with **adb**.

Identifying the UNIX release & hardware architecture

You've now got a set of system crash files. Maybe they are from your own system; maybe someone else forwarded them to you for analysis. If they are from your own system, you might opt to jump right into **adb**. However, if they were forwarded to you with little or no information, you may first need to figure out what type of system the files originated from. Doing this is surprisingly easy by using the UNIX **strings** command.

The **strings** command is a simple UNIX utility that searches sequentially through any type of file, looking for a sequence of four or more ASCII characters. The matches are displayed to the standard output device. When using **strings** as a system crash dump analysis tool, it is important to remember that an image of memory both on a live system and in a postmortem file contains pieces of user files, email messages, data packets being shipped between systems, and other, nonkernel-related data. When the **strings** command is used on an image of memory, some of this data will be seen, along with the strings and messages built into all the loaded device drivers and kernel routines.

So, while **strings** is very handy for looking at core files, be aware that it is also going to generate a lot of output! The bigger the image of memory, the more output you can expect to see. A simple forced crash on a lightly used SPARCstation™ 1+ generated over 40,000 lines of **strings** output! On a heavily used SPARCcenter 2000, over 100,000 lines is not unusual at all. Printed, that's well over three reams of paper!

Tucked away in the heart of the kernel are ASCII strings that describe the release of the operating system. These strings can be found by running **strings** on the **vmcore** file and using the UNIX **grep** command to search for key words. For example:

Figure 6-1   Using the strings command on a vmcore file

```
Hiya... strings vmcore.0 | grep SunOS
(#)SunOS 5.3 Generic September 1
@(#)SunOS 5.3 Generic September 1993
>@SunOS
SunOS Release %s Version %s [UNIX(R) System V Release 4.0]
@(#)SunOS 5.3 Generic September 1993
@(#)SunOS 5
@(#)SunOS 5.3 Generic September 1993
*0SunOS
@(#)SunOS 5.3 Generic September 1993
@(#)SunOS 5.3 Generic September 1993
@(#)SunOS 5.3 Generic September 1993
Hiya...
```

We now know what operating system was in use. What hardware architecture is the system based on? **Grep**'ing about, we find a nice string that tells us which system architecture was in use. In this case, it was a Sun SPARCstation 1+, which is a sun4c/65, a revved-up version of the sun4c/60.

```
Hiya... strings vmcore.1 | grep machine
Using default machine type Sun4c/60
setaudit:machine
xdr_bp_machine_name_t
Hiya...
```

This is enough information to get us started. We now know that we can use any sun4c system running Solaris 2.3 to do further analysis by using **adb**, that is, once we are done with the **strings** utility and other UNIX commands. If **grep**'ing for "machine" didn't prove helpful, we could **grep** for "Sun" instead. By the end of the long output, we would have no doubt which hardware architecture was in use!

The message buffer, msgbuf

When the system is up and running, it maintains a ring buffer known as the message buffer. This contains the information that you often see on the system console and later in the **/var/adm/messages** files. When the system panics or crashes, the panic-related messages appear on the console. However, they may not get written out to the **/var/adm/messages** file. Again, we can use the **strings** command to read this ring buffer. Before doing so, let's make sure you fully understand the nature of the ring buffer.

A ring buffer, as in the case of the message buffer, is a data area of fixed length. The message buffer on Solaris systems is known as *msgbuf*. Since *msgbuf* is a ring, the starting and ending points of the data within the ring are constantly rotating as the buffer is updated. When we dump the strings of a core image, we don't know where the most recent messages start.

Since the ring buffer is of fixed length, only the most recent information will be found there. If the system was booted months ago, you are not likely to find the boot messages in *msgbuf*. Instead, you will only see the more recent messages, including the panic messages.

To look at the *msgbuf* of a system crash dump, use the following as an example. This **strings** output is from the **vmcore** file generated by a bad trap / data fault generated by following the instructions in Chapter 5. Note that in this example, we are piping the output of **strings** into the UNIX **more** command so that only one page of output is displayed at a time.

Figure 6-2   Using the strings command to view the message buffer, msgbuf

```
Hiya...  strings vmcore.1 | more
Generic
Data fault
arc/
esac
done
shift `expr $OPTIND - 1`
if [ $# -gt 1 ] ; then
echo $USAG
stealing page f00d92a0 pfnum c4 for prom          (The message buffer starts here)
stealing page f00e1478 pfnum 2ee for prom
mem = 28672K (0x1c00000)
avail mem = 26963968
Ethernet address = 8:0:20:9:85:7e
root nexus = Sun 4_65
sbus0 at root: obio 0xf8000000
dma0 at sbus0: SBus slot 0 0x400000
esp0 at sbus0: SBus slot 0 0x800000 SBus level 3 sparc ipl 3
sd3 at esp0: target 3 lun 0
sd3 is /sbus@1,f8000000/esp@0,800000/sd@3,0
<SUN1.05 cyl 2036 alt 2 hd 14 sec 72>
sd6 at esp0: target 6 lun 0
sd6 is /sbus@1,f8000000/esp@0,800000/sd@6,0
Unable to install/attach driver `isp'
```

Figure 6-2   Using the strings command to view the message buffer, msgbuf

```
root on /sbus@1,f8000000/esp@0,800000/sd@3,0:a fstype ufs
zs0 at root: obio 0xf1000000 sparc ipl 12
zs0 is /zs@1,f1000000
zs1 at root: obio 0xf0000000 sparc ipl 12
zs1 is /zs@1,f0000000
cgthree0 at sbus0: SBus slot 3 0x0 SBus level 5 sparc ipl 7
cgthree0 is /sbus@1,f8000000/cgthree@3,0
cgthree0: resolution 1152 x 900
Unable to install/attach driver 'stc'
dump on /dev/dsk/c0t3d0s1 size 66012K
Feb 27 16:47:07 su: 'su sys' succeeded for root on /dev/console
Feb 27 16:48:01 sendmail[178]: network daemon starting
pseudo-device: vol0
vol0 is /pseudo/vol@0
audio0 at root: obio 0xf7201000 sparc ipl 13
audio0 is /audio@1,f7201000
Feb 27 16:50:37 su: 'su root' succeeded for kbrown on /dev/pts/2
Feb 27 17:07:30 su: 'su root' succeeded for kbrown on /dev/pts/3
Feb 27 17:09:51 su: 'su root' succeeded for kbrown on /dev/pts/1
Feb 27 18:15:43 su: 'su root' succeeded for kbrown on /dev/pts/3
BAD TRAP
sh: Data fault
kernel read fault at addr=0x0, pme=0x0
Sync Error Reg 80<INVALID>
pid=556, pc=0xf000aaa8, sp=0xf0331670, psr=0x4000c4, context=3
g1-g7: 0, 0, fffff80, 0, f03319e0, 1, ff467800
Begin traceback... sp = f0331670
Called from f0050668, fp=f03317e0, args=f0331844 0 f033184c 0 0 ff35be08
Called from f0093b68, fp=f0331850, args=0 0 1 0 f03318b4 f00c5b70
Called from f00245e4, fp=f03318b8, args=f0331e94 f0331920 0 0 4f074 f00b5218
Called from f0005acc, fp=f0331938, args=f00bc334 f0331eb4 0 f0331e90 fffffffc
   ffffffff
Called from 13c24, fp=effff678, args=4f074 effff6d8 3a 2f 1 4dc00
End traceback...
panic: Data fault
syncing file systems... done
1617 static and sysmap kernel pages
  56 dynamic kernel data pages
 168 kernel-pageable pages
   0 segkmap kernel pages
   0 segvn kernel pages
  51 current user process pages
1892 total pages (1892 chunks)
dumping to vp ff1e9d84, offset 116888
?PbM
 p-p
/opt/SUNWspro/ma
/Xinitrc
?PbM
```

Figure 6-2   Using the strings command to view the message buffer, msgbuf

```
/sbin/sh
-8.y              (We quit out of "more" at this point)
Hiya...
```

Since the system had just recently booted, the boot-time messages were still in *msgbuf*, including a very detailed description of the system's hardware configuration. Also, you can see the *syslog()* messages from the UNIX **su** command showing when user kbrown became root. These are messages that also were displayed on the system console.

This procedure all works because the message buffer area is kept in low memory and will appear close to the beginning of the core file. When you use **strings** to read the core file, you'll see the messages (remember that they may not appear to be in the right order, because the "beginning" of the buffer output may really be in the middle), followed by fairly random garbage once you're past the end.

Once you've passed the *msgbuf* area, watching the **strings** output is *usually* boring and useless. However, there are times when you might need to read more than just the messages data. Read on!

Strings and the case of the unknown customer

Recently, a customer mailed an unlabeled tape to a support engineer in Sun's UK Answer Centre. No note was sent with the tape. No return address was on the envelope. It seemed there was no way to figure out where the tape had come from, so we would have to wait for the customer to call and claim it.

Ah, but maybe the customer had been clever and put helpful information on the tape, something like a **README-FIRST** file. So, we read the tape. The only files it contained were **unix.0** and **vmcore.0**. At least now we knew that the files were from a Solaris 2 system by virtue of the file names. Had **unix.0** been named **vmunix.0**, we would know that the files were from a Solaris 1 system.

Using the techniques described above, we quickly learned that the system was a large SPARCcenter 2000 server running Solaris 2.3. However, we still didn't know whose SC2000 the files came from. The engineer involved knew many SC2000 customers. In hopes of finding more clues, we watched the **strings** output for a long time. Fortunately, we didn't have to read all 48,613 lines (over 850 printed pages) of it!

In reading the **strings** output, it became apparent that the SC2000 was used for inventory control of some sort. There were a lot of drugstore items with pricing and stocking data. This alone narrowed down our list.

Then, just when we were pretty sure which customer might have sent the tape, the customer's company name (the real name has been changed) appeared on our screen in banner-sized letters!

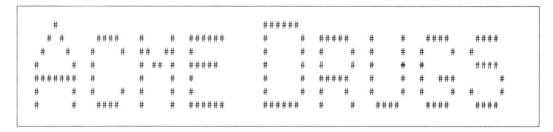

As it turned out, the system's **/etc/motd** or message of the day file contained this banner, some welcoming messages, and the latest system news for folks to read when they log in. Just prior to the crash, someone must have logged in, as the **/etc/motd** file was still in memory at the time of the crash.

Without the **strings** command, we would have had to wait for the customer to contact us.

Process status utilities: ps & pstat

On a lot of UNIX systems, you'll find that some of the status commands used regularly by system administrators can actually be used on postmortem files! This, however, is not always the case. If the commands appear to work, by all means use them!

For example, on Solaris 1 systems, the UNIX process status command, **ps**, can be used on the **vmunix.X** and **vmcore.X** files. To do this, after your favorite options append the **ps -k** option and specify the name of the **vmunix** and **vmcore** file. For example:

```
ps -laxk vmunix.3 vmcore.3
```

The Solaris 1 **pstat** command can also be used on your **savecore** files. No additional option is needed. For example:

```
pstat -T vmunix.3 vmcore.3
```

Neither of these commands exists for use against Solaris 2 crashes; however, as you'll soon see, other commands are available.

Network status: netstat

On both Solaris 1 and Solaris 2 systems, the UNIX **netstat** command can be used with your postmortem files. No special option is needed. For example:

```
netstat -d vmunix.5 vmcore.5
```

Unfortunately, some of the options don't work on **savecore** files even if you request it, so when using **netstat**, compare the output to the output you get when **netstat** is run on the system being used for analysis work. If the output is the same, you can assume that the command wasn't using the crash files.

NFS status: nfsstat

Just as with the **netstat** command, you can use the **nfsstat** command on your system crash dump files. No special option is needed, just the names of the unix and core file.

```
nfsstat -n vmunix.2 vmcore.2
```

As with the **netstat** command, always compare the output of the **nfsstat** command run on the live system with the output for the postmortem files, just to make sure you are really getting system crash data.

Address resolution protocol status: arp

The UNIX **arp** program can be used with postmortem files to extract information from the address resolution protocol table. Like many UNIX commands, you need only append the name of the unix and core files to the command line.

```
arp -a vmunix.1 vmcore.1
```

As always, compare the output to that from a live system to make sure it's reporting statistics for the **savecore** files.

Interprocess communication status: ipcs

The **ipcs** command is used to report status on the interprocess communication facilities: shared memory, message queues and semaphores. **ipcs** exists on both Solaris 1 and Solaris 2 systems. To use **ipcs** against your crash dump files, use option **-C** followed by the corefile name and **-N** followed by the namelist name. For example:

```
ipcs -a -C vmcore.4 -N vmunix.4
```

Again, compare the output to that from a live system to make sure you're viewing the proper data.

If you aren't familiar with **ps**, **pstat**, **netstat**, **nfsstat**, **arp**, or **ipcs**, please refer to the manual pages.

The crash program

Solaris systems provide a program called **crash** that was specifically written for use in examining memory on both live systems and in postmortem files; **crash** can be used to print out various structures and tables of the kernel in easy-to-read formats.

On Solaris 1 systems, the **crash** program can be found in the **/etc** directory. On Solaris 2 systems, it lives in the **/usr/sbin** directory.

While it is tempting for us to include a whole chapter or two on how to use **crash**, we would rather just refer you to the manual pages. However, since Solaris 2's process status, **ps**, command doesn't run on postmortem files, we will show you how to get the process status by using the **crash** program instead.

Figure 6-3   Using the crash utility to get process status information

```
Hiya...  crash -d vmcore.0 -n unix.0
dumpfile = vmcore.0, namelist = unix.0, outfile = stdout
> help p
p [-e] [-f] [-l] [-w filename] [([-p] [-a] tbl_entry | #procid)... | -r]
        tbl_entry = slot number | address | symbol | expression | range
process table
alias: proc
        acceptable aliases are uniquely identifiable initial substrings
> p -e
PROC TABLE SIZE = 490
SLOT ST  PID  PPID  PGID   SID   UID PRI CPU   NAME        FLAGS
   0 r    0     0     0     0     0  98  69 sched          load sys lock
   1 r    1     0     0     0     0  98  32 init           load
```

Figure 6-3   Using the crash utility to get process status information

```
 2 r    2     0     0     0     0  98  13 pageout        load sys lock nowait
 3 r    3     0     0     0     0  98  80 fsflush        load sys lock nowait
 4 r  369     1   369   369     0  98  14 sac            load jctl
 5 r  370     1   370   370 11628  98  69 sh             load
 6 r  331   323   323   323     0  98  13 lpNet          load nowait jctl
 7 r  261     1   261   261     0  98   2 keyserv        load
 8 r  259     1   259   259     0  98  80 rpcbind        load
 9 r  267     1   267   267     0  98  64 ypbind         load
10 r  269     1   269   269     0  98  14 kerbd          load
11 r  279     1   279   279     0  98  80 inetd          load
12 r  286     1   286   286     0  98  80 automountd     load
13 r  290     1   290   290     0  98  18 statd          load
14 r  292     1   292   292     0  98  45 lockd          load
15 r  303     1   303   303     0  98  28 syslogd        load nowait
16 r  323     1   323   323     0  98  28 lpsched        load nowait
17 r  313     1   313   313     0  98  50 cron           load
18 r  332     1   332   332     0  98  37 sendmail       load
19 r  373   369   369   369     0  98  20 ttymon         load jctl
20 r  528   523   520   520     0  98  61 adb            load
21 r  496     1   495   495 11628  98  11 fm_flb         load
22 r  407   370   370   370 11628  98  80 openwin        load
23 z  399   370   399   370 11628  98  80 zombie         load
24 r  372   369   369   369     0  98  21 listen         load nowait jctl
25 r  492     1   492   477 11628  98  80 maker4X.exe    load
26 r  411   407   370   370 11628  98  12 xinit          load
27 r  412   411   412   370 11628  98  80 Xsun           load
28 r  413   411   413   370 11628  98 107 sh             load
29 r  432   279   279   279     0  98  23 rpc.ttdbserver load
30 r  421     1   421   370 11628  98  17 fbconsole      load
31 r  520   517   520   520 11628  98  80 sh             load
32 r  428     1   428   370 11628  98  35 vkbd           load
33 r  431     1   431   370 11628  98  52 ttsession      load
34 r  435   413   435   370 11628  98   4 olwm           load
35 r  436   435   435   370 11628  98  24 olwmslave      load
37 r  444     1   413   370 11628  98  41 clock          load
39 r  523   520   520   520     0  98  51 sh             load
40 r  451     1   413   370 11628  98  77 cmdtool        load jctl
41 r  454   451   454   454 11628  98  61 sh             load
42 r  471   435   471   471 11628  98  80 x_cdplayer     load
43 r  517   435   517   517 11628  98  80 cmdtool        load jctl
> q
Hiya...
```

Use of the **p** command with the **-l** option in **crash** is interesting, giving you the user credentials information. Basically, this is who owns the process. The output of the **-l** option is very long, so we'll just show a snippet of it here.

Figure 6-4   Process credentials as displayed by the crash utility

```
   SLOT ST  PID  PPID  PGID   SID   UID PRI CPU    NAME         FLAGS
    20 r    528   523   520   520     0  98  61 adb             load

        Session: sid: 520, ctty: vnode(fc5acd04) maj( 24) min 1)
        Process Credentials: uid: 0, gid: 1, real uid: 0, real gid: 1
        as: fc1ef550
        wait code: 0, wait data: 0
        sig: effff178    link 0
        parent: fc451800        child: 0
        sibling: 0 threadp: fc4dc600
        utime: 41       stime: 20        cutime: 0        cstime: 0
        trace: 0        sigmask: effff178        class: 0
        lwptotal: 1     lwpcnt: 1        lwprcnt: 1
        lwpblocked: 0
```

This is the section of the output for the **adb** process that was running at the time of the crash. The crash dump in question was caused by the **adb** session in Chapter 5, when we set *rootdir* to zero and caused the system to panic.

Again, if you want to experiment with the **crash** command, go for it! However, please note that some early versions of **crash** were a bit buggy.

Summary

Sometimes, we will jump right into **adb** to analyze a crash dump. Other times, we might want to run other commands against the postmortem files. If you have favorite UNIX status commands, try them on the crash dump files. If they work, use them!

It's time to move on to the next chapter, where we will introduce you to **adb**.

Introduction to adb

Before we talk about analyzing system crash dumps with **adb**, let's talk about **adb** itself. The UNIX **adb** command is one of the oldest and most readily available UNIX debuggers. Although **adb** doesn't provide flashy features such as a graphical user interface and the ability to work directly with source code, it is fairly straightforward and, among UNIX gurus, is accepted as the kernel debugger of choice. **adb** is not limited to examining kernel crashes, but better tools are usually available for finding problems with user programs and application packages.

The name **adb**, or absolute **debugger**, comes from the fact that **adb** deals primarily with absolute addresses, normally hexadecimal, and global symbols. It doesn't know about source files, line numbers, local (automatic) variables, or internal function labels. **adb** works best with assembly language and uncomplicated C code.

adb understands simple, one- or two-character commands that allow you to control the execution of a process on a live system, control the operation of **adb**, and display the contents of memory or a file in numerous different formats. **adb** is well suited for work on both live kernels and postmortem files generated by system crashes.

adb, while simple and straightforward in nature, offers a very powerful feature called **adb** macros. We will briefly discuss **adb** macros in this chapter, simply as a concept, later exploring macros in much greater depth.

Other debuggers

Throughout this book, with a few exceptions, we will be working with **adb**. However, since you will run into other debuggers, let's talk about some of them now before we continue our discussion about **adb**.

dbx, dbxtool, & debugger

On Sun systems, you'll find at least five other debuggers. Three of these, **dbx**, **dbxtool**, and **debugger**, are excellent tools for debugging user-level programs and applications. They are rather sophisticated in nature, they work with the program source code, and they are designed to be more user-friendly. However, all three require special compiler options to be used to create debuggable object files that include the symbol table.

The kernel is not built with the special options, so there is no advantage to be gained by using these debuggers. Also, **adb** is the only debugger that understands how to work with kernel address mappings, and it has macro files (more about these later) to help dump out kernel data structures.

The kernel resident absolute debugger, kadb

A bootable sibling of **adb** exists on many UNIX systems. Known as the kernel absolute debugger, **kadb** is booted up instead of a UNIX kernel. **kadb** then loads in and executes a kernel, allowing for setting of breakpoints and live modifications and examinations of the kernel. **kadb** also has a macro facility; however, it differs from the **adb** macros feature in that the available macros must be prebuilt into the **kadb** executable.

You'll find that if you can use **adb**, you'll feel pretty comfortable using **kadb**. However, having said that, your first couple of experiences using **kadb** may surprise you a bit. When the system "drops" into **kadb**, in other words, when **kadb** takes over and you see the **kadb** prompt, everything else stops! You will no longer have a window system, you won't be able to run background processes, and the system will be inaccessible to anyone but the person looking at the **kadb** prompt on the console. Keeping this in mind, you would be wise to have another system handy for access to source code and any other tools you might need while working within **kadb**. Failing that, you might want to keep handy some printouts of the routines you plan to examine.

The crash program

Another debugging tool you'll find on some UNIX systems is the **crash** program. We've already seen an example of when we might want to use **crash**; however, in general we still prefer to use the tool and the macros that the UNIX kernel developers use. That, of course, means **adb**. We hope that, by the end of this book, you too will be convinced that **adb** is your kernel debugger of choice!

adb hardware & software requirements

From our discussion about the **savecore** program, one of the hardware requirements you've come to understand apropos of system crash dump analysis is the need for disk space. When systems consisted of 8 megabytes of memory, a set of **savecore** files wasn't too much of a disk hog. However, with today's system memory configurations reaching beyond the 1 gigabyte mark, one system crash dump can present a bit of a storage challenge.

Once we have a set of **savecore** files, we will want to use **adb** to analyze them. For this, it is best and easiest to move the **savecore** files to a system that has the same kernel architecture and operating system release running on it. Of course, analysis can be done on the system that crashed, assuming the system is back up and running.

Note – It is possible, *through much manipulation of libraries, programs, and directories,* to analyze postmortem files on a system with a different kernel architecture and OS; however, we will not be discussing the details of how to do this in this chapter. However, you will find much more information about this on the Panic! CD-ROM.

As an example, let's say you have postmortem files from a Sun SPARCcenter 2000 server running Solaris 2.4. The SC2000 is one of the systems in the sun4d kernel architecture family. For your analysis work, you will want to find a sun4d running Solaris 2.4. The system needn't be a SC2000. A SPARCserver 1000, also a sun4d system, running the same OS will do the job for you.

If you don't know the kernel architecture of a system, run either the **/usr/ucb/arch** or **uname -a** command on it. The example below is from a SPARCstation 20. Note that without the **arch -k** option, only the general hardware architecture is listed and not the more specific kernel architecture, which is what we are most concerned about.

```
Hiya...  arch
sun4
Hiya...  arch -k
sun4m
Hiya...  uname -a
SunOS kadb 5.3 Generic_101318-61 sun4m sparc
Hiya...
```

Architecture & OS mismatches: Some adb error messages

If you attempt to use **adb** on a system crash dump of a kernel from a system of differing kernel architecture, you will get various error messages. Below are some examples.

The crash dump files on which we attempted to use **adb** below were from a Sun-4™/400 system, a system from the sun4 architecture family. The system was running Solaris 1.1 (SunOS 4.1.3). The analysis system in use was a SPARCstation 20, a sun4m, running Solaris 2.3.

```
Hiya...  adb -k vmunix.0 vmcore.0
Cannot adb -k: vmunix.0: not a kernel namelist
Hiya...
```

This next example, run on the same SS20, shows an attempt to use **adb** on a system crash dump from an SC2000, a sun4d architecture. The SC2000 was also running Solaris 2.3, so while the architectures don't match, the operating systems do. This, however, is not enough to allow **adb** to work with the files.

```
Hiya...  adb -k unix.2 vmcore.2
Cannot adb -k: unix.0: can't find swapinfo
Hiya...
```

This next example, also done on the SS20 running Solaris 2.3, shows what **adb** thought of an SC2000 Solaris 2.2 crash.

```
Hiya...  adb -k unix.5 vmcore.5
Segmentation Fault - core dumped
Hiya...
```

Here's an example of a sun4m running Solaris 2.2 being used to **adb** a sun4m 2.3 crash.

```
Hiya on s4m-22...  adb -k unix.7 vmcore.7
Cannot adb -k: vmcore.0: uncondense error on kvtopdata: Error 0
Cannot adb -k: vmcore.0: unable to read kvtopdata
Cannot adb -k: vmcore.0: unable to read kvtopdata
Hiya on s4m-22...
```

Below is how **adb** on a sun4 system running 4.1.3 reacted to a sun4d 2.3 crash.

```
Hiya on s4-413...  adb -k unix.9 vmcore.9
Cannot adb -k: cannot mmap vmcore.0's bitmap: Invalid argument
Hiya on s4-413...
```

adb on another sun4d system, a SPARCcenter 2000 running an early version of Solaris 2.4, had a unique reaction to the same sun4d 2.3 crash. It reported problems but actually didn't refuse to try working with the files. However, further commands within **adb**, commands which we will be discussing later on, proved that this was definitely still a mismatch.

```
Hiya on p4d-2000a-24...  adb -k unix.9 vmcore.9
physmem fd87
Unable to locate current proc;no regs available.
$c
PR_BASE()
data address not found
$<threadlist
                 thread_id e00b1800
?(?) + dffff758
main(0x0,0xffffffff,0x1,0x0,0xe00ee110,0xe00d35a0)
data address not found
$q
Hiya on p4d-2000a-24...
```

Finally, here's an example of what it looks like when we get a good match!

```
Hiya on p4d-1000a...  adb -k unix.9 vmcore.9
physmem fd87
```

In this successful example, **adb** reported the number of pages of memory on the system and then silently awaited our first command.

In the next chapter, we will discuss the actual commands you might use while in an **adb** session. First, though, more about **adb** and **kadb**.

The distribution of adb

We've stated that **adb** is part of the standard UNIX operating system. However, as Sun's Solaris operating environments become more and more modular, even in how they are packaged for installation, we should be a bit more specific about where you'll find **adb**.

The **adb** program is a part of the Debugging group of software on Solaris 1 systems.

On Solaris 2 systems, the **adb** software (not including the man pages) is in four packages:

- SUNWcar   Where **kadb** is found.

- SUNWkvm   Where **adb** and the **adb** macros are found.

- SUNWtoo   Where you'll find the **/usr/bin** symbolic link for **adb**. This is also where you'll find the **savecore** and **strings** programs.

- SUNWesu   Where the **adbgen** utilities are found. **adbgen** is a program that helps the programmer generate **adb** macros.

The different uses of adb & kadb

Whether you want to use **adb** to look at a user program that dumped core, to look at a live, running system, or to examine the postmortem files of a system that crashed, you will usually use **adb** with two files: the object file and the core file.

The object file

The executable object file can be either a program or a kernel. The file contains the symbol table and the executable code. The symbol table is not required; however, without it, you can't use the symbolic features of **adb**.

The object file serves two purposes. First, you can examine the initialized data values in the executable to find the contents of variables when the program or kernel was first loaded. Second, the symbol table is kept within the executable object file. The symbol table enables **adb** or any other debugger to match symbolic names with real addresses. While **adb** doesn't really care, humans seem to respond better to functions or variables that have names rather than just hexadecimal addresses.

The core file

The second file is the core file. When used for postmortem analysis of a program or a kernel, the core file is an image that reflects a snapshot of the memory in use by the failed program or kernel at the time of failure. When a live system is viewed, the core file reflects the memory currently in use by the kernel.

If you, for whatever reason, don't have access to both the object file and the core file, you can specify a dash, "**-**", in its place on the command line when you invoke **adb**.

Using adb on crash dumps

User programs, utilities, and kernel core files can be debugged with **adb**. Programs that crash may leave a file, called **core**, in the current working directory. This **core** file can be examined along with the executable file to identify the cause and location of the error. Of course, if you don't have the source to the program, you will find debugging to be a lot of work! Remember, you will be working with assembly code.

In Chapter 3, "The savecore Program", we talked about how system crashes are captured. **savecore** files normally include all of the kernel data space, if not the entire contents of physical memory. The **adb -k** flag is used when analyzing system crash dump **savecore** files and live systems, because **adb** needs to do a lot of work with address translation for the kernel data space.

We'll briefly explore both types of crashes, program core dumps and system crash dumps, later on in this chapter.

Using adb on live systems

As we've already mentioned, **adb** is not limited to debugging postmortem files. As a matter of fact, it is common practice to use **adb** to modify or tune a running system in hopes of gaining better performance. **adb** can also be used to modify the kernel so that the next reboot will change the system's behavior.

By default, **adb** is used to only look at or read the object and core files. However, by use of either the **-w** flag when invoking **adb** or the **$W** command within **adb**, **adb** can be used to write to the files.

Note – You must be *extremely* careful when working on live system kernels, since a write to the wrong location can have disastrous effects, as you've already discovered in Chapter 5, where we crashed your own system!

The kernel resident absolute debugger, kadb

In some cases, it may be easier and more productive to take over a crashed machine and examine the system right then and there as opposed to looking at a system crash dump later. This obviously works best on a system that can be left down long enough to let you perform some diagnosis at your leisure. Servers with 500 users all breathing down your neck don't allow for a calm, quiet, analysis session.

If you are in a position to debug a live system, **kadb** is the debugger you will use. **kadb** is made available by actually booting the debugger initially instead of the operating system. **kadb** then loads in and starts the rest of the kernel. When something causes a panic, **kadb** takes over and leaves the system more or less in the state in which it died. At this point, **kadb** is ready to work with you.

The interactive capability of **kadb** can have major advantages when, for example, you are looking at panics caused by a device driver you are trying to install and debug. The driver is loaded, the device is available, which is not the case when looking at a set of postmortem files, and all of the kernel data is right there. Using **kadb**, you can set breakpoints and treat the kernel just like a great, big, user program, stepping through its execution, examining and modifying values on-the-fly.

Working with **adb** on system crash dump postmortem files doesn't provide this level of interaction with your patient, the system, since you are really dealing with a computer corpse at that point. Also, the process of panic'ing and dumping core alters the state of the system, occasionally just enough so that you lose critical crash information.

adb macros & /usr/lib/adb

We will be talking about **adb** macros in much greater detail in following chapters and using them throughout case histories. However, since this an introduction to **adb**, let's introduce you to the concept of **adb** macros for a moment.

Although **adb** has a very limited set of commands, they can be bundled into fairly powerful combinations of commands known as "macros." Macros are stored in individual files in a known directory. They are ASCII files that are invoked by name and are read in as if they were keystrokes you had typed from the keyboard. Where's the power in that, you might ask? Maybe we should let you discover that for yourself.

adb macros enable you to build a set of common commands, name them, save them, and invoke as them needed. Macros also can be designed to call other macros, allowing for even more analysis power with minimal effort on your part.

Numerous macro files are provided with Solaris 1 in the **/usr/lib/adb** directory. On Solaris 2 systems you'll find the adb macros in **/usr/kvm/lib/adb**. Most of the macros provided by Sun are used to print out commonly needed structures from the kernel, usually presented in easy-to-read formats.

Sun does not provide macros specifically intended for use with user program debugging, although some of the provided macros are helpful. For example, the macros that provide stack tracebacks can be used with user programs. Generally, if you have structures or lists for which macros might be useful, you will want to write and use your own macros.

We'll be talking about how to write your own macros in great detail in Chapter 14.

General startup syntax

While the general syntax for starting up **adb** is quite simple,

```
adb objectfile corefile
```

there are subtle differences, depending on what is being debugged. Let's cover the most common scenarios.

User program debugging

Quite often, **adb** is used to analyze user program core dumps. When a program dumps core, often the user will see an error message such as "Segmentation violation, Core dumped." The program core dumps are stored in the current working directory and are called **core**. This core file, paired with the object file or executable binary that fell over, can be examined by using **adb**.

adb can also be used to run user programs, allowing for breakpoints to be set, execution to be controlled, and data to be examined and modified on-the-fly.

The syntax used when invoking **adb** to examine a user program and its core file is quite simple. All you need is the executable binary, your object file, and an image of memory used by the program, the core file. If the core file is not specified, **adb** will look for a file named **core** in the current directory. If a dash, "-", is specified for the core file, **adb** will use the system memory to execute the object file. Here are a couple of examples.

```
adb a.out core
```

```
adb myprogram -
```

We will be using the second example later on in Chapter 11, "Symbol Tables."

While **adb** will work if there is no symbol table in the executable image, it won't be able to identify variables or functions by name. This makes identification of the location of failure extremely difficult, especially if the program is fairly large and you aren't an assembly language guru with tons of time on your hands.

If a stack traceback or examination of memory reports answers and addresses solely in hexadecimal, check the executable image to see if the symbol table has been removed from the object file. This removal of the symbol table is done via the UNIX **strip** command. Once the symbol table is **strip**'ed, there is no way to get it back in the object file.

If you find you need to debug a program that has no symbol table and you have the source code for the program, you would be wise to recompile it with the appropriate options so that the symbol table is attached. Do not **strip** the symbol table from the resulting object file. Run the newly compiled binary and work with any core files it generates. The time you spend recompiling will very quickly be returned to you as time saved from trying to hack your way through a **strip**'ed object file.

Examining system crash dump postmortem files

When examining postmortem system crash dumps, invoke **adb** with its **-k** option so that special kernel memory mapping is done within **adb**. On Solaris 1 systems, the object file is called **vmunix.X**, where *X* is the crash number assigned by the **savecore** program. On Solaris 2 systems, the object file is called **unix.X**. Both flavors of Solaris name the system crash dump core file **vmcore.X**.

We've already seen several examples of the syntax for starting up **adb** on a set of postmortem files. In general, the syntax is:

```
adb -k unix.X vmcore.X
```

Examining a live system: Solaris 1

The same general startup syntax is used to access a live, running system. However, the name of the object files is quite different in Solaris 1 and Solaris 2, so let's talk about them one at a time.

For Solaris 1, the startup command follows.

```
adb -k /vmunix /dev/mem
```

Here, since there is no crash file, the object file is the actual, booted, executing kernel, **/vmunix**, and the core file, **/dev/mem**, is the contents of physical memory at the current time.

You may have noted that there are two memory files in the **/dev** directory. These are **/dev/kmem** and **/dev/mem**. They are used for different purposes and only one will work with **adb**. The **/dev/kmem** device file is the "kernel virtual memory" for the current running kernel; thus, it accepts only virtual addresses in kernel space. The other device file, **/dev/mem**, corresponds to actual physical memory.

Since **adb** expects to find a core file created from a copy of physical memory pages, it automatically performs physical-to-virtual address translations internally in order to locate data. Therefore, you must give **adb** the file corresponding to physical memory so that the translations will get you something real.

Examining a live system: Solaris 2

Solaris 2 systems are very different at the kernel level from Solaris 1 systems. The kernel is much more modular than before, so various pieces that are loaded into memory do not necessarily come from the same file or even from the same directory.

/kernel/unix, the closest thing to Solaris 1's **/vmunix** file, is now only the "core" or heart of the system and will not contain the code or the symbols for other loadable modules or drivers. A new pseudo-device, **/dev/ksyms**, corresponds to the symbol table of all the currently loaded modules in the system.

In addition to being a file containing all of the kernel symbols, the **/dev/ksyms** device, when opened, effectively prevents modules from being *unloaded* on-the-fly. This helps to guarantee that the symbol table of what's in memory won't change from underneath you while you are trying to analyze it.

Be aware, however, that since modules are still being loaded on demand, the kernel may still increase in size while you are poking around, as previously unrequired sections are fetched from disk. So, new symbols may be *added*, but old ones won't disappear as long as **/dev/ksyms** is open.

The **adb** command to analyze a running Solaris 2 system is:

```
adb -k /dev/ksyms /dev/mem
```

Security issues

Earlier, we talked about the security issues of looking at system crash dumps. The live, running system also needs to be protected. Since the kernel image and the contents of memory are considered vital and since looking at memory could get around any permissions that might otherwise prevent you from looking at data on the system, the kernel and memory files are restricted. By default, only root can **adb** the live, running kernel.

On Solaris 1 systems, regular nonroot users who are added into group 2, the kmem group in the **/etc/group** file, may **adb** the running kernel. On Solaris 2, there is no special group that allows nonroot users to inspect and modify the kernel.

Other helpful files

In Chapter 10, we will be talking about the only portion of the source code that is supplied with most UNIX systems: the **/usr/include** header files. These files are distributed with the OS because they contain definitions that programmers may need to include in their programs.

The header files will play an important role, along with the **adb** macros, when we are using **adb** to try to figure out why our system bit the dust.

Now that we've introduced you to **adb** and shown how to start it up, let's get into some of the details of how to use **adb**.

adb: The Gory Details 8

So far, we've touched on a few of the **adb** commands without telling you much about how it all works. The absolute **debugger** is not highly sophisticated, but it does have a varied and powerful command set. **adb** allows you to examine and modify both the contents of memory and the actual data and code in programs.

In this chapter, we're going to discuss many of the **adb** commands. While your UNIX system might have come with excellent **adb** documentation, not all do. We hope that this chapter will help you recognize and understand the **adb** commands we will be using throughout this book and the **adb** commands used in the **adb** macros that you'll find on your own system.

Basic commands

There are a bunch of odd-looking command characters in **adb**, but they all follow some basic rules. There are commands to:

- Display the contents of memory or files
- Perform conversion and printing operations
- Control a process being debugged

and a bunch of others. The most common actions you will want to perform when looking at core files is to examine memory, so let's check out the display commands first.

Displaying data

As you no doubt recall, you will usually provide two input files to **adb**: the object file, which contains the code and the symbol table or namelist; and the core file, which contains the actual contents of memory. Since you may need to look at both of these, there are two separate display commands, one for each file. The general format for using either of these is the same.

```
address,count    command    formatting_information
```

You must provide some starting location, the address, when displaying anything.

The count specifies how many times the display should be done. It's not always used; if you don't specify anything, **adb** runs the command only once.

The command is a single character that tells **adb** where to find the data at the particular address you specified.

The formatting information specifies how much you want to display and how it should be displayed.

Now, let's look at each of these in more detail.

Addressing

adb will allow some different types of addresses that tell it where to go to begin the command. In general, you may have:

- A specific numeric address, in hexadecimal (which **adb** assumes is the base, by default) or perhaps decimal or octal if you wish

- The name of a variable or function

- An expression combining these, for instance, a name plus an offset value

Binary operators

You can perform arithmetic as you might expect when using symbol names and numeric addresses. **adb** offers several binary arithmetic operators that you can use when making expressions that will translate to an address or other numeric value. They include:

- + Addition. For example, the command **rmalloc+4?i** will display the instruction at the second word of the *rmalloc* function (4 bytes past the start of *rmalloc*).

- – Subtraction.

- * Multiplication.

- % Integer division (fractional addresses would be difficult to work with).

- & Bitwise AND operations, also known as conjunctions.

- | Bitwise OR operations, also known as disjunctions.

- # Rounding up the value on the left-hand side to the next nearest multiple of the value on the right-hand side. For example, **f032ea55#4** results in f032ea58. When writing **adb** macros, this is a clever way to realign **adb**'s current pointer to the next full-word address after displaying an ASCII string of unknown length.

- (and) Grouping expressions.

Aside from + and −, these operators are not commonly seen as part of expressions used to represent address values; however, they are all legal. You are more likely to encounter them inside macros. What you normally will use is a constant address, or a symbol name, with perhaps an offset forward or back.

Unary operators

There are five unary operators. They are:

- * Pointer to the contents of the location in the core file represented by the expression

- % Pointer to the contents of the location in the object file represented by the expression (@ is used instead on some versions of **adb**)

- − Integer negation

- ~ Bitwise complement

- # Logical negation

Of these operators, two appear consistently in macros. These are *, which indicates a pointer, and #. Let's talk about each of these in detail.

Pointers

Two unary operators act as pointers. Of these, the * is used the most often. Let's see an example of how it works.

The kernel variable *panicstr* contains a pointer to the string that was printed when the system panic'ed. To look at the string, you can perform two commands.

```
Hiya...  adb -k vmunix.3 vmcore.3
physmem 3f98
panicstr/X
panicstr:  0xf015f7a8
0xf015f7a8/s
0xf015f7a8:  zero
```

Or, you can use the asterisk to indicate that this is a pointer.

```
*panicstr/s
0xf015f7a8:  zero
```

This command uses, not the value in *panicstr*, but what it points to, as the address of the string we want to display.

We will be using the * unary operator quite often throughout system crash dump analysis.

Logical negation

Another unary operator worth discussing in detail is the # sign, also known as a hash symbol, tic-tac-toe, or a pound sign, depending on the country you live in. The # acts just like the exclamation point, !, in C programs. If the number it precedes is zero, then the result is one. If the number is non-zero, then the result is zero. This is known as logical negation. The result is either true, 1, or false, 0, and it's the opposite of the expression that follows.

We will put the # unary operator to good use when we move to the topic of macros later on.

Counts

The repeat count, which **adb** assumes is 1 if you don't say otherwise, is the number of times **adb** will execute the display command. Normally, this is some small number, although any expression can be used here.

The clever **adb** user will note that if the count turns out to be zero, **adb** will not perform the command at all. We will see how this can used to our advantage later on when we discuss **adb** macros.

Commands

There are two one-character data display commands, one for each possible file on the **adb** command line. They are:

- ? Examine and display data from the object file

- / Examine and display data from the core file

Let's cover each of these in detail.

The ? display command

The **?** command is most often used for displaying instructions, but sometimes you may want to look at data. The data in the executable object file is the value that a variable is set to when the program (or the kernel) initially is loaded into memory. An example C program code statement, such as:

```
int pencils = 100;
```

means that the variable *pencils* has an initial value of 100 when the program starts. This means you can look for *pencils* in the object file and expect to see 100 as the original value. On the other hand, a statement like:

```
char messages[4096];
```

just tells the compiler that you will want 4096 bytes worth of memory reserved for later use and to call that area of memory *messages*. This is known as "bss" (block started by symbol) space and just results in a notation in the object file that you will need an extra 4 kilobytes when you start up the program. Looking for *messages* with the **?** command will probably result in an error message such as "data address not found."

The / display command

The **/** command gives you the actual value of the variable when the machine or the program stopped, as stored in the core file. Note that you may find a name or a variable in both files. This is not unusual. It just means that the variable had an initial value that may have changed during execution, so the start value shows up in one place and the current value in another.

In some BSD-based kernels, executable code will appear only in the **vmunix.X** file, which must be examined with the **?** command. However, the loadable drivers will appear in the **vmcore.X** file, since they are put into kernel data space while the system is running.

With Solaris 2 SVR4-based kernels, most of the code is dynamically loaded, so normally you use the **/** command when looking at both code and data.

Formats

Reviewing the general **adb** command syntax, we see that the formatting information comes next.

```
address,count    command    formatting_information
```

As you might expect, there are a lot of format commands. Some of these deal with displaying different sizes of data in various formats, whereas others deal with methods of formatting the output. Let's first talk about the format commands used to display data.

Displaying data

Format display commands are all single-letter commands. With the data display commands, generally a lowercase letter indicates a "short" or simple value, and uppercase is used for "long" or more sophisticated displays. Let's go some of through them.

- **X**   Prints hexadecimal numbers. An uppercase **X** will display a long, 4-byte quantity, and a lowercase **x** will show a 2-byte short quantity.

- **D**   Prints a decimal number. **D** is for longs, **d** is for shorts.

- **U**   Also prints decimals, but as unsigned numbers. **u** is for short unsigned values.

- **O**   Prints unsigned octal (base 8). **o** is for short unsigned octal values.

- **Q**   Prints signed 32-bit octal values. **q** is for short signed octal values.

- **B**   Prints a single byte (8 bits) in hexadecimal. **b** prints a byte in octal.

- **F**   Used for floating-point. **F** prints a double-precision floating-point, which takes 8 bytes (64 bits). **f** prints a single-precision, 32-bit floating-point value.

- **s**   Prints a string, up to the first null byte. **S** does the same, but any characters that normally would not correspond to a printable character will be displayed as a "control" character. For example, a byte containing the number 1, which doesn't normally mean anything, will be output as "^A", a "control-A" character code.

- **c**   Prints a single character. Just as with the "S" strings format, a "C" prints nonprintable characters.

- **i**   Prints a full 32-bit word value as an instruction.

- **Y**   Prints a date value in string format. Date values are stored as the number of seconds since the beginning of (UNIX) time; not a useful number to most folks. The output from the **Y** command is much more intelligible.

Each of these format display commands will print one value. You can put several of these format commands together in any combination. You can also use a counter with any of them, which tells **adb** to repeat that particular format a certain number of times. Thus, if you put **XXX** in the format, it will print three long values in hex. **3X** will do exactly the same thing.

Formatting the output

adb also offers a few format display commands that are not used to print out data but are used to make the display more readable and useful. For example, you can print headings, move to a new line, or skip over data you're not interested in printing. The format display commands, shown below, are primarily used in macros.

- *text*   in quotes is printed as is. The text may be a label or heading, to make the output understandable.

- **n**   Prints a newline or goes to the next line of output.

- **t**   Causes **adb** to move to the next tab stop according to the multiplier you specify. If you specify **8t** in the format, **adb** will move to the next column that is a multiple of 8. You can use anything you want here, but **adb** does not assume an unlimited line length. Eighty characters is the normal width of a terminal screen, so **adb** will automatically move to a new line when you get out too far.

- **a**   Prints the current address of the data you're printing. This address is often used when displaying assembly code instructions, so you can keep each line labeled with the appropriate code location. For example, **rmalloc,20?ia** will display 20 (hex) instructions with the address on each line.

- **+**   Moves forward to another address, skipping over data. **–** moves backward. You must provide a count to tell **adb** how many bytes you're passing.

These commands are used most often inside macro files, but you can certainly type them yourself. Play around with these in your own commands if you'd like, and see what they do to your output.

Locations & sizes

adb keeps track of the "current location," the address it last used to start a display command. This is known as "dot," since you can use a dot or period (.) to reference it when building up an address expression. To redisplay something, you can use dot as the address for the command. If you need to back up, you can subtract something from the value of dot. For example,

```
./X
.-4/X
```

will display the contents of the current location as a hex value and set dot to the current location again, the same address. The second command says to back up four bytes and start the display there, effectively showing the value of the previous word. The value of dot will now be changed to the new starting address, or four back from where it used to be.

If you don't provide a new address, **adb** will continue to use the old one, the value of dot. This means you can redisplay the same data you did before, but using different formats, as shown below.

```
./XxxD
/D2X
```

These commands will use the same address for each display, since no new address was provided for the second one. This will show a long hex, two short integers in hex, and a long in decimal: a total of three full words. The next command displays exactly the same three words, but as a long decimal value and two full words in hexadecimal.

If you want to advance to the next sequential location, you need to provide a specific address or use an address consisting of just a plus sign (**+**).

Along with the current address, dot, **adb** also keeps a record of how much data was displayed last time or the number of bytes your format commands took up. This allows the + address to work correctly. **adb** knows how far to advance the current address, since it knows how much data got displayed. So, to output a bunch of data and then move on, you might use a command sequence like this:

```
./4Xxx20c4DX
+/5Xxxs
```

The use of **+** as the address allows you to keep from counting up all those sizes and calculating the correct offset from dot. Let **adb** do it for you!

Another **adb** shortcut concerns the format command string. If you don't provide one, **adb** uses what it had last time. To move through memory and repeat the last command, just type **+/** followed by a Return. **adb** will move the value of dot forward and reuse the old format string. Even easier, a simple return, with no address or format, means "move forward and reuse the last display command," so you can move through memory easily, repeating the last command, just by pressing Return.

You can also use a repeat count with the command, which acts just like retyping it or pressing Return that number of times. It *does* move the dot forward to the last set of data displayed. For example:

```
.,10/Xdd
```

would advance through the core file displaying 10 sets of data in Xdd format. Here is an example that demonstrates this feature of **adb**.

Figure 8-1   Viewing a file via adb

```
Hi, Kim...  adb my-file -
0?4X
0:             44726573      73616765      2c207768      656e2076
    (Hit return here)
0x10:          69657765      64206279      20612070      6572736f
    (Hit return here)
0x20:          6e207769      7468206c      6974746c      6520746f
+,5?4X
0x30:          206e6f20      6b6e6f77      6c656467      65206162
               6f75740a      74686973      20657175      65737472
               69616e20      61637469      76697479      2c207368
               6f756c64      206c6561      76652074      68652076
               69657765      72207769      74682061      2073656e
    (Hit return here)
0x80:          73652074      68617420      7468650a      686f7273
    (Hit return here)
0x90:          65206973      20686170      70792069      6e206869
$quit
Hi, Kim...
```

Note, as shown in the above example, when Return is pressed, only the format command string is repeated and not the command count.

Miscellaneous commands

A lot of special miscellaneous commands don't fit the general **adb** data display command syntax. Let's talk about some of them now.

Value conversion

The = command is used for conversion. Rather than looking up a value in memory and displaying it, the equals sign prints the value of the address field according to the format you specify. You can use this command for printing in different bases, for example, converting hexadecimal to decimal, or for displaying the actual hexadecimal address associated with a symbol.

Let's try a couple of examples of the = command. Below, we convert a hexadecimal value into date format. We also get the hexadecimal representation of the 4-byte character sequence "Hiya." (Yes, as shown below, **adb** can be run without any arguments.)

```
Hiya... adb
123456=Y
                    1970 Jan 14 14:24:06
'Hiya'=X
                    48697961
$q
Hiya...
```

The = command is also sometimes used in macros to print labels. You might see a line like the one below—

```
.="Top label"nnn
```

—with no actual display of a numeric value. All this command sequence does is print the string "Top label" and a couple of newlines. There was no request to display a data value from either the object file or the core file. In this example, the value of dot would not change.

Note – Even though there may be no memory reference involved, = can modify the value of dot. When using =, always remember that dot (.) may have changed.

$ commands

Of course, there are some useful commands that just don't fit in any major categories. This miscellaneous catchall set uses modifiers to the **$** command. These include:

- **$c**   Prints a C stack traceback. Originally, there were several different compilers for UNIX, and each had an individual code generator that used separate stack formats. This meant you needed a command to dump out C language stacks, Fortran stacks, or Pascal stacks. When the compilers were eventually modified to use a common code generator (and thus the same type of stack), the need for all these different commands went away, and the **$c** stack command is the one that survived. By default, **$c** will display six calling arguments. **$c**X, where X is 0 through f, can be used to specify how many arguments to display. You can also provide an address to **$c** (in front of the $) to tell **adb** "the top of the stack starts here." This combination is used in some macros to display stack tracebacks for various different stacks in the kernel.

- **$C**   Prints a C stack traceback and saved frame pointer and saved program counter values.

- **$r**   Displays the current values of the machine registers. There are lots of machine registers on SPARC; this command will show you their contents. Generally, this command is not too useful for kernel crash dumps, because the values displayed belong to the code in the *panic()* routine, but the stack pointer can come in handy.

- **$x**   (and **$X**) Displays the current values of the floating-point registers.

- **$<**   Reads a macro file. Think of it as "redirecting standard input" away from the keyboard to a file. When the file runs out of commands, control is returned to the user at the keyboard.

- **$>**   Sends output to a file, if you provide a filename. If the name is omitted, output returns to the screen for the following commands.

- **$v**   Displays **adb** variable values in octal.

- **$M**   Displays the names of the **kadb** built-in macros.

- **$q**   Quits, or exits, **adb**. For **vi** users, it usually takes two tries to get out of **adb**. After the familiar **:q** exit command results in a "bad modifier" error message, you remember "Oh yes, I'm in **adb**" and type the correct **$q** command. For those who are impatient, a Control-D will also exit **adb**.

There are other commands that are not commonly used. The man page for **adb** will give you the details on these and other exciting features.

Pattern searching

adb does have a limited ability to search for patterns. As a part of the display commands, you can ask for a matching pattern to be located. These will start at the given address and look in the appropriate file (? for the object file, / for the core file) until the value is found or **adb** runs out of data to look at. You can also provide a mask, which allows you to look for only certain bits. By default, the mask is **-1**, which scans for a complete match.

The command is **?L** or **/L** to search for full words, and **?l** or **/l** to look for short half-words. After the command, give the value followed by the mask. If **adb** finds a match, it will set dot to that address.

We will see an example of the pattern searching command in the one of the case studies later on.

Variables

adb maintains some internal variables for storing values. If you need to keep something around, there are commands available to store into and retrieve from local **adb** variables. These variables are restricted to single-letter or single-digit names, so you can have variables a through z, A through Z, and 0 through 9 in which to store things. Some of these have dedicated uses (a few of the numbers), and some are initialized when **adb** starts up, but in general you've got 50 or so places to stash things. Use the **$v** command to check the current usage of the **adb** variables.

As you'll see in Chapter 12, some of the **adb** macros use variables to temporarily keep addresses, so if you plan to use macros, check to see which variables they are using. You'll need to use names that the macros don't modify. Uppercase letters are generally a safe bet, since they are rarely seen in macro files.

The register names of the CPU, such as %i3, %l0, and %g6, are also available as "variables," but in this case these names really refer to the registers of the machine. Modifying these, especially when debugging a running program, will have an effect on the program execution and on the results of some operations.

A couple of commands are available to work with these variables and registers. The > command acts like redirecting standard output, or sending data: it stores the "address," the left-hand side of the command, into the variable. The opposite command, <, retrieves a value from a register and uses it as a value. For example, the commands shown below store the decimal value 1234 into variable *p*, take the value in *p*, copy it into Z, and then print the value in Z as a hex number.

Figure 8-2   Using adb variables

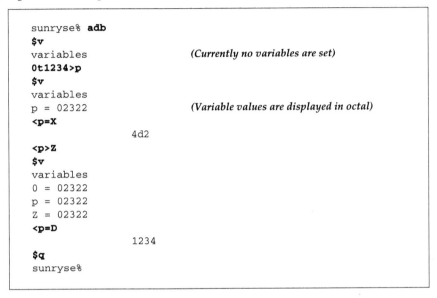

```
sunryse% adb
$v
variables                    (Currently no variables are set)
0t1234>p
$v
variables
p = 02322                    (Variable values are displayed in octal)
<p=X
                4d2
<p>Z
$v
variables
0 = 02322
p = 02322
Z = 02322
<p=D
                1234
$q
sunryse%
```

The < and > commands will also work on registers, to extract or modify their values. Thus <sp will get the contents of the current stack pointer register in the CPU.

Writing to the object and core files

adb is often used to modify the contents of a program or even the running kernel. This means writing into the object file or the core file, changing some of the values.

The normal mode of operation is viewing: You can look, but you can't touch. By adding the -w flag to the startup parameters for adb, you can use the write commands. These are essentially modifiers to the two display commands we saw before, which look at either the object file or the core file.

Using the **?** command, we can modify four consecutive bytes in the object file by using a **W** command with it. The bytes need not be full-word aligned. Here's an example that demonstrates this command.

Figure 8-3   Modifying the contents of a file via adb

```
sunryse% adb -w memofile -
123?X
0x123:          20746f20
123?W 100
0x123:          0x20746f20      =        0x100
123?X
0x123:          100
$q
sunryse%
```

This will *write* the value 100 (hex) into the four bytes starting at address 0x123 in the object file. Similarly, if we use a lowercase **w** command, we will write two bytes.

By use of **/**, modifications can be made to the core or memory file. (The above example did not have a specified core file.)

If you start out in read-only mode and decide that you really want to make some changes, the **$W** command will reopen the files as if you had started **adb** with the **-w** flag.

Note – Modifications to the object file and core file via **adb** are made immediately. If you change your mind about a modification, you will need to perform a second write command to put the original value back before any real damage is done.

Address map

The **$m** command will display the current set of addresses that **adb** thinks are valid. Just as your program, or the kernel, has sections of real code or data, **adb** keeps track of which areas of memory have pieces of the program or actual values in them. The map displayed by the **$m** command identifies what address ranges are considered "known" for each of the two files — object file and core file — along with some information about how **adb** will actually locate the correct place. In general, this is only useful when looking at user programs; it helps track down segmentation violations and shows where dynamic libraries have been mapped in.

Interactive debugging sessions (process control)

When discussing UNIX system crash dump analysis, it is easy to forget that **adb** is a general-purpose debugger that can be used interactively with running programs. When **adb** is used as an interactive debugger, there are a number of colon (**:**) commands to use for process and program control. These same commands can be used with **kadb**, the kernel absolute debugger, when working with the running kernel.

One of the primary uses for the colon commands is to set and remove breakpoints. Breakpoints are special instructions inserted into the code that cause the program (the kernel or a user utility) to stop and transfer control to the debugger. When a breakpoint is reached, program execution is frozen, allowing you to examine or change memory, look at registers, and even change the code if you desire.

The following breakpoint commands are available:

- *address***:b**   Sets a breakpoint at *address*

- **$b**   Displays all the breakpoints currently set up

- *address***:d**   Deletes a breakpoint at the *address*

- **:z**   Zaps (deletes) all the breakpoints

Once a breakpoint is reached, the following process execution commands can be used to interactively control program execution:

- **:r**   Runs the program (starts or restarts program execution)

- **:c**   Continues execution

- **:s**   Steps, executing only one instruction

- **:e**   Steps, treating called routines as one enormous instruction

- **:u**   Continues, stopping immediately after the next function call

We will be using some of these commands later on in another chapter.

Summary

As you have discovered in this chapter, **adb** is a powerful debugging tool that you'll be able to put to good use when trying to figure out why your system gave up the ghost. From our own experiences, we find that we often use **adb**:

- For dumping the stack out with **$c** or one of the stack traceback macros.

- To display the contents of the core file.

- For debugging, often just poking around, looking for things that "aren't right," following pointers, dumping out structures, and just examining the state of the data in general.

- For running various macro files, since most of them are used to display complex structures from the memory contents.

As you become more and more accustomed to **adb**, you'll find that your skills with **kadb** also improve since **adb** and **kadb** are so closely related.

Now that you have a good idea of what **adb** can do for you, let's move on and start putting it to use!

Initial Analysis Using adb 9 ≣

Now that we've collected some initial information about the system crash by using various UNIX commands, let's collect some more initial data by using **adb**. Before we start, however, let's talk about some assumptions we are making at this point.

In the next chapter, we will talk in depth about the header files in the **/usr/include** directory and how we can use them to gain more insight into the kernel. Shortly after that, we will discuss a very powerful aspect of **adb** known as macros, two of which we will use in this chapter. We will also cover the namelist (aka the symbol table) in another chapter. We are getting ahead of ourselves a bit in this chapter, but for now, our purpose is to jump right into **adb** and see it pump out some initial analysis data for us.

Starting an adb session

In the examples throughout this book, we will often show portions of an **adb** session already in progress, so let's quickly review how to start the **adb** session. The technique and syntax are the same for both Solaris 1 and Solaris 2 systems.

If you have a set of **savecore** files to work with, move them to a system that has the same kernel architecture and operating system release running on it. Once done, use the **cd** command to change to the directory where the **savecore** files are located, then start up **adb** with the general syntax:

```
adb -k unixfile corefile
```

As an example, on a Solaris 1 crash, looking at crash sequence number 3, the command would be:

```
Hiya... adb -k vmunix.3 vmcore.3
physmem 3f98
```

On a Solaris 2 crash, looking at crash number 3, the command would be:

```
Hiya...   adb -k unix.3 vmcore.3
physmem 3f98
```

In both cases, **adb** returns the number of pages of physical memory in hexadecimal and then waits for your first command. Note that most versions of **adb** do not offer the user any prompt at this point. Don't be fooled by this!

System identification

Often, it is helpful to know which system's **savecore** files we are looking at. This is especially true when you have a large collection of system crash dumps and don't remember which came from where. How do you sort out which dump came from which system?

In Solaris 1, the name of the system is stored in the kernel as *hostname*. In Solaris 2, the host name is kept in a structure called *utsname*. Both *hostname* and *utsname* are null-terminated strings—an array of characters where the last byte contains a zero. Using **adb**, we can examine those strings.

Yes, if we used the **strings** command as shown earlier, we might have spotted the system name; however, we wouldn't have been able to identify it as such in the context in which we were viewing it.

Other helpful system identification data can also be easily retrieved by using **adb**. Depending on the specific flavor of UNIX, this sometimes includes the architecture of the system, the domain name, and the hardware vendor. Let's first get some initial information from a Solaris 1 system crash dump.

Figure 9-1   Displaying initial system information from a Solaris 1 crash

```
Hiya...   adb -k vmunix.2 vmcore.2
physmem 3f98
hostname/s
_hostname:
_hostname:     sunny
version/s
_version:
_version:      SunOS Release 4.1.3 (DISKSUITE) #6: Thu Sep 23 17:25:03
               BST 1993 Copyright (c) 1983-1992, Sun Microsystems, Inc.
domainname/s
_domainname:
_domainname:   noname
```

Figure 9-1   Displaying initial system information from a Solaris 1 crash

```
cpu/X
_cpu:
_cpu:            72
sysname/s
_sysname:
_sysname:        SUNW,SPARCstation-10
$q
Hiya...
```

Now let's collect similar information from a Solaris 2 system. Remember that Solaris 1 is a BSD-based UNIX, whereas Solaris 2 is an AT&T SVR4-based UNIX. Although the average user may not see a big difference between these two popular flavors of UNIX, the two kernels differ greatly. Therefore, many of the symbol names within the kernel will be unique.

In this example, we will use an **adb** macro called **utsname**. We will be discussing macros in greater detail later on. For now, you just need to know that a macro is merely an ASCII file that contains keystrokes we feed **adb**, rather like UNIX command redirection. The **utsname** macro displays the same system information that the UNIX **uname** command with the **-a** option would show the user.

Figure 9-2   Displaying initial system information from a Solaris 2 crash

```
Hiya... adb -k unix.1 vmcore.1
physmem 1b24
$<utsname
utsname:
utsname:          sys   SunOS
utsname+0x101:    node maugrim
utsname+0x202:    release  5.3
utsname+0x303:    version  Generic
utsname+0x404:    machine  sun4c
hw_provider/s
hw_provider:
hw_provider:      Sun_Microsystems
architecture/s
architecture:
architecture:     sparc
srpc_domain/s
srpc_domain:
srpc_domain:      work.sun.com
$q
Hiya...
```

We now know a little bit about the identification of the system with which we are working. We know the name of the system, the hardware architecture on which the CPU is based, the release of UNIX it is running, and the domain, if any, that is in use.

Boot time, crash time, and uptime

UNIX systems keep track of the current time as well as the time when they were booted. The current time is usually easy to find, but sometimes the boot time is a bit trickier. In postmortem system crash dump files, the current time is actually the time of the crash.

The time of the crash can play a vital role in system crash dump analysis. For example, if you find you have several crashes from one system that all occurred at the same time but on different days, you are much closer to finding the source. In such cases, often a specific **cron** job turns out to be the program that is triggering the crashes.

Comparing the boot time to the current or crash time also provides useful information. Subtracting the crash time from the boot time gives the system uptime. A system that, according to the **savecore** files, was up for several months presents a different picture than a system that was up for merely a few minutes.

Looking first at a Solaris 1 system, let's get the boot time and the time of the system crash. These are conveniently stored in kernel variables *boottime* and *time*. UNIX time is maintained as the number of seconds since January 1, 1970. As you may recall from the previous chapter, in **adb** the /Y command says to show the 32-bit value stored in the specified variable as a date instead of, say, a hexadecimal value.

Figure 9-3   Displaying the boot time and crash time on a Solaris 1 crash

```
Hiya... adb -k vmunix.0 vmcore.0
physmem 3f98
boottime/Y
_boottime:
_boottime:      1993 Oct 25 13:02:25
time/Y
_time:
_time:          1993 Nov 3 00:14:06
$q
Hiya...
```

Solaris 2 also has a *time* variable but doesn't keep track of the boot time as a fixed value, as is done in Solaris 1. Instead, it keeps track of the 100ths of seconds that have passed since the system was booted. This value is kept in a kernel variable called *lbolt*, which is an abbreviation for "lightning bolts," or clock ticks.

To get the boot time on a Solaris 2 system, we have to get the *lbolt* value, divide it by 100 to get whole seconds, and subtract that value from the current or crash time. Within **adb** we can do this simple arithmetic and ask **adb** to display the result in time format.

Figure 9-4   Displaying the boot time and crash time on a Solaris 2 crash

```
Hiya... adb -k /dev/ksyms /dev/mem
physmem 1e16
time/Y
time:
time:              1994 Mar 13 21:12:49
time/X
time:
time: 2d8381d1
lbolt/X
lbolt:
lbolt: a50e3
2d8381d1-(a50e3%0t100)=Y
                   1994 Mar 13 19:20:09
$q
Hiya...
```

The % sign says to divide. The **0t** specifies that the next value is in decimal instead of the **adb** default base, hexadecimal. Instead of **0t100** we could have simply put 64, as 100 decimal is 64 hexadecimal. The **=Y** says to *show the result of the formula* in date format.

When calculating the boot time, you might find it easier to work in decimal. We will perform the same operation again, this time using all decimal values. We can easily do the division by 100 in our head by simply dropping the last two digits from *lbolt*.

```
Hiya... adb -k /dev/ksyms /dev/mem
physmem 1e16
time/D
time:
time: 763593169
lbolt/D
lbolt:
lbolt: 676067
0t763593169-0t6760=Y
                   1994 Mar 13 19:20:09
$q
Hiya...
```

Panic strings

We've learned what type of system we are dealing with, and we know when it was booted and when it crashed. The next thing we need to know is how it crashed. Was it a forced crash dump due to a hung system or did the system panic or trap on its own?

Whenever a system panics, the actual panic message is kept in a string pointed to by a kernel variable called *panicstr*. *panicstr* will contain the starting address for the panic string.

Both Solaris 1 and Solaris 2 use *panicstr* for this purpose, so we will show an example from one OS only. As you can tell from the name of the unix file, **vmunix.5**, we are looking at a Solaris 1 postmortem file.

Figure 9-5   Displaying the panic string

```
Hiya... adb -k vmunix.5 vmcore.5
physmem 15f90
*panicstr/s
_inprom+0x872: zero
$q
Hiya...
```

In this example, we see that the system panic'ed due to what is called a "panic: zero." While it is possible for a system to actually panic this way, usually this is caused by someone using L1-A to force a hung system to panic and then asking the system to resume execution at location zero. This is an illegal operation and results in the panic shown above. So, until we actually look deeper into the system crash dump files, we will assume for now that the panic was forced by the system administrator in response to a hung system.

The message buffer, msgbuf

We've talked about the message buffer, *msgbuf*, and have already seen how to find it by using the UNIX **strings** command. Now let's use **adb** and an **adb** macro to examine it. In this example, we are looking at a Solaris 1 system that trapped.

Figure 9-6   Displaying the message buffer via the msgbuf macro

```
Hiya... adb -k vmunix.0 vmcore.0
physmem 2fe3
$<msgbuf
0xf8002000:    magic        size         bufx         bufr
               63062        1ff0         d70          8b7
```

Figure 9-6   Displaying the message buffer via the msgbuf macro

```
0xf80028c7:      BAD TRAP
                 pid 2211, `my-menu': Memory address alignment
                 pc=0xf811a07c, sp=0xf88c5c10, psr=0x114018c4, context=0xc
                 g1-g7: 0, 8000000, ffffffff, 50, f8153c00, 0, 0
                 Begin traceback... sp = f88c5c10
                 Called from f8118f88, fp=f88c5c80, args=ff10c4d0 10a000 f8525a70 10a000 0
                    f81aaae8
                 Called from f80c360c, fp=f88c5cf0, args=ff10c4d0 10a000 f8525a70 0 0 10a000
                 Called from f80c3bfc, fp=f88c5d60, args=ff10c4d0 10a000 32000 fc e60ca0 0 0
                 Called from f80c60a4, fp=f88c5e10, args=ff10c4d0 1000 0 0 10a000 ff10cb60
                 Called from f812a450, fp=f88c5e70, args=10a000 ff10c4d0 1000 0 2 10a000
                 Called from f81284d0, fp=f88c5ee0, args=10a06c 0 2 0 f847241c f8 191400
                 Called from f8005c88, fp=f88c5f58, args=10009 f88c5fb4 10a06c 80 2 0
                 Called from 38218, fp=f7ffef40, args=0 382e0 1095ac 109c44 1 1
                 End traceback...
                 panic: Memory address alignment
                 <3>zs1: silo overflow
                 syncing file systems... done
                 00000 low-memory static kernel pages
                 01971 additional static and sysmap kernel pages
                 00000 dynamic kernel data pages
                 00341 additional user structure pages
                 00000 segmap kernel pages
                 00000 segvn kernel pages
                 00185 current user process pages
                 00305 user stack pages
                 02802 total pages (2802 chunks)

                 dumping to vp fce182c4, offset 42360
$q
Hiya...
```

When we later examine the **msgbuf** macro up close, we will see that the macro doesn't actually display the complete message buffer, only the most recently added messages. These are the messages that will be related to the crash. Again, to see the whole message buffer, you can use the UNIX **strings** command.

Note – There are times when the message buffer cannot be accessed via **adb** because *msgbuf* is not in the symbol table. Should this occur, simply use the UNIX **strings** command to view the buffer.

Stack tracebacks

In Chapter 17 and Chapter 18 we will be talking about the stack and stack tracebacks. Simply put, the stack traceback is a history of which routines called which and with what arguments. Nearly all initial system crash dump analysis using **adb** includes taking a look at the stack traceback, so let's show how that is done and we'll talk about it in greater detail later on.

Figure 9-7   Displaying the stack traceback

```
Hiya...  adb -k unix.0 vmcore.0
physmem 1e05
$c
complete_panic(0xf0049460,0xf05d03ac,0xf05d0238,0x3,0x0,0x1) + 10c
do_panic(?) + 1c
vcmn_err(0xf015f7a8,0xf05d03ac,0xf05d03ac,0x3cad8,0x2,0x3)
cmn_err(0x3,0xf015f7a8,0x0,0x18,0x18,0xf0152400) + 1c
die(0x9,0xf05d04c4,0x3,0x3a6,0x2,0xf015f7a8) + 78
trap(0x9,0xf05d04c4,0xf01822d8,0x3a6,0x2,0x0) + 598
fault(?) + 84
mutex_enter(0x0,0xd,0x64,0x1,0xd,0xf05d06ec)
lookuppn(0xf05d06e4,0x0,0xf05d06ec,0x0,0x0,0xfc01dd14) + 148
lookupname(0x0,0x0,0x1,0x0,0xf05d07f4,0x0) + 28
vn_open(0x3cad8,0x0,0x3,0xb40,0xf05d08ac,0x0) + a4
copen(0x3cad8,0x3,0xb48,0xf05d0920,0x3cad8,0xf0156628) + 70
syscall(0xf0160f3c) + 3e4
$q
Hiya...
```

The top of the stack tracebacks show the most recently called routine, in this case, *complete_panic()*. This stack traceback was from a Solaris 2.3 SPARCstation 20, which was crashed by setting *rootdir* to zero. Later on, we will learn how to discover the point at which the system became unhappy about the null pointer we had created.

Summary

Using **adb**, there is a lot of initial information that we can collect in a dump. This includes:

- System hostname
- System hardware configuration
- Operating system revision
- System boot time
- System crash time
- The panic message and whether the system was hung or crashed on its own
- The message buffer
- The stack traceback

Now that we have some initial information about our crash, we probably will want to go a bit deeper with our analysis work. Before we can do so, we need to explore some other topics.

However, having said that, if you have access to a bug database or, as in the case of SunService customers, the SunSolve CD, you are now armed with enough information to browse through the various databases provided on the CD to see if your system crashed due to a known problem for which a fix may already exist. If you have a SunSolve CD, use some of the information from your panic message and your stack traceback to search through the bugs and patches databases.

At this point, now that you have initial analysis data from **adb**, the odds are already more in your favor!

9

The /usr/include Header Files   10 ≣

The majority of UNIX system administrators in the world do not have access to UNIX source code. Many software support specialists also do not have source to refer to. However, most UNIX systems do come with **/usr/include** header files that are usually straight from the UNIX source tree.

In this chapter, we will talk about the header files, what they contain, and how we can use them when trying to track down why our system panic'ed. In the next chapter, we will take a look at the kernel symbol table or namelist and see how it relates to the **/usr/include** header files.

Both the **/usr/include** files and the kernel symbol table are big pieces in the overall puzzle that we are trying to piece together.

What is a header file?

Most C programmers are already quite familiar with header files. These are also frequently referred to as ".h" (pronounced "dot h") files because the filename usually has a **.h** suffix. When a large program is designed, the header file is used to store information that several routines within the program will want to address. For example, the programmer might want to define some common constants in a header file. He might also place commonly used structures in the header file as well as some external variables and function declarations. Macros are also commonly defined in header files.

The source for the routines that will use or include the information from the header file will begin with #include statements, at the head of the source—thus the name header file. Header files can also use the #include statement to bring in other header files at compilation.

The /usr/include directories

On most UNIX systems, you will find a **/usr/include** directory. On some UNIX systems, you may need to install a programmer's environment or package to see this directory. On others, it is part of the core UNIX system. On Sun's Solaris 2 systems, the majority of the **/usr/include** files are in the SUNWhea package.

Within the **/usr/include** directory, you will find several subdirectories. Note that each flavor of UNIX that you encounter may differ slightly here. On a Solaris 2.3 system, you will find a directory structure as follows. Each of these directories and subdirectories contains header files.

Table 10-1 Subdirectories of /usr/include

```
/usr/include
    ./admin
    ./arpa
    ./bsm
    ./des
    ./inet
    ./kerberos
    ./net
    ./netinet
    ./nfs
    ./protocols
    ./rpc
    ./rpcsvc
    ./security
    ./sys
        ./debug
        ./fpu
        ./fs
        ./proc
        ./scsi
            ./adapters
            ./conf
            ./generic
            ./impl
            ./targets
    ./vm
```

Let's briefly talk about what might be found in each of these directories.

/usr/include

If **/usr/include** were to have a miscellaneous area, this would be it. Anything that doesn't fit into one of the more specialized subdirectories described below will be found here. It is here that we find header files commonly used by the programmers *not* writing kernel code, network software, or device drivers.

/usr/include/admin

The header files here are all related to the administration framework products.

/usr/include/arpa

Here we find the header files relating to **ftp**, **telnet**, and other Advanced Research Project Agency (ARPA) products.

/usr/include/bsm

This directory contains the header files relating to the Basic Security Module. Here we find among other things, information about security auditing policies, audit queue controls, the various audit record structures, and the list of auditable events.

/usr/include/des

This directory contains the header files relating to the Data Encryption Set software.

/usr/include/inet

Here is where we find some of the header information relating to the Internet Protocol software.

/usr/include/kerberos

Yes, you guessed it! This is where the header files for Kerberos live.

/usr/include/net

This is where the low-level network interface header files can be found. Information about routing, the Address Resolution Protocol, and address families is tucked away here.

/usr/include/netinet

Here is where we find more information about the Internet Protocols. This includes:

- Address Resolution Protocol (ARP)
- Distance-Vector Multicast Routine Protocol (DVMRP)
- Internet Control Message Protocol (ICMP)
- Internet Group Management Protocol (IGMP)
- Internet Protocol (IP)
- Transmission Control Protocol (TCP)
- User Data Protocol (UDP)

/usr/include/nfs

If you're interested in digging through the Network File System structures, this is where you will find NFS® information. **Export** and **mount** option flags are found here, as well as various NFS limits, such as the maximum length of an NFS pathname. This is the directory we reference when looking at structures used by NFS.

/usr/include/protocols

This directory contains a few header files that relate to the **routed**, **rwhod**, **timed**, **dump**, and **restore** programs.

/usr/include/rpc

This is where we find information about the Remote Procedure Call software, **keyserv**, and more on Kerberos and DES authentication in relation to RPC. Also found here is information about boot parameters, more on exported directories, header files relating to the Port Mapper Protocol, and information about External Data Representation (XDR).

/usr/include/rpcsvc

This directory contains the header files for software serviced by RPC. Software represented here includes autofs, NFS, NIS+, and NIS (formerly known as YP).

/usr/include/security

Header files relating to the Pluggable Authentication Module (PAM) interface software are kept here.

/usr/include/sys

This directory contains the majority of the kernel header files as well as several subdirectories.

/usr/include/sys/debug

The Kernel Absolute DeBugger (**kadb**) is compiled using the header files found here.

/usr/include/sys/fpu

Everything you might need to know about the Floating-Point Unit structures, function, and variables is kept here.

/usr/include/sys/fs

Valuable information about the various local file systems exists in this directory. On Solaris 2.3, this information includes:

* autofs
* cachefs
* High Sierra File System (HSFS)
* Loopback File System (LOFS)
* PC (MS-DOS®) Compatible File System (PCFS)
* swapfs
* tmpfs
* UNIX File System (UFS)

/usr/include/sys/proc

Here is where we find the header information regarding the **/proc** file system.

/usr/include/sys/scsi

A few generalized and common header files exist here; the subdirectories listed below contain more specific information relating to the Small Computer System Interface (SCSI) hardware and supporting software.

/usr/include/sys/scsi/adapters

Information about the Enhanced SCSI Processor (ESP) chip is found here. This information includes register definitions, register manipulation macros, and clocking information for the chip. ESP options used in tuning ESP devices can also be found in this directory.

/usr/include/sys/scsi/conf

Global SCSI device configuration information is maintained here. This directory is also where we find the SCSI device structure.

/usr/include/sys/scsi/generic

Within this directory are the header files that define and describe standard SCSI command definitions, direct access mode operations, message codes, and other information from the SCSI specification.

/usr/include/sys/scsi/impl

This directory contains the header files that accompany each UNIX vendor's specific implementation of the standard SCSI interface.

/usr/include/sys/scsi/targets

Header information specific to SCSI targets is found here, including data about the SCSI disk (sd) and SCSI tape (st) devices.

/usr/include/vm

The header files in this directory define aspects of the virtual memory system. Here is where you will read about anonymous memory, how address space is structured, how hardware address translation is managed, and how virtual memory pages are handled.

CAUTION! The information in these **/usr/include** files is considered a part of the source code and may be changed dramatically in later releases without warning. Use the information in these files for debugging and for understanding how the system is structured, but don't depend on it remaining the same. Programmers who write their code based only on data in the header files should expect severe porting problems.

/usr/kvm/sys

On Solaris 1 systems, you will find another directory that contains header files. This is the **/usr/kvm/sys** directory. The header files contained here are used specifically during the build of a new executable kernel and, with a few exceptions, are the same files you would find in the **/usr/include/sys** directory.

/usr/share/src/uts

Solaris 2 does not contain a **/usr/kvm/sys** directory because the kernel is dynamically configured at boot time instead of being built and then booted. However, the nearest thing to this directory is the **/usr/share/src/uts** directory. In this directory, you'll find a collection of hardware-specific header files.

/usr/ucbinclude

Both operating environments have a **/usr/ucbinclude** directory that, as you might guess, contains header files that are specific to UCB (University of California, Berkeley) features and utilities.

Summary

On both Solaris 1 and Solaris 2 systems, there are over 1100 header files. These source files can be used to help gain insights into the operating system, aiding in your system crash dump analysis work.

As we continue, you'll see how we put the header files to use over and over again.

Symbol Tables

Without having access to the complete UNIX source, we have to learn to take full advantage of the header files in **/usr/include**. Reading through these files, we get an idea of what we might be able to see when poking around in the kernel. Another tool we use to help us do this is the UNIX **nm** command. Let's explore this command in detail.

Namelists & the nm command

nm displays the symbol table or namelist of an executable object file. On Solaris 1 systems, the executable object files are in assembler and link editor format. On Solaris 2 systems, objects are in executable and linking format, ELF. Some UNIX systems use the common assembler and link editor format, COFF.

The symbols in an executable object file can be one of several types. For the most part, we are interested in objects (variables, structures, and arrays) and functions. Using **nm**, we can get a complete list of all of the symbols, their types, sizes, and other information about each symbol. Using **nm** along with the UNIX **grep** command, we can obtain a list of just the objects.

It is important to remember that the kernel is really one great, big program. It is compiled from thousands of individual source files. On a Solaris 1 system, when running **nm** against **/vmunix**, you can expect to see over 7000 lines of **nm** output! On a Solaris 2 system, when running **nm** on **/dev/ksyms** (the location of the kernel symbol table for the dynamic kernel), over 10,000 lines is not unusual! Of those, maybe only a third are objects. However, to scale things down for a moment, let's look at a tiny program and see what its symbol table looks like.

A tiny example using Solaris 2

Let's write a small program that includes a small header file. Once compiled, we can take a look at the symbol table. Once we have that, using **adb**, we will look at the variables we have set in the program.

First, we have our header file, **tiny.h**.

Code Example 11-1   tiny.h

```
/*  tiny.h  */

#define BESTYEAR      66

struct mustang {
    float ragtop;
    int leather;
    int candyapple; } dreamcar;

struct highway {
    int speedlimit;
    int smokey; };

float beach_factor = 123.5;
```

Next, our little C program, **tiny.c**.

Code Example 11-2   tiny.c

```
/*  tiny.c  */

#include "tiny.h"

int whistles = 10;

main ()
{
    int tickets = 6;
    dreamcar.ragtop = 123.5;
    dreamcar.leather = 6;
    dreamcar.candyapple = 10;
}
```

This example, while maybe not the most exciting, demonstrates the relationship between the variables in the **.c** and **.h** files and the executable object file's symbol table.

When looking at the UNIX **/usr/include** files, you will see a lot of structures declared or described; however, not all of these will be immediately defined as actual variables. In **tiny.h**, we see the structure *mustang* being declared. In other words, we can see what a *mustang* structure looks like and what type of data it will contain. We also see that variable *dreamcar* is defined to be a *mustang* structure.

A structure type called *highway* is described or declared; however, it is not referenced in any definitions in either **tiny.h** or **tiny.c**. We encounter this type of situation a lot in **/usr/include** files. We have to dig through other **.h** files and, all too often, the source itself to discover which structures have been defined for use as a certain type of declared structure.

The difference between "declaring" a value and "defining" it may be a bit fuzzy for some, so let's try a silly analogy just to be on the safe side. You can "declare" to your friends what you would do *if* you won a million dollars. However, it is not until you actually have the money in your hand that you truly "define" how it is used. Declarations are the simply the descriptions of what might come to be someday. Definitions, in terms of programming, result in actual memory allocation.

Okay, back to the example. Note that **tiny.c** has a variable that is defined within the *main()* routine, while another is defined outside of *main()*. After compilation, which variables from **tiny.h** and **tiny.c** do you think will appear in the symbol table of the executable object file called **tiny**? Let's take a look!

For this example, we will use **nm** without any options on a Solaris 2.3 system, so expect to see a lot more than a few lines of output! We will highlight the symbols you are looking for so that they're easier to spot.

Figure 11-1   Using the Solaris 2 nm program to view tiny's symbol table

```
Hiya...   cc -o tiny tiny.c
Hiya...   nm tiny


Symbols from tiny:

[Index]     Value       Size     Type   Bind   Other  Shndx    Name

[1]     |         0|       0|FILE  |LOCL  |0     |ABS     |tiny
[2]     |     65748|       0|SECT  |LOCL  |0     |1       |
[3]     |     65768|       0|SECT  |LOCL  |0     |2       |
[4]     |     66076|       0|SECT  |LOCL  |0     |3       |
[5]     |     66780|       0|SECT  |LOCL  |0     |4       |
[6]     |     66984|       0|SECT  |LOCL  |0     |5       |
[7]     |     66996|       0|SECT  |LOCL  |0     |6       |
[8]     |     67032|       0|SECT  |LOCL  |0     |7       |
[9]     |     67220|       0|SECT  |LOCL  |0     |8       |
[10]    |     67232|       0|SECT  |LOCL  |0     |9       |
[11]    |     67244|       0|SECT  |LOCL  |0     |10      |
[12]    |    132784|       0|SECT  |LOCL  |0     |11      |
[13]    |    132788|       0|SECT  |LOCL  |0     |12      |
```

Figure 11-1   Using the Solaris 2 nm program to view tiny's symbol table

```
[14]    |    132924|      0|SECT  |LOCL  |0    |13     |
[15]    |    133012|      0|SECT  |LOCL  |0    |14     |
[16]    |    133020|      0|SECT  |LOCL  |0    |15     |
[17]    |         0|      0|SECT  |LOCL  |0    |16     |
[18]    |         0|      0|SECT  |LOCL  |0    |17     |
[19]    |         0|      0|SECT  |LOCL  |0    |18     |
[20]    |         0|      0|SECT  |LOCL  |0    |19     |
[21]    |         0|      0|SECT  |LOCL  |0    |20     |
[22]    |         0|      0|SECT  |LOCL  |0    |21     |
[23]    |         0|      0|SECT  |LOCL  |0    |22     |
[24]    |         0|      0|SECT  |LOCL  |0    |23     |
[25]    |         0|      0|FILE  |LOCL  |0    |ABS    |crti.s
[26]    |         0|      0|FILE  |LOCL  |0    |ABS    |crt1.s
[27]    |         0|      0|FILE  |LOCL  |0    |ABS    |values-Xt.c
[28]    |         0|      0|FILE  |LOCL  |0    |ABS    |tiny.c
[29]    |         0|      0|FILE  |LOCL  |0    |ABS    |crtn.s
[30]    |     67032|    116|FUNC  |GLOB  |0    |7      |_start
[31]    |    133016|      4|OBJT  |GLOB  |0    |14     |whistles
[32]    |    133020|      4|OBJT  |GLOB  |0    |15     |_environ
[33]    |    133036|      0|OBJT  |GLOB  |0    |ABS    |_end
[34]    |    132784|      0|OBJT  |GLOB  |0    |ABS    |_GLOBAL_OFFSET_TABLE_
[35]    |    132972|      0|FUNC  |GLOB  |0    |UNDEF  |atexit
[36]    |    132984|      0|FUNC  |GLOB  |0    |UNDEF  |exit
[37]    |     67220|      0|FUNC  |GLOB  |0    |8      |_init
[38]    |    133024|     12|OBJT  |GLOB  |0    |15     |dreamcar
[39]    |    132788|      0|OBJT  |GLOB  |0    |ABS    |_DYNAMIC
[40]    |    132996|      0|FUNC  |GLOB  |0    |UNDEF  |_exit
[41]    |    133020|      4|OBJT  |WEAK  |0    |15     |environ
[42]    |     67148|      0|NOTY  |GLOB  |0    |7      |__cg89_used
[43]    |    133020|      0|OBJT  |GLOB  |0    |ABS    |_edata
[44]    |    132924|      0|OBJT  |GLOB  |0    |ABS    |_PROCEDURE_LINKAGE_TABLE_
[45]    |     67248|      0|OBJT  |GLOB  |0    |ABS    |_etext
[46]    |     67244|      4|OBJT  |GLOB  |0    |10     |_lib_version
[47]    |     67148|     72|FUNC  |GLOB  |0    |7      |main
[48]    |    133012|      4|OBJT  |GLOB  |0    |14     |beach_factor
[49]    |     67232|      0|FUNC  |GLOB  |0    |9      |_fini
Hiya...
```

Does this **nm** output match what you expected to see?

The symbols that made it into the symbol table and are shown by the **nm** command are *dreamcar, beach_factor,* and *whistles.* The variable *tickets* did not end up in the symbol table because it was defined locally within the *main()* routine.

Note that *BESTYEAR* is not listed in the namelist because it doesn't exist after compilation. Instead, it's a definition of some constant or fixed value that is only referenced during the preprocessor phase in the compilation of **tiny.c**. In our example, we didn't even bother to use it.

Highway and *mustang*, being declarations, are also used only at compilation time. Both describe what structures of those type look like. After compilation, they are no longer needed.

Using **adb**, we are able to examine the symbol table objects *dreamcar*, *beach_factor*, and *whistles* during execution of our executable object, **tiny**.

A tiny example using Solaris 1

The default output of the **nm** command on Solaris 1 is much less informative than that from Solaris 2, though in this example it might appear to be simpler and more to the point. Once you get used to **nm**'s output, you will most likely choose to use it in piped commands, **grep**'ing for the information you are really interested in.

Recompiling **tiny.c** under SunOS 4.1.3, we get the following.

Figure 11-2   Using the Solaris 1 nm program to view tiny's symbol table

```
Hiya on s4-413...  cc -o tiny tiny.c
Hiya on s4-413...  nm tiny
00004000 d __DYNAMIC
000040a0 D _edata
000040b0 B _end
00004090 D _environ
000024b8 T _etext
00002290 T _main
00004098 D _beach_factor
000040a0 B _dreamcar
0000409c D _whistles
00002020 t crt0.o
00002020 T start
00002290 t tiny.o
Hiya on s4-413...
```

Different flavors of UNIX may have different **nm** options, so always be sure to read the man page for more information and a list of **nm** options that you can put to good use.

Using adb to look at tiny's variables

Now that we have some understanding about included header files and have used **nm** for a listing of the symbol table, we can use **adb** to look at the variables.

It is important to note that **adb** is not normally the first debugger you would reach for when debugging a user program. Tools such as **dbx**, **dbxtool**, and **debugger** are far more suitable. All three are easier to use and are much closer to the programming language we used to write our program, whereas **adb** is closer to the hardware's native language, in this case, SPARC assembly language. However, for the purpose of your education in working with the kernel, we will use **adb** now.

When **adb**'ing a program to be executed, **adb** starts off in an idle mode of sorts, waiting to see if we want to set up breakpoints before execution commences. Once our program is executing, we can watch our variables change as each SPARC assembly instruction is executed step by step.

Watch this Solaris 2 **adb** session on our tiny program and see if you can follow what is happening.

Figure 11-3 Running tiny under the control of adb

```
   Hiya...   adb tiny -
   main:b
   :r
   breakpoint      main:           sethi    %hi(0xfffffc00), %g1
   main?20i
   main:
   main:           sethi    %hi(0xfffffc00), %g1
                   add      %g1, 0x3b8, %g1            ! -0x48
                   save     %sp, %g1, %sp
                   mov      0x6, %o0
                   st       %o0, [%fp - 0x4]
                   sethi    %hi(0x20400), %o1
                   ld       [%o1 + 0x394], %o1         ! beach_factor
                   sethi    %hi(0x20400), %o2
                   st       %o1, [%o2 + 0x3a0]
                   ld       [%fp - 0x4], %o3
                   sethi    %hi(0x20400), %o4
                   st       %o3, [%o4 + 0x3a4]
                   sethi    %hi(0x20400), %o5
                   ld       [%o5 + 0x398], %o5         ! whistles
                   sethi    %hi(0x20400), %o7
                   st       %o5, [%o7 + 0x3a8]
                   ret
                   restore
   _init:          save     %sp, -0x60, %sp
                   ret
```

Figure 11-3   Running tiny under the control of adb

```
dreamcar/fDD
dreamcar:
dreamcar:    +0.0000000e+00  0                      0
beach_factor/f
beach_factor:
beach_factor:        +1.2350000e+02
whistles/D
whistles:
whistles:        10
tickets/D
symbol not found
:s
stopped at      main+4:         add     %g1, 0x3b8, %g1
:s
stopped at      main+8:         save    %sp, %g1, %sp
:s
stopped at      main+0xc:       mov     0x6, %o0
:s
stopped at      main+0x10:      st      %o0, [%fp - 0x4]
:s
stopped at      main+0x14:      sethi   %hi(0x20400), %o1
:s
stopped at      main+0x18:      ld      [%o1 + 0x394], %o1   ! beach_factor
:s
stopped at      main+0x1c:      sethi   %hi(0x20400), %o2
:s
stopped at      main+0x20:      st      %o1, [%o2 + 0x3a0]
:s
stopped at      main+0x24:      ld      [%fp - 0x4], %o3
dreamcar/fDD
dreamcar:
dreamcar:    +1.2350000e+02  0                      0
:s
stopped at      main+0x28:      sethi   %hi(0x20400), %o4
:s
stopped at      main+0x2c:      st      %o3, [%o4 + 0x3a4]
:s
stopped at      main+0x30:      sethi   %hi(0x20400), %o5
dreamcar/fDD
dreamcar:
dreamcar:    +1.2350000e+02  6                      0
:s
stopped at      main+0x34:      ld      [%o5 + 0x398], %o5   ! whistles
:s
stopped at      main+0x38:      sethi   %hi(0x20400), %o7
:s
stopped at      main+0x3c:      st      %o5, [%o7 + 0x3a8]
:s
```

Figure 11-3 Running tiny under the control of adb

```
stopped at      main+0x40:      ret
dreamcar/fDD
dreamcar:
dreamcar:   +1.2350000e+02  6                 10
$q
Hiya...
```

Let's now discuss in more detail what happened during this **adb** session.

Unlike what we will do with the postmortem files, we start **adb** specifying only the executable object file that contains a symbol table. The dash says that we don't want to examine a core file. If we were to analyze a core dump of **tiny**, then we would specify the core file in addition to the object file.

Note again that **adb** doesn't give us a prompt.

We start the session by setting a breakpoint at the beginning of *main()* and then begin execution of **tiny** by giving **adb** the **:r** command to run. Immediately, we stop at *main()*, where our breakpoint was set. Listing the first 20 instructions from the object file, we can see that the return instruction, ret, is down near the end. *main()* is a short routine, even in assembly code.

Before we go any farther, we check the contents of our variables in the core file, which in this case is simply memory. Since *dreamcar* consists of a floating-point word followed by two integers, we can specify **/fDD** to display it. The **f** says to display one single-precision (32-bit), floating-point word. The **DD** says to show two full-word (32-bit) integers in decimal.

While still at this breakpoint, we have **adb** display the current contents of *beach_factor* as a floating-point word, *whistles* as a full-word decimal value as well as the variable *tickets*. Since *tickets* is not in the symbol table, **adb** reports that it cannot be found.

Both *beach_factor* and *whistles* were assigned initial values when they were defined in our program. We can confirm this by using **adb**. **Tiny** hasn't started executing yet, but we see values assigned to both of these variables. Conversely, *dreamcar* has been allocated storage space in memory, but the memory still contains zeroes.

Let's execute some instructions. The **:s** command tells **adb** to step, executing only one assembly instruction at a time. As we step through the program, we can see where variables are being set via the store instruction, st. The first store instruction we encounter sets the variable *tickets* to 6. *Tickets* is a local symbol that is stored in the stack frame. There is no symbol name for it.

Stepping further, we check the value of *dreamcar* again after the next store. We can see that the first element of *dreamcar* has now been set. Continuing, we watch as *dreamcar*'s elements are assigned values. Soon we are done, so we exit **adb**.

A tiny summary

Using a header file, the symbol table, and **adb**, we've just stepped through the execution of a tiny C program. While this may have seemed quite trivial to some, we will soon be progressing to a much bigger program, the UNIX kernel. The concepts are the same, so if you are comfortable with this so far, you'll probably do just fine as we move on.

adb Macros: Part One

One of the most powerful and commonly used features of **adb** also happens to be one of the least well documented: **adb** macros. **adb** allows the user to read in **adb** commands from ASCII files instead of typing them by hand. These files, **adb** macro files, can contain very simple one line commands or more complex sequences that in turn can read in other macros, creating several layers of nested invocations.

The gurus who analyze UNIX system crash dump **savecore** files daily use macros often, saving themselves a lot of time as well as wear and tear on their fingers.

Even though **adb** macros are simply **adb** commands stored in a file, writing them is still a bit of a black art in its own right. Vendors, such as Sun, even go so far as to provide a tool to automatically generate **adb** macros so that the programmer need not write them from scratch. This tool is called **adbgen** and requires use of a C compiler.

Not everyone has access to a C compiler, so in this and the next two chapters we will not only tell you about some of the standard **adb** macros you might find on your UNIX system, we will also show you how to write and use your own macros without depending on **adbgen**.

The macro library

Most, but not all, UNIX vendors provide a directory containing **adb** macros. Since each flavor of UNIX differs at the kernel level, you can expect the macros to differ from vendor to vendor, from architecture to architecture, and, to a lesser degree, between operating system releases running on a vendor's hardware platform.

In Solaris 1, the standard **adb** macros provided by Sun are maintained in the directory **/usr/lib/adb**. On Solaris 2 systems, the macros are kept in **/usr/kvm/lib/adb**.

Reading and understanding macros

Since **adb** macros contain **adb** commands, you should first become comfortable with **adb** in general before moving on to macros. Once you are ready to tackle macros, probably the easiest way to get started is by looking at the macros provided on your UNIX system while trying out the commands on a live kernel or a set of system crash dump files. If you happen to start off with the more complex macros, it is quite easy to become discouraged rather quickly, so try to work with the simpler macros at first.

Invoking adb macros

The first thing we need to understand is that some macros start working at **adb**'s current address, dot (.), whereas others will specify a starting location internally.

While in **adb**, macros are called by using the command syntax:

```
$<macroname
```

If you need to feed the macro a new current address to work with, or a symbol name, you invoke it by using the syntax:

```
address$<macroname
```

In this chapter, we will explore macros that demonstrate examples of each syntax.

The utsname macro

We've already seen one macro in use on a Solaris 2 system, **utsname**. As a refresher, here is how we called the **utsname** macro while in **adb** analyzing postmortem files. Note that this macro is not given a specific address with which to work.

Figure 12-1   Using the utsname macro

```
Hiya...   adb -k unix.1 vmcore.1
physmem 1b24
$<utsname
utsname:
utsname:        sys   SunOS
utsname+0x101:  node  panic
utsname+0x202:  release  5.3
utsname+0x303:  version  Generic
utsname+0x404:  machine  sun4c
$q
Hiya...
```

In **adb**, **$<** says to bring in or execute a macro, in this case the **utsname** macro. If you like, think of this as being like UNIX I/O redirection. Unless we specify a full pathname, **adb** assumes we want to work with the **utsname** macro file stored in the **/usr/kvm/lib/adb** directory.

Let's take a look at **/usr/kvm/lib/adb/utsname**.

Code Example 12-1   The utsname macro

```
Hiya...  cd /usr/kvm/lib/adb
Hiya...  more utsname
utsname/"sys"8t257c
+/"node"8t257c
+/"release"8t257c
+/"version"8t257c
+/"machine"8t257c
Hiya...
```

The first thing this macro does is change our current location within **adb** to where the variable *utsname* is stored. The text **"sys"** is printed solely for the user's sake, helping him to understand what is being output. The **8t** says to tab out to the nearest tab stop located at a column that is a multiple of 8, then display up to 257 printable characters.

Now we move on to the next line of the **utsname** macro. We use **+** to advance our current location according to the previous display format we used. We print **"node"**, tab out for readability, and display up to another 257 characters.

Continuing to the last three lines, we repeat this whole process for **"release"**, **"version"**, and **"machine"**.

Now, how do we know what this macro is showing us? Well, if we poke around in the **/usr/include/sys** directory, we will find a header file called **utsname.h**. (Isn't that convenient? Don't count on such ease all of the time!)   Within **utsname.h** we find the following information, although it is not all clustered together as shown below.

Code Example 12-2   Excerpts from /usr/include/sys/utsname.h

```
#define _SYS_NMLN        257      /* 4.0 size of utsname elements */
                                  /* Must be at least 257 to        */
                                  /* support Internet hostnames.   */
struct utsname {
      char    sysname[_SYS_NMLN];
      char    nodename[_SYS_NMLN];
      char    release[_SYS_NMLN];
      char    version[_SYS_NMLN];
```

Code Example 12-2   Excerpts from /usr/include/sys/utsname.h

```
        char      machine[_SYS_NMLN];
    };

    extern struct utsname utsname;
```

Using what we have learned so far, we can see in **/usr/include/sys/utsname.h** that *utsname* is the name given to a type of defined structure. The five elements of this structure contain character strings of *_SYS_NMLN* or 257 decimal in length. Finally, we see that the *utsname* structure was used elsewhere (extern) to declare a structure variable, also called *utsname*. In this case, to see this structure's definition, we would have to look at the source. However, as we have seen by using the **utsname** macro, it is quite safe to assume that the declared *utsname* structure contains the system information we would expect to see there.

If you don't happen to have a set of system crash dump files to experiment with at this time and you want to look at the *utsname* structure on your own Solaris 2 system, go ahead and run **adb** on the running kernel. To do this, you will need to be root. As an example, here is an **adb** session that looks at an actively running system.

```
    Hiya... su
    Password:
    # adb -k /dev/ksyms /dev/mem
    physmem 1e15
    $<utsname
    utsname:
    utsname:          sys      SunOS
    utsname+0x101:    node     pasta
    utsname+0x202:    release 5.3
    utsname+0x303:    version Generic_Patch
    utsname+0x404:    machine sun4c
    $q
    #
```

Let's take a look at another relatively simple macro from the **/usr/kvm/lib/adb** directory on a Solaris 2 system and figure out what it does.

The bootobj macro

The **bootobj** macro is a three-line macro and, reading it, appears to show information about a file system. Here is the macro.

Code Example 12-3   The bootobj macro

```
Hiya...  cd /usr/kvm/lib/adb
Hiya...  cat bootobj
./"fstype"16t16C
+/"name"16t128C
+/"flags"16t"size"16t"vp"n3X
Hiya...
```

Unfortunately, unlike the **utsname** macro, execution of the **bootobj** macro starts at location "**.**", which means the current location. This is an example of a macro that we must call by specifying a symbol name or a new current address where the macro would start its work. The question is: For which file system or file systems was this macro designed to display data? We'll see if we can figure that out shortly. First, let's discuss what this macro does step by step.

The first line displays **"fstype"** for readability, tabs out to the display position that is a multiple of 16, then displays 16 characters. Note, unlike in the **utsname** macro, we are using an uppercase **C** modifier instead of the lowercase **c**. The difference is that the uppercase **C** says to show the contents of all 128 character positions whether or not they contain printable ASCII characters. When the value stored in memory is not printable, a "control character" representation (such as ^@ for a null byte) is printed instead.

The second line advances the current address and displays 128 characters, apparently a name of some sort, judging from the fact that we print **"name"** before the characters.

The last macro command line will generate two lines of output. The first line will have the words **"flags"**, **"size"**, and **"vp"** separated by tabs. The **n** says to print a newline. The **3X** modifier says to display the contents of three full-word addresses in hexadecimal.

By default, **adb** allows for 16 character positions for each full-word hexadecimal value displayed, with a maximum of four full words displayed per line, or **4X** if we were speaking in terms of **adb** modifiers. Knowing this about **adb**, the macro's author has the **"flags"**, **"size"**, and **"vp"** identifiers similarly tabbed out, using the **16t** modifier.

So, we now know what the macro does. Next, let's see if we can figure out with which kernel variables this macro was designed to be used. The first place we might look would be the namelist, which we can examine via the UNIX **nm** command. In this case, we will pipe the output of **nm** into the UNIX **grep** command, searching for **bootobj** or something similar. We are only interested in objects, such as variables and structures, instead of kernel routines and other symbols, so we use **grep** a second time to print out the **nm** OBJT matches only.

```
Hiya...   nm /dev/ksyms | grep -i bootobj | grep OBJT
Hiya...   nm /dev/ksyms | grep -i boot | grep OBJT
[469]    |4027923924|     52|OBJT  |LOCL |0    |ABS    |bootcode
[5034]   |4232978432|     12|OBJT  |LOCL |0    |ABS    |bootparam_addr
[6815]   |4027926848|      4|OBJT  |GLOB |0    |ABS    |path_to_inst_bootstrap
[7229]   |4028089244|    256|OBJT  |GLOB |0    |ABS    |kern_bootargs
[7402]   |4028089636|      4|OBJT  |GLOB |0    |ABS    |boothowto
[7482]   |4027920040|      4|OBJT  |GLOB |0    |ABS    |bootops
[7501]   |4028092332|      4|OBJT  |GLOB |0    |ABS    |kmacctboot
[8707]   |4028112416|      4|OBJT  |GLOB |0    |ABS    |netboot
Hiya...
```

Well, that wasn't very helpful. Next, we will dig through the **/usr/include** header files. It is probably safe to assume that **bootobj** has something to do with the booting sequence, so we will dig through the **sys** subdirectory as a starting point. If that fails to find what we are looking for, we can start the search at **/usr/include** next time.

In this example, we will use the UNIX **find** command to **grep** through all of the **sys** header files. If you aren't familiar with the **find** or **grep** commands, please refer to the man pages.

```
Hiya...   cd /usr/include/sys
Hiya...   find . -exec grep -i bootobj {} /dev/null \;
./bootconf.h:struct bootobj {
./bootconf.h:extern struct bootobj rootfs;
./bootconf.h:extern struct bootobj dumpfile;
./bootconf.h:extern struct bootobj swapfile;
Hiya...
```

Note – The use of **/dev/null** in the **grep** command **exec**'ed within the **find** command may have you wondering a bit. If only one filename is given for **grep** to search, we will not see the name of the file along with the matching strings. We are using **/dev/null** as nothing more than a second file name. Actually, any filename would have done. Try the same command with and without **/dev/null** specified, and you'll understand the significance of using it.

So, we have found that **/usr/include/sys/bootconf.h** defines a *bootobj* structure. We need to read this header file to learn more about this structure. Here is the portion of **/usr/include/sys/bootconf.h** that talks about the *bootobj* structure.

Code Example 12-4   Excerpts from /usr/include/sys/bootconf.h

```
/*
 * Boot configuration information
 */

#define BO_MAXFSNAME    16
#define BO_MAXOBJNAME   128

struct bootobj {
        char    bo_fstype[BO_MAXFSNAME];        /* vfs type name (e.g. nfs) */
        char    bo_name[BO_MAXOBJNAME];         /* name of object */
        int     bo_flags;                       /* flags, see below */
        int     bo_size;                        /* number of blocks */
        struct vnode *bo_vp;                    /* vnode of object */
};
```

```
 ll information in object is valid */
 object is busy */
```

 t of 16 characters reflecting a virtual file system
 ct name, a full-word integer flags value, another
 inally, a pointer (a full-word value) to a *vnode*
 is right in line with what the **bootobj** macro will

 declared for use. These are *dumpfile*, which we
 ese three variables will be in the symbol table.
 rough **nm**'s output.

```
Hiya...  nm /dev/ksyms | grep rootfs
[8662]   |4027916920|    156|OBJT |GLOB |0     |ABS   |rootfs
Hiya...  nm /dev/ksyms | grep swapfile
[1285]   |4028028788|      4|OBJT |LOCL |0     |ABS   |nswapfiles
[8378]   |4027917076|    156|OBJT |GLOB |0     |ABS   |swapfile
```

```
Hiya...   nm /dev/ksyms | grep dumpfile
[6059]   |4027917232|    156|OBJT |GLOB |0    |ABS    |dumpfile
Hiya...
```

Note that the sizes of *rootfs*, *swapfile*, and *dumpfile* are each listed as 156. This decimal value represents the size in bytes. Does it fit what we found in the *bootobj* structure? Absolutely!

16 chars + 128 chars + 3 full words = 16 bytes + 128 bytes + 12 bytes = <u>156 bytes</u>

We are now fairly confident what the **bootobj** macro was designed to examine. Let's use **adb** to look at all three variables on a live system   Remember, since the **bootobj** macro starts at the current address, we need to feed the macro a valid starting point.

Figure 12-2 Using the bootobj macro against three kernel variables

```
# adb -k /dev/ksyms /dev/mem
physmem 1e15
rootfs$<bootobj
rootfs:
rootfs:          fstype        ufs^@^@^@^@^@^@^@^@^@^@^@^@^@
rootfs+0x10:     name          /iommu@f,e0000000/sbus@f,e0001000/espdma@f,40000
                 0/esp@f,800000/sd@3,0:a^@^@^@^@^@^@^@^@^@^@^@^@^@^@^@^@^@^@^@^@
                 ^@^@^@^@^@^@^@^@^@^@^@^@^@^@^@^@^@^@^@^@^@^@^@^@^@^@^@^@^@^@^@^@
                 ^@^@^@^@
rootfs+0x90:     flags         size          vp
                 0             0             0
swapfile$<bootobj
swapfile:
swapfile:        fstype        ^@^@^@^@^@^@^@^@^@^@^@^@^@^@^@^@
swapfile+0x10:   name          ^@^@^@^@^@^@^@^@^@^@^@^@^@^@^@^@^@^@^@^@^@^@^@^@
                 ^@^@^@^@^@^@^@^@^@^@^@^@^@^@^@^@^@^@^@^@^@^@^@^@^@^@^@^@^@^@^@^@
                 ^@^@^@^@^@^@^@^@^@^@^@^@^@^@^@^@^@^@^@^@^@^@^@^@^@^@^@^@^@^@^@^@
                 ^@^@^@^@^@^@^@^@^@^@^@^@^@^@^@^@^@^@^@^@^@^@^@^@^@^@^@^@^@^@^@^@
                 ^@^@^@^@^@^@^@^@
swapfile+0x90:   flags         size          vp
                 0             0             0
dumpfile$<bootobj
dumpfile:
dumpfile:        fstype        ^@^@^@^@^@^@^@^@^@^@^@^@^@^@^@^@
dumpfile+0x10:   name          /dev/dsk/c0t1d0s1^@^@^@^@^@^@^@^@^@^@^@^@^@^@^@
                 ^@^@^@^@^@^@^@^@^@^@^@^@^@^@^@^@^@^@^@^@^@^@^@^@^@^@^@^@^@^@^@^@
                 ^@^@^@^@^@^@^@^@^@^@^@^@^@^@^@^@^@^@^@^@^@^@^@^@^@^@^@^@^@^@^@^@
                 ^@^@^@^@^@^@^@^@^@^@^@^@^@^@^@^@^@^@^@^@^@^@^@^@^@^@^@^@^@^@^@^@
dumpfile+0x90:   flags         size          vp
                 0             30200         fc2d7604
$q
```

To find out how these structures are initialized and later used, we would have to look at the source code.

We have learned a few new concepts by examining the **bootobj** macro, most importantly, how to attempt to establish what variables the macro was designed to be used with when its execution starts at the current location, "**.**".

Summary

To summarize, after looking at the **utsname** and **bootobj** macros, we have seen how to use the following **adb** commands within a macro:

*symbolname***/**	Change the current address
+/	Advance the current address
/"*printed text*"	Print text for our own use
/t	Tab over
/c	Print byte as a character (if displayable)
/C	Print byte as a character (or ^@ if not displayable)
/X	Print full word as a hexadecimal value
/n	Print a newline

In the next chapter, we will tackle some of the more complex macros and their features.

adb Macros: Part Two 13 ≡

In the previous chapter, we explored a couple of the simpler **adb** macros. Now we are going to discover the real power behind macros by exploring some of the more complex macros available to us.

Just as a warning, this chapter is not going to be light reading. If you've not had a good stretch or refreshed your coffee lately, now might be a good time!

Ready? Let's go!

The msgbuf and msgbuf.wrap macros

Let's tackle one of the more interesting **adb** macros now, one that shows some of the power that macros offer. We'll start with the **msgbuf** macros that display the message ring buffer we talked about earlier. These macros happen to be the same for both Solaris 1.1 and 2.3 systems. Here are the two macros used to display the *msgbuf* ring.

Code Example 13-1   The msgbuf macro

```
msgbuf/"magic"16t"size"16t"bufx"16t"bufr"n4X
+,(*(msgbuf+0t8)-*(msgbuf+0t12))&80000000$<msgbuf.wrap
.+*(msgbuf+0t12),(*(msgbuf+0t8)-*(msgbuf+0t12))/c
```

Code Example 13-2   The msgbuf.wrap macro

```
.+*(msgbuf+0t12),(*(msgbuf+0t4)-*(msgbuf+0t12))/c
msgbuf+0t16+0,*(msgbuf+0t8)/c
```

Yes, they look a bit hairy, but you'll fully understand them shortly!

Below is a portion of the **/usr/include/sys/msgbuf.h** header file that, as you might guess, describes the *msgbuf* structure. This is from a Solaris 2.3 system. The Solaris 1.1 version is quite similar, but does differ a bit.

Code Example 13-3 Excerpts from /usr/include/sys/msgbuf.h

```
#define MSG_MAGIC        0x8724786

struct  msgbuf {
        struct  msgbuf_hd {
                long    msgh_magic;
                long    msgh_size;
                long    msgh_bufx;
                long    msgh_bufr;
                u_longlong_t    msgh_map;
        } msg_hd;
}
```

As we saw in an earlier chapter, we use the **msgbuf** macro to print out the ring buffer known as *msgbuf*. The *msgbuf* structure maintains four values at the head of the buffer that are used to guide manipulation of the buffer.

The first word of the *msgbuf* structure, *msgh_magic*, contains a magic number, or in simple terms, a unique identifier number. The next word, *msgh_size*, contains the size of the message buffer in bytes. This size does not include the four words at the head of the buffer.

You'll remember from an earlier discussion that the message buffer is a data area of fixed length and is used as a ring, or rotating, buffer. As such, there are a few ways that the buffer could be managed by the operating system.

The method used by the Solaris systems is quite clever. Two pointers are maintained. One, *msgh_bufr*, points to the start of the most recently added message, and the other, *msgh_bufx*, points to the end of that message, which is where the next message will be written. These variables are byte offsets into the message buffer, with zero referring to *msgh_map*.

The messages we were looking for in *msgbuf* actually don't start until the fifth word, represented in the *msgbuf* structure by *msgh_map*. Don't let the fact that *msgh_map* is not a character array bother you. The Solaris 2 kernel magically makes sure that the structure is correctly allocated space in memory. In the Solaris 1 **msgbuf.h** header file, you will see a character array of fixed size in the *msgbuf* structure.

Since the message buffer is a ring buffer, sometimes *msgh_bufr* will be more than *msgh_bufx*, and sometimes it will be less. In other words, the beginning of a message does not necessarily always come before the end of the message in the ring. The programmer who wrote the **msgbuf** and **msgbuf.wrap** macros had to take this into account. We will see how he tackled this in a minute.

Here is a diagram of the *msgbuf* structure that shows it first with one message in it, and then again after a second message has been added. As each message is added to the *msgh_map* area, the pointers to the beginning and end of the most recent message, *msgh_bufr* and *msgh_bufx*, are adjusted accordingly.

Figure 13-1   The message buffer with one, then two messages in it

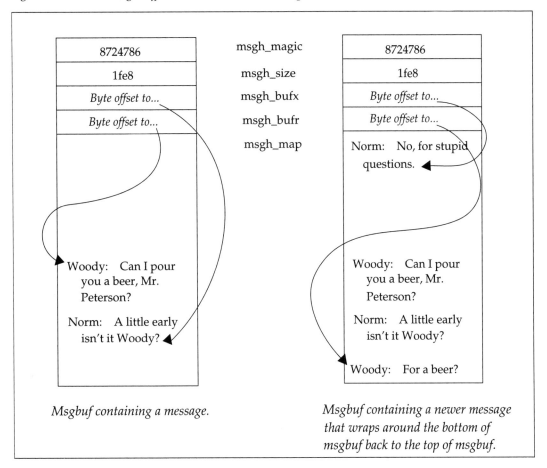

8724786	msgh_magic
1fe8	msgh_size
Byte offset to...	msgh_bufx
Byte offset to...	msgh_bufr
	msgh_map

Woody: Can I pour
you a beer, Mr.
Peterson?

Norm: A little early
isn't it Woody?

8724786

1fe8

Byte offset to...

Byte offset to...

Norm: No, for stupid
questions.

Woody: Can I pour
you a beer, Mr.
Peterson?

Norm: A little early
isn't it Woody?

Woody: For a beer?

Msgbuf containing a message.

Msgbuf containing a newer message that wraps around the bottom of msgbuf back to the top of msgbuf.

Calling another macro

New to our discussion on macros are two very powerful **adb** features used in the two **msgbuf** macros. These are:

- Calling another macro
- Command counts

As you explore the **adb** macro library on your system, you will find that both of these features are used quite heavily.

Let's start with the ability of a macro to call another macro. This can be done in one of two ways.

$<*macro2*	Execute *macro2*, but do not return to the calling macro
$<<*macro2*	Execute *macro2*, then return to the calling macro

In the **msgbuf** macros we will see the first calling method used. We will look at the second method in a short while.

Note – If, at any point, a macro generates an **adb** error, such as "symbol not found" or "data address not found," *all current macro execution immediately terminates.* This is true even if we are more than one level deep in macros and plan to return. Unfortunately, there is no way to capture or trap for these sorts of **adb** conditions. However, sometimes the clever macro programmer can work around this "feature" of **adb** by using the command count and combinations of unary and binary operators. As we walk through the **msgbuf** macro file and other complex macros, you'll see how this is done.

Let's take another look at the macros.

The msgbuf macro

```
msgbuf/"magic"16t"size"16t"bufx"16t"bufr"n4X
+,(*(msgbuf+0t8)-*(msgbuf+0t12))&80000000$<msgbuf.wrap
.+*(msgbuf+0t12),(*(msgbuf+0t8)-*(msgbuf+0t12))/c
```

The msgbuf.wrap macro

```
.+*(msgbuf+0t12),(*(msgbuf+0t4)-*(msgbuf+0t12))/c
msgbuf+0t16+0,*(msgbuf+0t8)/c
```

In **msgbuf**, the first line prints out the magic number, the buffer size, the offset to where the next message goes, and the offset to where the most recent message started.

Command count

You'll remember from Chapter 8, "adb: The Gory Details," that commands can be given a count saying to do something X number of times. As a reminder, here is the general syntax for **adb** data display commands.

```
address,count    command    formatting_information
```

The second line of **msgbuf** contains a command count (in this case, a formula that includes a bitwise AND) and a call to another macro, **msgbuf.wrap**. Note that we won't be returning from the **msgbuf.wrap** macro, by virtue of the **$<** calling method, and yet we have a third command line in this macro.

Q How would we execute the third line of the **msgbuf** macro?

A By not making the call to **msgbuf.wrap** at all.

The **,(*(msgbuf+0t8)-*(msgbuf+0t12))&80000000** translates into a count of how many times to call **msgbuf.wrap**. Rather silly, you might say, since we know that the **$<** calling method means we don't return. So, really, what we are looking for is whether to call **msgbuf.wrap** once or not at all. Here is where the macro programmer had to think about how to work with messages that had wrapped from the bottom to the top of the *msgbuf* ring buffer.

***(msgbuf+0t8)** gives us the *msgh_bufx* offset; the ending point for the most recent message. ***(msgbuf+0t12)** gives us the *msgh_bufr* offset: the starting point. If the start has a higher offset, then we know the message has wrapped around the bottom of the message buffer, which means special processing is needed to print out the most recent message because it is in two pieces. We compare the start and end by subtracting them. If the result is negative, we have a wrapped message.

Q   How can we test for a negative value within **adb**?

A   Negative values always have the high order bit set, so we test that bit by using a bitwise AND.

The **&80000000** tests to see if we got a negative value and thus have a wrapped message. If the high-order bit is set in the result of the subtraction, the final count will be 1 and we will call the **msgbuf.wrap** macro. If the high-order bit is not set, meaning that the end of the message is somewhere after the beginning, the final count will be 0 and we will not call the **msgbuf.wrap** macro.

adb does not offer conditional tests, such as "if" statements. However, through clever use of the features that do exist in **adb**, in effect, the formula for the command count actually performed this test:

```
if (start > end) msgbuf.wrap;
```

If we don't call **msgbuf.wrap**, we move on to the third line.

```
.+*(msgbuf+0t12),(*(msgbuf+0t8)-*(msgbuf+0t12))/c
```

In this line, **.+*(msgbuf+0t12)** is the new current address to work with. **,*(msgbuf+0t8)-*(msgbuf+0t12))** is the count and **/c** is the command. Can you figure out what this is going to do?

Starting at the beginning of the most recent message, *msgh_bufr*, we calculate the number of characters in the most recent message and print each one.

Take a look again at the **msgbuf.wrap** macro.

```
.+*(msgbuf+0t12),(*(msgbuf+0t4)-*(msgbuf+0t12))/c
msgbuf+0t16+0,*(msgbuf+0t8)/c
```

Unless we've lost you, you should now be able to figure out how this macro works. Remember that **msgbuf+0t4** contains the ring buffer size and **msgbuf+0t16** is where the messages actually begin. What we do in this macro is calculate the number of characters from the start of the most recent message to the actual end of the ring buffer and, starting at the beginning of that most recent message, print that many characters. This, in effect, prints the bottom end of the ring buffer.

The next line prints the top end of the ring buffer, printing all the way to end of the message.

The msgbuf macro in use

Let's take a look at a couple of system crashes. Both are from a SPARCstation 20 running Solaris 1.1.1. Both crashes were forced by modifying *rootdir*. The crashes were done within minutes of each other.

A unique feature of the message ring buffer is that it is given a fixed location within the memory of a system and is not initialized or cleaned out during reboots. Only a power-down or a reset of the system will result in clearing the message buffer. This means that in the case of back-to-back crashes, you may see more than one of them recorded in the message buffer. This works to our advantage when looking for some history about the system.

When looking at these crashes, note the *msgbuf* offset pointers. You'll notice that a gap seems to exist between the crash messages, which is quite true. What the **msgbuf** macros show us are the *most recent messages*. The messages that appeared during the boot-up are not the most recent. The crash messages are the most recent. However, if we look around, we will see that the boot-time messages are still in the buffer.

Figure 13-2   Viewing the message buffer via two methods while in adb

```
Hiya...   adb -k vmunix.0 vmcore.0
physmem 1f8c
$<msgbuf
0xf0002000:    magic          size          bufx          bufr
               63062          1ff0          1adb          1519
0xf0003529:    BAD TRAP: cpu=0 type=9 rp=f048bb1c addr=2 mmu_fsr=326 rw=1
               MMU sfsr=326: Invalid Address on supv data fetch at level 3
               regs at f048bb1c:
                     psr=404000c2 pc=f006c154 npc=f006c158
                     y: 3b000000 g1: 0 g2: 8000000 g3: ffffff00
                     g4: 0 g5: f048c000 g6: 0 g7: 0
                     o0: 0 o1: 4000 o2: d20 o3: 0
                     o4: 7 o5: 6 sp: f048bb68 ra: 0
               pid 326, `sh': Data access exception
               kernel read fault at addr=0x2, pme=0x0
               MMU sfsr=326: Invalid Address on supv data fetch at level 3
               rp=0xf048bb1c, pc=0xf006c154, sp=0xf048bb68, psr=0x404000c2, context=0x9e
```

Figure 13-2 Viewing the message buffer via two methods while in adb

```
              g1-g7: 0, 8000000, ffffff00, 0, f048c000, 0, 0
              Begin traceback... sp = f048bb68
              Called from f006c068, fp=f048bcd8, args=f048be0c 1 0 2f 0 0
              Called from f0040118, fp=f048bd38, args=f048be0c 1 0 f048be18 f048c000 0
              Called from f0035f88, fp=f048be40, args=0 0 f048beb4 0 f048be2014c00
              Called from f013fae8, fp=f048bec0, args=f048bfe0 1d8 f01ba1d8 f01ba3b0 00
              Called from f0005cd0, fp=f048bf58, args=f048c000 f048bfb4 f048bfe0 0 0 0
              Called from 886c, fp=effff778, args=1ee54 1e724 1e83c 1a400 1ee5c 0
              End traceback...
              panic on cpu 0: Data access exception
              syncing file systems... done
              01018 low-memory static kernel pages
              00432 additional static and sysmap kernel pages
              00000 dynamic kernel data pages
              00218 additional user structure pages
              00000 segmap kernel pages
              00000 segvn kernel pages
              00038 current user process pages
              00150 user stack pages
              01856 total pages (928 chunks)

msgbuf+10/s
0xf0002010:     SuperSPARC: PAC ENABLED
SunOS Release 4.1.3_U1 (GENERIC) #2: Thu Jan 20 15:58:03 PST 1994
Copyright (c) 1983-1993, Sun Microsystems, Inc.
cpu = SUNW,SPARCstation-20
mod0 = TI,TMS390Z50 (mid = 8)
mem = 32304K (0x1f8c000)
avail mem = 28893184
cpu0 at Mbus 0x8 0x224000
entering uniprocessor mode
Ethernet address = 8:0:20:1f:d9:aa
espdma0 at SBus slot f 0x400000
esp0 at SBus slot f 0x800000 pri 4 (onboard)
sd0 at esp0 target 3 lun 0
sd0: <SUN1.05 cyl 2036 alt 2 hd 14 sec 72>
sr0 at esp0 target 6 lun 0
ledma0 at SBus slot f 0x400010
le0 at SBus slot f 0xc00000 pri 6 (onboard)
SUNW,bpp0 at SBus slot f 0x4800000 pri 3 (sbus level 2)
SUNW,DBRIe0 at SBus slot e 0x10000 pri 9 (sbus level 5)
cgsix0 at SBus slot 2 0x0 pri 9 (sbus level 5)
cgsix0: screen 1152x900, single buffered, 1M mappable, rev 11
zs0 at obio 0x100000 pri 12 (onboard)
zs1 at obio 0x0 pri 12 (onboard)
SUNW,fdtwo0 at obio 0x700000 pri 11 (onboard)
MMCODEC: manufacturer id 1, rev 2
root on sd0a fstype 4.2
swap on sd0b fstype spec size 98784K
dump on sd0b fstype spec size 98772K
le0: Twisted Pair Ethernet
SuperSPARC: PAC ENABLED
SunOS Release 4.1.3_U1 (GENERIC) #2: Thu Jan 20 15:58:03 PST 1994
Copyright (c) 1983-1993, Sun Microsystems, Inc.
```

Figure 13-2 Viewing the message buffer via two methods while in adb

```
cpu = SUNW,SPARCstation-20
mod0 = TI,TMS390Z50 (mid = 8)
mem = 32304K (0x1f8c000)
avail mem = 28893184
cpu0 at Mbus 0x8 0x224000
entering uniprocessor mode
Ethernet address = 8:0:20:1f:d9:aa
espdma0 at SBus slot f 0x400000
esp0 at SBus slot f 0x800000 pri 4 (onboard)
sd0 at esp0 target 3 lun 0
sd0: <SUN1.05 cyl 2036 alt 2 hd 14 sec 72>
sr0 at esp0 target 6 lun 0
ledma0 at SBus slot f 0x400010
le0 at SBus slot f 0xc00000 pri 6 (onboard)
SUNW,bpp0 at SBus slot f 0x4800000 pri 3 (sbus level 2)
SUNW,DBRIe0 at SBus slot e 0x10000 pri 9 (sbus level 5)
cgsix0 at SBus slot 2 0x0 pri 9 (sbus level 5)
cgsix0: screen 1152x900, single buffered, 1M mappable, rev 11
zs0 at obio 0x100000 pri 12 (onboard)
zs1 at obio 0x0 pri 12 (onboard)
SUNW,fdtwo0 at obio 0x700000 pri 11 (onboard)
MMCODEC: manufacturer id 1, rev 2
root on sd0a fstype 4.2
swap on sd0b fstype spec size 98784K
dump on sd0b fstype spec size 98772K
le0: Twisted Pair Ethernet
```

Here we look at the second crash. Note that the offsets are both *less* than the offsets we saw in the first crash. This is because the boot messages wrapped around the bottom of *msgbuf*.

Figure 13-3 Viewing the message buffer of a subsequent crash

```
Hiya...   adb -k vmunix.1 vmcore.1
physmem 1f8c
$<msgbuf
0xf0002000:    magic          size          bufx          bufr
               63062          1ff0          979           38c
0xf000239c:    BAD TRAP: cpu=0 type=9 rp=f0413b2c addr=2 mmu_fsr=326 rw=1
               MMU sfsr=326: Invalid Address on supv data fetch at level 3
               regs at f0413b2c:
                       psr=404000c5 pc=f006c154 npc=f006c158
                       y: b3000000 g1: 40900ae4 g2: c1a0 g3: ffffff00
                       g4: 0 g5: f0414000 g6: 0 g7: 0
                       o0: 7 o1: ff1238d0 o2: 0 o3: f0047c08
                       o4: f0047c0c o5: f01efbc8 sp: f0413b78 ra: 1
               pid 243, `sh': Data access exception
               kernel read fault at addr=0x2, pme=0x0
               MMU sfsr=326: Invalid Address on supv data fetch at level 3
               rp=0xf0413b2c, pc=0xf006c154, sp=0xf0413b78, psr=0x404000c5, context=0xeb
               g1-g7: 40900ae4, c1a0, ffffff00, 0, f0414000, 0, 0
```

Figure 13-3   Viewing the message buffer of a subsequent crash

```
                    Begin traceback... sp = f0413b78
                    Called from f006c038, fp=f0413ce8, args=f0413d4c 1 0 2f f0413eb4 0
                    Called from f006ccbc, fp=f0413d58, args=0 0 1 0 f0413e3c f0413eb4
                    Called from f0036688, fp=f0413e40, args=1bfb0 ffffffff f0414a30 f0413eb4 0 0
                    Called from f013fae8, fp=f0413ec0, args=f0413fe0 60 f01ba1d8 f01ba238 0 0
                    Called from f0005cd0, fp=f0413f58, args=f0414000 f0413fb4 f0413fe0 0 0 0
                    Called from 7154, fp=effff9e0, args=1bfb0 effffd2a 18800 0 effffd2c 1bfb2
                    End traceback...
                    panic on cpu 0: Data access exception
                    syncing file systems... done
                    01018 low-memory static kernel pages
                    00430 additional static and sysmap kernel pages
                    00000 dynamic kernel data pages
                    00100 additional user structure pages
                    00000 segmap kernel pages
                    00000 segvn kernel pages
                    00038 current user process pages
                    00040 user stack pages
                    01626 total pages (813 chunksvail mem = 28893184
                    cpu0 at Mbus 0x8 0x22
.=X

                    f0002988
```

Phew! Well, that's probably enough about *msgbuf* and the **msgbuf** macros!

How are you doing so far? If you want to take a break from reading and have some fun with macros, make backup copies of the macros we've talked about so far and try modifying them. For example, see if you can redesign the **msgbuf** macros so that the *whole* buffer is displayed in the correct order! It will help warm you up for when you'll be writing your own macros from scratch later on.

The cpus, cpus.nxt, & cpu macros

Three macros, provided in **/usr/kvm/lib/adb** on Solaris 2 systems, display *some* of the information in the *cpu* structure for each CPU on the system. The *cpu* structure that these macros work with is defined in **/usr/include/sys/cpuvar.h**, as shown in this partial view of **cpuvar.h**.

Code Example 13-4   Excerpts from /usr/include/sys/cpuvar.h

```
  /*
   * Per-CPU data.
   */
  typedef struct cpu {
          processorid_t   cpu_id;          /* CPU number */
          volatile u_short cpu_flags;      /* flags indicating CPU state */
          kthread_id_t    cpu_thread;      /* current thread */
```

Code Example 13-4 Excerpts from /usr/include/sys/cpuvar.h

```
        kthread_id_t    cpu_idle_thread; /* idle thread for this CPU */
        klwp_id_t       cpu_lwp;        /* current lwp (if any) */
        struct cpu_callo *cpu_callo;    /* CPU callout list */
        struct fpu      *cpu_fpu;       /* currently loaded fpu context */
        /*
         * Links - protected by cpu_lock.
         */
        struct cpu      *cpu_next;      /* next existing CPU */
        struct cpu      *cpu_prev;
        struct cpu      *cpu_next_onln; /* next online (enabled) CPU */
        struct cpu      *cpu_prev_onln;
        /*
         * Scheduling variables.
         */
        disp_t          cpu_disp;       /* dispatch queue data */
        char            cpu_runrun;     /* scheduling flag - set to preempt */
        char            cpu_kprunrun;   /* force kernel preemption */
        pri_t           cpu_chosen_level; /* priority level at which cpu */
                                        /* was chosen for scheduling */
        kthread_id_t    cpu_dispthread; /* thread selected for dispatch */
        disp_lock_t     cpu_thread_lock; /* dispatcher lock on current thread */
        /*
         * Interrupt data.
         */
        caddr_t         cpu_intr_stack; /* interrupt stack */
        int             cpu_on_intr;    /* on interrupt stack */
        kthread_id_t    cpu_intr_thread; /* interrupt thread list */
        u_long          cpu_intr_actv;  /* interrupt levels active (bitmask) */
        int             cpu_base_spl;   /* priority for highest rupt active */
        /*
         * Statistics.
         */
        cpu_stat_t      cpu_stat;       /* per cpu statistics */
        struct kstat    *cpu_kstat;     /* kstat for this cpu's statistics */
        struct kern_profiling *cpu_profiling; /* per cpu basis */
        tracedata_t     cpu_trace;      /* per cpu trace data */
        /*
         * Configuration information for the processor_info system call.
         *
         * The pi_state field of this is filled in by the processor_info
         * system call code and is inaccurate at other times.  The rest
         * of the fields in cpu_type_info do not change after initialization.
         */
        processor_info_t cpu_type_info; /* config info */

} cpu_t;
```

Before we look at the macros that display information held in the *cpu* structures, let's try to get a feel for the layout of the data. The *cpu* structures are double-linked. This means that each structure points to the next structure and the previous structure.

The starting point of the *cpu* structures is pointed to by **cpu_list*.

For this diagram, we will say that there are four CPUs. To avoid a mess, we will point out the forward links only and let you draw in the backward links.

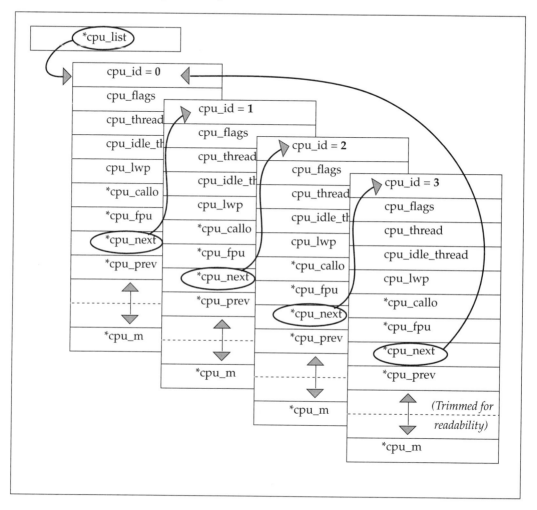

Figure 13-4 Data Layout in Four cpu Structures

Looking at the three macros that work with the *cpu* structures, we will see good use of the ability to write and read variables within **adb**. We will also see the logical negation command used. The power of **adb** and **adb** macros is well demonstrated by these three macros. Let's explore them now!

Here are the macro files:

Code Example 13-5   The cpus macro

```
*cpu_list>c
<c>e
<c,#(#(<c))$<cpus.nxt
cpu_list/X"(cpu_list ptr is NULL)"n
```

Code Example 13-6   The cpus.nxt macro

```
.>c
*(<c+0t28)>n
<c$<<cpu
0,#(#(<n))&#(#(<n-<e))=nn
<n,#(#(<n))&#(#(<n-<e))$<cpus.nxt
```

Code Example 13-7   The cpu macro

```
./"id"16t"flags"16t"thread"16t"idle_t"nDx16t2+2X
+/"lwp"16t"callo"16t"fpu"n3X
+/"next"16t"prev"16t"next on"16t"prev on"n4X
+$<<disp
+/"runrun"8t"kprnrn"8t"chsnlevel"8t"dispthread"16t"threadlock"nBBd8tXB3+
+/"intr_stack"16t"on_intr"16t"intr_thread"16t"intr_actv"n4X
+/"base_spl"nD472+
```

The **cpus** macro starts execution at *cpu_list*, which points to the first address of all of the *cpu* structures. We save the value stored at *cpu_list* into **adb** variable *c*. We also store it in variable *e*. As we'll see soon, *e* plays an important role in the **cpus.nxt** macro. The next line in **cpus** is the first really tricky one.

```
<c,#(#(<c))$<cpus.nxt
```

Starting at *cpu_list*, we will call the **cpus.nxt** macro *X* number of times, where *X* is once again a formula: **,#(#(<c))** . However, we already know that we never return from a macro called with **$<** syntax, so the only values of *X* that really matter are zero and non-zero. If non-zero, we will call **cpus.nxt** only once. Now, let's figure out what *X*, the count, is for this command.

In **adb**, the # says to logically negate the value. What is a logical negation? Simply put, it's the negative of logical true and false. If a value is true (non-zero), the logical negative is false or zero. If a value is false (zero), the logical negative is true or one.

Let's apply this to the statement above from the **cpus** macro, using **adb**. Comments have been added to the side to help you follow along.

Figure 13-5 Experimenting with logical negation in adb

```
Hiya...   adb -k unix.0 vmcore.0
physmem 1e05
cpu_list=X
                  f0170340        This is the address of cpu_list
cpu_list/X
cpu_list:
cpu_list:         f017caa0        This is what is stored at cpu_list
*cpu_list>c                       We save this into adb variable "c"
<c=X
                  f017caa0        Here is what is in variable "c"
#(<c)=X
                  0               Here is the logical negation of it
#0=X
                  1               Here is the logical negation of zero
#<c=X
                  0               Just to show parentheses were optional
##<c=X
                  1               And so on
###<c=X
                  0                   and so on
$q
Hiya...
```

The command `<c,#(#(<c))$<cpus.nxt` will call the **cpus.nxt** macro once, if and only if the content of *cpu_list* is non-zero. If **cpu_list* is zero, we don't call the **cpus.nxt** macro and, instead, continue to the command that prints out a message telling us that a null pointer was found.

Once we are in the **cpus.nxt** macro, we use the same ability to perform a simple "if" test; however, we also find a bitwise AND being performed.

We know variable *c* points to a *cpu* structure. Within the *cpu* structure, the eighth word, *cpu_next*, points to the next *cpu* structure. The ninth word, *cpu_prev*, points to the previous *cpu* structure. If there is only one CPU in the system, *cpu_next* and *cpu_prev* will both point to the one *cpu* structure. We set variable *n* to be the address of the next *cpu* structure.

We call the **cpu** macro to display lots of useful information about the *cpu* structure that the **adb** variable *c* is pointing to. Note that the *cpu* structure, as defined in **cpuvar.h**, contains much more information than the **cpu** macro actually displays. Also note, when reading **/usr/include/sys/cpuvar.h**, that the *cpu* structure has a lot of other structures built into it. This will give you headaches when you try to calculate the actual size of a *cpu* structure. We've been looking at Solaris 2 here. On Solaris 1 sun4m systems, the equivalent of the *cpu* structure (*PerCPU*) is exactly 1 megabyte in size!

When we return from the **cpu** macro, the current address is actually pointing to the beginning of the next *cpu* structure. Take another look at the **cpu** macro, specifically the last line, which is shown below.

```
+/"base_spl"nD472+
```

After printing out the decimal value of *base_spl*, the **cpu** macro advances the current pointer by 472 positions. Why? Since the *cpu* structures come one after another, the author of this macro had a choice. Knowing the *cpu* structure size, he took this route.

Another method would be to have the **cpus.nxt** macro simply set the current address to the *cpu_next* value we found. Either method is fine; however, the method chosen in this case requires that you know exactly how big the *cpu* structure is, and in this case, it is very large!

Okay, now comes the fun part....   0,#(#(<n))&#(#(<n-<e))=nn

Variable *e* contains the address of first *cpu* structure we found. Variable *n* now points to the next *cpu* structure. If *e* and *n* are the same, then we know we have walked through the loop of *cpu* structures and are done. In other words, if *n* minus *e* equals zero, we are done.

The **&** says to do a bitwise AND. For the command **=nn** to be executed, both sides of the **&** must equate to 1. If *(n-e)* equals zero, we know **##0** will result in zero, so **=nn** will not happen. The left side of the **&** is testing for a case where the *cpu_next* value was actually set to zero. While this shouldn't happen, the macro is ready for the possibility of a null pointer in *cpu_next*.

Do you remember what the command **=nn** does? It simply prints two new lines. Since we are only printing text, location 0 was safely used as the starting point for command execution.

The next command is nearly the same. The same tests are done with *n* and *e*. If there is another *cpu* structure to look at, we execute the **cpus.nxt** macro again, feeding it the pointer to the next *cpu* structure.

Summary

We've finished looking at the **msgbuf** and **cpu** macros. At this stage, we have seen how to use the following commands within a macro.

symbolname/	Change the current address
*symbolname/	Change the current address, using a pointer
+/	Advance the current address
/+	Advance the current address
/"*printed text*"	Print text for our own use
/t	Tab over
/c	Print byte as a character (if displayable)
/C	Print byte as a character (or a ^character if not displayable)
/X	Print full word as a hexadecimal value
/n	Print a newline
$<*macro2*	Call another macro without returning
$<<*macro2*	Call another macro and return
,*count*	Specify how many times to execute a command
&	Bitwise AND
#	Logical negation
>*a*	Write to an **adb** variable
<*a*	Read from an **adb** variable

Congratulations! You've gotten through some really tough macros. In the next chapter, we will challenge your new knowledge and invite you to try writing some **adb** macros of your own.

adb Macros: Writing Your Own   14

At this point, you've learned about header files, the only bit of the source provided to most UNIX users, and symbol tables. You've gained an understanding of how these two can be used together to learn more about the UNIX kernel. You've also learned a lot about the absolute debugger, **adb**, and we've looked at a few **adb** macros.

We now certify you as:

> *Dangerous Enough to Write Your Own* **adb** *Macros!*

In this chapter, we'll present you with macro programming tasks that will exercise your new knowledge. We will end the chapter with sample solutions. Let's get started!

Exercise 1:   Initial information

As you become accustomed to working with system crash dumps and doing so becomes more routine to you, you'll probably find that you develop a habit of initially checking the same information in each crash you analyze.

Task:
Write your own macro to collect some initial information from a live system or a set of system crash dump files. Here are some things you might want your macro to display:

- System name
- Boot time
- Crash time
- Panic message
- Stack traceback

Hint:
If working with Solaris 2, try to use the **utsname** macro, but keep in mind:

- Where will **adb** look for the macros you want to use?
- How do you return from a macro?

An example of output to aim for:

The following output is from a Solaris 2 system. Note that in this example, we are using the -I option of **adb** to specify the name of the directory where our own macros reside.

```
Hiya... adb -k -I /mymacros unix.0 vmcore.0
physmem 1e05
$<initial-info
                Initial Dump Information
                ========================
utsname:
utsname:            sys     SunOS
utsname+0x101:      node    pasta
utsname+0x202:      release 5.3
utsname+0x303:      version Generic_101318-45
utsname+0x404:      machine sun4m
srpc_domain:
srpc_domain:        sunservice.uk.sun.com        Domain name
time:
time:               1994 May 12 12:48:20    Time of crash
                    1994 May 12 10:23:55    Time of boot
cpr_info+0x2200:
                Panic string: Data fault

                Stack traceback

complete_panic(0xf0049460,0xf05d03ac,0xf05d0238,0x3,0x0,0x1) + 10c
do_panic(?) + 1c
vcmn_err(0xf015f7a8,0xf05d03ac,0xf05d03ac,0x3cad8,0x2,0x3)
cmn_err(0x3,0xf015f7a8,0x0,0x18,0x18,0xf0152400) + 1c
die(0x9,0xf05d04c4,0x3,0x3a6,0x2,0xf015f7a8) + 78
trap(0x9,0xf05d04c4,0xf01822d8,0x3a6,0x2,0x0) + 598
fault(?) + 84
mutex_enter(0x0,0xd,0x64,0x1,0xd,0xf05d06ec)
lookuppn(0xf05d06e4,0x0,0xf05d06ec,0x0,0x0,0xfc01dd14) + 148
lookupname(0x0,0x0,0x1,0x0,0xf05d07f4,0x0) + 28
vn_open(0x3cad8,0x0,0x3,0xb40,0xf05d08ac,0x0) + a4
copen(0x3cad8,0x3,0xb48,0xf05d0920,0x3cad8,0xf0156628) + 70
syscall(0xf0160f3c) + 3e4
$q
Hiya...
```

Exercise 2: DNLC, the directory name lookup cache

If you have discovered the fine art of kernel tuning, then you are already familiar with the directory name lookup cache. The DNLC maintains directory names and information about their *vnodes* in a cache in memory. The goal of this cache is to reduce actual disk accesses.

On a live system, we use the **-s** option to the UNIX **vmstat** command to see what the DNLC hit rate is. Unfortunately, **vmstat** *cannot* be run against system crash dump files. The example below is from a live system. The underlined output shows the statistics relating to DNLC performance.

Figure 14-1   Using vmstat to view the DNLC hit rate

```
Hiya...  vmstat -s
           0 swap ins
           0 swap outs
           0 pages swapped in
           0 pages swapped out
      166176 total address trans. faults taken
       25476 page ins
        5261 page outs
       37742 pages paged in
       25936 pages paged out
       11063 total reclaims
       11030 reclaims from free list
           0 micro (hat) faults
      166176 minor (as) faults
       25006 major faults
       24725 copy-on-write faults
       59393 zero fill page faults
      218960 pages examined by the clock daemon
          29 revolutions of the clock hand
       52878 pages freed by the clock daemon
        1103 forks
          31 vforks
        1108 execs
    16624282 cpu context switches
    15593437 device interrupts
      231838 traps
    28941879 system calls
      291807 total name lookups (cache hits 90%)
          39 toolong
      124902 user    cpu
       73504 system  cpu
    10051975 idle    cpu
       75699 wait    cpu
Hiya...
```

We see from the underlined output that the system is currently experiencing a 90% success rate in utilization of the DNLC. This is good. The kernel has only had 39 encounters of directory names too long (over 14 characters) to go into the cache. This is also good. But, is this all that we can learn about the DNLC performance? And are we limited to examining DNLC performance on live systems only? Hardly!

Task:

Write an **adb** macro that provides all the DNLC statistical information. Test your macro on a running system and compare the results to **vmstat -s** output.

Hints:

Read the **dnlc.h** header file for guidance.

The **vmstat** program uses the following section of code to calculate the hit rate.

```
nchtotal = ncstats.hits + ncstats.misses + ncstats.long_look;
printf("%9lu total name lookups (cache hits %lu%%)\n", nchtotal,
    ncstats.hits * 100 / nchtotal);
```

An example of output to aim for:

```
# adb -k -I /mymacros /dev/ksyms /dev/mem
physmem 1e03
$<dnlcstats
                   **   Directory Name Lookup Cache Statistics   **
                   ---------------------------------------------
ncsize:
ncsize:            600                 Directory name cache size
ncstats:
ncstats:           347153              # of cache hits that we used
ncstats+4:         34503               # of misses
ncstats+8:         10806               # of enters done
ncstats+0xc:       0                   # of enters tried when already cached
ncstats+0x10:      30                  # of long names tried to enter
ncstats+0x14:      32                  # of long name tried to look up
ncstats+0x18:      0                   # of times LRU list was empty
ncstats+0x1c:      1759                # of purges of cache
                   90                  Hit rate percentage
                   (See /usr/include/sys/dnlc.h for more information)
$q
#
```

Exercise 3: Swap information

On a live system, you can check the status of swap space through commands such as **vmstat** and, if you have a Solaris 2 system, the **swap** command. Unfortunately, neither command can be run against postmortem files.

Task:

On a Solaris 2 system, find the kernel structure that maintains swap space status and write an **adb** macro(s) that prints out some of this data.

Hints:

Each swap file will have its own *swapinfo* structure.

Each *swapinfo* instruction points to a *vnode* structure.

An example of output to aim for:

This example shows both the output of **swap -l** and our **adb** macro on a live system.

```
# swap -l
swapfile              dev   swaplo blocks   free
/dev/dsk/c0t3d0s1    32,25      8 197560 164264
/work/littleswap       -        8  32760  32592
#
# adb -k -I /mymacros /dev/ksyms /dev/mem
physmem 1e03
$<swapinfo
zs_softintr_id+0xffc:          Swap file: /dev/dsk/c0t3d0s1
cn_dip+0x4ed0:   Type:    3
                 Major:   32
                 Minor:   25
                 Blocks: 197560
                 Free:    164264

0xfc52c540:      Swap file: /work/littleswap
0xfc3b1c2c:      Type:    1
                 Major:   0
                 Minor:   0
                 Blocks: 32760
                 Free:    32592

$q
#
```

Try to match the output from **swap -l** instead of **swap -s**. **swap -s** reports on physical (anonymous) memory, as well as disk-resident swap space, and therefore involves a lot more work. If you do want to tackle anonymous memory, read the **anon.h** header file in **/usr/include/vm**.

Extra Credit Challenge: Which process on which CPU?

We haven't started talking about multiprocessor systems yet nor the analysis work involved with MP system postmortem files. However, if we were to give you the exact pointers, you already have the knowledge needed to write a set of macros that will print the names of the processes running on each CPU of an MP system.

Since we *are* giving you exact pointers, this exercise is for Solaris 2.3 systems only. To do the same for other versions of Solaris 2, you'll first need to look at the header files to verify the offsets in the structures you'll be traversing.

Task:

Write a set of macros that print the names of the processes running on each CPU. For more of a challenge, try to have your macros state if the CPU was idle.

Givens:

* The 3rd full 32-bit word of the *cpu* structure points to the executing thread's *thread* structure.

* The 4th word of the *cpu* structure points to the idle thread. If the executing thread and the idle thread are the same, that CPU was idle.

* The 41st (decimal) word of the *thread* structure points to the process or *proc* structure.

* The 152nd (decimal) word of the *proc* structure points to where the process name is kept as a string. (Use the 154th word for Solaris 2.4 systems.)

Hints:

Use the **cpu*** macros as a guide. However, use the *cpu_next* value to change the current address instead of trying to calculate an offset into the next *cpu* structure. If you use the offset method, as done in the **cpu** macro, you risk driving yourself crazy, as the offset for your macro will be quite different from the one used at the bottom of the **cpu** macro.

In **/usr/include/sys**, you'll find **cpuvar.h**, **thread.h**, and **proc.h** of interest should you wish to learn more about the structures your macro will be wandering through.

An example of output to aim for:

```
Hiya...  adb -k unix.6 vmcore.6
physmem bd90
$<proconcpu
ncpus:
ncpus:            Number of CPUS:  4

cpu0+8:           e1313ec0        Thread address
0xe1313f60:       e00ed880        Proc address
p0+0x260:         sched
                  This CPU was idle

                  Next CPU...
0xf5692408:       e134dec0        Thread address
0xe134df60:       e00ed880        Proc address
p0+0x260:         sched
                  This CPU was idle

                  Next CPU...
0xf5692008:       f5a31600        Thread address
0xf5a316a0:       f6be3800        Proc address
0xf6be3a60:       find /export/local -name core -exec rm {} ;

                  Next CPU...
0xf5682c08:       f6a7fc00        Thread address
0xf6a7fca0:       f6685000        Proc address
0xf6685260:       /opt/SUNWpop2/sbin/popd
$q
Hiya...
```

Note that in this example we did not specify a macro directory. Why not? Instead, we copied our macros to the **savecore** directory where the crashes are located. **adb** looks in the current directory for macros before going to the default **adb** macro directory.

Possible solutions

For every programmer who tackles a given problem, you can expect a different solution. This is also true when writing macros. It's important to remember that the only "wrong" solutions are those that generate incorrect results.

The rest of this chapter shows you the macros we used to generate example output for each exercises. We also offer some comments about the problems you may have encountered along the way, as well as some thoughts behind our own programming techniques.

Solution to exercise 1: Initial information

Did you find using the **utsname** macro a bit troublesome when specifying your own macro directory via the **-I** option of **adb**? If so, welcome to the group! It would be great if we could specify a pathlist with **-I**, but that's not the case, at least not yet!

adb does look for macros in the current working directory before going to the macro directory, so sometimes it's easier to just copy your macros to the directory where the system crash dump files reside.

Here is the macro we used to generate the example output shown earlier.

Code Example 14-1 The msgbuf macro

```
="Initial Dump Information"
="======================="
$</usr/kvm/lib/adb/utsname
srpc_domain/s15t"Domain name"
time/Y15t"Time of crash"
lbolt>a
*time-(*<a%0t100)=Y15t"Time of boot"
*panicstr/n"Panic string:"ts
=n"Stack traceback"
=n
$c
```

Note that we specified the full pathname of the **utsname** macro so that **adb** would find it.

Solution to exercise 2: DNLC, the directory name lookup cache

In our macro, the formula used to calculate the hit rate percentage is divided into two
statements to make it easier to follow. The result of the first step is stored in variable n,
which is then read into the formula in the second step.

Code Example 14-2   The dnlcstats macro

```
="**   Directory Name Lookup Cache Statistics   **"
="-------------------------------------------"
ncsize/D"Directory name cache size"
ncstats/D"# of cache hits that we used"
+/D"# of misses"
+/D"# of enters done"
+/D"# of enters tried when already cached"
+/D"# of long names tried to enter"
+/D"# of long name tried to look up"
+/D"# of times LRU list was empty"
+/D"# of purges of cache"
*ncstats+*(ncstats+4)+*(ncstats+14)>n
*ncstats*0t100%<n=D"Hit rate percentage"
="(See /usr/include/sys/dnlc.h for more information)"
```

The last line simply prints a reminder of where to read about the DNLC.

The interesting thing about this script is that it will produce inaccurate results when the
values used in the formula are too large. The integer math, multiplying by decimal 100,
then dividing, will eventually cause overflows and precision errors that **adb** will not
catch. You'll find many versions of the UNIX **vmstat** command that also report negative
or otherwise bizarre percentages once the values reach a certain size.

If your values become too large, consider dividing the values by an equal amount, such
as 100,000, then working out the percentage. An example of this second variation of
dnlcstats can be found on the Panic! CD-ROM.

Rebooting your system will reset all of the DNLC statistics back to zero.

Solution to exercise 3: Swap information

We used two macros to display the swapinfo data shown in the example output. Here they are.

Code Example 14-3   The swapinfo macro

```
*swapinfo>c
<c,##(<c)$<swapinfo2
="There is no swapinfo"
```

Code Example 14-4   The swapinfo2 macro

```
<c+0x10>n
*(<c+0x24)/"Swap file:    "s
*<c>v
<v+24/"Type:        "tD
*(<v+0x28)%3ffff="Major:   "D
*(<v+0x28)&3ffff="Minor:   "D
*(<c+0x18)*8="Blocks:  "D
*(<c+0x1c)*8="Free:       "Dnn
*<n>c
<c,##(<c)$<swapinfo2
```

In **swapinfo2**, we set variable v to point to the *vnode* structure. This unnecessary step is only done to make life a bit easier for the macro author, making it more apparent which values are being collected from the *vnode* structure and which are from the *swapinfo* structure.

The use of **0x** in address offsets is also added for readability and is unnecessary because hexadecimal is the default in **adb**. However, since we chose to use variable c to point to the current *swapinfo* structure, we didn't want to create confusion when we used the **1c** address offset.

Why are we multiplying the value of "Blocks" and "Free" by 8? We wanted to report the same numbers that the UNIX **swap -l** command would report. The *swapinfo* structure maintains the number of memory pages of swap space and free space. The **swap -l** command shows the number of disk blocks. Most Sun systems have memory pages that are 4096 bytes in size. Disk blocks are 512 bytes in size. Thus, there are 8 blocks per page. To find out the memory page size of your Solaris 2 system, use **adb** to examine kernel symbol *pagesize*.

Those with access to source will find that the **swap** command multiplies the *swapinfo* "Blocks" and "Free" values by "disk blocks per page," 8, just as we have done.

Looking at **swapinfo2**, you see that we display the major and minor numbers of the swap file by using the following lines. Were you able to figure out what these two **adb** command lines accomplish?

```
*(<v+0x28)%3ffff="Major:   "D
*(<v+0x28)&3ffff="Minor:   "D
```

The major and minor numbers are kept in the *vnode* structure as a single 32-bit word. The major number is 14 bits wide and the minor number is 18 bits wide. The following snippet from **/usr/include/sys/mkdev.h** confirms this.

```
#define NBITSMAJOR    14       /* # of SVR4 major device bits */
#define NBITSMINOR    18       /* # of SVR4 minor device bits */
#define MAXMAJ        0x7f     /* SVR4 max major value, max 128 dev's */
#define MAXMIN        0x3ffff  /* SVR4 max minor value */
```

The line ***(<v+0x28)%3ffff="Major: "D** grabs the 11th full word of the *vnode* structure, *v+0x28*, which is where the major/minor value is kept and divides it by hexadecimal 3ffff (18 binary bits set). In effect, this shifts the value 18 bits right, leaving only the high-order 14 bits, thus, the major number.

The second line ANDs the same major/minor value by 0x3ffff, so that only the low-order 18 bits are used to display a decimal value, thus, the minor number.

Extra Credit Challenge: Which process on which CPU?

If you were able to write macros that succeeded in meeting the requirements of this challenge, *Congratulations!* We are well aware that this was not an easy task!

We used two macros to generate the example output we showed earlier. Here they are.

Code Example 14-5   The proconcpu macro

```
ncpus/"Number of CPUS:   "Xnn
*cpu_list>c
<c>e
<c,#(#(<c))$<proconcpu.nxt
cpu_list/X"(cpu_list ptr is NULL)"n
```

Code Example 14-6   The proconcpu.nxt macro

```
*(<c+0t28)>n
<c+8/X"Thread address"
*(<c+8)>p
<p+a0/X"Proc address"
*(<p+a0)>j
<j+260/s
.,#((*(<c+8))-(*(<c+c)))="This CPU was idle"
0,#(#(<n))&#(#(<n-<e))=n"Next CPU..."n
<n>c
<n,#(#(<n))&#(#(<n-<e))$<proconcpu.nxt
```

Unless your job is centered around writing **adb** macros every day, it is unlikely that you will just whip out complicated macros such as these without some trial and error. In fact, we don't mind admitting that these macros tripped us up a bit!

Remember to refer to the macros that already exist, should you ever get confused.

As you discover new and exciting things in system crash dumps (and live systems), modify your own macros. The time and effort you put into writing and maintaining your own set of macros will pay off in the long run.

Now, before we move on to a new subject, talking about assembly language, go update your resume, adding "**adb macro programmer**" to your list of skills!

Part 2 — Advanced Studies

Intro to the Advanced Studies

To be successful in UNIX system crash dump analysis work, you need a variety of analysis skills and a good understanding of UNIX operating system anatomy. Without being able to comprehend how UNIX works, it is very difficult to identify how and why it fails.

This next section of *Panic!* introduces you to the more advanced topics. We will talk about assembly languages in general, and then SPARC assembly in detail. Overviews of the various components of the UNIX operating system are discussed. You'll read about stacks and stack tracebacks. We'll also cover traps and watchdog resets in great detail.

With the following chapters, we hope to increase your comfort level where the more advanced subjects are concerned. These are not, however, a substitute for advanced training.

If you are interested in reading and learning more about UNIX internals, a few excellent books are available, as well as UNIX Internals courses offered by UNIX vendors and UNIX training firms. We recommend these for the serious "guru-in-training."

Introduction to Assembly 15 ≡

Before you can really become proficient in the art of UNIX system crash dump analysis, you will have to be comfortable with an assembly language. Which assembly depends on the CPU with which you are working, as you'll soon understand.

We recognize that many system administrators may not yet feel they are proficient in any assembly language. With this in mind, we will now introduce you to the general concepts involved. In the next chapter, we will look closely at one assembly language: SPARC assembly.

High-level vs. low-level languages

Languages such as C, Pascal, Fortran, BASIC, and COBOL are often referred to as high-level languages. From a programmer's point of view, when writing in a high-level language, it doesn't matter what hardware platform the final program will run on. The programmer needn't learn the native language of each hardware architecture, because the compiler will generate the correct executable code for the programmer — object code that is written in the native machine language for that particular system. Looking at the generated assembly code, the programmer may not recognize his program; it will look very different from the high-level language in which he originally wrote it.

Assembly language is referred to as a low-level language. The assembly language programmer writes his code using the mnemonics for the machine's instruction set, as defined by the hardware. Instead of being compiled, the programmer's code is run through an assembler, which creates the final executable object file. Looking at this, the programmer will find no surprises; the code will be exactly what was written.

Every hardware architecture has its own native instruction set. The assembly code for each machine that you encounter will differ from the next. To help make UNIX easy to port from machine to machine, most of the UNIX source code is written in C. However, the sections of the code that are most tightly tied to the hardware, for example, interrupt- or trap-handling and stack manipulation, have to be rewritten (ported) in the destination hardware's native language.

The lowest levels of the UNIX kernel may also be written in assembly language to obtain performance gains. For example, the code that handles context switches, something that may happen thousands of times per minute, is best written in assembly language.

When we are analyzing a system crash dump by using **adb**, we will always be looking at native assembly code. Even if the kernel module we are examining was originally written in C, we will see the assembly instructions generated by the C compiler used to build the flavor of UNIX we are working with. Therefore, an understanding of assembly language is an important prerequisite to kernel analysis work. Unfortunately, since every native language is different from the next, we may find ourselves having to deal with several different assembly languages! However, don't despair! Once you understand the concepts, one machine language is pretty similar to the next (since they all have to do essentially the same things), and you will be able to pick up the new syntax fairly quickly. Just as all automobile engines have similarities, so do all computer processors and their native languages.

Assembly languages

In general, assembly language consists of mnemonics for the basic hardware instruction set, known as the machine language. This is the set of operations that the chip(s) will execute. It, by necessity, has a one-to-one correspondence with the CPU architecture, inasmuch as each machine type has a different set of instructions to go with the hardware.

Some machine architectures are complicated and provide a large, "rich" instruction set. This allows the assembly language code to be shorter and more efficient, because there are instructions that will do a specific task or that can do a great deal of work. Other machines are much simpler, at least in terms of hardware architecture, and provide fewer instructions to work with. It will normally take more code to do the same job because each one of the instructions is simpler and does less — although usually it gets done very rapidly.

The more complicated machines are known as CISC (Complex Instruction Set Computer) systems, while the more modern, simpler machines are RISC (Reduced Instruction Set Computer) systems.

Note – Older machines that were simpler because they just weren't able to do the work in hardware are not really members of the RISC class of systems — they're just simple and slow.

Assembly language can be the most efficient type of programming, in terms of getting the most work out of the machine in the least amount of time and space. An assembly programmer can take advantage of tricks because he knows the architecture and the job to be done.

There are some definite drawbacks, however, which make assembly programming less desirable and seldom used. It's certainly more difficult to read and debug and takes more programmer time to produce a working program. In fact, a study done a number of years ago showed that, on the average, a programmer could produce on the order of 10 lines of working, debugged code per day, over the lifetime of a project. It didn't seem to matter what language the code was written in, either; you could get 10 lines of C, 10 lines of Fortran, or 10 lines of assembly per programmer per day. As you might guess, it's much more efficient in terms of programmer time to use a higher-level language to do the job and let the compiler try to produce efficient, machine-language code.

CPUs constantly get faster, but assembly programming is still very slow and complicated. There are, of course, some times when you can't get away from it. For example, when you're dealing with certain aspects of the hardware or with parts of the environment that high-level languages don't cover (stack manipulation, for instance), then you're forced to use assembly to handle it. Fortunately, the UNIX kernel uses a fairly small amount of assembly source code.

Although UNIX is mostly written in C, when you are debugging you're going to need to know how the system works in terms of the machine language, assembly. You'll be seeing a lot of it.

Basic CPU structure (all CPUs are similar)

Most processors have some common characteristics and a standard sequence of steps they go through to execute a single instruction.

You will find *working registers*, which are essentially memory cells inside the CPU itself. Access to these locations is very fast, and, most of the time, instructions will use one or more of these registers to contain the data for the operation. Some CPUs offer the programmer a lot of working registers, some fewer. Some registers may be reserved for special use. Some may have special capabilities, such as automatically incrementing or decrementing the value they contain each time they are accessed.

In most CPUs you will see a *processor status register*, which will contain the state of the CPU, for example, whether it's in supervisor or kernel mode or in user mode. Various flags may exist that indicate the result of the most recent arithmetic operations (known as condition codes). It would be in the process status register that you might also find priority levels for handling interrupts and, possibly, error indication flags.

In all CPUs you will see a *program counter*, or a register that indicates where the CPU is getting instructions to be executed.

There may also be a *stack pointer* and some other dedicated or special-purpose registers that hold data relating to other, specific operations.

Instruction execution

Most of the CPUs you will encounter in the UNIX world are designed to execute instructions in a similar manner. A typical instruction sequence (cycle) would contain the following steps to execute one machine language operation.

- Check for an interrupt. See if there is an external device that needs attention. Based on the current priority of the processor and the priority of the request, this may result in an immediate "function call" to a special piece of code to handle this particular situation, in other words, take care of the other guy first.

- Fetch the next instruction. Using the program counter (PC) value, get the instruction to be executed from memory and load it into the CPU where it can be interpreted.

- Update the PC. Increment the program counter so that the next fetch will get the next instruction.

- Verify that the instruction is a recognized and legal instruction.

- Verify that the memory locations and registers requested for use by the instruction are accessible and available for use.

- Execute the instruction. This may require getting data from memory (a *load* operation) and/or putting a value into memory (a *store* operation).

- Now, loop back to the beginning and do it all over again.

Every CPU has to go through these basic steps to execute every single instruction. There are some tricks that hardware designers use to try to speed up this sequence, but you can't really get rid of any of the steps themselves.

Instruction pipelining

One common approach used to speed up instruction execution time is to overlap the steps of the instruction cycle. It may turn out that memory is not being used at all for the execution portion, so it would be more efficient to start the next fetch for the next instruction while the current instruction is being performed. This technique is known as "instruction pipelining."

To understand pipelining, think of an assembly line for automobiles. While one automobile is in the process of being built on the assembly line, several more will also be on the line, each at a different phase of its construction. The use of an assembly line doesn't necessarily speed up the manufacturing time of each individual car, but it has a dramatic effect on the overall production of the plant when measured over time.

As with the automobile assembly line, instruction pipelines do not make individual instructions run faster. However, a sequence of a dozen pipelined instructions may execute in the same amount of time needed to execute only a couple of nonpipelined instructions.

Imagine if one instruction had to go through all the way through the pipeline shown below before the next instruction could enter it. Next, imagine that five instructions could be in the pipeline at one time, each at a different stage in its execution.

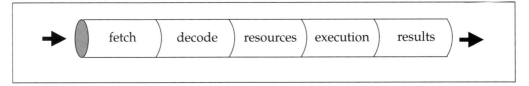

Figure 15-1 Some Possible Instruction Pipeline Stages

Now, think in terms of millions of instructions pr second passing through the instruction pipeline and the value of pipelining becomes quite clear.

Floating-point coprocessors

Another way to speed up overall program execution is to use *coprocessors* for certain types of instructions. The most common example of this is a Floating-Point Unit, which is used only for handling floating-point operations. The CPU will normally recognize an instruction as something that should be handed over to the FPU, allowing the CPU to continue with the next instruction. The FPU does its work asynchronously, taking as much time as it needs and possibly signaling the main CPU when the operation is complete. The CPU can proceed with other work in parallel.

Note – Do not confuse this concept with multiprocessor systems. Here, the FPU coprocessor is dedicated to performing only certain tasks. A true multiprocessor system normally has several CPUs, each of which runs concurrently and may have its own FPU.

Instruction types

On most machines, instructions can be classified into one of several different categories. These are fairly general, and some instructions may overlap the boundaries. Here are some common types of instructions:

- Arithmetic
  Basic numeric and logical operations, such as *add*, *multiply*, and *or*, require source operands and a destination for the result. These instructions often use registers to hold one or more of the values. The arithmetic result may also cause certain flags to be set in a processor status register for later reference.

- Memory reference
  Often the arithmetic instructions require the data to be resident in CPU registers and may leave the result there as well. This requires instructions to get data from the slower main memory into the registers, and to put the results back again. These instructions are known as *load* (get the data from memory and load into a register) and *store* (put the data currently in a register into memory) instructions.

- Transfer of control
  Loops, functions, and if-then-else constructs require execution to be able to go somewhere else to change the normal sequential flow of instructions. Transfers, known as *jumps* or *branches*, allow you to effectively change the PC contents and thus force the CPU to fetch from some other location. Often branches cover a shorter range than jumps but have the ability to branch conditionally, for example, to skip over some code if the result of the last arithmetic operation was zero.

- Input/output
  Some processors have special instructions for performing I/O, others don't. Those that lack the I/O instructions need another way to "talk" to devices. They communicate by making the devices look like memory and by using the normal memory reference instructions to get data or issue commands. This technique requires dedicating a range of memory addresses to be used for certain devices. The technique is known as memory-mapped I/O. Note that this technique is *not* the same as using the *mmap()* system call, which is at another, higher level of programming interface.

- Miscellaneous
  Some processors have a miscellaneous group of instructions that perform various tasks. These might include rotating a value within a register, clearing or setting specified bits, and performing no operation at all.

Instructions also have formats and addressing modes. Depending on what category the operation fits in, it may need to find some data to work with. There are many different methods of doing this. Some architectures provide different, or more, modes than others. Let's talk about some of these modes.

Instruction formats and addressing modes

Consider a machine that uses a stack for everything. If you need to add two numbers together, the CPU will take the top two numbers off the stack, add them, and put the result back onto the stack. For this particular *add* operation, the location of the data and the result is always the same. Nothing comes from memory, nothing is put into a register. This is known as a "zero-address" instruction. Everything is implicit.

A more common older architecture used one main register in the CPU for everything. This register, often known as an accumulator, was the main source or destination for all instructions. A *load* would get data from memory and place it into the register; a *store* would put it back to memory. An *add* needed to have a memory address specified; it would get the data from that location, add it to the value currently in the accumulator, and put the result there as well. This is a single address instruction—one source and the destination are always the same. Many of the old 8-bit microprocessors follow this scheme.

A double-address instruction would provide a source and a destination in the instruction code itself. This is most commonly used on machines with many registers in the CPU. An *add* would take a value from one register and add it to the value in another.

And finally, a triple-address instruction would indicate two source operands and a destination (usually using registers for all of them). This scheme would allow you to take a value from one register, add it to the value in another, and place the result in a third.

Aside from providing some interesting history, why are we telling you about all of this? Well, you'll soon find that the SPARC processor uses several of these formats for its instructions, especially the last. Triple-address instructions are used for all arithmetic.

Addressing and registers

Registers are essentially extremely high speed local memory that is resident in the CPU. They are used for many operations. Results are placed here, tests are performed on data here, and arithmetic is done on values in these registers. This is normally done for speed, inasmuch as register access does not involve going outside the CPU to make a bus access or a memory reference.

Registers can be used to hold addresses as well as data. One form of addressing, known as register-indirect, uses the value in a register as if it were a pointer: the data is fetched from the specified memory location. A modification of this, auto-increment mode, will not only use the register contents as an address but will automatically update the register so that it points to the next location. This can lead to some very efficient code. On the DEC® PDP-11 architecture, the C statement,

```
while (*d++ = *s++) ;
```

which performs the equivalent of a string copy, could be done in a two-instruction loop:

```
x:   movb   (r0)+,(r1)+    ; move a byte, increment both addresses
     bnz    x              ; branch back if the byte moved was not zero
```

In the above example, the CPU would take a source address from a register (r0), a destination address from another register (r1), and do a memory-to-memory move. The same instruction would update both the source and destination addresses appropriately and would set a flag based on the value of the byte it moved so that the following conditional branch would detect the case of a zero-byte and stop the sequence.

There is normally a corresponding auto-decrement mode as well. Unfortunately, SPARC does not use either of these modes. If you want to add a one to a register, a separate instruction is needed.

Another mode of addressing is known as PC-relative. This mode uses a value in an instruction or in a register as an offset from the location of the current instruction, adds the two, and finds the data address that way. This is *very* useful for PIC, or position-independent code.

Consider the requirements for writing a shared library, like **libc**. The library can be mapped into any arbitrary location in memory, depending on the program that uses it. This means that the code cannot ever use an absolute address of a variable, because it can't tell where that variable will be. Everything must be relative to the place at which the library was mapped.

With PC-relative addressing, the actual data address is irrelevant, as long as it doesn't change with respect to the code. SPARC does not have any PC-relative data addressing capabilities, which makes designing and writing position-independent code rather interesting for the programmer, to say the least.

Data in memory

Values contained in memory are usually accessible as bytes (8 bits), short words (16 bits), long words (32 bits), or double words (64 bits). Generally, specific instruction codes handle exactly one type of data. There may also be some that handle data as signed or unsigned values. A signed value might result in sign-bit extension when it is loaded into a register, whereas an unsigned value would force the unused bits to be set to zero.

Values that are stored in memory have two different forms they can follow. The most common is the "Big-Endian" scheme; that is, data needing more than one byte will have the high-order bytes stored first. For example, the long hex number 0x12345678 would be stored, on a SPARC system (a Big-Endian system), as the following sequence of bytes.

    0x12   0x34   0x56   0x78

Some architectures, notably the common Intel chips, use the reverse method. This would result in the sequence:

    0x78   0x56   0x34   0x12

when scanning memory from a low to a high address.

On to SPARC!

These are basic principles common to just about all machine types. Assembly languages will reflect these characteristics in the instructions and addressing modes that are available.

Now you should feel ready to move on to a specific assembly language. In the next chapter, we introduce you to SPARC assembly language.

Introduction to SPARC

In the previous chapter, we introduced you to general concepts of assembly language. As you learned, every CPU has similarities. However, every CPU also has features and concepts that make it quite unique. As such, each CPU's assembly language is also unique.

In this chapter, we introduce you to one assembly language, SPARC assembly. Due to the nature of assembly languages, we will also be introducing you to the SPARC processor and the concepts behind it and what makes it tick.

For those of you who enjoy learning about all the gory details, Appendix A goes into much further detail about both the SPARC (**S**calable **P**rocessor **ARC**itecture) hardware and the SPARC instruction set.

Basic characteristics of SPARC assembly language

There are some essential characteristics of SPARC instructions that come from the fact that the system is a RISC, Reduced Instruction Set Computer, architecture. Whereas some computer designs attempt to provide many instructions to do complex tasks, RISC machines are designed to be simple (at least in hardware), providing fewer but faster instructions. One consequence of this is that it may take more, sometimes many more, instructions to accomplish the same task that one CISC, Complex Instruction Set Computer, instruction would do.

For example, on a CISC processor, we might be able to execute one instruction to increment the current value stored in memory location 4000. Using a RISC processor, we might need to perform three instructions.

1. Read the contents of location 4000 into a register.

2. Increment the value stored in the register.

3. Write the value stored in the register back to location 4000.

However, the RISC machine can usually perform the longer sequence of code more quickly, getting the job done as fast or faster than the CISC machine.

While the RISC architecture may make life easier for hardware designers, compiler writers often bang their heads on walls trying to generate efficient code. However, since this is not a book for compiler hackers, we will concentrate on what you might encounter during debugging when looking at generated code: common instructions, common sequences, and common failings. We will be talking about the Version 8 specification for the SPARC chip. This is a 32-bit implementation; in other words, a full word is 32 bits wide. (Version 7 is quite similar, but lacks a few instructions. It is still a 32-bit specification, and Version 7 code runs fine on a Version 8 processor.)

Since the SPARC is a "simpler" machine, you will find some tradeoffs when it's compared to a CISC architecture. A potentially large instruction set was compressed into fewer, more frequently used commands, which can be executed very quickly. This means many common instructions appear to be missing. However, life is not all bad. One feature of the RISC architecture is that there are lots of registers to play with. These all hold one full word (32 bits) of information. Instructions, as much as possible, deal directly with these registers rather than going to memory for their data each time. This scheme provides some dramatic increases in speed of execution.

Registers contain the data for almost all instructions. Any arithmetic instruction, logical operation, or testing is done with all the values in registers. Parameters to functions and function return values are also set up in registers rather than being pushed onto the stack. Of course, there are a limited number of registers, and any parameters left over do have to be put someplace, so they are, in fact, stuffed onto the stack. But, as you'll see, it's much more expensive in terms of time and instruction space to access these values, or *any* data in memory, so as much as possible is done using the registers alone.

Data in memory is accessible as bytes (signed or unsigned), short 16-bit words (also signed or unsigned), long words (a full 32 bits), or double-words. There are some severe restrictions on where data can be placed, however. Short words *must* be stored on a 2-byte boundary (in other words, the address of a short must be even). A full word needs to go on a 4-byte boundary. And, reasonably enough, a double-word must have an address divisible by 8. If an instruction tries to access data in memory with a badly aligned address, this attempt will result in an immediate *Address Alignment Trap*, and the instruction will fail. When this happens in the kernel, the system panics, reporting a bad trap.

SPARC instructions

The first thing to remember when looking at SPARC instructions is that they are constrained by many factors. One we've already seen. Addressing must be done correctly. Another restriction is placed on the instructions themselves: they *must* fit into one word exactly. That means that all instruction codes are exactly 32 bits long, and will always start on a 4-byte boundary (an address where the lower two bits are always zeroes). Readers who have some previous experience with assembly language may be wondering how 32-bit addresses or constants are loaded into registers. The answer is, they aren't — not in one instruction, anyway. More on this later.

Yet another characteristic of SPARC instructions is that no instruction accesses memory directly with an address in the instruction code itself. Any memory reference requires an address in a register as everything is done register-indirect. This means that the address of a data value must be loaded into a register before the data can be fetched. When you consider that it usually takes more than one instruction to load up an address, you can see that referencing data in memory is a fairly complex and expensive operation. No wonder registers are popular, and no wonder there are lots of them!

SPARC registers

The SPARC specification defines a few special-purpose registers (generally accessible only to the kernel, if at all) and some working space.

- Processor Status Register (PSR) — Contains state (kernel/user mode), condition codes, and the CPU priority level.

- Program Counter (PC) — Address of the instruction currently being executed.

- next Program Counter (nPC) — Address of the next instruction. Used for prefetch of an instruction code.

- Partial Arithmetic Result (Y) — Primarily used for integer multiplication.

- 32 working registers (%r0 through %r31) — General-purpose 32-bit registers.

The CPU itself may have a large number of general-purpose registers available (from 40 up to 512), but an individual piece of code can access only 32 of these at any one time. This restriction is partly due to a design issue related to passing parameters.

Passing parameters when calling routines

Function calls are a common occurrence, especially with modular or recursive programs, so passing parameters needs to be fairly efficient. Since we've seen that access to memory doesn't fall in this category, it would be best if parameters were put in registers rather than on a stack in memory. There are several ways to do this.

First, we might have a lot of registers and dedicate a certain subset to be used for parameters. Thus, any routine that calls another would have to clear out that register set and put parameters there, which means lots of moving data from one register to another. This may be more efficient than putting data on the stack all the time, but it's still not very elegant.

A better method would be to give a subset of the registers to a function and make sure that any function that it calls would have a different subset with which to work. This approach is the one that was taken and leads us to the first interesting and potentially difficult concept to understand when dealing with SPARC systems.

Register windows

Regardless of the total number of general-purpose registers that the CPU contains, a function can see only 32 of them. There is a subset of the register set, a "window" into it, available for any given function. The kernel keeps a pointer to the current register subset in the processor status word.

Now, if each function uses a different set of registers, how does this help with passing parameters or results back and forth? The answer is to have these windows *overlap*, so that there are some registers (a subset of the window, if you will) in common. These shared registers can be used to pass parameters to a called function or to return a value to a caller. The registers available to a given function are shown below.

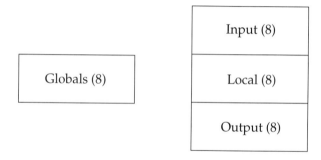

Figure 16-1   *Registers Available to a Given Function*

As you can see from the diagram, there are four sets of 8 registers, or 32 in all. The global registers are exactly that — accessible to all functions (all windows) as if they were really global variables. Everybody can see them.

The "window" that moves is composed of the 24 remaining registers. These are divided into groups of 8 and named more or less according to their function. The first 8, the input registers, are those into which the calling function will put the parameters that it wants to pass. In our current function, then, these registers contain the incoming data: the input to this subroutine. These 8 registers are the ones that overlap with the caller's window. The last 8, the output registers, will contain any data that this function passes on to someone else: outgoing parameters. These, then, overlap with the window of the *next* function, the one(s) called by this current bit of code. The local registers, the piece in the middle, don't overlap with any other registers and are purely local to this function.

These registers act like a "circular buffer," so it looks like an infinite set of windows are available. However, at some point you're going to run out, so there is a trap to the kernel when the next window would conflict with one already in use. This trap, known as a *window overflow*, will cause the system to save the conflicting window (the old data) on the stack. The reverse case, when a *window underflow* is caused by trying to back up to a window that has been put on the stack already, will result in another trap to the kernel to get the data and load it back into the desired register window.

Special instructions (`save` and `restore`) move to the next or previous register window, which may cause these special window underflow and overflow traps. Moving to a new window gets a new set of 24 registers, but since they overlap by 8, a `save` or `restore` will only move the window pointer by 16 registers. This gives a new function 16 registers plus 8 from the caller (or, when returning from a function, restores 16 registers and leaves the 8 output registers with the values placed in them by the old called function).

These registers are commonly named g (global), i (input), l (local), and o (output) in assembly language. The notation used starts a register name with a percent sign to distinguish it from a variable name, has one letter to indicate the type of register, and has one number from 0 to 7 to identify it. Thus, register `%i0` is the first input register, and `%g7` is the last global.

Register usage

Some conventions and some hardware requirements govern how these registers are used. From the software standpoint, a function assumes that the input and local registers belong to that function. Contents can be modified as the function sees fit. This means that the input registers can be used for parameters, local storage, temporary values, or all three. When a function returns back to the caller, then, that caller cannot depend on the values in its output registers (the overlap to the called function) still being there when the caller resumes.

The 8 output registers belong to the called function; their values cannot be assumed to be consistent across function calls. You will often see output registers used to hold temporary values in a function in between calls to other functions. Thus, a window overflow, when it has to save the old register contents to make way for a new function, will only save 16 registers (the inputs and locals) on the stack.

Now, parameters passed to a function must go in the output registers. This requirement obviously restricts you to passing eight parameters, right? Well, not quite. The excess has to be put somewhere else, that's all. (They go on the stack.) So, we have space for the first eight parameters in registers.

Unfortunately, that's not quite true, since there is additional information that would be nice to pass on to a subroutine. One vital bit, which that function will need in order to get back, is the *return address*, that is, where the call came from. That has to go in a register. In fact, one instruction (`call`) uses output register #7 (`%o7`) to hold the address of the call itself. This is done by the hardware; you have no choice in the matter. So one register is used for something other than a parameter, which bounces you down to seven, max.

There is, however, still more that needs to be passed on to the new function: the stack pointer. Since there is no dedicated stack pointer registers, one of the general-purpose registers has to be used instead. Output register #6 (`%o6`, also known as `%sp`) is used for this purpose, although it really could be any one of them.

Fortunately, this is it; the remaining six registers (`%o0` through `%o5`) are available for parameters. They are normally used in a left-to-right fashion: the first parameter goes in the first register (`%o0`), the next in the second (`%o1`), and so on. Thus, the new function sees its incoming parameters in `%i0` (the first), `%i1` (the second), and so on up to `%i5` (the sixth).

When more than six calling parameters are passed, the additional ones can be found on the stack — and we do have the stack pointer, since that's in the caller's `%o6` — which is our `%i6`. Our `%i7`, of course, is the caller's `%o7`, which contains essentially the return address.

The debugger cannot tell which of these six registers, if any, are really used for passing parameters, so usually a stack traceback will always display six parameters. The only way you can tell which of those six are used for incoming data versus temporary storage is to examine the source code (or, if you're really dedicated, by looking at the assembly code to see what they're used for.)

Global register zero

One other hardware feature concerns register contents. The first global register, `%g0`, is the assembly language equivalent of **/dev/null**. This register always contains zero. It doesn't matter what you try to put into it, the value will always remain zero. This is actually amazingly useful; you see `%g0` used quite often. We'll see some examples later.

SPARC instruction types

We'll just touch briefly on some of the SPARC instructions, so you can get a feel for what you'll be seeing in disassembled output. The operations can be divided into some basic functional types based on what they do.

- Load/store — Move data between a register and a memory location.

- Arithmetic/logical instructions — Do the real work, but only using data already in registers.

- Transfer of control instructions — Include subroutine jumps and conditional branches, as well as trap instructions that are used to issue system calls.

- Control register manipulation (normally done only by the kernel) — Allow the system to do things like indicate when a register window overflow should occur. These registers are not accessible to user programs, and you will only see these instructions in assembly-language kernel code.

- Coprocessor and floating-point instructions — Immediately pass off the special operation codes.

- Miscellaneous category — Instructions that just don't fit anywhere else. These include things like `flushi`, which clears the CPU instruction cache.

The load and store instructions we'll look at in more detail shortly. These are the only ones that reference memory. Therefore, any kernel panic resulting in a *data fault* message (an example of a memory access error condition) will most likely involve one of these instructions.

All arithmetic and logical instructions refer to registers or small constants in the instruction code itself. These cannot cause memory reference traps, because there is nothing that they can do except touch registers. The instructions include things like add, subtract, multiply and divide, plus the logical or Boolean operations: AND, OR, NOT, exclusive OR. These also come in two flavors: one that just does the operation and another that adds the action of setting condition code bits based on the result.

Delayed Control Transfer Instructions

The instructions of a routine are normally executed sequentially. However, there are often times when execution needs to skip over some instructions and continue at another, nonsequential location. Programmers often refer to this change in the order of program execution as a "branch" or "jump." And, appropriately, the instructions that perform this task are often called "branches" or "jump instructions."

In SPARC terms, we refer to all instructions that alter the order of instruction execution as "control transfer instructions."

There are basically two types of branches that may be performed by computers. These are:

- Unconditional branches — Simply change the order of instruction execution

- Conditional branches — Change the order of execution only when a certain condition is found to be true

Due to the pipeline, the SPARC processor is actually processing more than one instruction at a time. As you know, this is a big advantage when we are executing a sequential sequence of instructions. However, what happens when we need to test for a certain condition and, based upon the result, branch away from the sequence of instructions, *instructions that are already being processed in the instruction pipeline?*

On SPARC processors, all but one of the control transfer instructions will, unless specifically told otherwise, execute the instruction that immediately follows it into the pipeline. The instruction following the control transfer instruction is referred to as the "delay instruction" because it is executed during the time delay between execution of the control transfer instruction and execution of the instruction stored at the new location to which control was transferred.

Let's look at this concept from a programmer's point of view. See if you can figure out the order in which the following sequence of English commands might be executed on a SPARC processor.

```
1.  Load "5" into Register 1
2.  Jump to Step 7
3.  Load "10" into Register 2
4.  (other stuff)
5.  (other stuff)
6.  (other stuff)
7.  Store contents of Register 2 into location X
```

In this sequence, the execution sequence would be 1-2-3-7. Is this what you expected?

We load a 5 into Register 1. Next, we jump to Step 7. Since Step 7 was not part of the sequential order of instructions, it must be loaded into the instruction pipeline. Meanwhile, Step 3, which was nearly all of the way through the pipeline, is completed, and Register 2 ends up containing a 10.

Instead of the CPU sitting idle while waiting for the store instruction at Step 7 to be processed through the pipeline, the CPU is kept busy with the execution of the delay instruction, the instruction at Step 3. This is a much more efficient use of the CPU.

When you look at system crash dumps, you will often find nop instructions being used as the delay instruction. This instruction has no effect and is used to fill the delay time slot. Other times, you will see examples more like the one above, where a value is set and will be used *after* the branch is completed. It is up to the compiler or the assembly language programmer how to make best use of the delay instruction.

Later, when we talk about the stack, we'll see a very common use of the delay instruction.

Note – The Trap on Integer Condition Code, or Ticc instruction, is the only SPARC control transfer instruction that never executes the delay instruction.

Note – Most of the control transfer instructions have an annul bit that can be set to say "don't execute the delay instruction under certain conditions."

Looking at instructions in memory

For our purposes, we're mostly going to be looking at a dead program (or kernel) to see where we were and what the code was when the problem occurred. This means we're going to be looking at the machine language that was being executed and reading it as assembly code.

The **adb** utility has commands to examine memory and display the contents as instruction codes. **adb** performs *disassembly* of the binary back into mnemonics that are intelligible. The **i** format code does this for one instruction, one word. This is normally coupled with the **a** command to cause each word to be displayed with the associated symbolic address. Thus, an **adb** command to dump out 10 instructions in a row, starting at *main*, would look like:

```
main,10?ai
```

Now let's look at the actual instructions you are most likely to encounter when looking at a program or a kernel that faulted and died.

How load and store instructions can go wrong

There are two instruction types that are used to transfer data between the registers and main memory. These are the load and store instructions.

Load instructions get a byte, word, or some other data type from memory and place it into a register. Store instructions put the register's data back into memory. Each of these operations requires a source and a destination. For load, the source will be a memory location, and the destination will be a register. For store instructions, the source is a register, and the destination is a memory location.

Since the instruction itself must fit into exactly one 32-bit word, how do an instruction operation code, and destination register, and a 32-bit memory address all fit? They don't.

As we've mentioned, any instruction that references memory must have the address of the desired memory address already stored in a register. The memory access instruction then uses that register *indirectly* to reference the memory cell. In addition, there must be some information on the data type, whether signed, unsigned, short, long, and so on. This is normally encoded in the instruction itself, which means that we have a separate instruction code for loading a byte, as opposed to loading a full 32-bit word.

Any time you get a bad memory reference, the actual instruction where the fault occurred is almost guaranteed to be a load or a store instruction, since these are the ones that actually touch memory to get or save data.

For example, let's take a user program that died because of a segmentation violation (a bad memory reference). Looking at the PC (program counter) value will provide the address of the instruction that used the bad address, as shown below:

```
Hiya...   adb a.out core
$r
... {register output trimmed} ...
pc=0x4680
```

Looking at the instruction at that address with **adb**, we find:

```
0x1067c?i
0x1067c:        ld    [%i0], %l3
```

This is a common load instruction. It says to take a full 32-bit word from memory and put it into a register. The source is pointed to by the address in register %i0, and the destination is the local register %l3. Because the program faulted, the address used was incorrect; thus, the value in register %i0 refers to a memory location that is probably not mapped in. The location is not a part of the data segment of the executing program, a page fault could not resolve the address, and the program was terminated. These errors are commonly known as *data faults*.

Some of the load and store instructions you may encounter are:

- ld — Load a full word
- ldh — Load a half-word (16 bits)
- lduh — Load a half-word as an unsigned value (clear the upper bits to zero)
- ldb — Load a byte
- ldub — Load an unsigned byte
- st — Store a full word
- sth — Store a half-word
- stb — Store a byte
- ldstub — Load/store unsigned byte (used in Solaris 2 lock manipulation)

Use of some of these instructions (the full- and half-word loads and stores) may generate another type of fault, or trap, similar to that caused by a completely wild pointer: an alignment error. Again, the SPARC architecture imposes certain restrictions, and one of these is that data must be aligned in memory just as instructions must be.

If the instruction is a full-word load (ld), then the address used must be a multiple of 4, referencing a full word on a 4-byte boundary. Addresses that reference a half-word (a 16-bit quantity) must be aligned properly on an even 2-byte boundary. Bytes, of course, don't require any alignment, so this particular fault will never occur with one of the byte-specific instructions. An instruction using an address that is within bounds, but is improperly aligned, will fail. In this case, the program (or the kernel) will be terminated with an address alignment fault.

How branch instructions can go wrong

Another possible cause of addressing errors might be due to a transfer of control (a jump, or branch, or call to a function) where the destination did not exist, a jump to code that was not there. Of the three types of instructions for transferring control, only one is likely to result in an error.

The first, a conditional branch, is used normally after a test for some particular situation, such as two numbers being equal or the result of an arithmetic operation being non-zero. It is associated with loops and if statements and normally performs a relatively short branch to different code. Pointers don't enter into it. This branch is generated by the compiler and will only cause problems if the code should be present but somehow isn't. Of course, if the program uses self-modifying code or generates its own instructions, all bets are off!

The second, a call instruction, will transfer control to a function. Like a conditional branch, this uses a compiler-generated offset from the current location and is unlikely to jump to nonexistent code.

The third instruction is a long jump, or jump-and-link, `jmpl`. The `jmpl` instruction obtains the destination address from a register. Of them all, this is the one that will result in an error either because the address is way out of range or because it is not an even multiple of 4. The `jmpl` instruction is used in two places.

The first place is when calling a function where the address of the function is contained in a variable, as shown below.

```
(*func_ptr)(p1, p2, p3);
```

The second case, used in a very specific form, is when returning from function calls back to the invoking code. This latter case will generally be displayed by **adb** as a `retl` or `return` instruction, but it's really the same instruction code. If the faulting instruction appears to be a jump in the middle of a sequence of code, look for a bad function address as a parameter, or in an array, or as a structure element. If the instruction is decoded as a `retl` (usually immediately following a `restore` instruction) it is possible that you have stack corruption, because this is where the return address usually is obtained. This may be due to random pointers (a very hard thing to track down) or perhaps local arrays or strings that went past the expected maximum without checking and overwrote important stack structures.

These errors are detected at a different point in the execution of an instruction, because they result from an error during the fetch of an instruction code. These may appear as a *text fault*, an illegal attempt to access text or code.

How other instructions can go wrong

There are, of course, many more operations in the SPARC instruction set. Most of these deal with data manipulation in registers, for example, adding, testing, or multiplying. These operations do not reference memory. Instead, they require that the data be present in a register first, and the resulting value will also be placed into a register.

Register-only instructions will obviously not cause faults due to illegal memory addresses. The only cases where specific data values might cause a fault or a trap to occur would be divide-by-zero, various floating-point errors, or specific illegal or unexpected trap instructions.

You may also have the odd illegal instruction to deal with, but that's normally due to the program attempting to execute data as if it were code. These are pretty unusual, especially in kernel code. The most frequent errors occur when wild pointers are dereferenced and the machine tries to find data that just isn't there.

Finding trouble

These are the most common instructions that generate traps (faults) and abort the program or panic the system. Now you should be able to recognize the bad instruction and identify the address. Unfortunately, this is only a part of the story; many times you will be forced to backtrack in the code to see *why* the address in that register is wrong.

Reading assembly code is not a trivial exercise, but with this information and a bit of practice, you can often match the assembly to C source code (if you have it available) and identify the area or even the line of code where the problem occurred.

Want to learn more?

For those of you who love to know the details, we've provided much more information about the SPARC processor and the SPARC instruction set in the appendices.

Next, we are going to discuss a concept that we've already mentioned a few times; the stack. Now would be a good time for another stretch!

≡16

Stacks

Whenever one routine calls another, certain information about the calling routine must be saved so that, upon return, execution within the calling routine can be resumed where it left off. The information from the calling routine is saved in a structure of data known as a "frame" and is "pushed" onto what is referred to as a "stack."

During system crash dump analysis, stacks play a vital role. It is here where we find out who called whom and with what arguments. Although we can use **adb**'s **$c** command to get a C stack traceback, we will also want to be able to examine stacks by hand on some occasions. In order to be able to do that, we need to understand what a stack looks like. Before we talk about a specific architecture's stack format, let's talk about stacks in very generic terms.

A generic stack

The diagram below illustrates a simplified view of a stack frame. The only data this sample frame holds is a pointer to the previous frame, the program counter from the previous routine, and the arguments that were passed to the new routine.

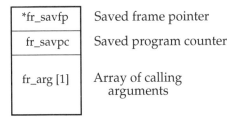

Figure 17-1 A generic stack frame

This simple frame layout is actually that used by the sun2 hardware architecture and probably other vendors' system architectures as well.

When one routine calls another routine, the three pieces of information diagrammed above will need to be loaded into a new frame that is placed or "pushed" onto the current stack. How this data gets moved onto the stack is implementation-specific. Soon, we will see how this is done on SPARC systems. For now, we'll just trust that it gets done for us.

As shown in the previous figure, the address of the caller's frame is saved in *fr_savfp* of the new frame. This provides us with a way of returning to the caller's frame.

The address, or program counter, of the instruction that caused us to jump into the new routine is stored in *fr_savpc*. This is used when it's time for us to return to the calling routine.

Finally, the arguments or parameters passed to the new routine are stored in the frame starting at *fr_arg*.

Now, keeping this as generic as possible, let's watch our stack grow as the result of a call to a new routine.

Here is a little program that calls a little routine, passing it three parameters. The little routine, *fred()*, actually does nothing at all.

```
main ()
{
   fred (1, 2, 3);
}

int fred (a, b, c)
int a, b, c;
{}
```

When we start running *main()*, an initial frame will be put on the stack. This is taken care of for us by the system. For now, we will demonstrate this initial frame as being filled with nulls or zeros. When we call *fred()*, a new frame will be put or "pushed" onto the stack for us. While we are actually in *fred()*, our stack will hold two frames, as shown in the next figure.

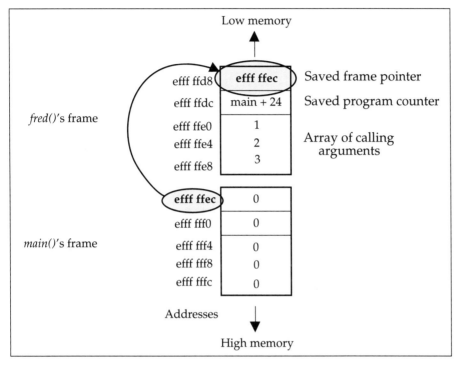

Figure 17-2   Stack frame example

When we are done executing *fred()* and need to return to *main()*, we will use the saved PC, the address of *main+24* in this example, as our reference of where to return within the main routine. This is in the current frame in *fr_savpc*. In many machines, this is the address of the instruction following the call to *fred()*. On SPARC, this is the actual address of the calling instruction, usually some sort of jump to subroutine or call instruction. Since we've already executed the instruction at *main+24*, we will not be executing the instruction referenced in the saved PC, but instead we will be using it as a reference for where to resume within the main routine.

As we return to *main()*, the original frame becomes our current frame. This is known as "popping" the stack. The area of memory that was used to store the stack frame we were using while in *fred()* is now considered free. If we were to call *fred()* a second time from *main()*, a brand-new frame would be constructed and pushed onto the stack.

Looking at the figure above, what may cause some confusion for you at this point is the direction in which the stack grows. Instead of starting at a low memory address and growing towards high memory, the stack starts in high memory and works its way down towards low memory.

Okay, that's the general concept. Now let's talk about SPARC frames in detail.

The frame structure

If you've been poking around in **/usr/include**, you may have already discovered the header files that describe your system's stack and the frames on the stack. These files are in different locations on Solaris 1 and Solaris 2 systems.

Solaris 1 header files

On Solaris 1, you will want to look in the **/usr/include** subdirectory for your system's architecture; **sun2**, **sun3**, **sun3x**, **sun4**, **sun4c**, or **sun4m**. Within that directory, you'll find the stack described in **asm_linkage.h**.

asm_linkage.h diagrams a stack and defines several stack-related functions and assembly language macros. However, **asm_linkage.h** does not describe the contents of a stack in any real detail. It just shows a nice diagram. To get the details of what a frame on the stack looks like, we have to look at **frame.h** which can be found in the same directory as **asm_linkage.h**.

Since the stack basically looks the same between the BSD-based SunOS and the SVR4-based Solaris 2, we will use a Solaris 2 system throughout the rest of this chapter.

Solaris 2 header files

On Solaris 2 systems, the stack is diagrammed in **/usr/include/sys/stack.h**; however, again, the actual definition of the *frame* structure is in **/usr/include/sys/frame.h**. First, let's look at a trimmed-down picture of **/usr/include/sys/stack.h**.

Code Example 17-1   Excerpt from /usr/include/sys/stack.h

```
/*
 * A stack frame looks like:
 *
 * %fp->|                             |
 *      |-----------------------------|
 *      |  Locals, temps, saved floats|
 *      |-----------------------------|
 *      |  outgoing parameters past 6 |
 *      |-----------------------------|-\
 *      |  6 words for callee to dump | |
 *      |  register arguments         | |
 *      |-----------------------------| > minimum stack frame
 *      |  One word struct-ret address| |
 *      |-----------------------------| |
 *      |  16 words to save IN and    | |
 * %sp->|  LOCAL register on overflow | |
 *      |-----------------------------|-/
 */
```

Here is the *frame* structure as described in this partial view of **/usr/include/sys/frame.h** on a SPARCstation 20 system running Solaris 2.3.

```
/*
 * Definition of the sparc stack frame (when it is pushed on the stack).
 */
struct frame {
        int     fr_local[8];            /* saved locals */
        int     fr_arg[6];              /* saved arguments [0 - 5] */
        struct frame    *fr_savfp;      /* saved frame pointer */
        int     fr_savpc;               /* saved program counter */
        char    *fr_stret;              /* struct return addr */
        int     fr_argd[6];             /* arg dump area */
        int     fr_argx[1];             /* array of args past the sixth */
};
```

Let's talk about the SPARC *frame* structure in detail.

The first eight integers in a frame, *fr_local [0]* through *fr_local [7]*, are the contents of the local registers %l0 through %l7. These are full 32-bit words. Local registers are used locally within a routine only and are not used to pass information to another routine.

The next six integers, *fr_arg [0]* through *fr_arg [5]*, contain the first six arguments a routine or procedure receives when being called. If more than six arguments were sent, we will find the remainder of them elsewhere on the stack.

The next word in the *frame* structure contains the address of the previous frame. In other words, this is a pointer to another *frame* structure. This corresponds to register %i6, which is the old stack pointer (%o6) belonging to the calling routine.

The next word, *fr_savpc*, contains the PC or program counter of the last instruction executed by the calling routine. When you look at this, you will usually find a call or jump instruction. When we "pop" the stack to return to the calling routine, this PC is used as the reference for where execution is to continue.

The next word, *fr_stret*, is specifically set aside for use by functions that return structures. The address of the returned structure is placed here.

The next six words, *fr_argd [0]* through *fr_argd [5]*, are used occasionally as a temporary storage space for the six arguments normally kept in the *fr_arg* variables.

And finally, we get to *fr_argx*. If more than six calling arguments were used, they would be placed at the end of the frame starting at *fr_argx*. Although we see *fr_argx* defined as an integer array of 1 in length, *fr_argx* represents the rest of the frame and can be of varying size, depending on the needs of the routines in use. What may surprise you, however, is that the frame containing the seventh and additional arguments will not be the same frame that contains the first six calling arguments. We will come back to this later. For now, it is important to note that SPARC stack frames do not have a fixed size.

Instructions that affect windows & frames

In the previous chapter, we briefly discussed the concept of windows that provide limited views of the general-purpose registers on the SPARC processor. Let's explore windowing a bit more now.

There are two SPARC instructions that directly affect the register windows:

* `save`
* `restore`

Both of these instructions also affect the stack. We will cover each of these in detail in a moment.

Windows diagrammed

There are several ways to diagram the concept of windowing. As we discuss the `save`, `call`, and `restore` instructions, the method used below will help you visualize how the instructions affect the window view.

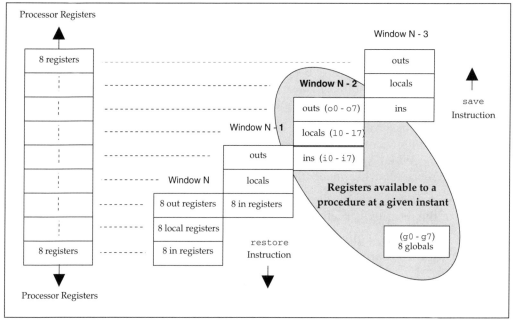

Figure 17-3   Processor registers and their corresponding window names

The save instruction

On SPARC systems, when a routine calls another routine, usually the first instruction of the new routine will be a `save` instruction. The `save` instruction actually does a lot of work, but we have no fears about it not completing its tasks. The only trap that can occur during a `save` is a window overflow.

The `save` instruction is the only instruction that decrements the window pointer, thus preserving the current window. In other words, according to the previous figure, our window view would shift from Window N-2 to Window N-3. As you can see, this would mean that the old output registers, `%o0-%o7`, would be the new input registers, `%i0-%i7`. The old local registers, `%l0-%l7`, would be outside of our new window view; however, we would have access to a new set of eight local registers with which to work.

The second thing the `save` instruction does for us is to push a new, empty frame onto the stack. Using the caller's stack pointer for reference that is in the caller's register `%o6`, (yes, which will become the callee's `%i6`), the stack is grown downward by a certain amount and the new stack pointer is saved in the callee's own `%o6` register. Here is an example of a `save` instruction you might see. Note that `%sp` is simply another name for `%o6`.

```
save   %sp, -0x78, %sp
```

The first `%sp` refers to the caller's stack pointer stored in the caller's `%o6` register. The second reference to `%sp` refers to the callee's stack pointer, which is stored in his own `%o6`. This may be easier to understand if you imagine that the window shift takes place between the time the CPU deals with the first and second `%sp` of the `save` instruction.

The call and jmpl instructions

Were you surprised to learn that it is the responsibility of the callee and not the caller to shift the windows and adjust the stack via the `save` instruction? Let's look at how the calling routine affects the callee's registers.

The caller may invoke subroutines via either a `call` instruction or a `jmpl` instruction. The `call` instruction actually has the address embedded in the instruction itself as a 30-bit displacement from the current PC value. This signed offset allows the `call` instruction to reach any location in memory. The address of the `call` instruction itself is saved in register `%o7`.

```
call   disp30
```

A long jump (jmpl) instruction can be used to call a function if the address is contained in a register. In this case, the address of the jmpl is saved in whatever register is specified in the instruction, although this is normally %o7. A jmpl looks like the following, where *address* is the location of the routine we wish to jump to.

```
jmpl  address, %o7
```

This instruction says to jump to *address*, saving the current PC in register %o7. You know what we plan to do with that saved PC value, right? It's going to become the %i7 value after the save instruction is completed and will be put into the callee's frame at *fr_savpc*.

Note that the return address is not actually the place we wish to return to, but rather the place we came from.

The restore instruction

Maybe you've already guessed it! restore is the instruction that shifts the current window view back to the caller's window. The restore instruction basically pops the callee's frame off the stack, bringing us back to the previous window and the previous %sp or %o6. The contents of memory don't actually change.

The restore instruction does not return us to the calling routine. For that, we must perform a jump-and-link or jmpl instruction. It is during this jump instruction that we use the saved PC value in %i7. Again, this is the value we will see in the callee's stack frame at *fr_savpc*.

The synthetic SPARC assembly instruction, ret, does the jump for us and really is just the instruction shown below. This instruction says to jump to the location referenced in %i7 plus 8 bytes or 2 full words and save our current PC in %g0.

```
jmpl  %i7+8, %g0
```

Think of %g0 as the **/dev/null** of registers. Reading and writing to %g0 always results in a zero. So, even though we say to store the PC in %g0, nothing actually happens. All we are doing is jumping back into the calling routine.

The man in the back wants to know why are we jumping to the saved PC+8 instead of PC+4. A good question!

The architecture of SPARC processors includes a pipeline. This pipeline overlaps execution of instructions, so that while the call that got us here was being processed, the next instruction was being fetched and started. Therefore, while we are doing the jump to the new routine, we are actually also executing the instruction at PC + 4. When we return to the calling routine, we are returning to the next instruction that we have *not yet executed*, which is at PC+8.

Note – For conditional branch instructions, there is a way of saying "Please don't execute the delay instruction, just do the branch"; however, no such feature exists for `jmpl`.

Okay, now it's time for us to return to our calling routine. This is done with two instructions. The first is the jump instruction. The second command shifts the window. Remember, even though we have jumped, the `restore` instruction gets executed by virtue of the SPARC pipeline architecture — it's in the delay slot. So, finally, here is what you can expect to see at the end of a routine.

```
    ret
    restore
```

Window overflows & underflows

Hopefully, you've a funny feeling that there's still a piece missing, because there is. We've talked about how the SPARC registers are used and how our windowed view of them changes when the `save` and `restore` instructions are executed. But who actually writes the register values into the stack frame in memory?

The short answer is: the operating system.

There is a `WIM` (Window Invalid Mask) register that keeps track of which windows are in use. There's also a `CWP` (Current Window Pointer) field in the `PSR` (Processor Status Register) that keeps track of which window is currently in view. These are discussed in more detail in Appendix A.

Whether you have 40 registers available or 4000, there are a limited number of windows on any system. At some point in time, when we try to execute a `save`, we will run out of windows and have to start recycling those we've already used. This condition is recognized by the hardware, through use of the WIM and the CWP, and triggers a window overflow trap.

The window overflow trap must be processed by the operating system. When the operating system is UNIX, the kernel moves the window registers onto the stack in memory for safekeeping. It also handles the restoration of window registers via the window underflow trap, which occurs when you have restored so often you need to retrieve old information from the stack.

Window overflows and underflows start occurring early on in the execution of the UNIX operating system. It is only down in the lowest levels of the kernel that we would ever see instances where window overflows and underflows do not occur.

While technically incorrect, it is probably safe for UNIX users on SPARC processors to think of the `save` instruction as being the one that puts the values of the new input registers into the callee's stack frame. However, it is important to remember that for each different hardware architecture that you encounter, you will invariably find differences at this low level, both in the hardware involved and in the UNIX kernel for that hardware.

What have we got so far?

We've talked about the stack in rather generic terms and how it grows. We've taken a look at a specific hardware architecture's stack frame structure. We've gotten down into the intricacies of the SPARC processor, talking about registers and windows. We've explained the magic behind the SPARC assembly instructions used when moving from routine to routine. And we've talked about how the UNIX kernel supports the SPARC windowing concept and helps maintain the stack.

By now, you should be itching to see all of this work for you on your own system! In the next chapter, we will compile our simple little program and, executing it under the control of **adb**, we'll step through it, watching the registers change and our stack grow.

Stack Tracebacks 18 ≡

We've spent enough time talking about stacks. Now let's see the theory put to actual use. We will start by using the little C program below, which we will run under **adb**.

Code Example 18-1   little.c

```
main ()
{
  fred (1, 2, 3);
}

int fred (a, b, c)
int a, b, c;
{}
```

In **little.c**, shown above, the *main()* routine calls the *fred()* routine, passing it three integer values. The *fred()* routine does nothing except return to the *main()* routine.

Using **adb**, let's first look at the SPARC assembly instructions for *main()*.

Figure 18-1   Viewing little's main routine via adb

```
Hiya...  cc -o little little.c
Hiya...  adb little -
main,20?ai
main:           main:           save    %sp, -0x60, %sp
main+4:         mov     0x1, %l0
main+8:         mov     0x2, %l1
main+0xc:       mov     0x3, %l2
main+0x10:      mov     %l0, %o0
main+0x14:      mov     %l1, %o1
main+0x18:      mov     %l2, %o2
main+0x1c:      call    fred
main+0x20:      nop
main+0x24:      ret
main+0x28:      restore
```

Starting at main, we have requested to see the first 20 hex (32 decimal) instructions of *main()*. We've trimmed the output shown above to just show the *main()* routine.

Main() first executes a `save` instruction, which adjusts the stack pointer, growing the stack downward towards low memory by 60 hex bytes (96 decimal) or 24 words. If you look again at **frame.h**, you'll see that 24 words is the size of the smallest frame we would expect to see.

The `save` instruction will result in a new window, but when we actually get around to looking at the program with **adb**, the registers will have been flushed out to the stack by the kernel, since the program will no longer be running (it will be stopped and waiting).

Next, *main()* loads values into registers `%o0`, `%o1`, and `%o2` in preparation for passing them as parameters to *fred()*. Instead of doing this directly, the values are first loaded into local, or `%l` registers, then moved to the output registers. Why? You would have to ask the compiler that question. However, this was compiled without using the optimizer, which often results in rather inefficient code.

Next, we call *fred()*.

Figure 18-2 Viewing little's fred routine via adb

```
fred,10?ai
fred:           fred:           save    %sp, -0x60, %sp
fred+4:         st      %i2, [%fp + 0x4c]
fred+8:         st      %i1, [%fp + 0x48]
fred+0xc:       st      %i0, [%fp + 0x44]
fred+0x10:      ret
fred+0x14:      restore
```

In *fred()*, we execute another `save` instruction, thus pushing another frame of minimum size onto the stack. This is the first time we see `%fp` in use. `%fp` is simply another name for the caller's `%sp`. Using `%fp` as a reference, we save the incoming arguments from *main()* onto the stack. Why does this happen? Again, you'd have to chat with the compiler about this.

From *fred()* we return to *main()*, which in turn returns control to the routines responsible for managing the execution of object files for us.

The following diagram is offered to help you understand the relationship between `%fp`, or the frame pointer (the caller's stack pointer), and `%sp`, the callee's stack pointer.

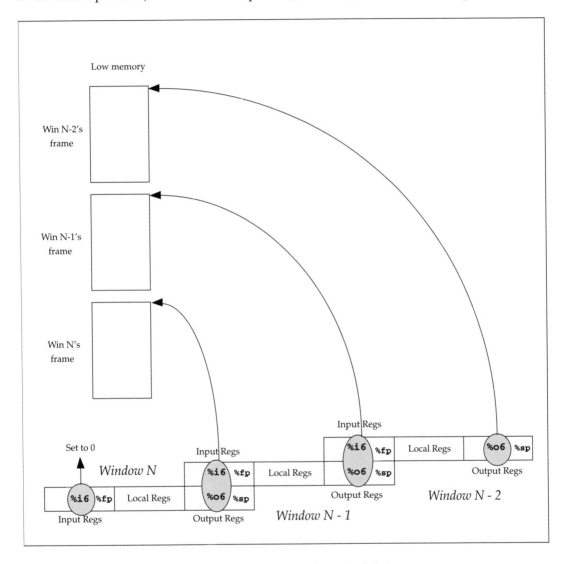

Figure 18-3 Relationship between `%fp` Frame Pointers and `%sp` Stack Pointers

Okay! Let's get back to **adb** now and watch the stack grow! If this is your first time walking a stack with **adb**, you might want to do this on your own computer while using this example as your guide. To help you, we will embed comments throughout the **adb** session.

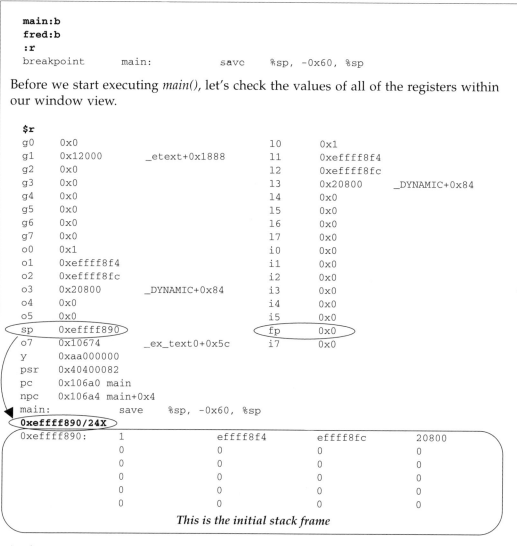

```
main:b
fred:b
:r
breakpoint        main:          save     %sp, -0x60, %sp
```

Before we start executing *main()*, let's check the values of all of the registers within our window view.

```
$r
g0    0x0                              l0    0x1
g1    0x12000      _etext+0x1888       l1    0xeffff8f4
g2    0x0                              l2    0xeffff8fc
g3    0x0                              l3    0x20800      _DYNAMIC+0x84
g4    0x0                              l4    0x0
g5    0x0                              l5    0x0
g6    0x0                              l6    0x0
g7    0x0                              l7    0x0
o0    0x1                              i0    0x0
o1    0xeffff8f4                       i1    0x0
o2    0xeffff8fc                       i2    0x0
o3    0x20800      _DYNAMIC+0x84       i3    0x0
o4    0x0                              i4    0x0
o5    0x0                              i5    0x0
sp    0xeffff890                       fp    0x0
o7    0x10674      _ex_text0+0x5c      i7    0x0
y     0xaa000000
psr   0x40400082
pc    0x106a0 main
npc   0x106a4 main+0x4
main:             save     %sp, -0x60, %sp
0xeffff890/24X
0xeffff890:    1             effff8f4       effff8fc       20800
               0             0              0              0
               0             0              0              0
               0             0              0              0
               0             0              0              0
               0             0              0              0
```
This is the initial stack frame

At this point, we are about to start executing *main()*. So far, all we have on the stack is an initial stack frame, shown above, which contains mostly zeroes. We will step, executing the `save` instruction, and see how the registers have changed.

```
:s
stopped at      main+4:        mov     0x1, %l0
$r
g0    0x0                               l0    0x40400080
g1    0x12000      _etext+0x1888        l1    0x106a0        main
g2    0x0                               l2    0xf0000000
g3    0x0                               l3    0x0
g4    0x0                               l4    0x4
g5    0x0                               l5    0x4
g6    0x0                               l6    0x7
g7    0x0                               l7    0xf05aa938
o0    0x10081                           i0    0x1
o1    0x0                               i1    0xefffff8f4
o2    0xf01822d8                        i2    0xefffff8fc
o3    0x0                               i3    0x20800        _DYNAMIC+0x84
o4    0x0                               i4    0x0
o5    0x0                               i5    0x0
sp    0xefffff830                       fp    0xefffff890
o7    0xf004146c                        i7    0x10674        _ex_text0+0x5c
y     0xaa000000
psr   0x40400087
pc    0x106a4 main+0x4
npc   0x106a8 main+0x8
main+4:        mov     0x1, %l0
0xefffff830/24X
0xefffff830:    40400080       106a0        f0000000       0
                4              4            7              f05aa938
                1              efffff8f4    efffff8fc      20800
                0              0            efffff890      10674
                3              efffff8f4    4              efffff8fc
                5              efffff9a4    0              0
10674/i                                          Saved PC
_ex_text0+0x5c: call    main                 Saved Frame Pointer
efffff890/24X
0xefffff890:    1              efffff8f4    efffff8fc      20800
                0              0            0              0
                0              0            0              0
                0              0            0              0
                0              0            0              0
                0              0            0              0
```

We have executed the `save` instruction at the beginning of *main()* and have seen that we now have two frames on the stack. Note that register `%l0` in the new frame has junk in it. We will let execution continue to our next breakpoint at *fred()*.

```
:c
```

```
breakpoint        fred:            save    %sp, -0x60, %sp
```

Here we demonstrate a way to examine the current values of individual registers.

```
<sp=X
                  effff830
<fp=X
                  effff890
<o0=X
                  1
<o1=X
                  2
<o2=X
                  3
$r
g0    0x0                              l0    0x1
g1    0x12000       _etext+0x1888      l1    0x2
g2    0x0                              l2    0x3
g3    0x0                              l3    0x0
g4    0x0                              l4    0x4
g5    0x0                              l5    0x4
g6    0x0                              l6    0x7
g7    0x0                              l7    0xf05aa938
o0    0x1                              i0    0x1
o1    0x2                              i1    0xeffff8f4
o2    0x3                              i2    0xeffff8fc
o3    0x0                              i3    0x20800       _DYNAMIC+0x84
o4    0x0                              i4    0x0
o5    0x0                              i5    0x0
sp    0xeffff830                       fp    0xeffff890
o7    0x106bc        main+0x1c         i7    0x10674       _ex_text0+0x5c
y     0xaa000000
psr   0x40400086
pc    0x106e0 fred
npc   0x106e4 fred+0x4
fred:              save    %sp, -0x60, %sp
```

Before we execute the `save` instruction in *fred()*, we see above that main's output registers are ready to pass the three calling parameters to *fred()* in %o0, %o1, and %o2.

```
:s
stopped at        fred+4:          st      %i2, [%fp + 0x4c]
```

Having stepped, the `save` instruction is done. The window shift has been performed and we see that our registers have changed accordingly. What were the output registers for *main()* are now the input registers to *fred()*.

```
$r
g0    0x0                              l0    0x40400085
```

g1	0x12000	_etext+0x1888		l1	0x106e0	fred	
g2	0x0			l2	0xf0000000		
g3	0x0			l3	0x0		
g4	0x0			l4	0x80		
g5	0x0			l5	0x80		
g6	0x0			l6	0x7		
g7	0x0			l7	0xf05aa938		
o0	0x10081			i0	0x1		
o1	0x0			i1	0x2		
o2	0xf01822d8			i2	0x3		
o3	0x0			i3	0x0		
o4	0x0			i4	0x0		
o5	0x0			i5	0x0		
sp	0xeffff7d0			fp	0xeffff830		
o7	0xf004146c			i7	0x106bc	main+0x1c	
y	0xaa000000						
psr	0x40400084						
pc	0x106e4	fred+0x4					
npc	0x106e8	fred+0x8					

```
fred+4:          st      %i2, [%fp + 0x4c]
0xeffff7d0/24X
0xeffff7d0:    40400085        106e0          f0000000          0
               80              80             7                 f05aa938
               1      Calling  2     Parameters  3              0
               0               0                 effff830        106bc
               0               0                 ef7df7c8        0
               2               2                 7               ef7fc3ac
```

fred()'s frame

106bc/i ◄─── Saved PC

```
main+0x1c:     call    fred           Saved Frame Pointer
```

effff830/24X ◄───

```
0xeffff830:    1               2                 3               0
               4               4                 7               f05aa938
               1               effff8f4          effff8fc        20800
               0               0                 effff890        10674
               3               effff8f4          4               effff8fc
               5               effff9a4          0               0
```

main()'s frame

10674/i ◄─── Saved PC

```
_ex_text0+0x5c: call    main           Saved Frame Pointer
```

effff890/24X ◄───

```
0xeffff890:    1               effff8f4          effff8fc        20800
               0               0                 0               0
               0               0                 0               0
               0               0                 0               0
               0               0                 0               0
               0               0                 0               0
```

the initial frame

Finally, as we step through *fred()*, we watch the incoming arguments being stored onto *main()*'s stack frame.

```
:s
stopped at          fred+8:             st          %i1, [%fp + 0x48]
:s
stopped at          fred+0xc:           st          %i0, [%fp + 0x44]
:s
stopped at          fred+0x10:          ret
```

Before we return to *main()*, here we take a look at *main()*'s stack frame. Note that in the tail end of the frame, we now have copies of the parameters with which we called *fred()*. These are stored in *fr_argd*, or frame argument dump area. You can refer again to **frame.h** to confirm this.

```
<fp/24X
0xeffff830:     1               2               3               0
                4               4               7               f05aa938
                1               effff8f4        effff8fc        20800
                0               0               effff890        10674
                3               1               2               3
                5               effff9a4        0               0
```

We end this demonstration here. However, if you wish to continue stepping through to completion, feel free to do so. See if you can predict what will happen to the registers and windows as you step through the restore instructions.

What have we accomplished here? We've walked through a very simple, little program, examining the stack as it grows and watching the window registers shift. What is important to understand is that whether we are debugging a simple program or part of a UNIX kernel, the concepts of the stack and "walking the stack" are the same.

Congratulations! You are now another *BIG* step closer to being able to analyze UNIX system crash dumps!

Compiling with optimization

You might be wondering why the particular compiler we used to generate our little object program created so much code for a program that basically didn't do anything. Good question. Remember that each compiler you encounter may generate slightly different assembly language code; however, your program will still generate the results you require of it. If we compile using optimization, we get a very different set of assembly instructions. For that matter, if we were to compile the program using a different compiler altogether, we can expect to see different assembly code again.

Let's take a quick peek at the same program compiled with optimization. The output has been trimmed, as displaying 10 hex (16 decimal) instructions was more than enough.

Figure 18-4 Little's assembly code after compilation with optimization

```
Hiya...  cc -o little -O little.c
Hiya...  adb little -
main,10?ai
main:         main:             mov      0x1, %o0
main+4:                   mov      0x2, %o1
main+8:                   mov      0x3, %o2
main+0xc:     mov       %o7, %g1
main+0x10:    call      fred
main+0x14:    mov       %g1, %o7
main+0x18:    unimp     0x0
main+0x1c:    unimp     0x0
main+0x20:    unimp     0x0
main+0x24:    unimp     0x0
fred:         jmp       %o7 + 0x8
fred+4:                 nop
```

From this we see that the compiler was clever enough to not even bother with generating assembly code to create new stack frames for *main()* and *fred()*. The compiler, however, did generate code to prepare the calling arguments and to call *fred()* as our original C code requested. So, in effect, this optimized code is still a perfectly valid representation of our program. In fact, it's even closer to the original source: *fred()*'s code consists of a jump back to where it came from.

The trouble with more than six arguments

If there were never routines written with more than six arguments, we could forget about stacks for a while and move onto another topic. Unfortunately, there are such routines within the UNIX kernel, so we really need to talk about this.

Let's refer to **/usr/include/sys/frame.h** again for a moment.

```
/*
 * Definition of the sparc stack frame (when it is pushed on the stack).
 */
struct frame {
        int     fr_local[8];            /* saved locals */
        int     fr_arg[6];              /* saved arguments [0 - 5] */
        struct frame    *fr_savfp;      /* saved frame pointer */
        int     fr_savpc;               /* saved program counter */
        char    *fr_stret;              /* struct return addr */
        int     fr_argd[6];             /* arg dump area */
        int     fr_argx[1];             /* array of args past the sixth */
};
```

Quickly, let's review what happens when we execute the `save` instruction upon entering a new routine. A new stack frame is created, the window is shifted, and possibly a window overflow trap occurs. The kernel will process the trap, copying the former output registers (aka the new input registers) onto the new stack frame. We are okay so far, right?

Now, if the calling routine needs to send more than six arguments to the callee, it cannot pass them through the window registers, as we have already used all of the overlapping registers. Looking at the *frame* structure, we see that the arguments past the sixth are to be loaded into the *fr_argx* array. We are still okay, right?

Here's the problem. Timing! We can't load up the callee's frame *fr_argx* array prior to calling the callee. The callee's frame doesn't exist yet! So, exactly where and when do we load up the additional parameters?

The answer is: in the caller's frame, in his own *fr_argx* array, before we invoke the callee.

We've seen that the compiler can be quite clever. When it comes to this scenario, the compiler creates assembly code that has the callee routine referencing not only his own frame, pointed to by `%sp`, but also the caller's frame via `%fp`.

Compile the following program on your own system. We recommend you compile first with optimization. After you get through the optimized version, try a straight compile for fun.

Here's the program, **nine-args.c**.

```
/*
 *   Demo file to show how the compiler produces
 *   SPARC assembly code to handle more than 6
 *   calling arguments.
 *
 */

main()

{
  printf ("Main calling fred.\n");
  fred (1, 2, 3, 4, 5, 6, 7, 8, 9);
}


int fred (i1, i2, i3, i4, i5, i6, i7, i8, i9)
int       i1, i2, i3, i4, i5, i6, i7, i8, i9;
{
  printf ("args are %x, %x, %x, %x, %x, %x, %x, %x, %x\n",
          i1, i2, i3, i4, i5, i6, i7, i8, i9);
  george (0x111, 0x222, 0x333, 0x444, 0x555, 0x666, 0x777, 0x888, 0x999);
}


int george (k1, k2, k3, k4, k5, k6, k7, k8, k9)
int         k1, k2, k3, k4, k5, k6, k7, k8, k9;
{
  int value;
  printf ("args are %x, %x, %x, %x, %x, %x, %x, %x, %x\n",
          k1, k2, k3, k4, k5, k6, k7, k8, k9);
}
```

For demonstration purposes, we will compile this program with optimization and show you what the whole stack looks like just after we create *george()*'s frame. Since we are expecting to see additional information in the frames, we will be displaying more than 24 words per frame (the minimum frame size).

After we walk through the stack, we also will show you the SPARC assembly program the compiler generated. This will allow you to try running the program on paper in case you don't have a computer handy. Yes, we highly recommend you try this method of program execution, especially on those nights when you are convinced you absolutely cannot fall sleep.

```
Hiya...  cc -O -o nine-args nine-args.c
Hiya...  adb nine-args -
george+4:b
:r
Main calling fred.
args are 1, 2, 3, 4, 5, 6, 7, 8, 9
breakpoint        george+4:        ld      [%fp + 0x5c], %l0
$r
g0    0x0                                10    0x0
g1    0x4da000                           l1    0x0
g2    0x0                                l2    0x0
g3    0x0                                l3    0x0
g4    0x0                                l4    0x40
g5    0x0                                l5    0x40
g6    0x0                                l6    0x7
g7    0x0                                l7    0xef7b3804    __daytab+0x3b4
o0    0x0                                i0    0x111
o1    0xeffff790                         i1    0x222
o2    0xeffff770                         i2    0x333
o3    0x209ff       _ex_shared1+0x47     i3    0x444
o4    0x1                                i4    0x555
o5    0x0                                i5    0x666
sp    0xeffff740                         fp    0xeffff7b0
o7    0xef78b5a0    _fprintf+0x1dc       i7    0x107c4       fred+0x6c
y     0xa0000000
psr   0x40400083
pc    0x107ec george+0x4
npc   0x107f0 george+0x8
george+4:        ld      [%fp + 0x5c], %l0
```

We'll help you with george's frame. We've put the arguments for *george()* into squares. Can you find the arguments for *fred()*?

```
0xeffff740/26X
0xeffff740:       0               0               0               0
                  40              40              7               ef7b3804
                 [111]           [222]           (333)           (444)
                 [555]           [666]          (effff7b0)      (107c4)
                  0               13              40400085        ef78b4a0
                  ef78b4a4        0               80              80
                  ffffffff        7ff                      Saved PC
(107c4/i)◄
fred+0x6c:        call    george                   Saved Frame Pointer
(effff7b0/26X)◄
0xeffff7b0:       999             888             ef78b4a4        0
                  80              80              7               ef7b3804
                  1               2               3               4
                  5               6               effff828        10734
                  0               f               1               2
                  3               4               5              [777]
                 [888]           [999]
```

```
10734/i
main+0x3c:      call     fred
effff828/26X
0xeffff828:     9          8          10678      0
                100        101        7          ef7b3804
                1          effff8f4   effff8fc   20800
                0          0          effff890   106cc
                effff890   106a0      0          4
                0          2          ef7b0c50   7
                8          9
106cc/i
_ex_text0+0x5c: call     main
effff890/24X
0xeffff890:     1          effff8f4   effff8fc   20800
                0          0          0          0
                0          0          0          0
                0          0          0          0
                0          0          0          0
                0          0          0          0
```

main's frame (annotation)
the initial frame (annotation)

And here are the actual assembly instructions that were generated by the compile we used in this example. We'll see you in the next chapter where we will introduce you to the UNIX kernel. Until then, sweet dreams!

Figure 18-5   Viewing nineargs's assembly instructions via adb

```
main,50?ai
main:          main:            save     %sp, -0x68, %sp
main+4:        sethi    %hi(0x20800), %l0
main+8:        call     _PROCEDURE_LINKAGE_TABLE_ + 0x54
main+0xc:      add      %l0, 0x1c0, %o0
main+0x10:     mov      0x7, %l0
main+0x14:     mov      0x8, %l1
main+0x18:     st       %l0, [%sp + 0x5c]
main+0x1c:     mov      0x1, %o0
main+0x20:     mov      0x2, %o1
main+0x24:     mov      0x3, %o2
main+0x28:     mov      0x4, %o3
main+0x2c:     mov      0x5, %o4
main+0x30:     mov      0x6, %o5
main+0x34:     st       %l1, [%sp + 0x60]
main+0x38:     mov      0x9, %l0
main+0x3c:     call     fred
main+0x40:     st       %l0, [%sp + 0x64]
main+0x44:     ret
```

Figure 18-5   Viewing nineargs's assembly instructions via adb

```
main+0x48:      restore
main+0x4c:      unimp   0x0
main+0x50:      unimp   0x0
main+0x54:      unimp   0x0
main+0x58:      unimp   0x0
main+0x5c:      unimp   0x0
fred:           save    %sp, -0x78, %sp
fred+4:         ld      [%fp + 0x5c], %l0
fred+8:         mov     %i0, %o1
fred+0xc:       st      %l0, [%sp + 0x60]
fred+0x10:      mov     %i1, %o2
fred+0x14:      ld      [%fp + 0x60], %l1
fred+0x18:      mov     %i2, %o3
fred+0x1c:      st      %l1, [%sp + 0x64]
fred+0x20:      sethi   %hi(0x20800), %l1
fred+0x24:      ld      [%fp + 0x64], %l0
fred+0x28:      add     %l1, 0x1d4, %o0
fred+0x2c:      mov     %i3, %o4
fred+0x30:      mov     %i4, %o5
fred+0x34:      st      %i5, [%sp + 0x5c]
fred+0x38:      call    _PROCEDURE_LINKAGE_TABLE_ + 0x54
fred+0x3c:      st      %l0, [%sp + 0x68]
fred+0x40:      mov     0x777, %l0
fred+0x44:      mov     0x888, %l1
fred+0x48:      st      %l0, [%sp + 0x5c]
fred+0x4c:      mov     0x111, %o0
fred+0x50:      mov     0x222, %o1
fred+0x54:      mov     0x333, %o2
fred+0x58:      mov     0x444, %o3
fred+0x5c:      mov     0x555, %o4
fred+0x60:      mov     0x666, %o5
fred+0x64:      st      %l1, [%sp + 0x60]
fred+0x68:      mov     0x999, %l0
fred+0x6c:      call    george
fred+0x70:      st      %l0, [%sp + 0x64]
fred+0x74:      ret
fred+0x78:      restore
fred+0x7c:      unimp   0x0
fred+0x80:      unimp   0x0
fred+0x84:      unimp   0x0
fred+0x88:      unimp   0x0
fred+0x8c:      unimp   0x0
george:         save    %sp, -0x70, %sp
george+4:       ld      [%fp + 0x5c], %l0
```

Figure 18-5 Viewing nineargs's assembly instructions via adb

```
george+8:        mov      %i0, %o1
george+0xc:      st       %l0, [%sp + 0x60]
george+0x10:     mov      %i1, %o2
george+0x14:     ld       [%fp + 0x60], %l1
george+0x18:     mov      %i2, %o3
george+0x1c:     st       %l1, [%sp + 0x64]
george+0x20:     sethi    %hi(0x20800), %l1
george+0x24:     ld       [%fp + 0x64], %l0
george+0x28:     add      %l1, 0x204, %o0
george+0x2c:     mov      %i3, %o4
george+0x30:     mov      %i4, %o5
george+0x34:     st       %i5, [%sp + 0x5c]
george+0x38:     call     _PROCEDURE_LINKAGE_TABLE_ + 0x54
george+0x3c:     st       %l0, [%sp + 0x68]
george+0x40:     ret
george+0x44:     restore
_ex_text1:       save     %sp, -0x60, %sp
_ex_text1+4:     call     _ex_text1 + 0x10
```

18

A Kernel Overview

In general, looking at kernel crashes requires at least a basic knowledge of what the kernel is *supposed* to do — since you're looking for instances where it failed to do it! For those who have not had the opportunity to examine the internal structure of an operating system, this chapter attempts to provide a quick look at some of the basic functions, requirements, and structures you'll need to know about.

An operating system kernel could be considered the "Master Control Program" for the machine, everything that is connected to it, and anything that runs on it. One of the basic functions of an OS is to control resources. Under this heading you will find memory, CPU time, disk space, and access to external devices like tapes or terminals. As a side benefit of this whole process, the kernel will also prevent users from stepping on one another's code or data — *corruption* of resources is another area of vital concern.

The UNIX kernel is no different from any other kernel; the same basic requirements hold. It was designed with timesharing in mind, so there is an emphasis on switching rapidly between several processes that are ready to run, giving the illusion that all users have an equal shot at getting things done.

Major sections

Let's take a look at some of the major sections of the kernel code, broken up by function. Some of these are:

- Process control. This function includes starting, suspending, and terminating processes, signal handling for responding to external events, and setting or changing priorities. The UNIX system calls *fork* and *exec* are handled by this section.

- IPC (Interprocess communication). Allowing processes to communicate without interfering with the operation or data of the other process is done by IPC. This can be through a pipe or by using shared memory, semaphores, or messages (part of the System-V IPC suite).

- Scheduling. Deciding who gets to run next, and for how long, is a vital part of any system. Choices made here will determine overall performance of the system.

- I/O. Input and output requests include opening and closing, or reading and writing data on files or devices. Device setup and control (such as baud rate settings on a terminal or modem line) are also done here.

- Networking. Communicating between machines requires various protocols to be established and followed. This is done with Streams modules in the Solaris 2 kernel.

- File system management. There are lots of different ways to arrange data on disk. This arrangement is known as a *file system,* and there are various known types with specific properties. These include UFS (the UNIX File System, for local disks), NFS (the Network File System, for accessing files on other systems as if they were locally resident), HSFS (the High Sierra File System, also known as ISO-9660 format, for CD-ROM). In SunOS and Solaris 2, handling these types has been further subdivided into type-independent "virtual FS" code and file system-, format-specific code.

- Memory management. This function covers both the memory that is available to a given process and how the kernel manages the hardware that keeps track of all this memory.

- Accounting/monitoring/security. Accounting is generally desirable in one form or another. It allows you to monitor and analyze resource usage. If nothing else, you will want to be able to find out who has used up all your disk space! Security may be a separate major area of the code but is also usually involved in basic operations like accessing files: Users want the ability to keep other users from examining and modifying their data.

Let's look at some of these sections in more detail, since these are the most common areas you will be examining when working with **savecore** files.

Entering the kernel

Once the machine is booted, there are only two ways in which the kernel code will be run: if a user makes a system call or if a device requests attention. These might be considered as the only two entrances into the kernel. A large portion of the kernel is devoted to handling user requests. This involves identifying the system call, validating the parameters, and heading off to the right area of the kernel to do the real work. The other entrance (from hardware signals) is via the device drivers, which handle the specific details about controlling various devices. One of these devices may in fact be the clock, which "ticks" every 100 milliseconds on Sun systems. This is also one way in which the scheduler gets invoked; if enough time has elapsed, the current user process may be suspended to allow another one to get some work done.

The following figure presents a fairly broad overview of the kernel and its component parts. The system call handling is one way — the only way — for user processes to get the kernel to do work for them. At the other end, devices can request attention through a device driver, which may involve other pieces of the kernel as well.

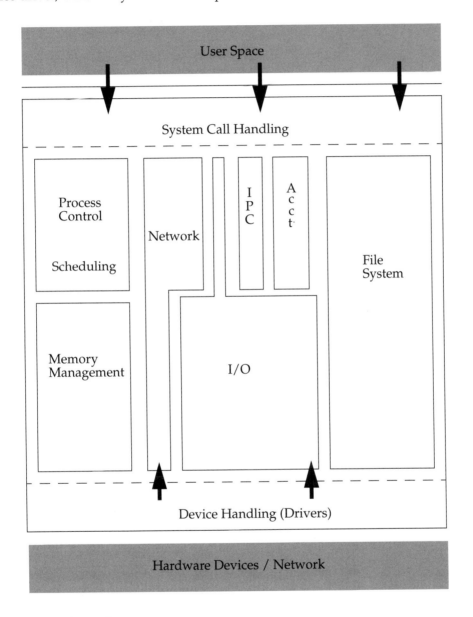

Figure 19-1   Kernel Overview

Let's move back to system calls. From a system programmer's standpoint, these requests look almost like a subroutine call to a kernel-level function. In actuality, the user program will issue a "software trap" instruction of some sort (dependent on the type of hardware) and will end up transferring control to the kernel temporarily in order to handle the system request. These system calls are the only way the user can access those facilities that are tightly controlled by the kernel. These normally include all the hardware (tapes, terminals, disks, etc.), memory, and any other user programs, plus software facilities such as IPC and pseudo-devices.

System calls exist to manipulate files (*open, close, read, write*), devices (*ioctl*), memory (*mmap, sbrk*), other processes (signals, IPC, *fork, exec*), and the process's own environment (resource limits, priority, current directory). Every UNIX user program and utility does its work by using the appropriate system calls to find and manipulate the proper data.

Kernel system call handling generally goes through these basic steps:

- Enter the system, identify the system call (verify that this is a legal request), and branch to the right system call handler.

- Validate parameters (Is the file open? Is this process allowed to access this data? Is the buffer address legal and mapped in?)

- Do the work, which may involve devices, network accesses, or other processes.

- Return any error conditions to the user as a special numeric code.

Error return values are placed inside a special variable in the U-area (the *user* structure) or the *thread* structure, each of which contains per-process information needed by the kernel. Any error is returned as the result of the system call, along with an error flag to distinguish error codes from legitimate return values. The flag is the carry-bit in the processor status register (PSR) for SPARC systems. Error values are placed by the system call code in **libc** into the global variable *errno*, which is actually resident in **libc** itself.

Scheduling: processes and threads

The kernel scheduler is the section that decides what should be run next and starts it up. This usually involves a *context switch*; the complete set of state information for the currently executing code must be saved so it can be continued later, and state information for another process must be loaded to resume *its* execution. This context data includes the complete set of registers in the CPU, the stacks (user stack and kernel stack), and the pages that were in use and in memory for that process.

One of the major changes between the kernel in SunOS 4.x and in Solaris 2 was the modification to allow multiple threads of control within one user process. A thread of control could be viewed as a place where work is being done. For some programs, it's possible to do some things in parallel: One section of the program can essentially be run independently of another. For "single-threaded" systems like the original UNIX kernel, actually doing this would require you to create a new process to run independently and do the work separately. Modern "multithreaded" kernels do allow several parts of a user program to be active at once, usually because they provide more than one CPU, which could be simultaneously running user code. There is no reason to restrict these processors to working with different user programs, so if the code allows it, more than one thread of control could be active and in execution at one time. This means that in SunOS 4.x, the *process* is the basic scheduling entity. In Solaris 2, one of the process's *threads* is what gets scheduled. In either case, the system still needs to keep track of processes and process-specific information, as well as scheduling parameters, state information, and a kernel stack. This is done with several structures; we'll look at each version of the OS separately, although there are many things in common.

SunOS 4.x

The main pieces of information needed by the scheduler are contained within the process table.

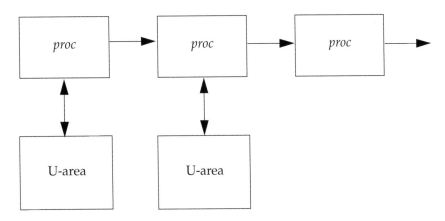

Figure 19-2 SunOS 4.x Process Table

The process table is a linked list of *proc* structures that describe processes and their various states. Those that are actually runnable are normally linked together on a separate list. Each process table entry contains enough information to schedule that process and to find the rest of it in case it's been swapped out to disk. This set of structures is used and updated primarily by the scheduler, but other things may change a process into a "runnable" state. Often device driver interrupt routines will do this when I/O is completed or when data arrives to be read.

The information needed to actually run the process is contained in the U-area, or *user* structure. This area includes pointers to open files, the current working directory, the effective user ID, and the context (register contents, PC value, stack). This may be swapped out to disk if necessary; the kernel maintains a pool of U-areas for active processes and swaps idle structures out to make room. When analyzing a core dump, you may not see any information about what a process is doing if it has been idle for a long period: all the information about that process's state, including the kernel stack, is not in the core file because it was not in memory.

Process structures are defined in **/usr/include/sys/proc.h**; the definition of a *user* structure can be found in **/usr/include/sys/user.h**.

Solaris 2

In Solaris 2, the information needed to run an individual thread of control is contained in a kernel *thread* structure rather than in the process's *user* structure. This makes the U-area significantly shorter (since a lot of information was pulled from it), so the remainder is now attached to the end of the process table structure, and a linked list of threads is attached to each process. Thus, each process table entry contains all the process-wide information, but each possible thread of control has its own structure containing the necessary state information. Along with the *thread* structure is an *lwp* structure, one per thread. The *lwp* structure contains the less commonly used data about a particular thread (accounting, for instance). Just as the U-area in SunOS 4.x contained process information that could be swapped out, the *lwp* contains thread information that can be swapped to disk if necessary.

These structures are defined in various **/usr/include/sys** header files. Look for **thread.h**, **proc.h**, **usr.h**, and **klwp.h**. (Note that **lwp.h** does *not* refer to kernel *lwp* structures!)

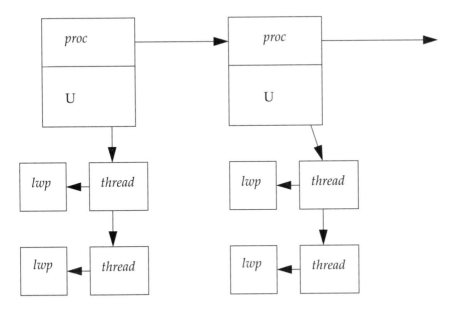

Figure 19-3 Solaris 2 Processes and Threads

Here, you can see that the per-process information contained in the U-areas and *proc* structures includes a pointer to a list of structures containing information about each thread of control. Normally, processes contain only one thread. It takes special coding, libraries, and initial design work to build a multithreaded process. The kernel itself does have multiple internal threads that all link to the process table entry for **sched**, the scheduler. These "system" threads are scheduled and handled just like user program threads, although with a higher priority. They include NFS handlers, Streams management functions, interrupt service routines, and the page daemon.

File systems

The piece of the kernel that deals with file systems is the part that determines disk organization, for instance, what actual disk blocks on what device you need to access in order to perform a read, or directory lookup, or file creation. However, there are many different ways of organizing disks. In an attempt to make some of the facilities in the kernel share standard interfaces, there are some *virtual* layers, in file handling in particular, which insulate the basic kernel functions from the details about file system organization and file types.

In SunOS 4.x and Solaris 2, a VFS (Virtual File System) layer handles the basic details of mounting and unmounting file systems without worrying about their underlying structure. Device- or file-system-specific code is invoked indirectly to perform the needed operations for mounting, unmounting, getting statistics, or flushing data out to the device.

UNIX File Systems (UFS) are the most common systems, with NFS (Network File System) a close runner-up. A new entry in the list is HSFS, which handles a format compatible with DOS CD-ROM. Other new types include procfs to define and handle **/proc**, which in Solaris 2 is a pseudo-file system without any real files, just processes. All of these file system types have a common set of operations that must be performed, and specific code for each different type handles the details of how these operations are done. A Virtual File System structure contains a pointer to an array of functions that "do the job." Nobody cares, at the VFS layer, what kind of file system is underneath as long as the appropriate functions have been provided.

Files, inodes, and processes

Speaking in a generic sense, the "inode" or index node is the source of all knowledge about a file. There are actually different types of inodes, used for different types of files. In addition, a "virtual" layer was imposed in the middle to remove the necessity for identifying various file types. In the beginning, the inode was used to describe a UFS local file, and it held all the data defining where that file lived, its attributes, ownership, and other vital information. When other file system types were introduced, it became necessary to define a *vnode* (a virtual inode) that would point to the actual inode with the real file system and type-specific access information. Thus, we now may have a *vnode* that points to an *inode* (UFS), an *rnode* (a remote file system—NFS), an *snode* (indicating a special file, or a device), a *tmpnode* (used for tmpfs), or (new in Solaris 2.3) a *cnode* (for cachefs file systems). Most layers of the system deal with vnodes until they really need to access the file data pointed to by that vnode.

UFS directory entries on disk really contain just an inode number and a name, which allows multiple names to refer to the same file by using the same inode (index, or file) number. (The format of a directory entry for both SunOS 4.x and Solaris 2 is described in **/usr/include/sys/dirent.h**.) The filename is used only when opening a file; from then on a "handle" (file descriptor) is used by the program to refer to the file and read to the vnode.

Several tables in the kernel keep information about open files in one way or another. As usual, all these tables and structures are linked. The links are set up to make finding the vnode easy for the user process. Let's assume the user wants to read data from a file. The following figure shows the various structures that are referenced and the pointers that are followed, in order for a program to open a file, get a file descriptor, and use that descriptor to retrieve some data from the file.

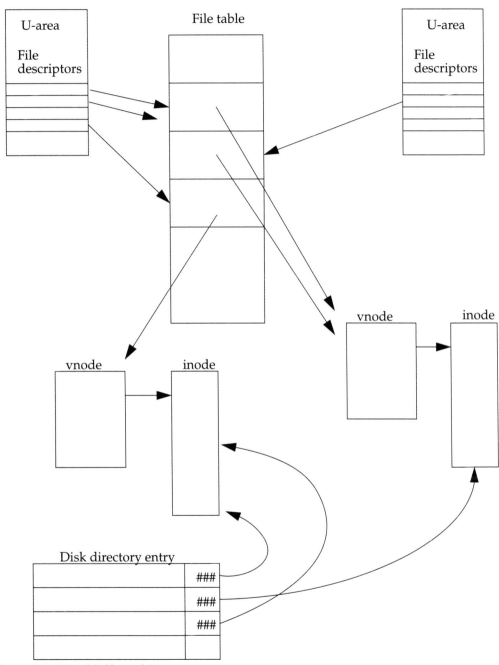

Figure 19-4   Kernel Tables and Structures

As you can see, the kernel must pass through the following structures before it can find the real location of the data that the user wants to read.

- The U-area (*user* structure) keeps an array of pointers for file references. There is one pointer (one array element) per open file. The file descriptor that the user program gets from an *open()* system call is an index into this array. These array elements really just contain pointers to:

- A file table entry, which contains the modes with which a file was opened (read-only, read-write) and the current "position" within that file where the next I/O operation will take place. Every separate *open()* request generates a new file table entry. There is only one file table in the system. Each file table entry contains a pointer to:

- A *vnode*, which identifies some generic characteristics of the file and points to:

- the real *inode* (for UFS files), *snode* (for special device files) or *rnode* (for remote networked files), which tells you, finally, how to get to the actual data.

At the bottom of the picture, directory entries (out on disk) also indicate the inode by means of an index or file number kept in the directory itself. These would be used during an *open()* request to translate the name of the file into an inode. You should note that no table in the kernel actually contains the filename once that file has been successfully opened.

There are pointers from *user* structures (U-areas) down to vnodes and inodes, but there are no pointers back up from vnodes to U-areas. You also find pointers (index numbers) from a directory entry to an inode, but not from the inode back out to the directory. Essentially, this is a many-to-one relationship at each stage — and there is no way to establish a single link back the other way. A commonly asked question is "How can I tell who has this file open?" Unfortunately, it's not an easy question to answer. You can identify a vnode associated with the file, but then you need to search every file table entry to see if it points to that vnode. Once you have a list of file table entries that refer to that particular file, then you need to search every U-area in the system to find all the pointers to those file table entries. The **fuser** program in Solaris 2 will locate processes that are using certain files, but it does require super-user access to search the kernel tables. The same thing holds for finding filenames on disk. If you know the inode, you must search every directory entry to see if that name refers to the desired inode. A program called **ncheck** helps you do this for disk files on a single file system.

Memory Management

Managing memory has several levels of software as well. High-level functions keep track of memory associated with each process, but low-level hardware specific code must handle the mechanics of dealing with the memory management unit (MMU) and setting up the virtual addressing. These lower-level functions are known as the *hat* (Hardware Address Translation) layer.

Higher-level, more generic functions keep track of the ranges of memory addresses that are valid for a particular process address space and identify pages that are in use.

Each process has an address space (*as*) structure associated with it, defining the valid segments of the address space and what their attributes are. For user programs, each individual segment will eventually point to a vnode. This vnode is used to identify the file you will need to fetch data from when it can't be found in memory or to store pages in when they have to be removed (paged out). The *as* structures also allow the system to identify a segmentation violation; a page fault results in a search down the list of valid segments to find the appropriate address range. If the address isn't found, it's a segmentation violation and a SEGV signal is sent to the process.

In addition, each page of physical memory that is not initially grabbed by the kernel at boot has a *page* structure associated with it, indicating how that page is being used. (Locked-down kernel pages will not have such a structure because they are dedicated to the kernel, and cannot be used for any other purpose). It's not always possible to get from a page structure back to "who's using it," but sometimes you can get general information on the page state ("on the free list" versus "locked down" or in use). Each *page* structure does contain information about what file it belongs to and which page within that file the data came from.

These are some of the more commonly examined areas of the kernel. This is not because most errors occur here, but because these are often the starting points when looking for information on the state of the system and the processes (or threads) running on it.

This was just a kernel overview

In the next ten chapters, we will explore different aspects of the kernel in much more detail. Ready? Let's move on, starting with Virtual Memory.

≡ 19

Virtual Memory   20 ≡

Many systems use what is known as "virtual memory." It doesn't mean that you almost remember what happened yesterday but instead refers to how a program will see the environment in which it's running.

Virtual memory means that a user program thinks that the whole machine belongs to it. The entire range of addresses that the CPU could reach (the address space of the processor) looks like it belongs to that program, and there is nobody else to share with. It means that a program does not have to be restricted by the physical parameters of the hardware on which it's running. The hardware and the kernel will take care of the insignificant little details like other users trying to use the system or a distressing lack of physical memory on the machine.

The idea is that a program may use a range of memory addresses so large that the actual physical memory that exists on the machine cannot hold it all at once — and it doesn't have to. Real memory is treated more like a "cache" of commonly or recently used chunks of memory. The hardware (and supporting kernel code) will detect an attempt to access a data value that is not actually resident in the physical memory on the machine, find the appropriate disk block with that data, load it into the system, and let the user program continue with its access as if nothing had happened. What the user sees as "real memory" bears little or no relationship to the actual amount of memory present. And, as you might expect, the addresses that a user program references also are unrelated to the actual location of the data: The hardware performs translations on these "virtual" addresses and turns them into real physical addresses of real physical memory.

Now, this does require some hardware support at several points. First, the CPU must be able to "freeze" the execution of an instruction that is trying to reference nonexistent memory. This will allow it to be continued or restarted when the address is made valid. The system must also have a way of mapping the addresses that the user needs to arbitrary physical locations. These physical addresses may actually change over time as data is moved out of memory and back in again. Also, memory normally must be organized in some way so that chunks of it can be manipulated easily. Usually, this is done by defining memory in terms of fixed size *pages*. All these capabilities are standard on most modern CPUs. The Memory Management Unit (MMU) takes care of the translations, signals the processor when a translation fails (there is no place in real physical memory that currently corresponds to the desired location), and usually determines the organization of physical memory (whether or not it is split into pages, and how big those pages are).

Virtual memory processing in the kernel consists of managing the physical memory as a collection of pages, which is used to hold as much of a user process as is possible. When total user requirements exceed the number of available memory pages, then the kernel attempts to store some of the pages out on disk until needed, keeping only the most recently accessed pages in memory.

Memory inside Sun's UNIX kernel is also set up as a range of virtual addresses. As far as the kernel is concerned, memory is considered to be of two types: kernel memory and everything else. In general, kernel memory is allocated and locked down. User memory can be tossed out to disk at any time, so that the pages can be reused for something else more pressing; for example, to satisfy a request for more memory from a higher priority process, to increase the kernel's supply of pages, or even to receive data from an important disk read request.

The free list

The system keeps a linked list of free (currently unassigned) pages in memory, known as the *free list*. For performance and to handle emergencies, the kernel tries to keep a certain minimum amount of memory in the free list at all times. If the list shrinks to a point where something must be done to get more pages, the **pagedaemon** is started up. The **pagedaemon** attempts to find some space by taking pages away from processes — but only old pages that (hopefully) are not in use. To find space, it makes a pass through a section of the page list, cleaning out the "referenced" bit. After a short time, it makes another pass through the same pages and checks to see if they have actually been referenced during that period. If not, these pages are candidates for theft, and the kernel will move them onto the free list for possible use by somebody else. Of course, if the page has been modified at some point, it will have to be written out to disk before being reused, but there is also a "modified" bit in the page information to let the kernel know. (These are known as *dirty pages*, since they have been scribbled on).

The algorithm used by the **pagedaemon** is called the "clock hands" method. Think of memory as a big ring like the outside of a clock face with two hands moving around this ring, separated by a bit of space (time). One hand cleans out the referenced bit in the status field, and the following hand looks for untouched pages. The "handspread" (amount of time between the actions of the hands), how often the page daemon runs, when it is started up, and how much memory it checks in one pass are all tunable parameters in the kernel.

Note that when a page is put onto the free list, it is not cleaned out: The data that was there is still available. Thus, if a program that lost one of its pages needs it back again, there is a good possibility that the page, even though it is not mapped into this process's address space, is still in memory (on the free list) with the same information still in it. In this case, the process can grab it back again. This is known as a reclaim, or a soft page fault, because it does not require any disk I/O to retrieve information.

To make this scheme work better, the pages that are put onto the free list can be placed in the front (and therefore used first) or stuck on the end. For example, pages used for a program's stack space might be put on the front of the list when that program exits, because the data in those pages is of no earthly use to any other process. However, pages that contain data from a disk file are stuck on the back end of the list, because somebody might need them later on. So if somebody runs the **ls** program, reads all the pages of code into memory, and exits, all those pages will, of course, have to go on the free list. But the next time **ls** is run, there is a good chance that all the necessary pages are still in memory, still on the free list, still with the correct contents — and no disk (or network) activity is necessary in order to get **ls** back in operation again.

Swap space

The system swap space is "raw disk," a collection of disk blocks the kernel can use as it wishes, without any specific structure associated with it. This can be a complete disk partition or perhaps a swap file. The kernel will use these pages as a backing store, or place to put pages that have to be saved for later use and cannot be retrieved from some file elsewhere. Swap space is used to hold the pages that are bumped out of main memory and cannot be put back into a named file. These may be pages used for a stack, or data space for which a program has allocated memory. Such pages, known as "anonymous" pages, don't have a home anywhere else and need a temporary shelter on swap space.

In the SunOS 4.x kernel, the pages in main memory are considered to be merely a cache for pages on disk. This means that when a new page is requested by a process for anonymous use, that page immediately must have corresponding disk space in swap reserved for it, so that in case it does need to be pushed out to disk there will be a place to put it. This is fairly straightforward but does have some disadvantages.

One disadvantage is that the total amount of pages (virtual memory address range) in use by *all* the processes in the system for data can be no larger than swap space. This doesn't count code that can be retrieved from an executable file, or memory-mapped data files, but any private data must be backed up by a swap page.

As another disadvantage, the amount of physical memory usable by programs is restricted by the amount of swap that has been defined. If you have a machine with 500 megabytes of main memory but only 100 megabytes of swap, much of your physical memory will be useless because there is not enough swap space to back up all the pages on disk. You may never actually have to page anything out — there may never be a small enough free list to force the page daemon to start running — but the system still requires that reservation, "just in case."

In Solaris 2, these restrictions have been relaxed somewhat. The method is more intelligent: The total amount of virtual address space available to processes is the sum of swap plus physical memory. Systems can be built (if enough physical memory is available) without any swap space at all. These systems, of course, are going to have a lot of trouble creating a system core file: There's no place to put it!

Page faults

What is a page fault? When a program tries to reference a memory location and the translation step done by the MMU indicates an error, the CPU is interrupted right in the middle of the instruction (since it can't finish). This is generally because there is no valid page in memory to reference. It is then the kernel's responsibility to decide whether this address really is valid (usually because a copy of the page does exist on disk somewhere). If so, it has to get that page loaded up and let the user program with the offending instruction try again. If the address really *is* bad — the user program shouldn't even be trying to get at that location — then the kernel will signal the program with a SIGSEGV, which normally kills the program. So, a page fault is a reference to data that is not in memory, but might still be valid because it could be loaded from disk. If the data can be found, this is a legitimate reference and the data has to be fetched. If the reference doesn't refer to any data (it's not in that process's address space), it's an illegal reference. Kernel software determines when a page fault is valid and when it is completely erroneous.

A page fault may also refer to a legal address (but one that is not set up in the MMU), and the desired data is already loaded in memory because somebody else needed it, for example, the part of the standard I/O library (**libc**) containing *printf()*. When processing a page fault, the kernel will first check to see if the page is already around and, if it is, will just map that existing page into the address space of the current process. This means pages might be shared among many different processes at the same time (which makes calculations like "how much memory is my program using" rather difficult to do correctly). Finding a page in memory results in a *soft page fault*: the only action the kernel needs to do is connect it. A hard page fault is one that needs actual disk I/O to complete, since nobody else has the correct page in memory at that time.

Working set, or resident set

Physical memory is not allocated to or associated with a user process until it is required. And, when the program doesn't need it any more or hasn't used it for a long time, it is taken away (the translation in the MMU is turned off) and the page is used for something else or put on the free list. Of course, if the data in the page has been modified, it will first have to be saved out on disk. The real memory pages associated with a process are called the *resident set*, meaning this is the set of pages currently resident (physically present) in memory and belonging to that process. This is somewhat complicated by the fact that some pages may actually be used by more than one process at the same time. For example, the pages that hold the code for the shared library **libc** are going to be required by many different programs simultaneously. However, since nobody should be changing these pages (in fact, they're not allowed to), there is no reason to have more than one copy of the data in memory at one time. It makes much more sense to have multiple MMU translations for that page so that many processes can be reading the same data. This does not require that the page be located at the same virtual address for each process that needs it. It does mean that several translations of virtual addresses may result in the same *physical* location and will thus find the same page. These pages, since they are mapped in by more than one process, will be counted as a part of the resident set for *each one* of these processes.

Keeping track of pages

Many, in fact, most, of the physical pages on the machine will be usable for many purposes. The kernel needs to keep track of these pages and identify who owns them or what data they contain. Every page not dedicated to the kernel's use must have a data structure describing that page —strangely enough, called a *page* structure. There is one for every page on the machine (except for the kernel pages locked down at boot time). Thus, if you add memory to your system, you will be increasing the kernel data space requirements (although not by much) to keep track of it.

The *page* structure has some interesting information in it. There is a pointer to a vnode, which indicates what file the data in this page comes from. There is a flag that notes that the page is "dirty" — which just means that it has been modified and these changes need to be saved on disk someplace. Another flag indicates that the page is not currently associated with a process but is on the free list. Pointers keep all the pages on the free list linked together. More pointers link the pages with data into a list organized by vnode so the kernel can find them.

The *page* structures are allocated in kernel memory fairly soon in the boot process. They are created as a single array, sized according to the amount of physical memory available on the system. The address of the start of the array is kept in the kernel variable, *pages*, and the end of the list is pointed to by *epages*.

Page structures are defined in the **/usr/include/vm/page.h** header file.

Keeping track of process space

Every process has one single "address space," which is actually a list of separate sections, or chunks, of the total virtual address range. These chunks compose the set of valid addresses that the process can use — the ones that hold real data. To keep track of all these, the process table entry (*proc* structure) contains a pointer to an address space (*as*) structure. The *as* structure points off to a linked list of segments, or address ranges, kept in sorted order.

Each segment has a special structure (the *seg* structure) to define it that tells the kernel where that particular segment starts and how long it is. When a page fault occurs, it is easy for the kernel to run down this list and check to see if the desired address is really part of an existing segment. If not, the program receives a *segmentation violation* signal: there is no segment containing this address, so it was out of bounds. If the address really is part of a valid segment, it means that the desired data (page) was probably not in memory, and the kernel has to find the data and set up the MMU to point to it. In order to do this, each segment structure points to some data that is specific to the type of file to which this segment refers. It might be a regular disk file that has been memory-mapped. It might be a file that can be read but not modified. It might be the stack, which doesn't actually refer to a disk file at all. For example, the special data will contain information about how a page fault is satisfied, or how the system should handle a *sync* system call over this range of addresses.

There are several segment types. Among these are *seg_vn*, which is a segment that refers to data in some vnode, and *seg_dev*, which refers to some device, like a frame buffer, that has been mapped in by that process. The following diagram shows all the structures and how they are linked together.

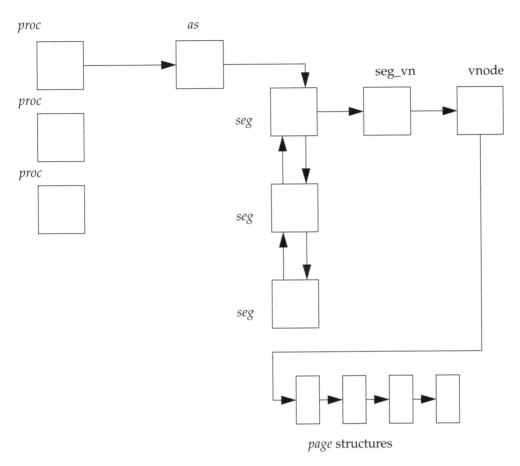

Figure 20-1 Process Space Structures

Anonymous memory

Programs very often require memory that is not associated with a file. For example, *malloc()* may expand the program's data space or the stack might grow by another page. Neither of these actions needs data from a file to satisfy a page fault. For these cases, the only real requirement is a brand-new page that is initialized to zeroes and that can be saved someplace if it has to be paged out. This is known as *anonymous* memory, since it is not associated with a specific, named, disk file. The kernel will reserve some space in swap to hold the image in case paging out is required at some point. You will often hear anonymous memory loosely referred to as swap space (which *is* disk space in SunOS 4.x, but not necessarily so in Solaris 2), because that's where it lives.

In the 4.x kernel, a whole collection of routines deals with anonymous memory. These routines do such things as:

- Reserve space with a call to *anon_resv()*
- Find out information about the pages with *anon_getpage()*
- Allocate a zero filled page with *anon_zero()*
- Remove a reference to a page with *anon_decref()*

In Solaris 2, anonymous memory is treated like a regular file. A special unnamed vnode is assigned to keep track of all swap space, so that the regular vnode processing code will work on anonymous space. The special *anon* routines have been removed.

Kernel functions

You'll find two types of kernel routines dealing with memory. The first set contains all the functions that implement the kernel's version of *malloc()* — "give me some space." These functions keep a kernel free memory list and expand the kernel's data space (and physical size) as necessary. These functions deal with the kernel's need for more memory and have nothing to do with a user program's memory requests.

The other type of function deals with setting up virtual address mappings for user processes: keeping track of their address space, handling page faults, and dealing with swapping and anonymous memory. We'll deal with them in a moment; first, let's look at the various versions of handling the kernel's requirement for memory. This will not be an in-depth treatment but will briefly cover the functions and their purpose so that you can recognize the names when you see them.

malloc(): SunOS 4.x

There are some differences between the OS version of *malloc()*, although the end result is the same. In the SunOS 4.x kernel, there are two distinct methods of requesting or allocating memory inside the kernel's address space, depending on what you're going to use it for. One method will just take pages as necessary and add them to kernel space. This method attaches the new pages to the kernel address space in an area known as the *heap*. The heap is "generic" memory: it can be used for anything. Most commonly, it is used for data structures that are dynamically allocated as the kernel needs them. These memory requests will fail if there are no pages on the free list and the kernel can't wait around for some to become available.

The other method of memory allocation uses "resource maps," which define a range of virtual addresses intended for a specific purpose: the kernel pulls a chunk from a map of already allocated and locked-down memory. For these allocations, running out of space is usually an error, and the request will fail. The space used for *mbufs*, for example, is a fixed size. When the system runs out of memory for network data buffers, you will see error messages on the console and the system will probably start losing incoming data.

What are resource maps? A map is a low-level kernel structure used to keep track of things. It is intended to hold a list of free space for some particular resource. (The map structure is defined in the header file **/usr/include/sys/map.h**). In 4.x, resource maps are used for describing kernel virtual address space, performing *mbuf* allocations, keeping track of swap space, and DVMA (I/O direct to memory) operations, among others. There may actually be higher-level functions that perform the act of allocation, but these routines will keep track of the data with resource maps. Each of these maps consists of a fixed-length array of structures describing a range of free space, which may correspond to actual memory, disk blocks, or a set of unused structures. In fact, the map may be used for units of bytes, pages, or disk blocks. The maps themselves, the arrays, are set up at boot time, although the space they keep track of may not have been allocated yet.

The resource map contents (the array entries) are handled by two functions, *rmalloc()* and *rmfree()*. These routines deal with arbitrary maps, since they are all in the same format, so for any stack tracebacks or panics that involve these functions you will need to discover which map is being processed. Resource allocation can fail (or hang) for a couple of reasons: Either the map is empty (the resource is completely exhausted) or it has become so fragmented that there is nothing big enough to satisfy the request. In fact, if a new bit of free space has to be added in to an already badly fragmented map, there may not be any place to put that information: The array could be full. In this case, a message is printed on the console ("rmap overflow") and that bit of free space is thrown away. It can only be recovered and reused by rebooting the system.

One of the kernel maps describes the range of memory known as *heap space*. The heap functions work just like a user-level *malloc()*. If a request can be satisfied from a list of free (available) memory that already belongs to the kernel, that memory will be "recycled." If more memory is needed, then new pages are obtained from the system free page list and inserted into the kernel heap space by being added to the resource map.

If there is memory in the free list, it is kept in a special form (a tree structure), so there are some special functions that deal with getting free memory from the heap:

- *kmem_alloc()* — Returns a pointer to an allocated block of memory (or a null, if the request failed).

- *new_kmem_alloc()* — Is essentially the same but takes an additional parameter. In fact, *kmem_alloc()* calls *new_kmem_alloc()*. The additional parameter is a flag that tells the function whether it can wait (sleep) if memory is not available.

- *kmem_zalloc()* — The same as *kmem_alloc()* with a *bzero()* call added to clear the memory to zeroes.

- *new_kmem_zalloc()* — *new_kmem_alloc()* with a bzero.

You may also see some very similar but separate routines that grab space from different small pools of memory. These pools each keep their own free list, which is not based on a *map* structure; the functions are intended to provide a faster allocation method for specific, dedicated memory areas. These functions correspond to the above list and have very similar names:

- *kmem_fast_alloc()*
- *new_kmem_fast_alloc()*
- *kmem_fast_zalloc()*
- *new_kmem_fast_zalloc()*

Although their purpose is similar to the whole idea behind resource maps, the functions are not implemented the same way. All in all, many different but very similar routines manipulate memory. A lot of consolidation was performed in Solaris 2 to eliminate some of this confusion.

malloc(): Solaris 2

Many of the same routine names have been kept in Solaris 2 for compatibility, but the allocation scheme behind the names is substantially different. There are still resource maps, but the heap in its original form is gone; there are now *pools* of memory with chunks of various sizes that are used for general purpose memory allocation. The pools are filled when needed by pages grabbed from the free list. Plus, in a radical turnabout, excess free pages are actually returned to the system free page list!

kmem_alloc(), *kmem_zalloc()*, and *kmem_free()* are defined in the list of kernel support functions known as the DDI/DKI (section 9F in the manual pages). These routines behave to the outside just as they did in 4.x: a size in bytes is requested, a flag will indicate whether the caller can wait (sleep) for the request, and either a pointer to the memory space or a null is returned. There are internal differences corresponding to the new organization of free memory.

The new lower-level functions *kmem_allocspool()* (to control the "small" buffer pool) and *kmem_allocbpool()* (for the "big" buffer pool) are routines to add to the available pools of free buffers if it becomes necessary. These functions request chunks of memory and split them up. Small buffers are chunks of memory from 8 bytes up to 256 bytes in length. Big buffers range from 512 bytes up to 16 kilobytes in length. Buffers are maintained in lengths that are powers of two; each level up is twice the size of the previous level. If a request for a particular size cannot be filled, a larger buffer (the next size up) will be requested and split in half: one half going to the requestor, the other back to the free pool. If no memory is available all the way up the chain, a call to *kmem_getpages()* will grab pages from the free list, perform a call to *rmalloc()* to allocate kernelmap (page table) entries, and add the new kernel pages to the buffer pool.

Resource maps are still around in Solaris 2. The map structure itself is different, and there are fewer maps in the kernel. Some maps are set up at boot time, and others are built dynamically when the appropriate module is loaded. Refer to the header file **/usr/include/sys/map.h** for the definitions.

Virtual memory routines

Now let's move on to the next set of kernel memory functions: those dealing with the chunks of virtual address space in use by the various processes on the system.

A substantial part of the kernel is devoted to virtual memory processing. Some of these routines handle very specific hardware details, which we won't get into because they will be different for every architecture and MMU. However, the sections dealing with more generic, "virtual" topics can be covered. These are functions that manipulate the address spaces of processes (and the *as* structure) and the individual segments (*seg* structures), page-handling routines, and a general high-level interface to the *hat* layer, for hardware address translation.

Along with these you will find more specialized routines handling anonymous memory, swap space, and the *seg_vn* structure, which deals with segments that refer to actual vnodes (files). There are some common naming conventions that should enable you to identify functions in each of these areas, although we will touch on only a few specific function names.

Let's start at the highest level and work down. The include files, which define the structures we're interested in and often list the important routines, are all contained in the **/usr/include/vm** directory for both SunOS 4 and Solaris 2.

Address spaces

Every process has its own address space, so every process table entry contains a pointer to an address space structure just for that process. The structure serves mostly as an anchor for a list of segments, which describe the valid ranges of virtual addresses that each individual process has. The structure contains global pieces of information, such as a flag that indicates that the entire process is locked in memory, and a count of the number of physical pages actually in use by this process (the *a_rss* field: the resident set size).

A few functions deal with the address space as a whole. Some of these are:

- *as_segat()* — Find and return the segment that contains the specified address.

- *as_alloc()* — Allocate a new address space structure.

- *as_dup()* — Create a copy of an existing structure.
- *as_fault()* — Handle a fault at the given address for "size" bytes. This function is the one eventually called to handle a page fault.
- *as_unmap()* — Unmap all the segments that cover the given address range.

There are more functions; they have similar names and deal with various requirements at this level: locking and unlocking address ranges, finding an empty memory range for mapping something in, adding a segment to the list, and so forth.

Segments

Segments are individual chunks of continuous address space, generally with separate characteristics (such as belonging to a particular file). Each segment structure (*struct seg*) contains a base address and a size, links to other segments that belong to the same process, and a pointer to a list of functions. This list, defined in the *seg_ops* structure, contains addresses of functions that perform a certain set of operations specifically for the given type of segment. These operations include things like:

- Unmapping a portion of a segment
- Removing an entire segment and any hardware mappings for the pages
- Handling a page fault that occurs inside this segment
- Performing a sync
- Returning a pointer to the vnode that is associated with this segment

Some actual functions for the different segment types are:

- *segvn_unmap()* — Do an unmap operation on a *seg_vn* type of segment. A *seg_vn* is one that refers to a file (a vnode). A memory-mapped file would be a *seg_vn* type.
- *segdev_free()* — Free a segment that referred to a device. A frame buffer would be handled as a *seg_dev* type of segment.

There are also some generic segment handling functions that deal with the segment structures themselves.

- *seg_alloc()* — Allocate a segment for the specified address range and attach it to the list of segments for a particular address space structure.
- *seg_attach()* — Insert a segment structure into a list of segments. Called by *seg_alloc()* to actually do the work.
- *seg_unmap()* — Is a front end to the segment-specific unmap operation.

- *seg_free()* — Remove a segment structure from the list and actually free up the structure. This function also calls the segment type-specific free function to take care of releasing any resources used by the segment.

Segments are another "virtual" layer, like vnodes, to allow a range of addresses to refer to many different things (a file, a device like a frame buffer, anonymous memory) but still be handled at a high level in a standardized way.

Pages

Individual pages on the machine that are not permanently dedicated to the kernel are tracked by a *page* structure. This structure keeps some state information about a page and a pointer to the vnode to which the data in this page belongs. A list of pages organized by vnode and offset (how far into the "file" this page belongs) keeps track of pages containing data for specific vnodes. If a user wants a certain piece of data from some file, the kernel can rapidly find out if that data is already resident in memory.

There are many functions that deal with pages: finding them, freeing them, hashing them, locking them. These all deal with pages above a hardware level and are generally similar across versions of the OS. Some that you may see are:

- *page_lookup()* — Find a page. Given a vnode and an offset, look through the pages in memory to see if it is there. If it is but it's "in transit" (i.e., being loaded up), the caller will sleep and wait for the I/O to finish.

- *page_hashout()* — Remove a page from the list of pages, based on the vnode/offset data pair.

- *page_reclaim()* — Grab the page from the free list and attach it to the list of pages associated with a vnode. This implements a "soft page fault" where the data is still in memory although not directly entered in a process's address space.

There are a lot more page functions. The *page* structure and the list of page related functions are defined in **/usr/include/vm/page.h**.

The hat layer

Some work can be done at a level independent of the actual MMU hardware to keep track of mapping and virtual-to-physical translation information. A large portion of this is just concerned with defining the operations and necessary supporting structures. In the 4.x kernel, a list of functions was defined and then implemented in machine-specific code files. In Solaris 2, the same approach was taken as with vnodes, *vfs* structures, and segments; a set of operations was defined for each type of MMU, and the generic *hat* routines just call the appropriate machine-dependent functions after some setup and error checking.

The functions are fairly consistent across the OS versions. The definitions appear in the include file **/usr/include/vm/hat.h**, and contain routines like:

- *hat_memload()* — Load a given page into the translation hardware.

- *hat_fault()* — Try to resolve a fault with the existing translations.

- *hat_pagesync()* — Get the hardware information into the page structure (the referenced/modified status) and reset the hardware.

- *hat_getkpfnum()* — Return the kernel "page frame number" (the actual physical page number) for a given kernel virtual address.

- *hat_unload()* — Unload a mapping from the hardware.

In 4.x, these are the functions that actually do the work. In Solaris 2, these functions will immediately call another routine directly related to the particular hardware on that system. A function such as *srmmu_memload()* will deal with the intricacies of the SPARC Reference Memory Management Unit.

We're now down pretty close to the hardware. Failures in these functions or in routines that they call are quite possibly due to hardware problems, in part because these functions are some of the most heavily used routines in the kernel. If you see problems at this level, you will at least have a pretty good idea what hardware to look at!

Scheduling 21 ≡

Process (or thread) scheduling is done by the kernel to make sure that everybody gets a fair share, nobody hogs the system, and nobody prevents others from getting their work done. Each process is allowed to run for only a certain amount of time before it is bounced and the CPU is switched over to another process. The basic mechanisms of scheduling, however, changed dramatically between SunOS 4.x and Solaris 2. It was turned into a more tunable, table-driven process. In addition, a real-time facility was added to the kernel in Solaris 2, and the whole process of deciding who got to run next was redone.

SunOS 4.x

The older system design has been tweaked over a number of years and is quite stable and reliable. However, it was originally intended for a single-processor, timeshared system. The emphasis is on running lots of highly interactive user programs, switching back and forth to give everyone fairly even performance. CPU-bound (heavy processing) programs are deliberately placed in a lower-priority bracket to give interactive programs, like editors, a better response time. Processes that have not been active for a long time and have been off the CPU, or swapped out, are also given a boost in priority to get them back into the system.

Users (and administrators) of the system have very limited abilities to change this scheme. The **nice** command will essentially add a constant to the priority of the process and force it to be placed in a different level. Users can only *lower* their priority by using a positive nice value. Administrators (super-users) can use a negative nice value, causing their processes to be run sooner, perhaps even before some system daemons. Doing so, of course, makes the system administrator somewhat unpopular with the long-suffering user community who can't get any work done. (The answer, of course, is for the administrator to rename that game program to **cc** so nobody can tell.)

There are 32 different run queues, which are ordered by priority. If more than one process is in a run queue at a particular level, they are executed in round-robin fashion, that is, a process that exceeds its CPU-time allotment moves to the back of the list and must wait for everyone else at that level to have a chance before running again. In practice, this rarely happens. Most processes run into a blocking situation where they have to give up the CPU voluntarily and wait for something else to happen (I/O, for example) before they can continue running. In addition, since CPU-bound processes are penalized, they generally find themselves moving down to a lower-priority run queue rather quickly. A fairly complicated formula is used to compute the process priority (and eventual run queue), based on the amount of CPU time the process has used, its former priority value, the nice number, and the amount of memory the program is using, among other things.

The important kernel functions used to put processes on the run queues or take them off are:

- *sleep()* — Voluntarily give up the CPU because there is nothing more to be done right now. This function calls *swtch()* to let another process run.

- *wakeup()* — Put a process that was sleeping onto the appropriate run queue. If the newly readied process has a higher priority than the one currently executing, set a flag (*runrun*) and try to bump this other one off. The flag is checked as part of trap and interrupt processing to see if the original process should be allowed to continue running.

- *setrq()* — Put the given process at the end of the appropriate run queue.

- *remrq()* — Remove the first process from the head of the given run queue. This function is called by various kernel housekeeping functions as well as by the kernel code that prepares to run another process.

These functions all move processes around on the queues. The actual code to perform a context switch is contained in two routines, *swtch()* and *resume()*.

The first, *swtch()*, can be called (via *sleep()*) by a process or by the scheduler if it decides that the current process needs to be bumped off the CPU. The function finds the next process that should be allowed to run. The second function, *resume()*, actually restores the state of a process and returns control to the process. The *swtch()* function will call the idle loop if there is nothing to run and will just spin around watching the CPU lights move, if there are any. (Actually, the LED bouncing-light pattern, on those systems that have the lights, is updated in the clock-tick interrupt code, but the pattern will be updated only if the clock tick happened to interrupt the idle loop.)

A substantial portion of the context switch code and queue manipulation is written in assembly language. It is quite complex. There was a very large descriptive comment in the old UNIX source code for the PDP-11, describing how a context switch was performed. The last line of the comment said, "You are not expected to understand this."

Solaris 2

Numerous substantial changes were made in the Solaris 2 scheduler. Part of them made the scheduling simpler and more easily tunable. The end result was a table-driven scheduler and the capability for administrators to completely confuse the entire system by loading their own tables. The table construction is not complex, but you should be careful about making major changes blindly. If you are analyzing a system that is performing strangely, it might be worthwhile verifying that the tables are still the originals.

Scheduling is now performed on a thread basis rather than on a process basis. This allows different threads of control within the same process to be run independently and with unique priorities.

Threads will also have scheduling classes associated with them. Each scheduling class has its own set of parameter tables to control dispatching and its own kernel code to process them. The normal class for user processes is "timeshare," but there is now a real-time scheduling class available. Real-time threads have a higher precedence than any other thread on the system except for interrupt service routines. Real-time will also take priority over system daemons and internal kernel threads. If a real-time process gains control, particularly in a single processor system, and gets into a loop, the only solution may be to halt and reboot the machine. (This is one easy thing to look for when debugging a hung system: Make sure no user processes running with real-time priorities have taken over the machine.)

There are now 170 possible priorities (dispatch queues), of which 60 are given to timeshare threads, 40 are allocated for kernel operations, 10 are reserved for interrupt services, and the remaining 60 are available for real-time work. The same basic functions must be performed as in the 4.x kernel, so *swtch()* and *resume()* are still around to do the actual thread selection and thread startup. Some new functions manipulate the dispatch queues, based on the parameter tables defining the class characteristics (for both timeshare and real time). The tables are the most important part; they specify what queue a thread will move to for its next turn to run.

For timeshare threads, the dispatch parameter table contains several columns:

- A priority (queue) number

- A time quantum in milliseconds (ranging from 10 to 100)

- The queue a thread is moved to if it uses up all its time

- The revised priority of a thread if it hasn't used up its time (and thus deserves a better shot next time)

- The amount of time remaining in which to try to use up that quantum (typically 5 seconds)

- The priority temporarily assigned to the thread after it returns from a sleep. Generally, the priority is higher than normal to allow a thread that was waiting for I/O to complete to get in promptly and use that data. This gives interactive processes a slightly better response time.

Real-time threads are controlled by a much simpler parameter table, because a priority for real-time is usually based on the job a thread has to do rather than the amount of time it has used up. These threads do not change priorities; their table contains a time quantum and that's about all. This allows multiple threads at the same real-time priority level to cycle among themselves until they're finished, sleeping, or a higher-priority task comes along.

Along with the tables defining general class characteristics, every thread has associated with it a *scheduling class* structure, which contains information used by the appropriate scheduling functions to help identify the proper dispatch queue. This information includes the current priority numbers, nice value, amount of time left in this thread's quantum, and various flags. Look in **/usr/include/sys** for **ts.h** and **rt.h** to find the scheduling class structure definitions for timeshare and real-time threads.

The internal kernel threads, such as the page daemon, the STREAMS service procedures, and the NFS daemons, also have a scheduling class, which is really just timeshare with a slightly higher priority setting. These system threads run at a priority above normal timeshare users, but below real-time.

In Solaris 2, interrupts have scheduling priority levels as well. Interrupt processing is more sophisticated; there is a separate thread for most interrupt priority levels, so a service routine may actually sleep and wait for some busy resource. This means that interrupt handlers can be scheduled and thus need a set of queues for their own use. These are always the highest-priority threads on the system.

How you change it

In the SunOS 4.x kernel, the only thing you really can change is the nice value associated with a process. The algorithm is hardcoded; it would be necessary to replace the subsystem with new functions in order to change the way the scheduler works.

In Solaris 2, it's obviously possible to manipulate the scheduling dispatch tables. A utility, **dispadmin**, can be used to dump out the tables and replace them.

The nice value still exists and is used essentially the same way — to artificially adjust the selection of the dispatch queue by some constant number. Another utility, **priocntl**, can manipulate the scheduling parameters and the basic class for a particular process or an individual thread within a process.

In general, the scheduling algorithm in the SunOS 4.x kernel is fixed and unchanging, but fairly robust. Panics or traps occurring in this area are normally due to hardware problems. They get escalated and fixed promptly if they are software related. However, there haven't been any major software changes in this area for quite a while.

The Solaris 2 mechanism is simple, but the table setup could have unexpected repercussions if the numbers are just slightly wrong. The errors, though, should show up as performance issues rather than system crashes.

File Systems 22 ≡

A file system is a formal, structured way of organizing data on some sort of medium, like a disk. You want to be able to rapidly find the information you've put out there and access it efficiently. The format of the file system may depend on the type of disk, the speed of access, or the kind of data you have stored there. If you've got a disk full of video clips or sound files, it might be advisable to arrange them in contiguous files so the data transfer will be as fast as possible. If the disk is going to be used for a bulletin board or news system, you need to optimize it to handle lots of very short files that will be updated or replaced frequently. SunOS has various types of file systems that it understands, but from the top level they all look the same because of software layers that perform standard, common tasks in the same way for any file system type.

Most file systems are supported only on some sort of random-access device, like a disk. These are known as *block* devices, because they normally store and retrieve data in fixed-length chunks, or blocks. Hardware devices such as a tape drive cannot support a file system structure, since there is no way to locate a random block on the tape without starting at the beginning and reading sequentially through the tape until you find the data you want. (There actually was a form of tape that supported blocking, but it was a short-lived product. The medium was cheap, but the performance was much too slow.)

There are various methods of keeping track of data on a block device. Some are more efficient for certain purposes but perform very poorly under particular circumstances. The UNIX file system was designed originally to be simple and to support timesharing, where many users would probably access fairly short files on a pretty random basis. In fact, trying to keep files in contiguous disk blocks was of no benefit, since it was more likely that another disk request from an entirely different user would be made before the next disk block in the "contiguous" file was requested. This design, now known as UFS, for the UNIX File System, was enhanced by the University of California at Berkeley (the designers of the BSD UNIX releases) and eventually distributed as the Berkeley Fast File System, which is currently used on the Sun disks for both Solaris 2 and SunOS 4.x systems.

Basic disk structure

You've probably seen pictures of disk layouts before, describing the disk as a pie. Far be it for this book to be different; think of a disk surface divided up into slices — like a pie.

As the disk spins, a read head sitting in one position will describe a circle over the surface, entering into each slice. The data in a slice, known as a sector, is the basic element of data storage on a disk surface. This is what a read or a write deals with. Fine so far, but eventually you're going to run out of room on this one circle, and you'll need to move to a new one. Since most disk drives involve more than one disk surface, in fact containing many two-sided platters, it turns out that they have multiple read/write heads stacked on top of each other, one for each surface. This gives you a bunch of stacked circles, known as cylinders, to play with. Sooner or later, though, this, too, will fill up, and it will be time to move on.

The next step is to move to an adjacent circle, or cylinder. Most disks have hundreds of cylinders available. However, there is a disadvantage in going to another cylinder to find data: The disk head must move. This operation, known as a *seek*, is the most expensive operation in disk I/O. Much of the work in optimizing disk layouts for faster access has been in minimizing the number of seeks performed, or at least keeping them as short as possible.

The old original

The initial UNIX file system structure was quite suitable for the small disks of the time. It had a master table at the beginning, giving information about the structure and layout of the disk data. This was known as the superblock. Following this was an index, or table, of information about every file on the disk. This contained file "nodes" that told the system how to actually locate the file data, which was kept farther out in a general data area making up the rest of the file system. These were known as index nodes, or inodes, and kept everything about the file except the name. On the rest of the disk were found the data files themselves, including directories (which were treated just like regular files) that associated a name with the data. Directories were a slightly special case, and the data in them was rigorously formatted: There was a 14-character name, followed by a 2-byte index number that identified the inode for the file.

This entire structure was quite restrictive, but it was sufficient — for a while. The first method of expanding this structure was to put more than one file system on a disk. The physical disk was partitioned into a maximum of eight different areas, each of which could have a different, independent file system on it. This was very significant when larger disks became available, because with this basic file system structure, you were limited to a 16-bit number to identify the inode, meaning you could only have 65,000 files in a file system.

The BSD file system

Work done at Berkeley to expand and enhance UNIX included massive changes to the file system structure. The basic idea was to try to minimize seeks. The first change was to intermingle inodes with the data, thus having the information about the file close to the contents of the file. After you open up a file, you are probably going to issue a read (or write) request quite soon thereafter, and the disk will be in a better position to satisfy that request. This concept is referred to as "cylinder groups," that is, grouping related data in the same bunch of cylinders. Other changes involved decisions on where to put the data in a file, keeping track of the free blocks on the disk, and doing I/O in larger-sized chunks rather than in small disk-sector sized pieces (which are normally 512 bytes). All in all, the developers were quite successful in speeding up the disk and making much larger file systems possible. The BSD file system has become a de facto standard for UNIX systems.

Broadening horizons

It soon became desirable to have UNIX understand other file system types, especially for transportable media, and to be able to access data on remote systems. The combination of these led to a more "virtual" or object-oriented approach to dealing with files and file systems. A VFS, Virtual File System, layer was inserted in the kernel to make referencing other types of file system structures possible. Below this virtual layer you could put routines to do general tasks on different layouts, for example, remote systems, CD-ROMs, and floppy disks.

The same concept was extended to cover files within a file system, since an inode was very UFS-specific. A "virtual inode," or *vnode*, was defined to describe files in general terms. It also contained a pointer to functions that would implement general operations in a specific kind of file system for a certain type of file. When the kernel starts getting down to the level where file system-specific code takes over, the vnode's type-specific functions will be invoked.

VFS functions

The virtual file system layer provides a standard way to deal with file system types without having to know anything about them. There is a *vfs* structure to hold general information of interest, such as the vnode on which this file system is mounted. The blocksize, some flags (like "mounted read-only"), and a list of function pointers round it out. The function list holds pointers to code for each file system type. These correspond to standard operations that need to be done for all file systems:

- *vfs_mount()* — Mount the file system and make it accessible.

- *vfs_unmount()* — Unmount the file system.

- *vfs_root()* — Get the root vnode (the top of the file system)

- *vfs_statvfs()* — Get statistics and information about the file system structure. (This function is known as *vfs_statfs()* in SunOS 4.x.)

- *vfs_sync()* — Do a sync operation: Update the file system.

- *vfs_vget()* — Convert a file ID into a real vnode pointer.

- *vfs_mountroot()* — Mount the root file system at boot time.

- *vfs_swapvp()* — Return a swap vnode pointer.

The definitions of the various VFS structures can be found in the header file **/usr/include/sys/vfs.h** on both SunOS 4.x and Solaris 2 systems.

Any user system calls relating to a file system (such as *mount* or *umount*) will go through the VFS structure. The remainder of the functions are primarily for internal kernel use to traverse the file system tree.

Vnodes

The organization and use of a *vnode* structure is similar to that of a vfs structure. Some general information about the file is not dependent on the type of the file system that holds it. This information includes a reference count, indicating how many structures are referencing the vnode (essentially an "open" count); a file-type code; a pointer to the *vfs* structure for the file system in which this file appears; a pointer to a list of pages that currently contain data from this file. There is also a "vector" of vnode operations, composed of a list of functions to perform certain tasks. The actual routine names will be file-type specific, but they must all implement the same basic operations. This is a fairly long list (documented in the header file **/usr/include/sys/vnode.h**), which includes operations such as:

- *vop_open()* — Perform an *open* system call.

- *vop_getattr()* — Obtain attributes from a file. These attributes include things like owner, size, update time, and permissions.

- *vop_lookup()* — Perform directory search operations.

- *vop_create()* — Create a new file.

- *vop_remove()* — Delete a file.

- *vop_rename()* — Rename a file or directory. This operation may actually change the location of the file in the directory hierarchy.

- *vop_mkdir()* — Create a new directory.

- *vop_fid()* — Build a "file identifier" structure, which uniquely identifies a file inside a particular file system.

- *vop_getpage()* — Read in from the file all the pages that make up a given range of data (pass in an offset and a length).

- *vop_map()* — Perform an *mmap* system call (calls *as_map()* to set up the new mapping).

These operations take care of all the system calls that need to access data specific to a file, and they perform various housekeeping functions, for example, I/O on the file or locating a file in the file system.

General VFS & vnode operations

Some general operations performed with vnodes or the VFS structure are not dependent on file system type, so there are functions to deal with these. Some of these just deal with filenames (paths), such as *lookuppn()* (look up path name), which processes a user-supplied filename, traversing the directories to find the actual desired file. Others handle the *dnlc*, or directory name lookup cache. This cache keeps a list of frequently used pathnames and a pointer to the vnode resulting from this path, making common searches much faster. Rather than actually traversing the entire path and searching all the intermediate directories, the name can be found immediately in the cache. Some of these functions are *dnlc_enter()* and *dnlc_lookup()*.

Other generic functions handle common vnode operations that do not need specific information about the file to do their job. They also implement higher-level checking or validation on system calls that may eventually go through the vnode operations list to finish with type-specific functions. These generic functions include:

- *vn_rele()* — Release a vnode by decrementing the reference count and actually removing it once the count drops to zero.

- *vn_rdwr()* — Perform actual read/write operations.

- *vn_create()* — Build a new vnode.

Many of these routines will eventually need to find out file-specific information or will need to have lower-level functions do some of the work to take care of details that are file system specific, like how the directories are organized and how a new file is actually created.

Let's examine a few of the functions that the UFS-specific code provides.

UNIX File System (UFS)

The UNIX File System (UFS) covers what you might think of as "normal" files on a local disk. The contents of this file must be accessed through the file system, because only the UFS code knows how to locate the blocks on the disk.

There are several sets of UFS functions: those dealing with the virtual file system and its needs, those handling vnode and inode related requests, and those managing the details of the file system organization, keeping track of superblocks, cylinder groups, and free fragments.

VFS operations are fairly obvious; they provide low-level support for the standard file system operations, such as mounting. A *ufs_mount()* function would be the place where the contents of the superblock are checked for validity, to make sure that the user is trying to mount a real file system instead of a swap device.

Vnode operations are a bit more numerous, but still just implement the inode-specific details of system calls and functions on files. The function *ufs_readlink()*, for example, would find and read the value of a UFS-style symbolic link.

The bulk of the UFS code deals with managing the internal structure of the file system on disk. We won't get into much here, since the details of the internal file system structure could fill a book by themselves, but you will find functions to allocate and free inodes, blocks, and file fragments; manage the free blocks and fragments; search, create, and update directories.

- *ufs_dirlook()* — Look for a file name in a directory. (Known as *dirlook()* in SunOS 4.x.)

- *ufs_direnter()* — Create a new directory entry. (Again, *direnter()* in SunOS 4.x.)

- *ufs_dirfixdotdot()* — Set up the appropriate ".." entry in a new directory. (As above, there is no *ufs_* prefix in SunOS 4.x.)

- *ufs_ialloc()* — Allocate an inode in the file system.

- *ufs_freesp()* — Free all storage space associated with the given inode.

Some renaming was done in Solaris 2 to accommodate all the other file system types the kernel might have to deal with, since UFS is certainly not the only one, although it may be one of the most common.

Other file systems

The initial push for redesigning the file system handling code was the introduction of NFS, or the Network File System. Suddenly, files could no longer be accessed directly, since they were not necessarily local and they were not necessarily UNIX files! There is nothing to prevent a completely different system with a unique OS from offering its files for access over the network. This flexibility meant that file system type information or file information had to be divided: into the parts that were general and could be used by any machine; and into the parts that were entirely specific to that file or file system type, on that system, and would have to be handled by the local system itself.

Once the new design was implemented, the set of file system types that could be handled locally was also increased, even to the point of creating "pseudo" file systems that actually didn't have a file system, files, or real devices. Solaris 2 has a greatly expanded repertoire when it comes to handling file system types.

Some of the more common file system or disk formats you will find:

- HSFS — High Sierra (ISO 9660) CD-ROM disks.

- PCFS — PC format (DOS) diskettes.

- lofs — "loop-back" file system. A currently mounted file system or directory can be mounted onto another point in the file system hierarchy, creating essentially two paths to the contents.

- procfs — process file system. In Solaris 2, this file system, normally mounted on **/proc**, contains one "file" entry for each process on the system. Opening one of these files can provide access to information about the process. This information is used by such programs as **ps**, which requires some data from the kernel about the state, size, and time consumption of the given process. procfs is a replacement for the **kvm** libraries, which allowed programs to actually open up kernel data space and read the internal tables directly.

- specfs — Handles special files (devices) directly.

- tmpfs — Uses swap space to hold a temporary variable-sized file system to be used for **/tmp**.

- and, of course, NFS (the original) — Mounts and accesses file systems that are controlled by other machines elsewhere on the network.

Some examples of supporting routines for these other file system types are:

- *hsfs_getattr()* — Get information about a file on a CD.

- *nfstsize()* — Check the network interfaces and return the preferred NFS transfer size.

- *tmp_mount()* — Create and mount a file system in swap.

- *spec_badop()* — Prove the "error" routine for many of the VFS functions applied to devices. For example, how can you issue a *statvfs* system call on a terminal device when there is no file system there?

As you can see, every file system type provides the same general functions to access the data that resides there. Most system calls are processed at various levels: the general level to validate the parameters, then at the vnode level to do file-oriented things, and then at the file or file system-specific level to take care of accessing real data if needed. These are usually well named functions, and can be easily recognized as referring to a specific type of file system.

Hardware Devices and Drivers   23 ≡

Proper handling of various devices attached to a computer system is essential. A machine is useless if it can't communicate with the users, save data in disk files, or output results. A major piece of the kernel is composed of code to talk to and control hardware. This is known as the *device driver* layer in the kernel; it is the "interface layer" between the specific hardware attached to a particular machine and the kernel itself. Generally, an operating system is written to handshake with this driver layer through a standard set of functions, structures, and conventions. We'll take a quick look at the requirements and format of a device driver in both the SunOS 4.x kernels (BSD-based) and the Solaris 2 systems (SVR4-based).

Drivers and device control

A device driver is written to control a very specific piece of hardware. Usually if you change to a different device or install a new one on your system, you will also have to add or update the software that handles it — the driver. If the device comes with a circuit card you plug into the machine (of course, while the power is turned off), you'll most likely be installing software, too. Because every piece of hardware is designed with different chips, organized differently, and has different command sequences to make it do its job, it needs specific driver software written to understand that particular hardware. There are some standardized interfaces, like SCSI, the Small Computer Systems Interface, that will often allow you to plug in a compatible peripheral device and communicate without problems, but even these sometimes require new or special drivers.

There are generally two major parts to a device driver: interpreting user requests passed through the operating system and attending to service demands from the device itself. The first part is concerned with data transmission between the user and the device via the operating system and must conform to whatever conventions have been established by the kernel. The second part, interrupt service, is more concerned with the state of the hardware (recognizing error conditions or unexpected events) and handling them. Generally, interrupt routines are very short and have limited interaction with the main kernel. They are also high priority and may interrupt normal kernel processing, so they have to be careful about what they manipulate.

Once a system call has been issued by a user program, the kernel has some basic steps it goes through. The first actions are validation and verification: Check the request to make sure it's valid; check the various parameters passed in by the user to be certain they are in range, or refer to valid addresses, or contain proper commands. Once this part is done, more specific code is invoked to handle the actual request. If it involves I/O or some other action that requires access to a device, the kernel must invoke the necessary function in the driver. The driver code itself will finish the work, passing a result code or some data back to the kernel, which hands it back to the user.

For example, let's say you want to read from a tape device. The kernel will process the **read** system call in general terms, then call a read function, which makes sure the file descriptor is correct and you have permission to do the operation. It will finally get to the point where it has to access the data, and to do this it has to find the right device and tell it what to do. The driver *read()* routine is called. Normally, for tape drives, the driver will not have the data already available, so it will have to allocate a buffer, and set up and issue a command to the tape drive hardware to initiate a read. This may take some time, and it's not worth waiting around for the device to finish when the system could be doing real work somewhere else. The driver therefore does a *sleep()*, which essentially freezes the current program and the request it was making, saves the whole thing, and allows the system to switch over to another process.

Eventually the tape device finishes the I/O transfer. The buffer is full of data, and the kernel should be notified that the device is ready for the next command. An interrupt is issued, the driver interrupt service code is invoked, and a *wakeup()* is sent to the suspended (sleeping) program. This notifies the kernel that this program can be scheduled to run again. When the kernel switches back to this process, the data is passed out to the user program and the system call returns.

This is the general flow of a system request that uses hardware and indirectly calls the driver functions. We'll take a look at some of the specific routines that may appear in device driver code and what they're used for.

SunOS 4.x drivers

Device drivers in the Solaris 2 kernel are quite a bit different from the older BSD-style 4.x versions. Part of this difference stems from some major changes to the internal structure of the kernel itself. There have also been changes in hardware that make revisions in the driver/kernel interface necessary. But let's look at the structure of the older drivers first.

The 4.x kernel is basically static. You must build a customized kernel that incorporates all the software you anticipate needing and configure it for the expected environment. If any of this changes, you must create a new kernel. If you add new hardware, you will also have to rebuild the system to add the new driver(s), unless you had the foresight to include them earlier. The drivers must be resident in the kernel for the device to function.

You may include drivers for devices you don't need or don't have, if you anticipate adding them or you don't care about the wasted space for the code.

Autoconfiguration

Since there may be drivers for hardware that doesn't exist when the system is booted, the kernel must have a way to identify devices that *are* present. One of the requirements for drivers is that they provide a function the kernel can call to look for the device. This function, called a *probe()* routine, returns a true/false indication. If the device is present and functional, the kernel will print a message indicating that it has located the device and enabled the driver. This procedure is done as a part of the boot sequence and is the cause of all the device identification messages you see on the console.

Device switches

If you want to add a device to the system, you must include the driver in the kernel and tell the kernel how to get to it. You do so through the device switch tables. In the file **conf.c** (in **/usr/kvm/sys/sun**), you will find two arrays of structures, *bdevsw* and *cdevsw*. These structures define the functions provided in the device driver that are available to the kernel. There are two different types of devices, corresponding to the two tables. The bdevsw table is the *block device switch*; it handles things like disk drives, which normally perform I/O transfers in fixed-size pieces and are capable of handling a file system on that device. The cdevsw table is the *character device switch*; it takes care of everything else. Many of the entries are the same, but block devices have some different requirements and usually are more difficult to set up. In general, the entries in the switch tables are driver functions that the kernel can call. They will take care of the specific hardware details for various system calls. You will see an entry in the table identifying driver *open()*, *close()*, *read()*, *write()*, and *ioctl()* functions for every device.

From the point of view of a user, a device is identified by a device file, which is almost always in the **/dev** directory. The long listing of a directory entry for a device file (with the **ls -l** command) contains much of the basic information about the type of device behind the file. The file type field, which is the first character on the line in the 'ls -l' output, will show either **b** or **c** for a "special" (device) file. This indicates whether the device is block- or character-based, in other words, which device switch table will be used to find the driver functions. The numbers you see instead of the file size are known as the device *major* and *minor* numbers. The major number is used as an index into the appropriate switch table (it selects the driver); the minor number is passed to the driver code as a possible logical unit number. Some devices, like tapes, will encode various extra pieces of information in that minor number, like the density, whether or not to rewind afterwards, and the actual unit number of the tape drive.

In the SunOS 4.x kernel, there is a limited ability to create and use loadable device drivers. These are drivers that are not configured into the system at boot time but can be loaded later. They are not often used and are difficult to debug because the symbol tables for the drivers themselves are not loaded with them. About all you can do is identify the fact that you are looking at code in a loaded driver and tell which one it is. Loaded drivers will appear in the data space of the kernel, so if you cannot locate the instruction codes you want to examine in a **vmunix.X** file, try looking for it in the **vmcore.X** file. If it appears there, you can see if it's in a driver by looking at the list of *vddrv* structures (defined in the **/usr/include/sun/vddrv.h** file) pointed to by the kernel variable **vddrv_list**. These "virtual device driver" structures, one per loaded module, will contain information about the driver, such as the start address and size of the code. This will allow you to find out if the instructions you are interested in do appear in the address range that corresponds to code for a particular driver. The name of the module can be found in the *vdlinkage* structure, which is pointed to by the very first word of *vddrv*.

Driver code

The code in a SunOS 4.x device driver can be divided into several sections, dealing with different requirements. The part that deals with user system calls is known as the top half of the driver. These are the functions that are listed in the device switch table and are directly called by the kernel. The bottom half of the driver is the interrupt service code, which is invoked directly by the hardware. Finally, the probe and attach routines are responsible for verifying the existence of the device and setting it up at boot time.

Numerous support functions are available in the kernel for the drivers to call when necessary. These are documented in the *Writing Device Drivers* manual for SunOS 4.x systems. Some of these are:

- *copyin()* and *copyout()* — Move data to and from user space
- *iowait()* — Sleep, waiting for I/O to complete
- *mballoc()* — Allocate Main Bus resources for I/O transfers
- *physio()*, — Lock down user memory in preparation for data transfers
- *splx()* — Set a processor priority level and possibly block out interrupts
- *uiomove()* — Move data around, using *copyin()* and *copyout()*

The 4.x BSD driver structure is complex, but it has been around for a long time and is well understood by many people. However, it is not particularly consistent in many ways, and the Solaris 2 interface definitions establish some needed standards for driver writers.

Solaris 2 drivers

Device drivers in Solaris 2 are all loadable kernel modules. Drivers are no longer configured into the system and are not always resident. Instead, they are loaded only when needed, and perform all the initialization necessary at that time. Some new requirements are imposed on drivers because of this, so the format has changed slightly;

new routines must be written, new structures must be maintained. In addition, the interface between the kernel and all device drivers is more firmly established. There is better documentation, and a more rigorous standard helps drivers to communicate.

The Device Driver Interface/Driver Kernel Interface (DDI/DKI) specification provides a list of the required functions a driver must provide, a definition of structures that both drivers and interface functions use, and a set of internal support routines that drivers can call. Along with this goes the requirement that device drivers use *only* those documented routines and structures: Anything else is subject to change without notice.

There are specific parts to a driver in Solaris 2, similar to those in the SunOS 4.x kernel. One section must deal with various aspects of loading and unloading modules in the kernel. One part handles initialization of the device: *probe* and *attach* are still present, and an additional routine, called the *identify* function, is needed for newer, smarter hardware known as "self-identifying devices." The functions that deal with system calls are known as the user level, and the interrupt level contains service routines as before.

Various structures define the available driver functions. The user-level functions are contained in a *cb_ops* structure (similar in concept to the *cdevsw/bdevsw* setup for SunOS 4.x kernels). A *dev_ops* structure holds the addresses of the configuration functions, along with a pointer to *cb_ops*. A *modldrv* structure holds loadable driver information with a pointer to *dev_ops*, and a *modlinkage* structure tops everything off by pointing to the *modldrv* information. During initialization and loading, a call to a function *mod_install()* will pass the head of this chain of structures to the system, which will allow it to find out all the necessary information to hook the driver into the kernel.

Driver functions

A naming convention established early on in the life of the UNIX operating system helps keep the names of driver functions consistent. A short driver identification (it used to be only two characters long, but that has expanded over time) is attached to the basic name of the function. Thus we have routines like:

- *stopen()* — Handles an open request on a SCSI tape drive
- *sdread()* — Performs a SCSI disk read
- *idwrite()* — Writes to IPI disks
- *ptcioctl()* — Interprets ioctl requests on pseudo-terminals
- *cg6_poll()* — Checks the CG-6 frame buffer
- *fdstrategy()* — Sets up floppy disk I/O requests
- *zsintr()* — Responds to serial character interrupt requests

Each driver has some standard routines which it must provide, and these are easily recognizable in stack traces. They serve the following functions, among others.

- *open()* — For a user open request
- *close()* — Called on the last user close request
- *read()* — Handles a read system call
- *write()* — Processes a write system call
- *strategy()* — Used for disk requests (block devices only)
- *ioctl()* — Sends special requests or commands to the driver
- *mmap()* — For devices capable of being mapped into memory
- *probe()* — Determines whether the device is present
- *attach()* — Called after probe returns true, finishes setting up the device
- *intr()* — Handles interrupt requests

All these names will appear in most drivers for both SunOS 4.x and Solaris 2 systems. The actual function name you see in a stack traceback will, of course, be prefaced with the name of the device, such as *sdopen()* for an open function in the **sd** (SCSI disk) driver code.

Identifying driver functions involved in a panic or hang situation may help to isolate the problem. If a user-level (or top half) function is involved, the driver may be invoking kernel support routines with bad parameters or setting up data incorrectly for these functions to use. An interrupt service routine appearing in the traceback could indicate problems with the device hardware itself, data structures that were not correctly set up for an interrupt to reference, or possibly an error in locking (a race condition). Drivers are very complex, and it's easy to miss a small requirement that has drastic implications later on. While it's certainly not always true that driver code in a traceback automatically indicates a driver problem, it may be worth checking to see if the problem only occurs when the device is in use.

Real hardware

Let's cover a few hardware terms you may see batted around and make sure that you have a basic understanding of what they mean.

- MMU
  The Memory Management Unit is the hardware piece that controls mapping a virtual address into a real physical memory address. If the mapping fails, the MMU will signal the CPU with an interrupt (a page fault) and let the kernel figure out what to do about it. The MMU is set up by the kernel at boot time, and even the kernel code itself uses the MMU to perform memory accesses. The mappings are done in terms of pages, which are short chunks of memory of a fixed size, usually 4 kilobytes (older Sun-4 systems use 8-kilobyte pages). These mappings use Page Table Entries (PTEs) to describe allowable actions and the actual physical page to be used.

You will not see a device driver specifically for an MMU. The code to support this hardware is in the virtual memory subsystem. In most Sun systems, the drivers will use virtual addresses to set up and perform input and output operations. Device accesses and I/O transfers will go through the MMU and thus use virtual rather than physical addresses.

- Cache
As a means of speeding up memory accesses, frequently used bits of memory are often *cached* (copied into a local, high-speed storage area). If the data is present in the cache, it will be fetched from there immediately without even touching memory. There are complex methods to keep cache contents up-to-date and consistent with real physical memory contents. There may be some requirements for a driver to ensure that caching is done properly, since I/O (which references memory) may require the cache to be flushed out or reloaded.

- SCSI (Small Computer Systems Interface)
SCSI is a type of I/O bus used for access to multiple devices. It's a fairly well defined interface specification, originally developed for small microcomputer systems (hence the name). It allows for one main CPU (an *initiator*) and seven devices, or controllers, to be present.

- ESP (Enhanced SCSI Processor)
The ESP, known as the host adaptor, is the interface between the SCSI bus and the main I/O bus (SBus) on a SPARC machine. It issues SCSI requests, receives responses, and sets up data transfers between the devices and memory.

- SCSA (Sun Common SCSI Architecture)
The SCSA is not really hardware, but it's related. SCSA is a standard to define how a device driver, such as a SCSI tape driver, should communicate with the host adaptor. Since host adaptors may vary on different systems, this standard provides a way for drivers to be more hardware-independent in this area (they need only be written for a device, not for the device plus the host adaptor!).

- SBus
The SBus is the I/O bus (data path) for SPARCstations and later Sun systems. Older systems used the VMEbus for I/O, but a requirement for faster throughput and higher-speed devices led to the development of a newer bus. The ESP, graphics displays, and the Ethernet controller are connected to the SBus. Most SBus devices are known as "self-identifying" because the actual hardware contains a read-only memory with code to identify the device on that circuit card to the kernel.

- MBus
The MBus is the internal data path between one or more processors and memory or devices. It is the main machine bus for the sun4m architecture family.

- XDBus
  With the development of yet faster processors and multiprocessor systems, the MBus was found to be too limited and slow. A newer internal bus was developed for the larger server systems (sun4d family).

- Ethernet
  One of the original network implementations, Ethernet is a simple and popular method of connecting machines. Since it just needs a cable, it's flexible and easy to install. Speed and distance limitations restrict its applications, but it is still very useful for Local Area Network (LAN) setups. Messages can be sent directly to a specific machine on the wire or as a broadcast, received by everything on the net.

- PROM (Programmable Read-Only Memory)
  Every Sun system has a PROM that performs power-on testing, identifies a console, and either interacts with a user or automatically boots up a specific system from a specific device. There are two types of PROMs on Sun systems. The older one is fairly primitive but does have a set of commands available for basic hardware debugging. The newer version, known as the OpenBoot PROM, actually contains a FORTH interpreter along with a sophisticated command language.

  Some examples of useful commands can be found in Chapter 27, "Watchdog Resets," since they are the only thing available for debugging this particular condition.

- DMA (Direct Memory Access)
  DMA is used by devices to perform I/O without directly involving the CPU. Older or slower input and output is often done by having the processor communicate directly with the device for each word or character transferred. This involves a great deal of overhead, which severely limits the speed of an I/O operation.

  An alternate approach is to have the device itself perform the transfer directly to or from the main memory of the machine, signaling the CPU when it's finished. This procedure, known as DMA, is used by most high-speed devices (disk, tape, and network interfaces); the alternate method is called "polled I/O" because the device must be polled (queried) for each data element. The CPU, when setting up a DMA transfer, must provide the device with a starting address in memory (a buffer location), a transfer size (byte count), and then issue a command to start. It will be interrupted by the device when the transfer is completed or when something unexpected happens (like an I/O error).

  Sun systems generally use DVMA, or Direct Virtual Memory Access. The addresses used by the device for memory accesses are all *virtual* addresses, and all data transfers go through an MMU.

Drivers and crashes

In general, although debugging drivers is supposedly the responsibility of the driver writer, bugs can sneak past even the most dedicated tester. Unless you wrote the code yourself or have access to the author, most of your debugging will be limited to trying to verify that the driver is causing the problem. There are some basic steps you can perform that will help.

- Monitor the use of the device, if possible, and see if crashes can be associated with initial access or heavy use of the driver.

- Look for console messages that may identify hardware problems. Many drivers will log error conditions.

- See if the driver has options you can set, either via the **/etc/system** file or by using **adb** to modify the data in the running kernel, that will print debugging information.

- In Solaris 2, try using the **/etc/system** file to set the high-order bit in the variable *moddebug*. Setting the bit will instruct the system to print a message on the console every time a kernel module is loaded or unloaded.

- Examine all the processes on the system to see if any of them are using the suspect device. The stack tracebacks for each process on SunOS 4.x (with the **traceall** macro) or thread on Solaris 2 (with the **threadlist** macro) might allow you to identify the fact that a device is actively in use, even though the driver functions do not actually appear in the stack trace for the process that caused the panic.

Especially when working with new drivers, getting several core dumps may be a necessity. Having more than one crash to look at will help to identify common features or characteristics. And last but not least, since drivers deal so closely with hardware, what appears to be a driver problem may just be an indication that the device itself is having trouble. Cabling, line termination, and even power supply problems can have drastic and very misleading effects.

Interprocess Communication 24 ≡

Interprocess communication, also known as IPC, covers the facilities offered by the operating system to allow processes to share information. In general, a process can access only its own address space, so the only way data can be shared is if that data can be found in a common area. The simplest answer is to put the data into a file, but this is slow, imposes lots of overhead (especially if the data won't be needed again), and presents some problems with synchronization and locking. The real answer is to make the kernel provide some way to ship data back and forth without involving physical I/O.

The first attempt used *pipes*. These were implemented as short (4K) kernel buffers that would allow one process to write data in and another process to pull data out. Normal read and write operations were used, but the data never left the kernel. The main problems with this method were a limited transfer rate (small buffers) and the fact that the pipe had to be set up by a common parent process. You couldn't set up a pipe to talk to an already running daemon, for example.

Several extensions appeared. AT&T created named pipes (fifos), with an entry in the file system, which allowed unrelated processes to communicate. The BSD kernel used the network communications facilities (sockets) to set up data paths between processes on the same machine with UNIX domain sockets, which also used an entry in the file system.

More choices became available when message queues, semaphores, and shared memory facilities were added to the kernel. These were applicable to processes on the same machine and could not be used for network applications. Sockets continue to be a primary method for data transfer between processes on different machines, although in Solaris 2 these became library functions; the underlying implementation now uses the Transport Level Interface (TLI) and Streams.

We'll concentrate here on the SVR4 IPC facilities that have been in SunOS kernels since before release 4.0: *messages*, *semaphores*, and *shared memory*.

To use each of these different facilities, a user process must create a "pseudo-file," that is, something with a name or key to identify it, an owner, access permissions, sizes, and so forth, although the pseudo-file never makes it out to the file system. This object is created by a system call that defines some kernel tables and is "opened" by another system call when a process wants to use it. Messages allow short chunks of data to be passed to one or more mailboxes, semaphores provide a set of kernel-maintained counters, and shared memory provides some common pages that can be mapped in to each process's address space. Generally, shared memory is coupled with another type of IPC to coordinate updates to this common memory.

Some tuning is usually required if any user wants to make extensive use of these. The kernel includes basic IPC capabilities but they are limited in scope. The SunOS 4.x GENERIC configuration file includes these as options. If the system calls fail mysteriously, it is advisable as a first step to make sure that the options were not commented out or deleted in the kernel you are running.

Tunable parameters are defined (or at least listed) in the manuals. A description of the appropriate variables or values and their meanings is contained in each section below for the different IPC types. While these rarely appear in system panics, they can affect the behavior of user programs and the performance of the system. We've included a discussion of the kernel structures and variables to help analyze these problems.

Semaphores

Semaphores are often considered (and used) as an on-off flag. They are actually implemented as short counters that contain positive values. Think of them as if each contained a count of the number of "things" available for use. User programs can use them to control common resources (files or shared memory areas) not already controlled by the kernel.

Semaphores are allocated in sets. Each set has one ID number (*semid*) associated with it. A user program, when it wants a semaphore, must "open" a previously created set. Many semaphores can be in one set, subject to some tuning parameters. The semaphore number itself (the index into the set) is an unsigned short, which will allow over 65,000 semaphores to be associated with one ID. Each semaphore is kept as an unsigned short value. Generally you "request items" from a semaphore by decrementing it, and you release/restore those items by incrementing. A request will cause the process to be blocked if the value in the semaphore is not big enough. The request size can be added to a semaphore "undo" value when a request succeeds. This undo number is added to the semaphore value if the process exits and the semaphores are released, which prevents a semaphore from keeping a count low after the requestor is long gone.

Tunable parameters for semaphores

For Solaris 2, some parameters are described in Appendix A of the manual *Administering Security, Performance, and Accounting*. This appendix lists the variables that can be adjusted using the **/etc/system** file. These values are stored into the *seminfo* structure and used to initialize the semaphore tables when the **semsys** kernel module is first loaded. (These tables and maps will not be deallocated when the module is unloaded.)

The variables are not really well defined in the manual, so we'll go over them here.

- *seminfo_semmap* — Defines the size of the free space map for the actual semaphore structures, which come from a common pool. This map (see the **map.h** header file in **/usr/include/sys** for a description of resource maps) identifies contiguous blocks of free semaphore structures in the pool, so the maximum size you really need is half the total number of semaphores in the system (to handle the worst case: every other structure in the pool is in use).

- *seminfo_semmni* — Defines the number of semaphore identifiers that can exist in the system. This variable controls the total number of sets available or the maximum number of semaphore groups that can be declared simultaneously.

- *seminfo_semmns* — Is the total number of semaphores in the system (the size of the pool of semaphore structures).

- *seminfo_semmnu* — Declares the total number of *undo* structures in the kernel. Each structure will be associated with one semaphore that has been updated by a process (or thread) using the *sem_undo* flag with that operation.

- *seminfo_semmsl* — Gives the maximum number of semaphores per ID, or the set size. In the SunOS 4.x kernel, *seminfo_semmsl* is given as a short, allowing up to 32,767 semaphores in one set. In Solaris 2, this has been changed to an unsigned short. It's still probably best to keep *seminfo_semmsl* to a reasonable value.

- *seminfo_semopm* — Defines the maximum number of simultaneous operations that can be performed on a set of semaphores (i.e., the total number of semaphores you can update or check in one *semop* system call.)

- *seminfo_semume* — Is the maximum number of *undo* entries per process. A table of undo entries is constructed for each process that wants to perform undo operations.

- *seminfo_semusz* — Is the size in bytes of the *sem_undo* structure. This is listed as a tunable parameter but is rather pointless to change. This variable is set by default to the size of the undo entry itself times the number of entries per process (*seminfo_semume*) added to the basic size of the *sem_undo* structure.

- *seminfo_semvmx* — Set by default to 32767. This is the maximum semaphore value. Since this is an unsigned short value, it could conceivably be set as high as 65535.

- *seminfo_semaem* — Is the maximum value allowed for the *undo* structure (adjust-on-exit number). Any attempt to have a semaphore operation modify this to a value larger than 16384 will result in an error.

Every structure in the kernel that is allocated for semaphores is based on these values. An idea of the various sizes of these structures can be obtained from the **sem.h** header file. Most of the structures are not very large.

For a SunOS 4.x system, there are fewer tunables, but they control basically the same parameters.

The tunables are documented in the *System and Network Administration* manual under "Advanced Administration Topics, Tuning IPC System Parameters." These values are set in the kernel configuration file with options statements, in the form

```
options NAME=value
```

These values are:

- *SEMMNI* — Maximum number of sets
- *SEMMNS* — Total number of semaphores in the system
- *SEMUME* — Maximum number of undo entries per process with non-zero values
- *SEMMNU* — Maximum number of processes that can have undo's

The other existing parameters are considered to be untunable and are fixed constants.

Internal variables

The **sem.h** include file also defines some global variables that enable you to find these structures in the kernel.

- *struct semid_ds *sema* — Pointer to the pool of semaphore id structures, which contain the pointer to the semaphores themselves.
- *struct sem *sem* — Address of the semaphore pool.
- *struct map *semmap* — Map pointer, indicating the semaphore allocation map.
- *struct sem_undo **sem_undo* — Pointer to a list of per process undo tables.
- *int *semu* — The actual undo structure pool. (It's not really a pointer to an integer.)
- *struct seminfo seminfo* — Contains the tunable information.
- *struct sem_undo *semunp* — Is declared only in the Solaris 2 header file as a pointer to the head of an undo chain. This variable and the next both exist in SunOS 4.x.
- *struct sem_undo *semfup* — Pointer to the undo free chain.

Internal structures

The semaphore structures are all defined in the **sem.h** include file. You have one *semid_ds* structure per set, one *sem* structure per semaphore, and one *sem_undo* structure for every process that is using a backout, or *semadj*, value. This *sem_undo* structure contains an array of *undo* structures, each of which contains a value for adjust-on-exit, a semaphore ID to define the set it applies to, and a semaphore number to identify the individual semaphore in that set.

Each *sem_undo* structure contains a fixed-length array of *undo* entries, even though not all of them may be used.

Functions

The following functions appear in both SunOS 4.x and Solaris 2 to handle various semaphore operations, including the system calls, initialization, and cleanup.

- *seminit()* — Takes no parameters and returns nothing. It is responsible for semaphore table initialization, map setup, and space reservations. In Solaris 2, this function takes the tunable parameters and sets the *seminfo* structure accordingly.

- *semexit()* — Cleans up and handles undo operations when a process exits.

- *semsys()* — Is the system call entry point. It handles initial processing of the user arguments. In SunOS 4.x, these arguments are obtained from the *user* structure. In Solaris 2, a pointer to a "user argument structure" is passed in as a parameter, along with a location for the return value. In SunOS 4.x, the return value is placed, again, in the *user* structure.

- *semctl()*, *semget()*, and *semop()* — Performs the actual processing for the specific system calls. In SunOS 4.x, they take no parameters. In Solaris, they receive the user argument and return value pointers.

- *semaoe()* — Updates the adjust-on-exit value in an *undo* entry.

- *semunrm()* — Clears out undo entries that belong to semaphores being removed or globally reset.

- *semundo()* — Backs out any semaphore operations that have been done when an error is detected.

- *semconv()* — Converts a user-supplied *semid* into a pointer to the actual semaphore header.

Messages

The IPC messages facility allows users to define a message queue ID number (essentially a mailbox) that can be used to hold messages for another process. Each message may have an associated type, which makes finding special (high-priority) mail easier. The queues themselves are configurable and probably need to be expanded if any major use is going to be made of them.

Tunable parameters for messages

Tunable parameters in Solaris 2 are listed in Appendix A of *Administering Security, Performance, and Accounting*. SunOS 4.x discusses them in the *System and Network Administration Manual* in the chapter "Advanced Administration Topics." They are somewhat different.

For Solaris 2, the following variables are defined as tunable.

- *msgmap* — Defines the number of entries in the free space map for messages. This map keeps track of free message segments.

- *msgmax* — Is a maximum byte count for an individual message.

- *msgmnb* — Keeps a queue from growing too large. This variable is the maximum byte count for all messages on that queue.

- *msgmni* — Defines the total number of message queues allowed. This variable allocates the *msqid_ds* data structures (queue headers).

- *msgssz* — Defines the message segment size. Messages are built of small segments (which should be an even multiple of the system word size). The total memory pool allocated to messages is derived from the total segment allowance multiplied by the size of each segment. A message will be built from the needed number of contiguous segments, allocated from the message map. The pointer to the message text will be derived from the starting segment number.

- *msgtq*— Is a maximum for the number of messages that may be outstanding. This variable defines the number of *msg* header structures that are allocated.

- *msgseg* — Defines the total number of message segments to allocate. This variable is a short and must be kept less than 32768 to avoid sign extension problems.

For SunOS 4.x kernels, some defined values can be overridden by options specified in the configuration file. Those options are:

- *MSGPOOL* — Defines the total amount of space available for messages. This will automatically be divided up into 8-byte segments. (In Solaris 2, this number is derived from the message segment quantity and size.)

- *MSGMNB* — Is the maximum number of bytes allowed on any one queue.

- *MSGMNI* — Is the total number of message queues (*msgid* instances).

- *MSGTQL* — Defines the total number of message headers (the maximum number of messages that can be waiting on all the message queues).

- *MSGMAX* — Is listed as "assumed not to require tuning." It is defined by default as the total number of bytes available for messages. Thus, it is possible to have one message use up the entire memory pool. It may be worth restricting *MSGMAX* if user programs have the potential to write massive missives.

Message tuning for both SunOS 4.x and Solaris 2 must be based on the number of queues desired, the type of messages being sent (small ones or large ones), and the expected number of them.

Internal variables

Messages are implemented in essentially the same way in Solaris 2 and in SunOS 4.x. The internal variables, structures, and routines are essentially the same.

Variables of interest are:

- *msg* — Points to the space available for messages. This is the "pool" of segments.

- *msgmap* — Defines the list of free space in terms of individual segments.

- *msgh* — Points to the start of the pool of message headers (*msg* structures).

- *msgfp* — Points to a list of individual message headers, which are linked together. This is a free list of unused *msg* structures.

- *msgque* — Points to the list of queue headers, which contain pointers to the beginning and end of the individual queues.

Internal structures

The important internal structures are defined in **/usr/include/sys/msg.h** for both Solaris 2 and SunOS 4.x systems. These include the *msgid_ds* data structure, which is the queue head, the *msg* structure, which identifies specific message parameters, including type and length, and the *msginfo* structure, which contains the message system parameters.

Functions

The handling of messages follows closely the semaphore routines, but messages are significantly simpler to deal with.

- *msginit()* — Performs initialization, memory allocation (in Solaris 2), and sets up the map information.

- *msgconv()* — Converts a message ID from a user into a pointer to a queue header (*msg_ds*) structure.

- *msgsys()* — Is the front end to the system calls.

- *msgctl()*, *msgget()*, *msgrcv()*, and *msgsnd()* — Performs the actual system calls.

- *msgfree()* — Takes a message that has been received and frees up the segments and the message header.

Shared memory

Surprisingly enough, shared memory is exactly what it sounds like — common memory shared between processes. This is, however, special memory that is allocated deliberately for this purpose; a chunk of swap space (so called "anonymous memory") is reserved and is **mmap**'ed in to whatever process requests this shared memory. As with semaphores and messages, a structure defines the ownership and permissions associated with this particular area. When a shared memory area is mapped in, the pages are mapped directly into the process address space. If another process maps that same shared area in as well, the pages are double-mapped: there is exactly one copy of the data, and anybody that touches it will have an immediate effect on everybody else's view of that data.

Tunable parameters for shared memory

Very few parameters are actually available, because little data is kept in the kernel other than the description of the memory area and some bookkeeping information. The tunable parameters are simply there to keep a user process from running wild and chewing up the entire system swap space.

For both versions of the kernel, the parameters perform basically the same functions. For Solaris 2:

- *shmmax* — Defines the maximum shared memory segment size, in bytes. The documentation indicates that this is set to 128 kilobytes, but in reality the default is 1 megabyte.

- *shmmin* — Indicates the minimum shared memory segment size. The default is 1, which is about as small as you can get.

- *shmmni* — Specifies the maximum number of shared memory identifiers. This parameter defines the size of the pool of *shmid_ds* structures available to describe shared memory segments.

- *shmseg* — Puts an upper limit on the number of attached shared memory segments per process. The default is 6. This number is checked only when a process attempts to attach another one. A current counter is kept in the *user* structure.

For SunOS 4.x, there are even fewer tunable parameters.

- *SHMSIZE* — Defines the maximum segment size (in kilobytes), 1 megabyte by default.
- *SHMMNI* — Indicates the total number of shared memory description structures in the kernel.
- *SHMMIN* — Is defined as 1, assumed not to require any tuning.
- *SHMMAX* (the size in bytes) — Is defined from *SHMSIZE* (the size in kilobytes).

There is no maximum number of segments per process in SunOS 4.x.

Internal variables

Since shared memory is considerably simpler to manage than some of the other IPC facilities, very few variables are of interest: *shminfo* is the structure that contains the tunable parameter values, and *shmem* points to the pool of descriptor structures.

Internal structures

The *shmid_ds* structure, defined in the **shm.h** header file, contains all the information about the shared memory area. It includes a pointer to the *anon_map* structure, which tells the system how to actually locate the swap space dedicated to the particular shared memory chunk.

Functions

The internal functions differ slightly between the two releases because the SunOS 4.x virtual memory system is slightly less sophisticated than that in Solaris 2 and more careful checking needs to be done in some places. The Solaris 2 version includes more accounting and some differences in the deletion of a shared memory segment. In addition, for compatibility, SunOS 4.x would allow a request with an address of zero under some circumstances to mean literally a mapping address into the first page, at location 0, rather than indicating that the system could put the page where it liked. This "feature" does not appear in Solaris 2.

The SunOS 4.x routines are:

- *shmat()* — Handles attach operations. *shmat()* immediately calls *kshmat()*.
- *kshmat()* — Performs the real work.
- *shmconv()* — Converts the *shmid* value into a pointer to the descriptive structure.
- *shmctl()* — Handles the control system call. It promptly calls *kshmctl()*.
- *kshmctl()* — Handles control functions from the *shmctl* system call.

- *shmdt()* — Handles detaches by calling the internal version, *kshmdt()*.
- *kshmdt()* — Performs detach operations.
- *shmget()* — Is another front end to the real function: *kshmget()*.
- *kshmget()* — Performs the shmget system call to allocate new shared memory segments.
- *shmsys()* — Is the front end to all the shared memory system calls: *shmat()*, *shmdt()*, *shmget()*, and *shmctl()*.
- *shm_vmlookup()* — Is an internal function to check for possibly conflicting virtual memory segments (to avoid hooking up the wrong one).

In Solaris 2, we have the following internal functions.

- *shminit()* — Performs the memory allocation request for the pool of *shm_ds* structures.
- *shmconv()* — Performs conversion of an ID number into a pointer to a header.
- *shmat()* — Attaches a segment to a process.
- *shmctl()* — Handles *shmctl()* system call functions.
- *shmdt()* — Detaches a segment from a process address space.
- *kshmdt()* — Is a common routine to do detaches. This can be performed with a detach call or by exiting.
- *shmget()* — Handles the system call to create a segment or find an existing one.
- *shmsys()* — Is the front-end checker for all the system calls.
- *sa_add()* — Adds this record to the *segacct* list, which is kept in the *proc* structure. This is a linked list of *segacct* structures.
- *sa_del()* — Deletes this record from the *segacct* list.
- *sa_find()* — Searches the list of accounting structures and finds the one that corresponds to this address.
- *shmfork()* — Duplicates the parent's segacct records in the child. The new process has access to the same segments that the parent has.
- *shmexit()* — Detaches all shared memory segments from a process doing an exit.
- *shm_rm_amp()* — Removes all references to this anonymous memory. This means all processes have detached it and an IPC_RMID request has been issued.

One of the allowed control functions is to lock the pages in memory. The following functions deal with locking and unlocking the segment.

- *lock_again()* — Pages should be in memory, so just lock them down.

- *check_locked()* — Checks to see if this segment is already locked.

- *shmem_lock()* — Attaches the shared memory segment to the process address space and locks the pages.

- *shmem_unlock()* — Unlocks this shared memory segment.

Common functions

A couple of common functions are used in all routines. They are defined in the **ipc.h** header file.

- *ipcaccess()* — Checks access permissions for all types of ipc requests. (The SunOS 4.x version uses the current *user* structure to identify the user and group information).

- *ipcget()* — Looks for a matching key and passes back a pointer to the appropriate entry. A structure will be allocated if requested (by the flags) and the key does not exist. The function returns an error status. In Solaris 2, the error code is returned or a zero for success. In SunOS 4.x, a pointer to an *ipc_perm* structure is returned on success, and a zero (null pointer) is returned on error, with the appropriate error code set in the *user* struct.

For each of these facilities, a header structure is maintained for each item allocated. This identifies the allowed operations with a permissions structure and provides parameters indicating the size, number of semaphores, or pending messages. These structures are all allocated from a pool, an array of structures whose size is determined by the tunable parameters. The identifier value returned to the user is used to produce an index into this array by taking this ID modulo the number of structures. This allows you to identify the appropriate header structure, given the ID number. This is distinct from the *key*, which contains a unique identifying code to be used by a process or group of processes to keep their data straight. This value is passed in when creating or locating some IPC facility; the ID value is like a file descriptor, which the user program uses to find the appropriate structures quickly.

Why all this?

The primary purpose of this chapter was to provide information on how Interprocess Communication works. IPC doesn't often appear in core dumps, but when it does, nobody seems to have a clear understanding of how things should look. The information in this chapter should help you to recognize the functions, identify variables, and verify the contents. Remember, analyzing crashes is usually devoted to identifying things that are wrong. To do that, you need to know what's right, what is legal, and the interactions and relationships between the pieces.

STREAMS 25 ≣

The STREAMS facility replaces the old BSD serial character I/O mechanism. The replacement was done to clean up some of the procedures in order to make them more efficient, portable, and extensible. It was first introduced in SunOS version 4.0. The Solaris 2 version of STREAMS is not much different from the SunOS 4.x implementation; some changes were made to support multithreading, but the basic internal structure remains unchanged.

The STREAMS specification defines a set of system calls, kernel functions, and interface requirements to handle general serial character I/O. It can support terminals (ttys), pipes, and a lot of network protocols. The kernel functions that perform the work are divided up into loadable modules, all of which deal with the same basic method of passing data back and forth (message blocks, or *mblks*, placed in linked lists called *queues*).

STREAMS structure

An individual Stream is composed of various pieces:

- Stream head, which is the piece responsible for dealing with user requests via system calls. The Stream head supplies users with data from message blocks to satisfy their read requests and turns user writes into messages that are passed on down the Stream.

- Device driver, which talks to the actual hardware and places/grabs data from queues. Some Streams talk to "pseudo-device" drivers, which just emulate the action of hardware (the pseudo-terminal driver, for instance).

- Individual STREAMS modules, which filter and manipulate the data as it passes through the Stream.

The advantage of this approach is that the modules are essentially completely independent. You can arrange a Stream to do whatever kind of data processing you want by putting the appropriate modules into the Stream in the right order. There is a default set (for tty Streams), but user-level *ioctl()* calls can push any desired modules onto any Streams they own.

Here is a simple diagram of a Stream.

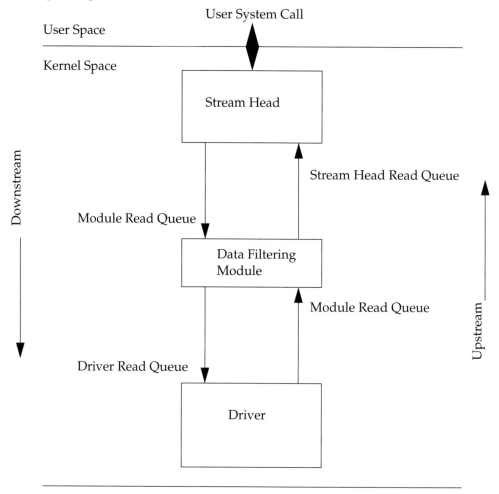

Figure 25-1 *Stream diagram*

User-level code will create the Stream initially by opening a STREAMS device. The user program can control and change the modules that are placed on the Stream as well as their order. The user program uses normal system calls to do this: *ioctl()*, *write()*, *open()*, *close()*, *read()*.

Note that all the pieces of a Stream live in kernel space: the driver, the Stream head, the queues, and the modules are all kernel text or data.

The "head" of the Stream is the connection to user space. Data coming from a user process and going to the driver (and probably eventually to a real device) is noted as coming downstream. The opposite direction is called, strangely enough, upstream.

Modules, drivers, and Stream heads have a *queue* for data going from one to the other in each direction. In other words, a queue connects modules (and the driver at one end, and the Stream head at the other). In between any two of these elements is a structure to handle the data being passed from one to the next one in the sequence. Each queue is essentially treated as a read "list" for the appropriate piece, and moving data from one Stream element to another involves putting data (messages) onto the read queue of the appropriate element. Thus, every module will have two queues associated with it: one for data going downstream, which is to be read and processed by this module; and another for data going upstream, which also must be handled. A module will also be able to pass data on to the next module's read queue once any filtering operation is done.

Data structures

Streams are often described as linked lists of data structures. Since all message passing is done the same way, regardless of what a module might do to the data internally, we can ignore the modules themselves for the moment and view individual Streams as a set of queues with related structures hanging off the sides.

Queues are always allocated in pairs: one for the upstream side and one for downstream. The structures for each side are as follows:

- *queue* structure — Keeps track of the data. This contains pointers to a *qband* and a *qinit* structure.

- *qband* structure — Identifies priority bands (also called out-of-band data)

- *qinit* structure — Identifies the processing procedures for the module. This points to *module_infr* and *module_stat* structures.

- *module_info* structure — Holds initial values and setup.

- *module_stat* structure — Contains statistics.

The *queue* structure also has:

- a pointer to the first message on the queue, if any
- a pointer to the last message on the queue

Each *queue* structure contains a pointer to the next queue in the chain and can identify its paired queue (same module, going in the opposite direction) with a macro.

Here is an illustration of the data structures.

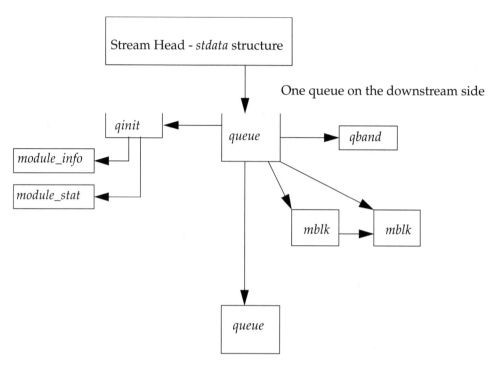

Figure 25-2 Queue data structures

When looking at a running kernel or a crash, identifying and locating active streams is slightly different from SunOS 4.x to Solaris 2.

- In SunOS 4.x, the kernel variable *allstream* points to a linked list of active *stdata* structures, each of which identifies a stream head.

- In Solaris 2, *stdata* structures no longer contain links. An encompassing structure (*shinfo*, for stream head info) contains the *stdata* structure plus a couple of links, forward and back. A pointer to the start of a linked list of *shinfo* structures is contained as the first element of the global *Strinfo* array.

   The header file **strsubr.h** in **/usr/include/sys** includes a definition of the *strinfo* structure. The *Strinfo* array contains these structures. The first element is the one of interest, but the others may be relevant if you're searching through Streams. The second, for example, is a list of all the *queue* structures.

Pipes

In early versions of UNIX, pipes are implemented as kernel buffers and are basically unidirectional: You can have only one reader and one writer on a pipe. BSD UNIX changed this to use sockets (network connectors). In SunOS 4.x, pipes are in fact implemented internally as UNIX domain socket connections.

In Solaris 2, pipes are implemented by using STREAMS, so they are also true bidirectional data paths. They look like two Stream heads linked together, with no device driver or modules to get in the way. Data that is written to a pipe will be turned into a Streams message and sent off to the queue for the other end. The following figure illustrates the concept.

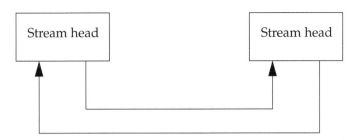

Figure 25-3 Pipe implementation

A user still gets two file descriptors from a *pipe(2)* system call. A write to the first descriptor delivers data that can be read from the second descriptor at the other end of the pipe, and vice versa — with the distinction that the data paths are separated. A process cannot read data that it has written, as could be done with old UNIX pipes.

Since a pipe is just like any other Stream, it can have modules pushed on it. There is, however, a concept of a "midpoint" in pipes, so a module must be popped off the same end from which it was pushed. There are also some tricky semantics regarding data flow (specifically with regard to flushing data from the stream). The *STREAMS Programmer's Guide* has more information if you want to play with these.

Basic functions

Each STREAMS module, driver, or Stream head uses a couple of standard functions to process and move data. The modules and drivers must provide them (they are a part of the module or driver code), but they are standardized and follow some specific rules. Each module has a local *put()* procedure associated with it for each direction, which controls putting data (message blocks) on the appropriate input queue for this module. In other words, each module must provide a function to receive incoming data and stash it somewhere, usually on its own queue. You will find a read-side put procedure to place data on the upstream queue, and a write-side put procedure to put data on the downstream queue. One of these functions will be called (indirectly) by some other kernel piece that has data it wishes to pass to this particular module. If little or no processing is to be done, the put procedure may actually use a kernel function called *putnext()* to call the put procedure for the *next* module rather than stacking data up in its own queue. Thus, a put may call the next put in the next queue, which calls the next, and so on until either the end of the Stream is reached or something stops the progression of data. This could be either a need to do some extended processing or the fact that the next queue is full.

If the data cannot be passed directly on, for whatever reason, the *put()* procedure will have to place the message in the queue associated with its module and cause a service procedure to be scheduled. This service procedure will do whatever processing is necessary and will call the *put()* procedure for the next queue when it is done. In Solaris 2, a special kernel thread for each CPU in the system runs all the service procedures. In SunOS 4.x, procedures are run periodically: checks are made before returning to user mode to see if any service procedures are ready to be run. Service procedures might be run just before a user process resumes execution or as a part of clock-tick processing.

Flow control can be implemented if a service procedure exists for a module: a put (or a service procedure that wants to pass data onwards) will use a routine called *canputnext()* to see if the next queue in the stream has room, that is, if a put will work. If not, the data is stuffed back in the queue for the original module and the procedure goes away, to try again later. When the next (full) queue empties out enough to receive more data, the service procedure of the preceding queue will automatically be scheduled to run, and this time the put call should work.

Put procedures can be called from interrupt level (by a driver), by writes from a Stream head, or by service procedures. This means put procedures, as well as service procedures, cannot make any assumptions about the context in which they are run (especially about working with the *user* structure). They also cannot block or sleep.

Support functions

The STREAMS functions provided by the kernel are documented in the man pages, section 9F, "DDI/DKI Functions." The DDI/DKI is the set of supported routines for use by driver or module writers. We'll point out a few you might see:

- *allocb()* — Allocates buffers. This routine returns a pointer to a linked message block and data block pair, since one must be used with the other, plus a data buffer of the specified size. If no space is available, this routine should return immediately with a null pointer.

- *copyb()* — Creates a new copy of a message; message block, data block, and data are duplicated. This routine uses *allocb()* to get the space.

- *copymsg()* — Copies a complete message, possibly consisting of multiple message blocks.

- *dupb()* — Creates a message block that points to the same data block (and data buffer) as an existing message block.

- *dupmsg()* — Proceeds through a list of message blocks, using *dupb()* for each, to create a new set of message block headers referring to the same data as the original.

- *esballoc()* — Allocates a message that points to a data buffer already allocated and provided. It makes provisions for a *callback function*: one that will be called when the buffer is freed. Since it has not been allocated by the STREAMS functions, something else must take care of returning the buffer to a free list or reusing it somehow. Otherwise, the buffer will be thrown away, and a nice memory leak will result.

- *freeb()* — Frees a message block. If the data block it refers to is not pointed to by any other message, then that data block and buffer will be freed as well.

- *freemsg()* — Performs the *freeb()* function on all blocks of a message.

- *put()* — Places a message directly on the supplied queue. This routine can be used by a module to place data on its own queue. Note that this is a system routine; individual modules will have to name their own *put* procedures to be something unique.

- *putctl()* — Creates a control message, fills it in with the right type code, and puts it on the specified queue. It will not pass any data along (many control messages don't need any). If necessary, *putctl1()*, a variation of *putctl()*, will create and put a control message with one byte of data (supplied as a parameter).

- *putnext()* — Calls the *put()* procedure of the next queue in sequence.

- *qprocson()* — Actually makes the queues available for use. This is an initialization function that "enables" the put and service procedures of a module. There have been instances when a device driver interrupt service function attempted to use the put procedures of newly pushed modules, or of the driver itself, before *qprocson()* was completely finished. This can result in unpleasant things, like panics.

This list doesn't cover all the STREAMS support functions, but these are some of the more commonly used ones and some that have been seen on stack tracebacks of hung or crashed systems.

Digging around inside

Let's examine a Stream. This exercise should be something you can do on your own system. The only exercise requirement is that you be able to run **adb** on your kernel.

In order to do this on a running system, we need to first make sure that there is something in a Stream to look at. To ensure this, we're going to run a program that generates a lot of output and then press Control-S to stop the printing—the output will be backed up in the queues for this Stream. Then, we have to actually locate the queues. This part is going to provide some nice practice in following pointers through the operating system (which was Solaris 2.3 for the example). The *user* structure contains a table of open files (what your file descriptors refer to). These point to file table entries. These in turn contain pointers to the vnode of the open file, which contains a pointer to the Stream head. From there we can find the queues. Trivial, isn't it?

Well, let's start. Bring up a terminal window that will be our test site. The type of window doesn't matter, but the shell you run in it should probably not be the C shell (since it does some rather odd things with file descriptors). For the example, our default was **csh**; we just started up **sh** as a subshell and ran the commands from there. Once you have the Bourne shell, run the **tty** command, which will identify the terminal name. This is necessary to be able to identify the proper process in a **ps** output list. You may also wish to echo $$, the process ID of the shell itself.

```
% sh
$ tty
/dev/pts/3
$ echo $$
2236
```

Now, in this window, start up a command that generates a lot of output, and press Control-S quickly to prevent the command from completing. We used **sleep 5;ls -l /dev** for the sample. As long as the output device (the Stream going to the window) is blocked, the characters will be backed up inside the queues in this Stream and we should be able to find the output and recognize it.

In another window, preferably one with a scroll bar (because you will be backing up over a lot of output), let's look around. First, you need to be able to find the process table entry for the command you just started, or the shell that ran it.

```
# ps -lft pts/3
8 S chris 1028 1025 63  1 20 fc13e800  206 fc13e9c8 Nov 29    pts/3    0:02 csh
8 S chris 2236 1028 20  1 20 fc1d3000  162 ff603a46 19:35:39 pts/3    0:00 sh
```

The last line is the line of interest; it's the shell. Note that no **ls** is listed— it finished already and exited, even though all its output is still pending.

We'll have to start up **adb** on the kernel to see if we can find anything. Use the ADDR field from the **ps** output (fc1d3000) as the address of the process (the *proc* structure pointer). There are other ways to find this value, but this is the easiest.

```
# adb -k /dev/ksyms /dev/mem
physmem 4f0d
```

Now, dump out the process table entry. We're just doing this to verify the fact that this is a real *proc* structure, and that the values in it do match what we expect to find.

```
fc1d3000$<proc
0xfc1d3000:
                lbolt           cid             exec            as
                0               0               ff3df408        fc1e43b0
0xfc1d3010:
                uid
                1847
                lock
0xfc1d3014:     owner
                0
0xfc1d3014:     lock    type    waiters
                0       0       0
0xfc1d301c:     crlock
0xfc1d301c:     owner
                0
0xfc1d301c:     lock    type    waiters
                0       0       0
0xfc1d3024:
                cred            swapcnt         stat    wcode   wdata
                ff8ff780        0               2       0       0
0xfc1d3034:
                ppid            link            parent
                1028            0               fc13e800
0xfc1d3040:
                child           sibling         next            nextofkin
                0               0               fc1ef000        fc13e800
0xfc1d3050:
                orphan          nextorph        pglink          sessp
                0               0               0               ff40f380
0xfc1d3060:
                pipd            pgidp
```

```
                    ff82d830           ff82d830
 . . .
```

We'll stop listing it here; you will see a bit more output. Let's take the *ppid* field, which should contain the PID number of the parent process. It seems to be 1028, and if we look back at the **ps** output, we see that the parent process ID is in fact this number. Good so far. Now, the pipd label from the macro is actually, if you look at the process structure definition, referring to the *pidp*, or PID structure pointer. (Check the *proc* structure in the header file **/usr/include/sys/proc.h**.) There is a macro to dump out PID structures, so let's check.

```
ff82d830$<pid
0xff82d830:     bits               pid
                300003d            2236
0xff82d838:     pglink             link
                fc1d3000           0
```

And we see that the pid value is 2236, which does match our process ID. (This particular *pid* structure appears to contain a pointer back to the same process table entry. This is really a pointer to the *process group leader*, which happens to be the same process in this instance.) Next, look at the *user* structure for this process by using the **proc2u** macro, which needs the address of the process table entry again as a starting location.

```
0xfc1d3000$<proc2u
0xfc1d31b0:
                execid             execsz            tsize
                32581              12a               0
0xfc1d31bc:
                dsize              start             ticks           cv
                0                  2ee0c88b          2bed603         0

 . . .

0xfc1d3260:     psargs
                sh^@^@^@^@^@^@^@^@^@^@^@^@^@^@^@^@^@^@^@^@^@^@^@^@^@^@^@^@^@
                ^@^@^@^@^@^@^@^@^@^@^@^@^@^@^@^@^@^@^@^@^@^@^@^@^@^@^@^@^@^@
                ^@^@^@^@^@^@^@^@^@^@^@^@^@^@^@^@^@
0xfc1d32b0:     comm
                sh^@^@^@^@^@^@^@^@^@^@^@^@^@^@^@^@

 . . .
```

```
             flist
0xfc1d3594:  ofile
             ff601640       ff601640       ff601640       0
             0              0              0              0
             0              0              0              0
             0              0              0              0
             0              0              0              0
             0              0              0              0
...
```

We've extracted just the interesting pieces here. First, the *psargs/comm* fields contain the process name and full command line. Both of these contain **sh**, along with a lot of nulls. Are we running the shell in that window? Yes, we are. This matches.

Look at the *ofile* table: this is the list of open files. We see that the first three entries, corresponding to file descriptors 0, 1, and 2 (standard input, standard output, and standard error) are all set and are all the same. They are in fact "clones" or duplicates of one another, all referring to the same device. In other words, everything is pointing to pts/3, the pseudo-tty associated with the window. No big surprise, but it's nice to see confirmation of what we expect. Now, each one of these table entries is a pointer to a file table structure. Take the address and run the *file* macro on it.

```
ff601640$<file
hwc_debug+0x633c:               next        prev            flag    count
                ff40ebc0        ff82d900    3           8
hwc_debug+0x6348:               vnode       offset
                ff457004        0           cb8a
hwc_debug+0x6354:               cred
                ff8ff780
```

(Be careful with some of this **adb** output. Note here that the labels are pushed out to the right because the address that's printed is quite long. In this case, it looks like they are over the wrong column. Go by number rather than the actual printed position).

The output indicates that the vnode referenced by this file table entry is out at address 0xff457004. Let's display that.

```
ff457004$<vnode
0xff457004:    flag      refcnt            vfsmnt            vop
               0         2                 0                 spec_vnodeops
0xff45701c:    vfsp                stream            pages
               f00c81fc            ff5ff700          0
0xff457028:    type                maj<<2   min      data
               4                   60       3        ff457000
0xff457034:    filocks
               0
```

These numbers and addresses look good. There is a reference count of 2, which seems reasonable; at least it's not some ridiculously large number or negative. (Why 2? This number corresponds to the number of "open" requests actually issued for this particular vnode. One was from the **shelltool**; to find the other, we'd have to look through every file table entry to find another occurrence of this vnode, and trace that back to a process.) We see that the operation structure pointer for this vnode refers to *spec_vnodeops*, indicating that this is a "special file" or a device. Again, something we would expect: this *is* a pseudo-terminal.

There is a "stream" pointer listed as well. Looking at the *vnode* structure definition (**/usr/include/sys/vnode.h**), this can be seen as:

```
        struct stdata    *v_stream;          /* associated stream */
```

So we want to look at an *stdata* structure, actually. Looking in the **adb** macro directory, we find something that has exactly that name, so let's use it and dump this data out.

```
ff5ff700$<stdata
hwc_debug+0x43fc:                wrq          iocblk       vnode    strtab
               ff603a54          0            ff81cc04     ff2fe87c
hwc_debug+0x440c:                flag         iocid        iocwait
               4010282           2459f        0
hwc_debug+0x4414:                sidp         s_pgidp      wroff
               ff600b90          ff82d830     0
hwc_debug+0x4420:                rerror       werror       pushcnt
               0                 0            3
hwc_debug+0x442c:                sigflags     siglist      eventflags
               0                 0            0
hwc_debug+0x4438:                eventlist
               0
hwc_debug+0x443c:                list         dummy        events
```

	0		0		0		
hwc_debug+0x4448:		mark		closetime		rtime	
	0	5dc		0			

Again, the labels are a bit off, but the first pointer is labeled *wrq*. If we check the definition of the *stdata* structure (**/usr/include/sys/strsubr.h**), this appears to be a queue pointer for the write side:

```
struct queue *sd_wrq;          /* write queue */
```

Since we're looking at output, let's follow this. Again checking in the macro directory, we find a *queue* macro.

ff603a54$<queue

0xff603a54:	qinfo		first		last		next
	f00b4e98		0		0		ff82ee54
0xff603a64:	link		ptr		count	flag	
	0		ff5ff700		0		4020
0xff603a74:	minpsz	maxpsz	hiwat	lowat			
	0		0		0		0
0xff603a84:	bandp		nband				
	0		0				

The queue structure is defined in the **stream.h** header file. This one appears to be empty: the first data block and last data block pointers are null, and the number of bytes on the queue (in *count*) is zero. There is a next queue, which refers to the *queue* structure for the next module in the Stream, so let's follow the chain.

ff82ee54$<queue

0xff82ee54:	qinfo		first		last		next
	ff263eb0		0		0		ff82d254
0xff82ee64:	link		ptr		count	flag	
	0		ff87f640		0		822
0xff82ee74:	minpsz	maxpsz	hiwat	lowat			
	0		ffffffff		12c		c8
0xff82ee84:	bandp		nband				
	0		0				

This again appears to be empty. Let's stop for a moment here and see where we are in the Stream. Looking in the *queue* structure again, the first pointer in the struct, labeled *qinfo* in the macro output, is a *qinit* pointer. A macro exists, so let's check it out.

```
ff263eb0$<qinit
ttycompatwinit:
ttycompatwinit: putp            srvp            qopen           qclose
                ff2621d8        0               ff262040        ff262164
ttycompatwinit:
ttycompatwinit: minfo           mstat
                ff2621d8        0
```

OK, except for one thing: notice that the label on the second line is exactly the same as the label on the first one, and the data appears to be the same as well. This is not right. In fact, if we look at the macro itself, it appears to be erroneous.

Code Example 25-4   The qinit macro

```
% cat qinit
./"putp"16t"srvp"16t"qopen"16t"qclose"n4X4+
./"minfo"16t"mstat"n2X
%
```

If you think back to the **adb** chapter, you may recall that **adb** will remember the last place you started displaying data as "dot." The second line uses the value of dot again as a starting point, and displays the same data as the first line, using a different format! This line should read:

```
+/"minfo"16t"mstat"n2X
```

If your macro looks like the broken one, you might consider fixing it.

Note – The macros are generally reliable, but we want to emphasize the need for caution, checking everything, and never making any assumptions when dealing with broken kernels.

However, we will check the *qinit* structure and dump it out manually. Again from **stream.h** we can find the definition of the structure.

Code Example 25-5   The queue information structure as defined in /usr/include/sys/stream.h

```
/*
 * queue information structure
 */
struct  qinit {
        int     (*qi_putp)();           /* put procedure */
        int     (*qi_srvp)();           /* service procedure */
        int     (*qi_qopen)();          /* called on startup */
        int     (*qi_qclose)();         /* called on finish */
        int     (*qi_qadmin)();         /* for future use */
        struct module_info *qi_minfo;   /* module information structure */
        struct module_stat *qi_mstat;   /* module statistics structure */
};
```

What we want to look at is probably the *module_info* structure, because this one contains the name of the module itself.

Code Example 25-6   The module information structure as defined in /usr/include/sys/stream.h

```
/*
 * Module information structure
 */
struct module_info {
        ushort  mi_idnum;               /* module id number */
        char    *mi_idname;             /* module name */
        long    mi_minpsz;              /* min packet size accepted */
        long    mi_maxpsz;              /* max packet size accepted */
        ulong   mi_hiwat;               /* hi-water mark */
        ulong   mi_lowat;               /* lo-water mark */
};
```

There's no macro for this one, so we'll have to dump this out manually as well. (Note: there are a lot of "mod"-something macros in the **adb** library directory, but none of them are appropriate. Most of them deal with loadable modules in the kernel, not with Streams data.)

Looking back at the *qinit* structure, we see five pointers to functions followed by two pointers to structures. Dump these out, first five, and then two on another line.

```
ff263eb0/5XnXX
ttycompatwinit:
ttycompatwinit: ff2621d8        0               ff262040        ff262164
```

```
            0
            ff263e98        0
```

The first structure pointer (the next to the last value dumped) should be a pointer to a *module_info* structure. This has an unsigned short as the first element followed by a long pointer. Warning! The compiler, when it generates space for this structure on a SPARC machine, will make sure the second element, the pointer, starts on an even 4-byte boundary. It inserts two extra bytes of padding after the short ID number field. We will need to dump the short for the ID field, another short that we ignore completely, and the full word, the one we want, beyond that. (This is one place where a good macro would help. Incidently, **adbgen** would automatically take care of that needed padding.)

```
ff263e98/xxX
ttycompatmoinfo:
ttycompatmoinfo:            2a      0      ff263ef8
```

This should be a string pointer, so we can display what it points to with the **s** command:

```
ff263ef8/s
ttcoinfo+0x2c:   ttcompat
```

And we see that we are looking at the **ttcompat** module, which is indeed something we should expect to see on a tty stream.

After that little detour, let's go back to our empty queue and follow on to the next one.

```
ff82d254$<queue
0xff82d254:     qinfo            first           last          next
                ff25b958         0               0             ff602354
0xff82d264:     link             ptr             count   flag
                0                ff8c2a40        0             822
0xff82d274:     minpsz   maxpsz  hiwat   lowat
                0                ffffffff        1             0
0xff82d284:     bandp            nband
                0                0
```

This again is empty. Let's grab that *qinit* pointer and see what it is.

```
ff25b958/X
ldtermwinit:
ldtermwinit:      ff258fac
```

It's pointing to a global structure labeled *ldtermwinit*—the *init* structure for the write side of the **ldterm** module, which seems appropriate. We won't do more, but feel free to make sure the name is **ldterm** if you want to. Move on to the next queue structure in the stream.

```
ff602354$<queue
hwc_debug+0x7050:                qinfo           first         last        next
                ff2a1220         fc1caf80        fc17ad00      ff602e54
hwc_debug+0x7060:                link            ptr           count   flag
                0                ff40b5c0        26272         82a
hwc_debug+0x7070:                minpsz   maxpsz hiwat   lowat
                0                200             0             0
hwc_debug+0x7080:                bandp           nband
                0                0
```

Now, this one looks significantly different. We have a real first pointer, a last pointer, and a fairly large count field of over 26,000 bytes. Looking at the *queue* structure definition again, the first pointer and last pointer should be indicating *msgb* structures. We don't see an **msgb** macro, but we do find one for an *mblk*. If you look a couple of lines down in the **stream.h** header file, you may see a declaration —

```
typedef struct msgb mblk_t;
```

— that is a clue that the *mblk* macro applies here. You might also dump the macro contents out and look at them, checking the headers, types, and offsets against the structure contents to make sure they match. Let's use it.

```
fc1caf80$<mblk
0xfc1caf80:     next            prev            cont
                fc1aaa00        0               0
0xfc1caf8c:     rptr            wptr            datap
                fc1cafc0        fc1cafcb        fc1cafa0
0xfc1caf98:     band    flag
                0       0
```

According to the *msgb* structure definition, *rptr* and *wptr* are character pointers to data in the buffer, so we should be able to see some output. Note again that this is *not* null-terminated, so using the **s** (string) **adb** format to dump it out may produce extra garbage characters at the end. The *wptr* value indicates the point at which a write would be started, so data should lie *before* this, starting at the read pointer. Subtracting the two pointers gives a value of 0xb, or 11 characters to look at. We'll use the **adb** format command **c**, which just prints one character, but give it a repeat count so we get the entire string.

```
fc1cafc0,b/c
0xfc1cafc0:     total 326
```

Promising. Definitely promising. This is indeed something we might see as the first line of output from an **ls -l** command. This doesn't look like 11 characters, though. Let's print them out with the uppercase **C** command, which displays nonprinting characters in coded form:

```
fc1cafc0,b/C
0xfc1cafc0:     total 326^M^J
```

A ^M code (Control-M) happens to be a carriage return in ASCII, and a Control-J is a linefeed. This is something that **ldterm**, one of the standard serial I/O STREAMS modules, does to lines of output: turn the newline into a return/linefeed pair.

Move on to the *next* message block in the list, following that next pointer from our mblk:

```
fc1aaa00$<mblk
0xfc1aaa00:    next            prev            cont
               fc214280        fc1caf80        fc216480
0xfc1aaa0c:    rptr            wptr            datap
               fc1aaa40        fc1aaa80        fc1aaa20
0xfc1aaa18:    band      flag
               0         0
```

Looking at the data, we see:

```
fc1aaa40,40/c
0xfc1aaa40:    lrwxrwxrwx  1 root        29 Nov 28 11:36 arp -> ../devices/p
```

This is a truncated line. However, there is a continuation pointer in the *mblk* header, which also points to another *mblk*.

```
fc216480$<mblk
0xfc216480:    next            prev            cont
               0               0               0
0xfc21648c:    rptr            wptr            datap
               fc2164c0        fc2164d3        fc2164a0
0xfc216498:    band      flag
               0         0
```

We have a little bit of data (0x13 bytes), so let's see what's there.

```
fc2164c0,13/c
0xfc2164c0:    seudo/clone@0:arp
```

This, when tacked on to the previous output, says that the **arp** entry is a symbolic link pointing to

../devices/pseudo/clone@0:arp

which is correct. Let's go on to one more line of output (the *next* message) and see what we have.

```
fc214280$<mblk
0xfc214280:      next            prev            cont
                 fc1aab00        fc1aaa00        fc1aac00
0xfc21428c:      rptr            wptr            datap
                 fc2142c0        fc214300        fc2142a0
0xfc214298:      band    flag
                 0       0


fc2142c0,40/c
0xfc2142c0:      lrwxrwxrwx  1 root          12 Nov 28 11:39 audio -> /dev/sound

fc1aac00$<mblk
0xfc1aac00:      next            prev            cont
                 0               0               0
0xfc1aac0c:      rptr            wptr            datap
                 fc1aac40        fc1aac44        fc1aac20
0xfc1aac18:      band    flag
                 0       0


fc1aac40,4/c
0xfc1aac40:      /0
fc1aac40,4/C
0xfc1aac40:      /0^M^J
```

Here again, the line is split into two messages, but putting them together results in pretty good-looking output.

So, we've followed a trail of pointers through a lot of structures in the kernel and found what we had hoped to find: the output that was supposed to come to our suspended window. This should be good practice for looking at Streams in crash dumps, as well as chasing pointers through various structures in the kernel. Be sure, until you become familiar with the various macros and the structures they dump, to do some double-checking: Make sure the macro is the right one, and maybe even verify the value of one or two of the fields manually. And remember, you learn best by doing; use those macros and **adb** commands until you become familiar with them, and your debugging sessions will proceed quickly and smoothly.

Trap Handling

A trap, in SPARC terms, is something that causes an immediate branch to kernel code —
an interruption of the normal stream of instructions. This interruption can be due to a
user request (a system call) or some external event (a page fault, a disk interrupt, or a
keystroke). In either case, the interrupt is processed by hardware and very low-level
software, so understanding how traps work and how they are handled requires some
understanding of the architecture of the system. The CPU hardware will identify the type
of the trap and attempt to get to the right place to handle it; the kernel must set up some
control registers to make sure the appropriate trap handling code can be reached.

Once the system has started up and user processes are running, a trap is the only way the
kernel will get control of the CPU from a user program. A trap is the means by which a
user request is processed (the kernel is running on behalf of a user program) and the way
a device is controlled (the kernel is running because of some external request).

Kinds of traps

Two basic kinds of traps can occur: synchronous and asynchronous. Synchronous traps
are caused by, or during the operation of, an instruction. These may be actual trap
instructions or hardware errors, such as bad address alignments, bad addresses (bus
timeouts), illegal instructions, floating-point coprocessor errors, and so on. These traps
are taken immediately; the hardware stops the operation of the current instruction in its
tracks and heads for kernel space.

A synchronous trap will occur *before* it changes any state in the processor. Thus, if the
trap is caused by a "repairable" hardware fault, then the instruction can and should be
restarted to recover from the problem once the trap handling is completed. Page faults
are a good example of this. You need to be able to get the page into memory, map it in to
the process address space, and then let the instruction try again, now that the data is
really there.

Asynchronous traps can be "requested" at any time but will be recognized and processed
only after an instruction has completed. These traps are due to external events such as
interrupts; they do not affect the operation of an instruction but just cause a break in the
instruction stream. It's as if a subroutine call to the kernel were invisibly inserted into the
code.

Both types of traps can occur in user programs and inside the kernel. Both cause a switch to kernel or supervisor mode and a transfer of control to the kernel trap code, where the software will decide what to do about it. Thus, a page fault from a user program is generally acceptable: the kernel will load in the appropriate page and let the instruction continue. A page fault from the kernel, however, is bad news, and the trap code will stop with a panic.

Trap sequence

The hardware will perform a set sequence of operations, regardless of whether the trap is a synchronous fault or an asynchronous interrupt. Interrupt requests, page faults, illegal instructions, or system calls will all be handled the same way. The trap recognition sequence transfers control to the kernel and enters kernel or supervisor mode, with information saved about where the trap occurred and what kind of trap it was.

- Further traps are disabled by clearing the Trap Enable bit in the PSR (Processor Status Register). This prevents further traps or interrupts from being recognized while in the middle of processing this one, which will avoid having a second trap overwrite data the system needs to keep in order to return from the current trap.

- The pS bit, previous S bit in the PSR, is set to the current S bit value to preserve information about where this trap came from. If the S bit was set, the CPU was already in supervisor mode or in the kernel. If the S bit was clear, the trap occurred while user code was executing. This is referenced by the kernel trap-handling code to determine what the proper response should be to certain traps.

- The S bit is set. This indicates that you are now in supervisor mode.

- The CWP (Current Window Pointer) is decremented to move to the next register window: this move does *not* cause a window overflow trap even if the move is into an invalid register window. It is the responsibility of the software to identify this case and handle it. This particular feature does put some interesting restrictions on the code that actually handles the traps.

- PC and nPC contents are stuffed into %11 and %12 of the *new* trap window (since the local registers are the only ones guaranteed to be available at this point).

- The tt (Trap Type) field of the TBR (Trap Base Register) is set, based on what kind of fault or request occurred. This identifies the address of the trap-handling code for the specific trap.

- The PC and nPC are set to the value of the TBR (and TBR+4). This forces a branch to these locations, which have been set up to contain a short piece of code to get to the correct routine to handle the particular type of trap received.

Thus the trap sequence as performed by the hardware looks like:

- Recognize the trap.
- Get to a new window (an implicit save instruction).
- Set TBR according to the trap type.
- Force a branch to the trap instructions — the address in the TBR.

Turning off the Enable Traps bit is necessary, but since doing so also delays interrupt recognition, this has to be done for as short a time as possible. The code must also be carefully written; if a trap is requested (a page fault, for example) while traps are "disabled," a watchdog reset will occur.

The current window pointer (CWP, in the Processor Status Register) indicates the registers that are in use. Since registers behave like a circular buffer, this acts as a circular list pointer, so it will cycle around through the complete register set. Sooner or later, it will overlap, when the "new register window" it indicates is not actually free for use. This case is the source of a window overflow trap (or a window underflow, when moving in the other direction), and because a trap at this point would cause a watchdog reset, the CWP may in fact be changed to point to an invalid window. For this reason, the hardware and software in the trap-handling process can only use the *local* (%l0–%l7) registers. No other registers can be touched. This will produce a nonstandard stack frame on the stack: one in which, for example, the return address (in %i7) is not really a valid pointer.

The Trap Base Register is normally set up once during the initialization of the system to point to some page boundary. It looks like this:

Trap Base Address	Trap Type				
20 bits	8 bits	0	0	0	0

Figure 26-1 Trap Base Register

You will notice that the lower bits are always zeroes, and the next eight bits are the trap type field — filled automatically, based on the type of the trap as determined by the hardware. This means that if the base address register was initialized by the kernel to start at location 0x4000, then a trap type 1 (which is a text fault or an instruction access problem) would cause the type field to be set to 1, the lower bits are zeroes, and we are thus branching immediately to location 0x4010. For an illegal instruction (trap type 2), the hardware sends us to 0x4020. There's not a lot of space between these two addresses (four words, in fact), so the "trap code" generally consists of an immediate branch off to someplace else — where we've got enough room to do some real work! You now can see why the trap-handling code is written in assembly language.

Trap frames

A trap frame is not structurally different from any other type of stack frame; there is no magic distinguishing characteristic that identifies it as such. However, there are a few things you can look for, since traps don't happen all that often and are handled by special code.

Trap frames have the address of the instruction that caused the trap (or, in the case of an interrupt, the instruction that is just ready to execute) in local register %11 and the next PC in local register %12. This is done, as we mentioned before, by the hardware. The software function handling the trap may do other things with the registers, but normally, at least the PC address is available in %11.

Synchronous traps resulting from an instruction will usually have a frame from a "fault" function or "trap" function appearing in the stack trace right after (above) the trap frame. Asynchronous faults, usually due to external device interrupts, can be recognized by the interrupt-handling code. This may be a clock function ("hardclock") or a specific piece of code dedicated to one particular interrupt level (level10). Return addresses on the stack that refer to these functions (interrupt or fault handlers) normally indicate an immediately preceding trap frame. Look for a frame with a code address in %11 and normally that address plus 4 in %12. Device interrupts are usually recognizable by the names of the interrupt service routines; these generally end in "*int*"—for example, *zsint()* might be a service routine for the ZS (serial keyboard/mouse) device.

Trap types

Each trap type has a unique identifying number, which is used to modify the Trap Base Register and direct the CPU to the correct trap-handling routine. The types are assigned by the SPARC chip specification and correspond roughly to their priority. (Trap priorities only matter when simultaneous trap or interrupt requests are present). Some of these may become familiar to you after seeing some Bad Trap panics: a *data fault*, for instance, is trap type 9.

The most common trap types and their meanings are listed below.

Table 26-1 Common trap types

Trap Type	Trap Description
1	Illegal instruction access (text fault)
2	Illegal instruction
3	Privileged instruction
4	Floating-point disabled
5	Window overflow

Table 26-1 Common trap types (Continued)

Trap Type	Trap Description
6	Window underflow
7	Memory address alignment error
8	Floating-point exception
9	Data access exception (data fault)
17	Interrupt level 1
18	Interrupt level 2
	up to
31	Interrupt level 15
128	Software trap #0
	up to
255	Software trap #127

The first traps, up to the hardware interrupts, are synchronous: they are caused by or occur during an instruction. The various interrupt levels are asynchronous; level 15 is the highest priority. Software traps are those caused by the trap instruction, which has a type code from 0 to 127 embedded in the instruction as a constant or supplied in a register. Generally, only a few software trap codes are valid. One of them is used to issue system calls. (This code changed in Solaris 2, from a trap 0 to a trap 8 instruction. This enables the kernel to distinguish between system calls issued from statically linked SunOS 4.x binary executables and those issued from a Solaris 2 or Binary Compatibility library).

Returning from traps

The system must be able to return to the code that was interrupted or that caused the trap. There is one specific instruction, `rett`, which does a "return from trap" operation. This undoes the sequence of events that took place when the hardware recognized the trap.

We've mentioned watchdog resets a few times now. Let's move on to the next chapter where we discuss them in greater detail.

Panic! UNIX System Crash Dump Analysis

Watchdog Resets 27 ≡

Sometimes a system will die with a "watchdog reset" message on the console and will drop into the boot PROM (or possibly reboot automatically). It's not a panic: The system is no longer in control, it's not dumping memory to disk, and the CPU has done a *reset*.

What is a watchdog?

Watchdog resets usually indicate a software problem, although the root cause may be hardware related. The immediate cause is a trap, like a page fault, that occurs in the middle of handling another trap. The kernel processes a trap with the Enable Traps bit in the Processor Status Register reset (turned off), which prevents the CPU from accepting another trap until the initial processing of the first one is complete. This means that another trap is not supposed to be generated until the system has done enough work to successfully handle the first trap. If for some reason a trap is caused during this period, the system has to take the trap — but it can't because the bit is off, so it quits right there. This is a watchdog reset — an unrecoverable situation that essentially forces a reset of the CPU.

The only thing you can do after a watchdog reset is reboot the machine. Due to the nature of watchdog resets, not even use of the kernel absolute debugger, **kadb**, will allow you to capture watchdog resets as they happen. There are, however, as you'll see shortly, a few OpenBoot PROM commands you can use to get some status information before you do that reboot.

sun4d systems

On the Sun SPARCserver 1000 and SPARCcenter 2000 systems (sun4d architecture), there are actually two different types of watchdog resets.

The first one is as described above, when a single CPU finds itself in trouble and causes the system to drop into the PROM.

The second is a more drastic problem caused by a major hardware failure. In this case, called a *system watchdog*, the entire system is rebooted automatically: No PROM **ok** prompt appears, and you will not have the opportunity to attempt to debug it. During this process, some information is saved into the NVRAM (NonVolatile Random Access Memory).

/usr/kvm/prtdiag: A special sun4d command

In the case of a *system watchdog* on a SPARCserver 1000 or SPARCcenter 2000 system, there is one command you can run after the system reboots and comes back up again. The **prtdiag** utility is only available on sun4d systems and only prints information about the last system watchdog, so it's not useful for a normal CPU watchdog reset. However, it will assist in identifying the bad hardware that caused the system reset.

Can you get a core file?

Not usually. The catastrophic nature of this event means that even if you do see a boot PROM **ok** prompt, it's likely that the CPU registers have been corrupted already, and running a **sync** command will either fail or will give a core dump that is useless—one that is unreadable, or has no good information left in it to examine. It is always worth a try, but there are some other things you should do first.

What do you do next?

Once you have the boot PROM **ok** prompt, you can use some special PROM commands, shown below, to dump out information about the state of the system when it received the watchdog. This information includes the actual instruction that caused the problem and a stack trace of how it got there. Note that some of these commands start with a dot.

- **.registers** — Displays many of the kernel internal CPU registers.

- **.locals** — Dumps out the registers in the current register "window." These are the registers that were in use at the time of the crash.

- **.psr** — Prints the Processor Status Register contents in a readable format.

- **ctrace** — Displays the return stack (similar to a **$c** command in **adb**).

- **wd-dump** (*sun4d architectures only*) — Displays watchdog information on the console, including the PC value, which is the location of the instruction that caused the crash.

It would be best to run every one of these commands. They all have useful information that will help you decipher where and why the system reset itself.

Unfortunately, at this point the kernel is not running, so you can't save this information to a file. You'll have to copy the information down on paper for later reference and analysis.

An alternative console device

Transcribing data from the console screen to paper is not much fun. One way around this is to use another system as a console server and **tip** into one of the tty ports from a command-tool window. You can then run commands from the other system and save the output. It does mean, however, that you have to set up your crashing system ahead of time so that the console is on one of the tty ports.

Watchdog analysis

Since you may not get a good core file, the PROM commands will be necessary to give you the current state of the system at the point of failure. You may be able to look at other things in a core image, such as the other processes and their stacks, but much of the data about the currently running process or thread will be unavailable. The PROM commands may allow you to find the routines, at least, that were in use at the time the reset occurred.

Since watchdog resets only occur when the system is processing traps, the actual PC value will not be of much use: You can guarantee that it's going to be in the kernel trap-handling code. The trace information is the most important and useful output.

Note that when you are using the PROM, the kernel is not running and the symbol table is not available to the PROM code. This means your output from the PROM commands will be entirely in hexadecimal. All you can get is raw numeric addresses. Once the system is rebooted, you can try to associate these with the functions in the kernel by running **adb** on the live system, using the command **address/i** to display the instruction and location of each address taken from the stack trace.

This is one instance where it may actually be better to run the debugger on **/kernel/unix**, for Solaris 2, rather than on the standard **/dev/ksyms**. You cannot be sure that the modules loaded on a rebooted system will be the same, or in the same order, as they were loaded on the original crashed system. The only locations where you can guarantee that the names are correct will be those in the static, booted kernel. The SunOS 4.x kernel is already static, so the addresses can be applied to the newly booted system without any fear that things will have moved around.

Summary

Analyzing watchdog resets is not an easy task. A few PROM commands can be put to use; however, you may not always get useful information from your efforts.

If multiple watchdog resets occur, you may be able to obtain consistent results and identify the functions involved. Although watchdog resets are the result of a software problem, they are often related to (or caused by) a specific piece of hardware. This will hopefully be recognizable from the stack traces.

When dealing with a system suffering from watchdog resets, be prepared to look at the whole system, both the hardware and the software, for trouble spots.

For further reference

The Solaris 2 *OpenBoot Command Reference Manual* will provide a great deal of information about the PROM setup and available commands. The PROM includes a FORTH language interpreter, so there are a large number of sophisticated operations you can do with it, including defining your own command set. To some extent you can debug with it just as with **adb** or **kadb**, including setting breakpoints and examining memory. It is less user friendly in that the symbols are not available, but for those emergency situations where you don't have **kadb** loaded, the PROM can allow you to examine and modify the kernel, the machine state, and even devices.

Interrupts 28 ≡

You're familiar with interruptions already; you get them every day — a request for something special, right now. You might possibly delay it by locking your door, but the sources rarely go away, and you'll have to take care of it sooner or later.

A computer interrupt is the same thing: something out there wants immediate attention. This request appears as a hardware signal delivered to the CPU. Each interrupt has with it a priority, relating to how soon the system should take care of the situation. Some interrupts are more like completion signals: "The task you gave me is finished, and I'm waiting for something else to do. " This case is not a high priority, since neglecting it for a while won't hurt anything (except perhaps performance). Other interrupts are more time-critical: a clock tick, for instance, won't wait for too long. Eventually the clock will request another interrupt as time passes. Miss too many of these and your system's notion of the time of day will be seriously off. Another example might be incoming data, which signals its arrival. Wait too long and it may be overwritten by new data — and you've lost it.

All of these situations require the CPU to stop what it's doing (eventually) and go off to execute some unique code that handles this special condition. This code is known as an *interrupt service routine*, and there is usually a separate routine for each possible interrupt that might occur. Since each interrupt has an associated priority, the system will normally associate the same priority with the service routine. This prevents lower-priority requests from interrupting a high-priority service function.

An interrupt is generally known as an *asynchronous event*, since it can occur at any time unrelated to the current code being executed by the machine. The CPU will check before fetching the next instruction to see if an interrupt has been requested and if it is at a high enough priority to be recognized. If the interrupt needs to be handled, the system will immediately perform some sort of function call or trap to the appropriate kernel code. As a part of this unexpected break in the normal flow of events (and code), the CPU must ensure that no state information is ever lost: the interrupted code must be able to pick up and continue exactly where it left off, as if nothing had ever happened.

SPARC systems

On a SPARC system, an interrupt is treated just like any other trap condition. The CPU will automatically execute a special trap sequence, based on the interrupt's priority level. The hardware will stuff a unique code into the Trap Base Register, which provides an address in kernel space. This is immediately used as the PC value for the next instruction. Interrupt- and trap-handling routines are invariably written in assembly language, although they may call C functions once the correct environment has been set up. These routines (both C and assembly) are generally given names reflecting the priority level of the interrupt that invoked them or the device they are intended to service. The C functions themselves are usually short and are not supposed to do much other than alert some other routine about a special event. Since they are I/O-related, they normally appear in device driver code. This means, of course, that they are part of the kernel and operate with all the rights and privileges pertaining thereto (and all the responsibilities).

Priority levels

The SPARC CPU has 16 priority levels, ranging from zero to fifteen. Level 0 is where user code executes: *anything* can interrupt users. Level 1 is sometimes known as "softclock"—the level at which the kernel does time-based housekeeping functions. This is a low enough priority that any hardware needing attention can get it: all devices interrupt at a higher level. The highest level of priority (15) is used to mask out everything except the highest level of interrupt, usually associated with a system shutdown or (in the case of the SPARCserver 1000 and SPARCcenter 2000) a potentially dangerous overheating condition.

SBus and VME peripheral devices have only seven levels of interrupt priority (and usually use only about four of them). These are mapped to internal CPU priority levels by hardware according to the following table.

Table 28-1 SBus and VME device interrupt priorities

CPU Priority	Interrupt/Device
Level 0	Spurious
Level 1	
Level 2	SBus/VME level 1
Level 3	SBus/VME level 2
Level 4	On-board SCSI devices
Level 5	SBus/VME level 3
Level 6	On-board Ethernet
Level 7	SBus/VME level 4
Level 8	On-board video (retrace)
Level 9	SBus/VME level 5

Table 28-1 SBus and VME device interrupt priorities (Continued)

CPU Priority	Interrupt/Device
Level 10	Normal clock (100 Hz)
Level 11	SBus/VME level 6, floppy drive
Level 12	Serial I/O (ZS)
Level 13	SBus/VME level 7, audio device
Level 14	High-level clock (kernel profiling
Level 15	Asynchronous error (memory errors)

Devices that interrupt at SBus/VME level 2 or 3 are normally disk or tape devices (the IPI disk controller, for example, interrupts at level 2). Bus level 4 is used for the somewhat smart ALM-2 serial I/O card; this does have some buffering capability and does not need attention quite as promptly.

Unfortunately, the mappings are not linear or consistent, but at least they are in order.

Note the difference between disk/tape and character input. Generally, any response to a CPU request is a low priority; it's just informative. Any unsolicited input occurs at a fairly high priority, since more may be arriving at any time. Also, unsophisticated hardware is generally handled at a higher priority, partly because the smarter stuff can take care of itself and requires little attention from the main processor.

For several reasons, the high-priority interrupt service routines are generally very restricted in what they can do. First, since they will most likely block out other requests that might occur at the same time or while the service routine is executing, they need to do their thing and get out fast. Second, since they may be associated with devices that are fairly high speed, they must avoid doing any extensive time-consuming processing or they will lose succeeding interrupts and possibly data. As a general rule, interrupt service functions, regardless of their priority, will do little more than save data in a safe place, signal some other function that the data is there, and possibly start up the next device request if one is pending.

Serial devices

TTY ports (serial input lines) are handled uniquely. Since the data is fairly volatile, it needs to be handled quickly. However, since it may involve some extensive work, especially when dealing with STREAMS, it can't all be done at a high-priority level. This results in a two-phased scheme.

Every incoming character for the standard serial ports (the ZS devices, which stands for Zilog Serial — the chip that handles them) results in an interrupt request. The hardware has a very small, two-character "silo," which it uses to store the character until the software function can get to it. If the CPU doesn't get there in time, the data will be overwritten, resulting in a "silo overflow" condition and an error message to that effect on the console. This situation means data was lost, although normally it's associated with the mouse and is not catastrophic. The interrupt service routine doesn't want to spend much time worrying about character processing, so it just grabs the character(s) from the silo and stuffs the data into a small circular "ring buffer," which normally holds about 256 characters. Very high speed input on the serial lines may result in the ring buffer being filled before the STREAMS code can get to it; this may result in a "ring buffer overflow" message. The interrupt service routine now sets a flag noting that data is available, and one of the housekeeping functions done at clock-tick time will take the incoming data and parcel it out to the correct Stream. The STREAMS code, also run periodically based on clock ticks, does whatever processing is necessary, such as recognition of special characters like Control-C, echoing back to the originator, or sending full lines of text to the user programs.

If the system is locked up at a priority level higher than 1, this may result in the L1-A (or Stop-A) key sequence apparently being ignored. It's not really ignored, but the system won't get around to processing it until the STREAMS code (at level 1) is allowed to run. This may never happen: the system looks (and is) hung. A "break" on an ASCII terminal used as a console (or unplugging the normal keyboard and plugging it back in again) may have better results, because this is actually a line condition rather than an incoming character and, as such, can be recognized and handled by the higher-priority ZS interrupt service routine.

Vectored interrupts

On some systems, especially those that are VME-based, the interrupt response sequence performed by the hardware may look something like this:

```
    Device: Interrupt request   -->>   CPU
            Acknowledgment      <<--   CPU
            Vector number       -->>   CPU
```

As a part of the hardware signal sequence, the device will supply a *vector* number to the CPU. This vector is an ID number associated with the device or card and helps the CPU get to the appropriate service routine quickly. Assuming that each device has a unique ID, the vector number is used as an index into an array of function pointers, and the interrupt recognition hardware in the CPU will actually make a call directly through the vector slot to the appropriate function. This way there's no overhead involved in identifying the device associated with the interrupt request and in locating the correct function to call. It's all done in hardware.

This does lead to interesting problems if more than one device attempts to use the same vector number. Hopefully, this is caught by the system during initialization. The system administrator must be very careful to make sure that conflicts do not arise when adding new hardware.

Polled interrupts

A simpler form of interrupt response has essentially one vector associated with each interrupt priority level. Interrupt recognition is faster and easier (in hardware) but requires the software to check each device that might interrupt at that particular priority level to see if it was the one(s) issuing the request. This is known as *polling*.

Some software complications result. Since the hardware cannot uniquely identify a device, the driver code for each device must have a function that checks to see if that particular piece of hardware was responsible. This is normally done by the interrupt service routine, which can be called at any time, whether or not an interrupt was pending. Thus, the interrupt service routine in a driver must first check to see if there really *was* an interrupt before proceeding.

Polling is the method used by SPARC. The CPU does not support a large vector; there is one per interrupt priority level, giving 16 slots. The first one, level 0, is not used—it actually holds a pointer to a spurious error function (no device should be able to interrupt at level 0!). For SPARC machines that handle VME boards (older Sun-4 systems and the 600 series), additional hardware receives and holds the vector information provided by the devices. This is made available to the software and is used to locate an interrupt service routine — but the hardware doesn't do it all for you, this time.

Interrupts in tracebacks

An interrupt is just another form of trap, so any interrupt response is going to operate the same way something like a page fault would. A special trap frame is stored on the stack, and an interrupt service routine is called from the vector. This function then polls various pieces of hardware at that interrupt level.

You can usually identify an interrupt by noticing a driver interrupt service function on the stack. These almost universally end in "int" or "intr," so something like *zsint()* would refer to the interrupt service function for the ZS device driver. Just before this in time (just below it on the stack trace), you should find a low-level assembly function that does the polling. Look for something like *level10()* as a function name, which would correspond to interrupt priority level 10 processing. Just below this on the stack will appear the stack frame that contains the PC/nPC values from the code being executed when the interrupt occurred.

Some interrupt priority levels are devoted to one device, just as if it were a real vectored interrupt system. This means the kernel software need not poll; it knows exactly which device caused the interrupt. The clock is the main device for which this is done, since the great frequency of clock interrupts (100 per second) demands efficiency in handling them. The function that handles the high-priority clock hardware "tick" is normally known as "hardclock"; "softclock" is the lower-priority housekeeping function invoked by hardclock when and if there is something to be done that is time-based (required periodically or after a certain elapsed time). This could include STREAMS service procedures, character data handling, callback functions (also known as *callout* functions), or signal generation, such as alarm clock signals delivered to user programs.

Callout functions are also known as delay functions or deadman timers; a driver or kernel routine will request that a function be invoked after a certain amount of time has passed. This may be a cleanup function, to be called if a device has not answered within a certain period of time, or merely some sort of delay function to send certain data out after a specified time has elapsed.

For an example of an interrupt from the keyboard appearing in a traceback, look at the third case study, "Hanging Instead of Swapping", which examines a hung system. In this case, recognition of the L1-A stop sequence appears on the top part of the stack. The interrupt itself occurred during the idle function; the trap frame contains a PC and nPC value from within that routine.

Multiprocessor Kernels 29 ≡

Early computers, and early UNIX systems, were designed with one main processor. In order to handle lots of "simultaneous" jobs, the kernel would rapidly switch back and forth between tasks, or processes, giving each a small slice of time, which gave the illusion of simultaneous, parallel activity. This was known as timesharing. A single task would only be interrupted and stopped if it needed a resource or some data that was not available (for example, if it requested input from a tape drive) or if it exceeded its time slice and another task needed to run.

The UNIX kernel was designed to fit this model. A process would run until it ran out of time or until it issued a system request that resulted in the process being blocked. At that point, the process would "give up" the CPU, and the kernel would change over to another process and continue where *that* one had left off.

One obvious way to make a system process more jobs in a shorter period of time is to add another processor, so that more than one user task could be performed literally simultaneously. This does cause some problems, most notably in the area of synchronization and protection of data. For example, if processor number 1 is busy scanning the list of free pages to secure some additional memory for its job, the second processor had better not be taking pages off the free list at the same time, or there is liable to be a conflict: Both processors may think that they got the same page off the free list, and both will try to use it for two different purposes. Systems can also end up in "deadlock" situations, where each processor has something in use that another one needs and ends up waiting for another resource that it can't get.

Data protection

In a single-processor system, the only case where data protection is required occurs during interrupt processing. Since an interrupt might appear at any time, if the kernel is working with data that could be accessed or modified during an interrupt service routine, that interrupt must be prevented or delayed until the data manipulation is finished. As soon as the kernel is done with that particular piece of data, it doesn't matter if it is interrupted, because there will no longer be any possible conflict. The standard method used by the UNIX kernel to protect data was to prevent interrupts during *critical sections* of code by increasing the priority level of the processor. This would delay recognition of the interrupt until the level was reduced again. If you examine kernel code, you will see many *spl()* calls; *spl* stands for *set priority level* and is a means of blocking out interrupts that might interfere with the current section of code and the data it is manipulating. Obviously, you don't want to block important interrupts for long, or you may find yourself losing data. Priority changes are done frequently around small sections of code to delay interrupt recognition for as short a time as possible. There are also priorities associated with interrupts, so you only need to set the CPU priority high enough to block out the service routine you are worried about.

This works fine for a single processor. However, when there are two CPUs in a system, issuing a call to set the priority level of one processor high, thus preventing it from receiving interrupts, will not affect the operation of the other processor at all, and the interrupt is likely to be recognized and handled by that CPU instead, which defeats the whole purpose of the *spl()* call. This requires a major change in approach and design in order to make a real multiprocessor system work.

SunOS 4.x multiprocessor systems

The SunOS 4.x multiprocessor kernels are a half-step toward a real multiprocessor system. In order to make a real multiprocessing kernel, a major rewrite of the kernel code would have been required. This was not really practical in the time available (the rewrite was called "Solaris 2"), so the old single-processor kernel was modified in an uncomplicated way to make it functional with more than one CPU. The idea was very simple: Since having more than one processor in the kernel at one time would cause lots of synchronization problems, don't let that happen. A "lock" was built at the kernel entry points so that only one processor could actually be executing kernel code at any time. Any other processor attempting to handle system requests and enter the kernel would be forced to wait until the first one was through and had released the lock. This was somewhat inefficient if several CPUs were attempting to enter the kernel at the same time, because only one would make it and the other(s) would just spin, waiting for the lock. However, for systems with a lot of CPU-intensive user processes, this would provide effective multiprocessing of user tasks on a single-threaded kernel.

Multiprocessor debugging on a 4.x system, then, is quite similar to debugging on a single processor system. At most, one CPU will actually be doing work in the kernel, so if there is a crash, there should only be one processor, one stack, and one set of data to worry about. The state of the other CPUs should be either idle, in user mode, or blocked at the kernel lock waiting to get in.

There are only a couple of changes to the kernel you should be aware of. The first is obviously the kernel lock and the code to handle it. The second is a per-CPU state structure. It was necessary to keep some information around specific to each processor, and a single structure was allocated to hold this. Although there are multiple copies of the structure (obviously at different addresses) in kernel space, to make the kernel code work without change, each structure, when active, is mapped in to a fixed kernel address to make all of the variables accessible at the same location.

SunOS 4.x lock code

Kernel lock manipulation is done in assembly language routines, that is, very low level kernel code. The main functions are:

- *klock_enter()* — Enter/grab the kernel lock. Spin if it's otherwise occupied.

- *klock_knock()* — Try it. Return a true/false indication (we got the lock, or somebody else has it already). Do not just sit there and spin.

- *klock_exit()* — Release the lock.

The kernel lock itself, *klock*, is a word containing a lock byte (the first, or high-order byte of the word) and an indication of which CPU owns it. The possible values are:

> 00000000 — The lock is free
>
> ff000000 — Somebody owns it but may not have finished setting things up
>
> ff000008 — Owned by CPU #0
>
> ff000009 — Owned by CPU #1
>
> ff00000a — Owned by CPU #2
>
> ff00000b — Owned by CPU #3

If you are working with a kernel crash on a multiprocessor machine, one of the first things to check is that the lock is owned by the correct CPU. With more than one processor working in the kernel, all bets are off, and data corruption is not only possible but likely. One possible example of this is where data in a CPU register (a parameter, for instance) does not match the value actually in the memory location where it came from. This could be caused by hardware, an interrupt service routine improperly masked out, or more than one CPU in the kernel at once.

SunOS 4.x CPU structure

The *PerCPU* structure is defined in **/sys/sun4m/OBJ/percpu_str.h** (this header file is automatically generated as a part of the original kernel build). The file defines a structure that is maintained for each CPU in the system, identifying the CPU (by ID number) and containing the kernel stack for this processor, a pointer to the current running process (*masterprocp* and *uUNIX*), and a lot of other data areas with specific information for this particular processor. A couple of magic fields to note: *cpuid*, *cpu_enable*, *cpu_exists*, and *cpu_supv*, which identify the CPU number, whether or not it is turned on, if it exists, and if this particular one is in supervisor (kernel) mode.

These structures appear in an array, *PerCPU*, one megabyte apart (starting at address *VA_PERCPU*), and one of them also shows up at a fixed virtual address (*VA_PERCPUME*). These addresses are defined in **/sys/sun4m/devaddr.h**. Unfortunately, there is not a macro to dump these structures out in a readable form, and they are much too large to blindly scan through. Think of this as "an exercise for the reader" to test out your macro construction skills.

Solaris 2

For the new Solaris 2 kernel, a major rewrite of the internal code was done to provide true symmetric multiprocessing. A different approach to protecting the kernel data had to be taken since the *spl()* method was effectively useless. Instead of putting a lock around a section of code that accessed critical data structures, the locks were put in the data structures themselves. Before accessing or modifying a piece of data, the code was made responsible for obtaining the correct lock. This would enable multiple processors not only to be running in the kernel simultaneously, but also to be running the same code. For example, if a piece of code modifies a thread structure, as long as multiple processors are not trying to access the *same* structure, multiple versions of the structure could be accessed or updated at the same time without any problems.

This does mean that each major data structure must be protected with a lock. There is a bit of a tradeoff here. If you have very few locks, it is very likely that a processor will need that lock to do its work. If you have a great number of locks, there will be fewer conflicts when the same lock is needed, but all the processors will spend a lot of their cycles grabbing and releasing locks. Solaris 2 has about 150 different types of structures protected with locks.

Atomic instructions

For a multiprocessor system to realistically implement some sort of locking and synchronization between the CPUs, some support in hardware is required. On a SPARC processor, there are a couple of atomic instructions, or operations guaranteed by the hardware to be uninterruptible. This allows any given processor to examine and possibly modify a lock in memory without fear of another processor getting in there in the middle. If this were to be done with normal instructions, it would be a fairly long process: it would take several operations to pull the lock out of memory, examine it, and put a new value back to mark the lock as "taken." Picture, if you will, two processors executing the same code within one instruction of each other, as illustrated in the next figure.

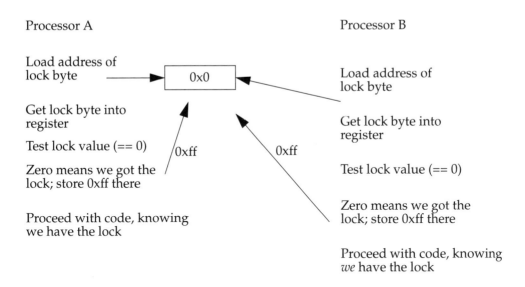

Figure 29-1 Two processors executing the same code within one instruction of each other

As you can see, this lock was a waste of time. There has to be a better way to implement a lock access in order to make the lock work reliably. Atomic instructions will allow a processor to test and set a lock in one instruction cycle, preventing any other processor from looking at the lock at the same time. The instruction used in Solaris 2 is `ldstub` (load/store unsigned byte), which will take a byte from memory and replace it with 0xff in one clock cycle. The processor can then look at the value and see what it got. If the byte in the register is zero, then the lock was not previously set, it is now 0xff by virtue of the instruction we just executed, and we have set the lock. If the value is 0xff, that means we replaced 0xff in the lock with 0xff, and somebody else got there first.

All locking in Solaris 2 is done at some point by using this `ldstub` instruction. The basic lock that utilizes this is called a mutex lock, for *mutual exclusion*. There are other types of locks in the kernel, but they depend on this type for synchronization at some point.

Note – There is another atomic instruction in the official SPARC instruction set, `swap`. This will replace a 32-bit word in memory with one in a register. It's not used. Some very early implementations of the SPARC processor did not include the `swap` instruction in hardware: it was emulated by the system. With no guarantee that this is a real atomic operation for all CPUs, it can't be depended upon for locking.

Mutex structure

The mutex lock structure is defined in the header file **mutex.h**. It contains several different definitions for varieties of mutex locks. The most commonly used is the adaptive mutex.

Code Example 29-1   The default adaptive mutex structure as defined in /usr/include/sys/mutex.h

```
/*
 * Default adaptive mutex (without stats).
 */
struct adaptive_mutex {
        uint_t  m_owner : 24;           /* 0-2  24 bits of owner thread_id */
        lock_t  m_lock;                 /* 3    lock */
        uchar_t m_type;                 /* 4    type (zero) */
        disp_lock_t     m_wlock;        /* 5    waiters field lock */
        turnstile_id_t  m_waiters;      /* 6-7 cookie for the turnstile */
} m_adaptive;
```

Note that this lock has the owner of the lock and the lock byte itself encoded into the first word of the structure. The owner field is in reality a mangled pointer to a *thread* structure describing the thread that obtained (and owns) the lock. This pointer compaction (32 bits into 24 bits) can be done by pulling a few tricks. First, the SPARC Application Binary Interface specification (the ABI) defines explicitly the lowest possible starting address of the kernel (which is also the highest available address in user space): 0xe0000000. Kernel addresses will only be larger than this, which means that the top three bits of any thread structure pointer are going to be all 1's, guaranteed. They get stripped off. Next, structures are placed on word boundaries, so the starting address will always be an even multiple of 4, which means the last two bits of the address are zero. This gives 5 bits, whose value we already know, but in order to fit this pointer into 24 we need an additional 3 bits taken off. To do this, the kernel will enforce a boundary condition for thread structures such that they always begin on an even 8-word address. This forces 3 more bits of zeroes at the bottom of the address and gives us 8 total whose value we know. The remaining 24 are put into the mutex structure.

Why go through all these contortions? Consider what happens when you release a lock. If another processor is currently examining that lock, there are a couple of things that might happen. If you clear out the owner field first, then release the lock byte, anybody looking at the lock will find it set and see a null pointer as the owner. Not good. If you clear the lock byte, and then the owner, the lock will be open for a period, which may allow somebody to grab the lock, set their thread pointer in the owner field, and proceed — only to have *your* processor zero out the owner field as the last act of releasing it. Also not good. It is mandatory to release the lock byte and clear the owner field in one blow, so they both have to fit in one full word that can be zeroed by one instruction.

There are two main types of mutex locks: the *spin lock* and the *adaptive mutex*. Spin locks are the simplest (they are essentially what was implemented for the SunOS 4.x MP kernel). Any processor that wants the lock will simply sit in a loop watching for it to be released. This waiting can obviously tie up a CPU and will only be done when the system can do nothing else, for instance, when in a high-level interrupt service routine. There is no way the processor can block the interrupt handler, so it has to wait in a loop.

The more common type of mutex is the adaptive mutex. This starts out as a potential spin lock; if the status of the thread that owns the lock is currently *ONPROC* (executing on a CPU at this instant), then the processor will spin. The idea is that locks are generally held for a short period of time, and it is likely that the lock will be released soon. This avoids the overhead of putting the current thread to sleep and performing a context switch. If, however, the thread that owns the lock either is sleeping or goes to sleep, there could be a long wait for this one to be freed, so the waiting thread blocks, goes to sleep on that lock, and does a context switch until the lock is released.

Other locks: semaphores, reader/writers, condition variables

There are other types of locks for other purposes, although most of them use the same basic lock (the mutex) as an underlying control mechanism.

Semaphores are used to control resources where a finite number of items, all the same, are available. If you need a buffer, for example, you can get one from a pool. If no more are available, then you sleep. This allocation mechanism needs a counter, which is implemented with a semaphore lock. Internal kernel functions to manipulate and set up semaphores are defined in the DDI/DKI kernel functions list, under *semaphore(9F)*.

Reader/writer locks allow many threads to access data in read-only form (to scan a list, for example). As soon as another thread needs to update that list, everything else must wait until the modification has been performed before looking at it again. Thus, we need a control mechanism to allow multiple readers *or* one and only one writer. The functions associated with these locks are defined in *rwlock(9F)*.

Condition variables are used, like mutex locks, when checking conditions or the availability of resources and for blocking if the conditions are not right. These are generally always used with an associated mutex lock: the lock is intended to make sure that the condition check is done atomically. If the check indicates that it is time to go to sleep, the thread can block on a condition variable (which contains the information on how to find this thread and wake it up again). Use of condition variables is controlled by *condvar(9F)* functions. The associated mutex routines are defined in *mutex(9F)*. Condition variables are not really a lock in themselves, but they are used to help with the synchronization of threads.

Blocking & sleeping

Normally, a processor that needs a lock of any type will try to grab it, and sleep (block) if it fails. What exactly *is* "sleeping"?

In BSD-based kernels, with one processor, a process inside the kernel (performing a system request) could encounter a situation where it could not proceed any further: it was blocked. Obviously it couldn't just sit there and spin, since that would lock up the processor and prevent anybody else from getting any useful work done. This means it had to stop, save its current state, and allow another process to pick up where *it* left off and continue running for a while. This was done with a *sleep()* function call, which effectively blocked the caller and did a context switch to another process. The *sleep()* call had two parameters: an address and a priority code. The address was really just a magic number (sometimes referred to as a cookie). It was used as a unique index into a hash table: this process was put in a queue, asleep, until something, somewhere, did a *wakeup()* with the same magic number as a parameter. This would result in the process being put back on the run queue, since the reason it went to sleep had gone. This magic cookie can be seen in the output of the **ps** command as the value in the *WCHAN* or "wait channel" column. The priority on the *sleep()* call indicated, among other things, whether this sleep was interruptible (e.g., an I-wait or a D-wait state in the **ps** output). If it was interruptible, or in I state, a signal would result in an "error return" from the sleep, a return back to the user, and usually an error code of *EINTR* being placed in the global *errno* variable.

Solaris 2 waiters

With Solaris 2, this method was revised somewhat. The new method involves creation of something called a *turnstile* (a first-in, first-out queue) with a unique ID value. Since there are so many locks and condition variables, it's impossible to have a separate queue for each one to hold waiting threads, so a pool of queues was defined. This pool is known as a set of turnstiles, which are more or less general-purpose queues for sleeping. When some thread needs to wait and there is no current set of sleepers, it will grab the next queue available from the list of turnstiles, put itself on that queue, and insert the information about which queue it used into the condition variable itself. Later threads that hit the same lock will add themselves to the end of the queue. Eventually, the lock is released, or the condition goes away, and the first sleeping thread on the queue gets to run. The functions that do this are *cv_wait()* and *cv_wait_sig()*, to sleep and await a wakeup call, and *cv_signal()*, to send the wakeup. The latter of the two *cv_wait* calls will also return if a real signal occurs. The condition variable is a short 16-bit location that is intended to contain a turnstile ID number (essentially a row and column number for the array of turnstile pointers). This was the only method of thread synchronization used up through Solaris 2.2.

In Solaris 2.3, a variation on the old hash table scheme was put back in. The condition variable address supplied to *cv_wait* is just used as the magic number in an old-style sleep. The Solaris 2.3 thread structure contains the address of the condition variable that was used to sleep on in the *wchan* field. If this field is non-zero, it is the address of some condition variable and the thread is blocked.

When looking at sleeping threads, then, a Solaris 2.0 through 2.2 thread will have the address of the condition variable as the first parameter of the *cv_wait()* function on the top of its stack trace. For 4.x and Solaris 2.3 (and greater), systems will use the *wchan* field to identify the address, or the "reason for sleeping." This value may help you identify threads or processes that are stuck on the same resource or event. If several seem to have the same *wchan* value (or condition variable address), examine the tracebacks for these to see if the reason for sleeping is innocuous (waiting for input from the keyboard, for instance) or potentially interesting (like sleeping in paging functions that really should be of a very short duration).

Turnstiles are defined and documented in the **/usr/include/sys/turnstile.h** header file. In particular the definitions of row/column sizes and how those are extracted from the 16-bit number in the turnstile are of interest. These will indicate which turnstile is in use, but unfortunately locating the actual list of waiting threads is impossible without digging into the source files.

Mutex locks

There are some differences with condition variables in Solaris 2, but mutex locks are all treated the same way. The mutex lock that allows sleeping, an adaptive mutex, contains a field, called *m_waiters*, in the structure. This field is the ID number of a turnstile, not a condition variable, and the turnstile queue contains the list of threads waiting for this mutex lock. Thus, you can find out if threads are waiting for a particular mutex by examining the waiters field to see if it is non-zero. In general, a thread that is waiting for a mutex should be put on a queue. In a crash dump, stack traces that show one or more threads actually spinning in the *mutex_enter()* function may be significant. It might be worthwhile finding the owners of these mutex locks and checking to see what *they* are doing. Remember, a thread will only spin if it thinks the owner of the lock is currently running and should be done soon. If this doesn't happen, you may have run into a deadlock situation with a loop: Each thread is spinning, waiting for the owner of a different lock to finish and release the first one. If you end up in a circle, each thread will spin forever. This can have a rather significant effect on performance.

29

Part 3 — Case Histories

Introduction to the Case Studies

Postmortem analysis of UNIX system crash dumps always involves the same initial investigative work. We begin the analysis by collecting information including:

- System identification
- System boot time
- System crash time
- Messages that appeared during the crash or hang
- Whether the system was hung, panic'ed or trapped
- Stack traceback

This data might be likened to a medical doctor's check of blood pressure, temperature, pulse, and respiration, followed by an open probe such as "So, what's wrong?", which is answered by the patient. The doctor may do this for every patient who walks into his office.

Using this initial information, the doctor then begins a more detailed analysis of the problem using information and data from further tests. Putting his experience and knowledge to work, he interprets the new data. In UNIX system crash dump analysis, once the initial information is collected, the UNIX guru also moves into a phase of more detailed analysis work.

The subsequent, detailed investigative work will often vary, based on what is found throughout the analysis process and how that data is interpreted. This interpretation is done by individuals, thus introducing a human factor to this absolute, numerical puzzle. One UNIX guru might see the data and decide to turn left in his analysis work, whereas another might turn right. Their analysis paths may cross a few times, but in the end, they will reach the same conclusions.

In the following chapters, we invite you to sit with us while we examine the postmortem remains of several different UNIX systems. You'll see how we interpret the data, adjust our analysis work based on that data, and decide whether the data is relevant. You'll witness successful and unsuccessful quests for information. You'll see clever use of **adb**. We'll also share with you a few of the more advanced "tricks of the trade."

We hope you'll enjoy these visits to the world of UNIX system crash dump analysis.

Pull up a chair, make yourself comfortable, and let's begin!

Network Troubles 30 ≡

For this example, we've got a system that panic'ed several times with essentially the same error: a bad pointer. The trace information indicated that it was a problem in the networking code in the kernel. It's an easy one to solve (or at least fix), because in this case a patch for the problem was readily available.

We'll go through the analysis procedures, take a short detour to verify that the problem was real, and look for a solution in the SunSolve bug and patch databases.

Initial analysis

This system was a fairly new SPARCstation 5, running SunOS 4.1.3_U1. (We'll verify that, leaving nothing to chance.) This means we need to analyze the crash on a comparable system: a sun4m architecture, running the same version of the kernel. Once we put the **savecore** files on the right machine, we can run **adb** and make sure we're working on the right system immediately.

Let's start out by checking the version of the OS we're dealing with.

```
sparc413: strings vmunix.1 | grep SunOS
SunOS Release 4.1.3_U1 (S5) #2: Thu Nov 24 10:35:22 PST 1994
```

So far, so good. We can now run **adb** with some degree of confidence that we're at least looking at the right version of the system. In the analysis, we should be able to find some verification that the system is correct by looking in the system message buffer.

```
sparc413: adb -k vmunix.1 vmcore.1
physmem    2fb1
*panicstr/s
_sizestr+0x9b:    Memory address alignment
```

The panic string printed on the console was "memory address alignment," which indicates that we have a bad pointer in the kernel someplace. A "data fault" message

313

would indicate a similar problem; both of these messages mean that an attempt to follow a pointer resulted in an error. It's a different kind of error, but it still relates to having a bad value in that pointer to begin with. This type of error is detected by hardware, which means we should be able to get some information out of the kernel message buffer. One of the most useful is the PC value, identifying the actual address of the instruction that tried to use the invalid pointer. Let's check the contents of the message buffer. There are two ways to do this. One way is to use the **msgbuf** macro, which will print just the information at the time of the fault. The other way is to dump the whole thing, which means we'll have to isolate the point where the messages wrap around. We'll take the second option. The command starts printing after the header, which in SunOS 4.x is 16 bytes (0x10) long. (In Solaris 2, it got a little bit larger—it's 20 bytes, 0x14.)

```
msgbuf+10/s
0xf0002010: VAC ENABLED
SunOS Release 4.1.3_U1 (S5) #1: Mon Sep 19 15:06:35 PDT 1994
Copyright (c) 1983-1993, Sun Microsystems, Inc.
cpu = SUNW,SPARCstation-5
mod0 = FMI,MB86904 (mid = 0)
mem = 48836K (0x2fb1000)
avail mem = 45682688
entering uniprocessor mode
Ethernet address = 8:0:20:20:28:b0
espdma0 at SBus slot 5 0x8400000
esp0 at SBus slot 5 0x8800000 pri 4 (onboard)
sd0 at esp0 target 3 lun 0
sd0: <SUN0535 cyl 1866 alt 2 hd 7 sec 80>
sd1 at esp0 target 1 lun 0
sd1: <Seagate ST12400N cyl 2617 alt 2 hd 19 sec 84>
SUNW,bpp0 at SBus slot 5 0xc800000 pri 3 (sbus level 2)
ledma0 at SBus slot 5 0x8400010
le0 at SBus slot 5 0x8c00000 pri 6 (onboard)
cgsix0 at SBus slot 3 0x0 pri 9 (sbus level 5)
cgsix0: screen 1152x900, single buffered, 1M mappable, rev 11
SUNW,CS42310 at SBus slot 4 0xc000000 pri 9 (sbus level 5)
zs0 at SBus slot 5 0x1100000 pri 12 (onboard)
zs1 at SBus slot 5 0x1000000 pri 12 (onboard)
SUNW,fdtwo0 at SBus slot 5 0x1400000 pri 11 (onboard)
root on sd0a fstype 4.2
swap on sd0b fstype spec size 70000K
dump on sd0b fstype spec size 69988K
le0: AUI Ethernet
syncing file systems... done
rebooting...
VAC ENABLED
SunOS Release 4.1.3_U1 (SS5) #2: Thu Nov 24 10:35:22 PST 1994
```

```
Copyright (c) 1983-1993, Sun Microsystems, Inc.
cpu = SUNW,SPARCstation-5
mod0 = FMI,MB86904 (mid = 0)
mem = 48836K (0x2fb1000)
avail mem = 45682688
entering uniprocessor mode
Ethernet address = 8:0:20:20:28:b0
espdma0 at SBus slot 5 0x8400000
esp0 at SBus slot 5 0x8800000 pri 4 (onboard)
sd0 at esp0 target 3 lun 0
sd0: <SUN0535 cyl 1866 alt 2 hd 7 sec 80>
sd1 at esp0 target 1 lun 0
sd1: <Seagate ST12400N cyl 2617 alt 2 hd 19 sec 84>
SUNW,bpp0 at SBus slot 5 0xc800000 pri 3 (sbus level 2)
ledma0 at SBus slot 5 0x8400010
le0 at SBus slot 5 0x8c00000 pri 6 (onboard)
cgsix0 at SBus slot 3 0x0 pri 9 (sbus level 5)
cgsix0: screen 1152x900, single buffered, 1M mappable, rev 11
SUNW,CS42310 at SBus slot 4 0xc000000 pri 9 (sbus level 5)
zs0 at SBus slot 5 0x1100000 pri 12 (onboard)
zs1 at SBus slot 5 0x1000000 pri 12 (onboard)
SUNW,fdtwo0 at SBus slot 5 0x1400000 pri 11 (onboard)
root on sd0a fstype 4.2
swap on sd0b fstype spec size 70000K
dump on sd0b fstype spec size 69988K
le0: AUI Ethernet
BAD TRAP: cpu=0 type=7 rp=fd002dc4 addr=0 mmu_fsr=0 rw=0
MMU sfsr=0: No Error
regs at fd002dc4:
    psr=48001c3 pc=f001c770 npc=f001c774
    y: 5800000 g1: 40007e2 g2: ff65cc0c g3: 0
    g4: 0 g5: fd009000 g6: 0 g7: f0189400
    o0: 805905c1 o1: 805908d9 o2: fd002e00 o3: ff65eb32
    o4: 0 o5: fd009000 sp: fd002e10 ra: f0189400
pid -1, `': Memory address alignment
rp=0xfd002dc4, pc=0xf001c770, sp=0xfd002e10, psr=0x48001c3, context=0x0
g1-g7: 40007e2, ff65cc0c, 0, 0, fd009000, 0, f0189400
Begin traceback... sp = fd002e10
Called from f001b8f0, fp=fd002e70, args=ff652a0c ff6492a4 0 5a9d4401 4
8059ffff
Called from f0017e04, fp=fd002ee0, args=ff65d48c 1000 12 1e3fe ff6492a4
ff652a0c
Called from f003b8dc, fp=fd002f40, args=ff649280 ff005000 14 2 20 ff641b8c
Called from f0005eb8, fp=fd002fa0, args=0 8 f001779c 0 48001e7 f018d3f0
```

```
Called from f002e4ec, fp=fd008e98, args=48000e1 8 ff000008 0 40000e6
f0180c00
End traceback...
panic on cpu 0:  Memory address alignment
syncing file systems... done
01050 low-memory static kernel pages
00527 additional static and sysmap kernel pages
00000 dynamic kernel data pages
00145 additional user structure pages
00000 segmap kernel pages
00000 segvn kernel pages
00000 current user process pages
00050 user stack pages
01772 total pages (1772 chunks)

dumping to vp fb004c1c, offset 125800
```

Well, this is a fairly long message buffer, but it does contain some items of interest. We've underlined a few of them so we can touch on those specifically.

First, the fourth line of the message buffer output indicates the CPU type, and yes, this is a SPARCstation 5 like it's supposed to be. There seems to be only one CPU module present on this machine, so it's a uniprocessor, even though it is of the sun4m architecture family. Lots of devices probe out, but nothing really unusual appears to be there. On the second page, we see a reboot. Note that the version of the kernel changed here: It's possible that this was related to the problem (new software or a new configuration may have been introduced here), but we don't know how long it was up before the system crashed or what the changes were.

Right after the boot sequence, we find a BAD TRAP message. This is our panic. The next line indicates that the MMU Synchronous Fault Status Register did not detect any error: This was a problem that was detected before it got to the MMU. A data fault that resulted from a completely wild pointer would probably display some flag settings in this register, indicating a memory access or a mapping problem. Below these we see the value of the PC (Program Counter), which is the address of the failed instruction. Following the register contents, the traceback information appears. This is a stack traceback performed by the kernel trap code, indicating what routines were called to get to the function where the fault occurred. You will note that these are all hexadecimal addresses, which makes interpretation slightly difficult.

This message buffer appears to be quite clean; no "overlap" is apparent. The machine either hasn't been up long or hasn't had much written on the console.

One of the useful things to look at is a stack traceback, to see where the system died and how it got there.

```
$c
_panic(0xf0168800,0xf01835f4,0x0,0x0,0xfd003,0xfd008e98) + b4
_badtrap(0x1c,0xfd002dc4,0x0,0x0,0x0,0xf0197c00) + 114
_trap(0x7,0xfd002dc4,0x0,0x0,0x0,0xffffffff) + 1c8
fixfault(?)
_in_pcbdetach(0x805908d9,0x805908d9,0xf018c400,0x63,0x89b,0x3c06915b)+5c
_tcp_close(?)
_tcp_respond(0xff652a0c,0xff6492a4,0x0,0x5a9d4401,0x4,0x8059ffff) + 7c
_tcp_input(0xff65d48c,0x1000,0x12,0x1e3fe,0xff6492a4,0xff652a0c) + 1878
_ipintr(0xff649280,0xff005000,0x14,0x2,0x20,0xff641b8c)+ 668
_softint(0x0,0x8,0xf001779c,0x0,0x48001e7,0xf018d3f0) +64
softlvl1(?)
_spl0(0x48000e1,0x8,0xff000008,0x0,0x40000e6,0xf0180c00) + 18
_idlework(0x0,0x1,0xfd00a800,0x0,0xf0429000,0x0) + 68
_main(0x44000e7,0xfb0042e0,0x1,0xe,0x80003,0xfb0042e0) + 3d4
```

Tracing from the bottom up, it appears that the system was idle; it came through the *idlework()* function. Following this, there was an interrupt (*softlvl1()*), then *softint()*, and then *ipintr()*, an interrupt service routine for "ip"). There is no physical device that goes by this name, but looking ahead on the stack it seems like this belongs to TCP/IP.

We then find several routines that start with "tcp," another part of TCP/IP (the Transmission Control Protocol networking code in the kernel). Right after this it enters the function *fixfault()*, then goes through the kernel trap code. So far, this looks like it is network related: a message came in, and, in the process of responding to it, the system found a bad pointer.

We can find the exact location of the faulting instruction by looking at the PC value, which is saved by the kernel trap code in a *regs* structure. The second parameter of the *trap()* function in the stack trace is the address of this *regs* structure with values obtained from the CPU registers at the time of the trap. (The first parameter is the actual trap type number, in this case 7, identifying a memory address alignment problem.). There is a macro to display *regs*, so let's see where the bad instruction was.

```
0xfd002dc4$<regs
```

0xfd002dc4:	psr	pc	npc	
	48001c3	f001c770	f001c774	
0xfd002dd0:	y	g1	g2	g3
	5800000	40007e2	ff65cc0c	0

0xfd002de0:	g4	g5	g6	g7
	0	fd009000	0	f0189400
0xfd002df0:	o0	o1	o2	o3
	805905c1	805908d9	fd002e00	ff65eb32
0xfd002e00:	o4	o5	o6	o7
	0	fd009000	fd002e10	f0189400

This gives us the values of the PC and nPC registers, all the globals, the Processor Status Register, and the output registers at the time of the trap. From here, we can extract the value of the PC and examine the instruction at that location. (The PC is also printed on the console by the trap function at the time of the crash, so we can double-check our address by getting the PC from the message buffer, which we underlined above.)

```
0xf001c770?i
_tcp_respond+0x20:      ld       [%o5 + 0x1c], %o5
```

This looks a bit strange, since the stack traceback we got above from **$c** showed a couple of routines after *tcp_respond()* before the fault code showed up.

Just to be on the safe side, let's double-check this stack traceback with the **stacktrace** macro in **adb**. This will give us a more verbose version, but hopefully the same image of the stack as we have here. Maybe it will help to explain why **$c** seems to give more output than it should.

We'll take this in pieces. Normally, of course, this all runs together in one massive burst.

```
<sp$<stacktrace
              l0           l1           l2           l3
              l4           l5           l6           l7
              i0           i1           i2           i3
              i4           i5           i6           i7
```

The first lines of output from the macro are just a set of headings, defining the registers placed in a stack frame. Locals (%l0–%l7) come first, followed by inputs (%i0–%i7).

Following this, the **stacktrace** macro will dump out the 16 registers stored in the beginning of a stack frame: 8 locals and 8 inputs.

0xfd002c40:	fd009b84	fd009000	fd009400	f018ead8
	f004898c	f017d100	fd002c40	0
	f0168800	f01835f4	0	0
	fd003	fd008e98	fd002ca0	f00f7a1c

0xfd002c40:	0xfd009b84	0xfd009000	0xfd009400	_panic_regs
	_panic+0xb4	_olv16	0xfd002c40	0
	_ldtab_initialized+0x434_trap_type			0
	0	0xfd003	0xfd008e98	0xfd002ca0
	_badtrap+0x114			

There are a couple of things to notice here. First, although you get two sets of numbers, they are the same stack frame. Note that the addresses on the left hand side are the same: both 0xfd002c40. This is the same set of data printed in two different ways. The first set of 16 numbers is just plain hexadecimal. The second set is printed symbolically or, if possible, as a variable name plus an offset. It's the same numbers, but sometimes it's easier to recognize significant addresses if you can see them as names, rather than as numbers.

You should also note here that the second set, when it uses names, may have trouble fitting everything on the line, especially for long names. In this case, the third line has only three numbers on it, so the fourth will appear as the first one on the next line, and the last one is on a line by itself. Just remember, the same amount of data is being printed, but the alignment may be off, so count the values, that is, go by number, not by position on the line.

You may recall from the discussion of stack frames that the %i6 register (the next to the last number in our display) is the old stack pointer, or the frame pointer. This gives us the location of the next frame on the stack, which will be displayed next in the same manner.

0xfd002ca0:	44001c1	f0056718	f00166a4	8
	10	10	7	44007e3
	1c	fd002dc4	0	0
	0	f0197c00	fd002d00	f00f7e54

0xfd002ca0:	0x44001c1	_sofree+0xbc	_in_pcbdetach+0x10	
	8	0x10	0x10	7
	0x44007e3	0x1c	0xfd002dc4	0

0	0	_fdkbuf+0x18	0xfd002d00
_trap+0x1c8			

Here again, we see the same set of data displayed twice (the address on the left is the same), but the second set is printed symbolically. The address of this frame is the same as the old %i6 value.

The next frame:

0xfd002d00:	44001c2	f00166e8	0	10
	20	48001c3	fd009b84	0
	7	fd002dc4	0	0
	0	ffffffff	fd002d68	f0005608

0xfd002d00:	0x44001c2	_in_pcbdetach+0x54		0
	0x10	0x20	0x48001c3	0xfd009b84
	0	7	0xfd002dc4	0
	0	0	-1	0xfd002d68
	fixfault+0x5c			

As expected, the next to the last address in the preceding register set is the location of the next frame. We're just following the chain.

You might also recall that the last value is the return PC address, or the location of the call to get to the current function. The first frame had a value of _badtrap+0x114; the second had _trap+0x1c, and this current frame shows fixfault+0x5c. We are obviously backing through some trap-handling code. At some point we should expect to see a trap frame on the stack: the frame with the PC value in register %l1. We know what the PC should be, since that was printed in the message buffer: down in tcp_respond().

0xfd002d68:	48001c3	f001c770	f001c774	40
	7	8	7	fd002d68
	805908d9	805908d9	f018c400	63
	89b	3c06915b	fd002e10	f001cac0

0xfd002d68:	0x48001c3	_tcp_respond+0x20		_tcp_respond+0x24
	0x40	7	8	7
	0xfd002d68	0x805908d9	0x805908d9	_arptab+0x2660
	0x63	0x89b	0x3c06915b	0xfd002e10
	_tcp_close+0x7c			

Well, what have we here? This looks like a normal stack frame, but the value in register %l1 has the PC value for the bad instruction, at just about the location where we might expect to see a trap frame on the stack. **adb** sometimes has trouble identifying a special trap frame, since it can look the same as anything else. You have to keep an eye out and recognize it from context, as we did here.

If this is the trap frame, then the *next* frame on the stack will have the set of registers in use by the code at the time the fault occurred.

0xfd002e10:	80590000	ff64ba80	8059ffff	805905c1
	ffff0000	0	ffff0000	0
	ff652a0c	ff6492a4	0	5a9d4401
	4	8059ffff	fd002e70	f001b8f0
0xfd002e10:	0x80590000	0xff64ba80	0x8059ffff	0x805905c1
	0xffff0000	0	0xffff0000	0
	0xff652a0c	0xff6492a4	0	0x5a9d4401
	4	0x8059ffff	0xfd002e70	_tcp_input+0x1878

Now we appear to be back on track. The return address here is inside *tcp_input()*, and the next stack frame, as we'll see, has a return address in *ipint()*. These follow the traceback information we got from the **$c** command. It looks like **adb** figured out there was a trap frame on the stack, possibly by recognizing the trap function name as a special return address, but it was off by one stack frame. The value in %l1 of the erroneous trap frame is indeed *_in_pcbdetach+0x54*, which is our missing "return address." In this instance, the built-in command gave us misleading information, although it wasn't drastically wrong.

The **stacktrace** macro, although more work to decipher, gives us a dump of exactly what is currently on the stack and leaves the interpretation to us. We can validate or correct what we got from **adb** by using the easy method.

Let's quickly dump out the rest of the stack traceback and verify that it matches what we expect — the output from **$c**.

0xfd002e70:	0	1	0	1f400
	5864e802	0	ff649280	0
	ff65d48c	1000	12	1e3fe
	ff6492a4	ff652a0c	fd002ee0	f0017e04
0xfd002e70:	0	1	0	0x1f400
	0x5864e802	0	0xff649280	0
	0xff65d48c	0x1000	0x12	0x1e3fe

```
              0xff6492a4    0xff652a0c    0xfd002ee0    _ipintr+0x668


0xfd002ee0:   805908d9      805908d9      1             f0189d30
              18            2000          ffffbfff      ffff
              ff649280      ff005000      14            2
              20            ff641b8c      fd002f40      f003b8dc


0xfd002ee0:   0x805908d9    0x805908d9    1             _loif
              0x18          0x2000        0xffffbfff    0xffff
              0xff649280    0xff005000    0x14          2
              0x20          0xff641b8c    0xfd002f40    _softint+0x64


0xfd002f40:   f018d000      30            8             6
              1             4000          dc00          f01869d0
              0             8             f001779c      0
              48001e7       f018d3f0      fd002fa0      f0005eb8


0xfd002f40:   _dk_time+0x20 0x30          8             6
              1             0x4000        0xdc00        _leservice+0x18
              0             8             _ipintr       0
              0x48001e7     _softcalls+0x240            0xfd002fa0
              softlvl1+0x18


0xfd002fa0:   44001c0       f002e554      f002e558      f0005ea0
              0             f017e010      44            fd008df0
              48000e1       8             ff000008      0
              40000e6       f0180c00      fd008e98      f002e4ec


0xfd002fa0:   0x44001c0     _idlework+0xd0 _idlework+0xd4 softlvl1
              0             _xlvl1+0x10   0x44          0xfd008df0
              0x48000e1     8             0xff000008    0
              0x40000e6     _wantmodules+0x23c           0xfd008e98
              _idlework+0x68
```

We'll stop here, since it's clear that the stack matches what we saw before. This last frame is interesting, however. Remember, a system call is a trap, a fault is a trap, and an interrupt is also a trap. Thus, if we see an interrupt service routine on the stack, we should see a trap frame below it someplace to reflect the interrupt itself. In this case, right below the *softlvl1()* function, we note a return address from inside *idlework()*. We can also see, however, that the %l1 register contains an address from inside the same function! (As an additional bit of evidence, %l2 should contain the nPC register, which is normally the PC plus 4. In this case, it does contain the value in %l1 + 4.) This looks like a trap frame as well: the *idlework()* function was interrupted as it was cycling through a loop looking for something to do.

Check the instruction

Let's take a slight detour now and verify that the instruction that caused the fault really was bad or, at least, had a bad pointer to work with. This is not necessary to the analysis, but it's a good idea (and a useful exercise) to double-check your conclusions and verify the data you're working with. If you're not clear on the details of how register windows and traps work, this might be a good time to review it before digging into this section.

The instruction that faulted was:

```
_tcp_respond+0x20:        ld        [%o5 + 0x1c], %o5
```

This is a load instruction, using the value in output register %o5 as a pointer. It will add the constant 0x1c to that address and use the result as the real location in memory which is wants to use. Grabbing a full word from that address, it will load it into output register %o5, replacing what was there. The instruction, however, faulted: it had a bad address. This means that the register values should remain untouched while a trap takes place, so that, if necessary, the instruction could be redone. Now, where do the output registers get put on the stack? Unfortunately, they don't show up at all! But all is not lost. Recall that a trap will get a new register window and will use *only* the local registers to save the address of the faulting instruction. So, the input registers for the trap frame itself are actually untouched; they contain the values that they had before the trap occurred. What are these registers in the new trap frame? These input registers are, in fact, the *output* registers of the preceding register window! So in this case, we can locate the value in register %o5 by looking in register %i5 of the trap frame itself.

We'll show you the frame again, since it's so far back there.

0xfd002d68:	48001c3	f001c770	f001c774	40
	7	8	7	fd002d68
	805908d9	805908d9	f018c400	63
	89b	3c06915b	fd002e10	f001cac0
0xfd002d68:	0x48001c3	_tcp_respond+0x20		_tcp_respond+0x24
	0x40	7	8	7
	0xfd002d68	0x805908d9	0x805908d9	_arptab+0x2660

```
        0x63           0x89b          0x3c06915b     0xfd002e10
        _tcp_close+0x7c
```

The eight locals are printed first, so the value in %i5 (the 14th number printed) would be 0x3c06915b. According to the instruction, we take this value, add the constant 0x1c to it, and use it as the address of a full word in memory. Hey, this is odd—literally! Trying to pull a full 4-byte quantity from memory starting at an odd address is illegal: it violates the alignment requirements for full-word values, which state that these must be on even 4-byte boundaries. Well, it looks like the CPU was right when it took a memory address alignment trap. This is a very bad address to use for a full-word pointer.

Bug check

We have enough information at this point to see if this might be a known bug, perhaps even with a known patch for it. We gave the SunSolve bug database (available on CD-ROM) two key words to search for: *panic* and *tcp_respond*. The search turned up three bug reports to check out.

- Bug Id: 1122457
  Category: kernel
  Subcategory: network
  Release summary: 4.1.3
  Synopsis: trash on net panic box w/"Data Fault" or "Mem addr align" null ptr
    tcp_respond

- Bug Id: 1151988
  Category: kernel
  Subcategory: tcp-ip
  Release summary: no-v4, 4.1.3
  Synopsis: panic in tcp_respond with data fault

- Bug Id: 1108657
  Category: network
  Subcategory: internet
  Release summary: 4.1.2
  Synopsis: in_cksum() caused system panic

All these look somewhat promising, especially the first two. The last was filed against 4.1.2, however, and from the description of the problem, it appears that it only shows up on FDDI links. We'll rule that one out, since the symptoms don't match.

The other two were filed against 4.1.3, not 4.1.3_U1. However, since the U1 release was primarily an upgrade with just bug fixes in it, they may still be applicable if those particular fixes did not make it into the new release. Let's check the patch database just to see if they were taken care of with an official patch.

Searching the patch description files for occurrences of either of these two bug numbers (1122457 and 1151988) gives us two matches.

- Patch-ID# 100584-06
  Keywords: loopback keepalive tcp_respond panic sigio exponential backoff
  Synopsis: SunOS 4.1.1, 4.1.2, 4.1.3: system freezes using loopback interface.

- Patch-ID# 102010-01
  Keywords: loopback keepalive tcp_respond panic sigio exponential backoff
  Synopsis: SunOS 4.1.3_U1: system freezes using loopback interface.

It looks like that problem was fixed in three releases by patch 100584, and it was ported to SunOS 4.1.3_U1 and given a new number, 102010. Let's try this patch and see if it solves the problem.

Resolution

Bug 1151988 included a stack traceback that almost exactly matched the symptoms we saw here. The patch #102010-01 README file explicitly noted that this particular bug was fixed by that patch. The patch was delivered to the customer, who applied it to the system. Extensive use of the network gave no further problems in this area (especially no further panics), and the system stabilized. Problem solved!

≡30

A Stomped-on Module   31 ≣

All too often, the root cause of a system crash cannot be located. When we are working with postmortem files, we are examining the last snapshot of the system. We can always find what caused the system to die, just as a coroner can find what finally ended a human life. However, finding the source of the problem, what actually caused the condition that caused the panic, or the death, is not always so easy. To say a person died of heart failure is easy. But finding the reason the heart stopped is not always as simple. The same is all too true with computers.

The crash dump that we are going to examine in this case study is a perfect example of a system that panic'ed due to an unknown cause. We will quite quickly and easily find the reason that the system failed; however, we may never know who or what caused the condition that resulted in the panic. Additional crashes from the system would be useful, but only in hopes of finding a commonality and, eventually, the real troublemaker.

This system crash dump was kindly provided by a Sun customer who wishes to remain anonymous. Information from the analysis has been modified somewhat to abide by his wishes. The reason for his anonymity is simple. We don't know what caused the crash and we suspect it will happen again. His customers would not be happy to hear that!

Let's take a look at the dump now.

Strings output

Since this is the first time **savecore** was used on this system, the **savecore** files are **unix.0** and **vmcore.0**. For starters, let's take a look at the strings in **vmcore.0** and find out a little about the system. We need to find out what type of system we are dealing with, and it would be nice to get an idea of what type of trouble the system got into.

Things of particular interest have been underlined to help you see what the trained eye looks for.

```
Hiya...  strings vmcore.0 | more
Generic 101318-41
Illegal instruction
g Level = 0
    11403144 bytes
```

```
Thu Jun 16 15:59:0
 saved
dump...
nc Module Version 1.23 loaded
Version 1.12 loaded
LC_CTYPE
CHRCLASS
LC_NUMERIC
LC_TIME
LANGUAGE
LC_COLLATE
LC_MONETARY
LC_MESSAGES
@>{]
BAD TRAP: type=2 rp=f0ac95bc addr=0 mmu_fsr=0 rw=0
CRHout: Illegal instruction
pid=24709, pc=0xfc69d458, sp=0xf0ac9608, psr=0x404000c4, context=931
g1-g7: fc69d440, 8000000, ffffff00, 0, f0ac99e0, 1, fc4c6200
Begin traceback... sp = f0ac9608
Called from f00ee640, fp=f0ac9668, args=fc61607c 80 fc6ca580 1 19f8309 fc61607c
Called from fc606ca0, fp=f0ac9760, args=fc61607c 80 fc6ca580 1 19f8309 fc61607c
Called from fc607a14, fp=f0ac9858, args=f0ac9e94 f0ac9920 f0ac9e94 1 fc607800 fc6ca580
Called from f0070898, fp=f0ac98b8, args=f0ac9e94 f0ac9920 0 0 0 fc607b04
Called from f0041aa0, fp=f0ac9938, args=f0160dec f0ac9eb4 0 f0ac9e90 fffffffc ffffffff
Called from ef790f04, fp=effff138, args=35 0 8d03 1 8 0
End traceback...
panic: Illegal instruction
syncing file systems... done
 3682 static and sysmap kernel pages
   90 dynamic kernel data pages
  288 kernel-pageable pages
    2 segkmap kernel pages
    0 segvn kernel pages
  180 current user process pages
 4242 total pages (4242 chunks)
dumping to vp fc21b404, offset 171664
93, Sun Microsystems, Inc.
pac: enabled - SuperSPARC/SuperCache
cpu0: TI,TMS390Z55 (mid 8 impl 0x0 ver 0x1 clock 50 MHz)
mem = 65536K (0x4000000)
avail mem = 57569280
Ethernet address = 8:0:20:1f:d9:aa      (Actual Ethernet address has been modified)
root nexus = SUNW,SPARCstation-10
iommu0 at root: obio 0xe0000000
sbus0 at iommu0: obio 0xe0001000
espdma0 at sbus0: SBus slot f 0x400000
dma1 at sbus0: SBus slot 0 0x81000
esp0 at espdma0: SBus slot f 0x800000 sparc ipl 4
esp1 at dma1: SBus slot 0 0x80000 SBus level 3 sparc ipl 5
sd1 at esp0: target 1 lun 0
sd1 is /iommu@f,e0000000/sbus@f,e0001000/espdma@f,400000/esp@f,800000/sd@1,0
<SUN1.05 cyl 2036 alt 2 hd 14 sec 72>
sd3 at esp0: target 3 lun 0
sd3 is /iommu@f,e0000000/sbus@f,e0001000/espdma@f,400000/esp@f,800000/sd@3,0
<SUN1.05 cyl 2036 alt 2 hd 14 sec 72>
sd6 at esp0: target 6 lun 0
```

```
sd6 is /iommu@f,e0000000/sbus@f,e0001000/espdma@f,400000/esp@f,800000/sd@6,0
sd18 at esp1: target 3 lun 0
sd18 is /iommu@f,e0000000/sbus@f,e0001000/dma@0,81000/esp@0,80000/sd@3,0
<SUN1.05 cyl 2036 alt 2 hd 14 sec 72>
Unable to install/attach driver 'isp'
root on /pseudo/md@0:0,blk fstype ufs
WARNING: forceload of misc/md_hotspares failed
obio0 at root
zs0 at obio0: obio 0x100000 sparc ipl 12
zs0 is /obio/zs@0,100000
zs1 at obio0: obio 0x0 sparc ipl 12
zs1 is /obio/zs@0,0
cpu 0 initialization complete - online
Unable to install/attach driver 'vme'
Unable to install/attach driver 'mcp'
Unable to install/attach driver 'mcpzsa'
Unable to install/attach driver 'vme'
Unable to install/attach driver 'mcp'
Unable to install/attach driver 'mcpzsa'
Unable to install/attach driver 'stc'
ledma0 at sbus0: SBus slot f 0x400010
le0 at ledma0: SBus slot f 0xc00000 sparc ipl 6
le0 is /iommu@f,e0000000/sbus@f,e0001000/ledma@f,400010/le@f,c00000
lebuffer0 at sbus0: SBus slot 0 0x40000
le1 at lebuffer0: SBus slot 0 0x60000 SBus level 4 sparc ipl 7
le1 is /iommu@f,e0000000/sbus@f,e0001000/lebuffer@0,40000/le@0,60000
dump on /dev/md/dsk/d30 size 102800K
t 3 0x0
sbusmem3 is /iommu@f,e0000000/sbus@f,e0001000/sbusmem@3,0
sbusmem15 at sbus0: SBus slot f 0x0
sbusmem15 is /iommu@f,e0000000/sbus@f,e0001000/sbusmem@f,0
Unable to install/attach driver 'xbox'
SUNW,bpp0 at sbus0: SBus slot f 0x4800000 SBus level 2 sparc ipl 3
SUNW,bpp0 is /iommu@f,e0000000/sbus@f,e0001000/SUNW,bpp@f,4800000
Unable to install/attach driver 'pn'
Unable to install/attach driver 'cgeight'
Unable to install/attach driver 'ipi3sc'
audio: no mmcodec device foundSUNW,DBRIe0 at sbus0: SBus slot f 0x8010000 SBus level 5 sparc
   ipl 9
SUNW,DBRIe0 is /iommu@f,e0000000/sbus@f,e0001000/SUNW,DBRIe@f,8010000
pseudo-device: vol0
vol0 is /pseudo/vol@0
Unable to install/attach driver 'xbox'
Unable to install/attach driver 'vme'
Unable to install/attach driver 'mcp'
Unable to install/attach driver 'vme'
Unable to install/attach driver 'mcp'
Unable to install/attach driver 'mcpzsa'
Unable to install/attach driver 'vme'
Unable to install/attach driver 'mcp'
Unable to install/attach driver 'mcpp'
Unable to install/attach driver 'stc'
Unable to install/attach driver 'isp'
Unable to install/attach driver 'qec'
Unable to install/attach driver 'qe'
```

(References to custom hardware and its driver have been omitted)

A Stomped-on Module   329

```
cseight0 at sbus0: SBus slot 1 0x800 and SBus slot 1 0xc00 and SBus slot 1 0x1800 and SBus
    slot 1 0x1c00 and SBus slot 1 0x2000 SBus level 5 sparc ipl 9
cseight0 is /iommu@f,e0000000/sbus@f,e0001000/cseight@1,800
cseight1 at sbus0: SBus slot 3 0x800 and SBus slot 3 0xc00 and SBus slot 3 0x1800 and SBus
    slot 3 0x1c00 and SBus slot 3 0x2000 SBus level 5 sparc ipl 9
cseight1 is /iommu@f,e0000000/sbus@f,e0001000/cseight@3,800
Hiya...                  (We quit out of more at this point as another set of reboot messages was showing up)
```

What did we learn from the messages ring buffer?

First, the system has the Solaris 2.3 jumbo kernel patch 101318-41 installed. This patch fixes several nasty kernel-related bugs. It's good to see that the customer has the patch installed.

Second, the system panic'ed due to a bad trap type 2, which is an illegal instruction.

Third, we see that the system has one CPU module, running at 50 megahertz clock speed. We will come back to this later.

Finally, we also discover that we are dealing with some unknown quantities: custom hardware and custom device drivers. We will remember this; however, we will try not to let it prejudice us during our analysis work. (Ahem! Please, no snickering!)

Analysis using adb

Let's jump into **adb** and find out what instruction caused the bad trap type 2. We will do this on a SPARCstation 20, a sun4m system as is the customer's SPARCstation 10. The SS20 is running Solaris 2.3. Underlined bits show you the information we used in some of the **adb** commands. Again, some of the **adb** output has been modified in accordance with the customer's wishes.

```
Hiya...   adb -k unix.0 vmcore.0
physmem 3e15
$<utsname
utsname:
utsname:          sys      SunOS
utsname+0x101:    node     anonymous
utsname+0x202:    release 5.3
utsname+0x303:    version Generic_101318-41
utsname+0x404:    machine sun4m
time/Y
time:
time:             1994 Jan 18 17:00:00
*time-(*lbolt%0t100)=Y
                  1994 Jan 16 19:50:45
$c
```

```
complete_panic(0xf0049460,0xf0ac94a4,0xf0ac9330,0x0,0x0,0x1) + 10c
do_panic(?) + 1c
vcmn_err(0xf015f608,0xf0ac94a4,0xf0ac94a4,0x80,0xffee2000,0x3)
cmn_err(0x3,0xf015f608,0x0,0x18,0x18,0xf0152400) + 1c
die(0x2,0xf0ac95bc,0x0,0x0,0x0,0xf015f608) + 78
trap(0x2,0xf0ac95bc,0xf0181d80,0x0,0x0,0x0) + ca0
sys_trap(?) + 1e4
mutex_exit(0x0,0x0,0xe26310ff,0x1,0x0,0x0)
mod_hold_stub(0xfc61607c,0x80,0xfc6ca580,0x1,0x19f8309,0xfc61607c) + 26c
0xf0ac95bc$<regs
0xf0ac95bc:     psr             pc              npc
                404000c4        fc69d458        fc69d4bc
0xf0ac95c8:     y               g1              g2              g3
                0               fc69d440        8000000         ffffff00
0xf0ac95d8:     g4              g5              g6              g7
                0               f0ac99e0        1               fc4c6200
0xf0ac95e8:     o0              o1              o2              o3
                0               0               e26310ff        1
0xf0ac95f8:     o4              o5              o6              o7
                0               0               f0ac9608        f00e7570
fc69d458/i
ipcaccess+0x18: unimp   0x0
ipcaccess/10i
ipcaccess:
ipcaccess:      save    %sp, -0x60, %sp
                ld      [%i2 + 0x4], %o0
                orcc    %g0, %o0, %g0
                bne,a   ipcaccess + 0x1c
                ld      [%i0], %o2
                ba      ipcaccess + 0x7c
                unimp   0x0
                cmp     %o0, %o2
                be,a    ipcaccess + 0x6c
                ld      [%i0 + 0x10], %i0
ipcaccess/10X
ipcaccess:
ipcaccess:      9de3bfa0        d006a004        80900008        32800004
                d4060000        1080001a        0               80a2000a
                22800013        f0062010
```

That was easy! The system trapped due to an illegal instruction in the *ipcaccess()* routine.

Walking the stack by hand

Let's dig a bit further and find out what the stack looks like. We'll start at the stack pointer stored in the trap registers. %o6 contains the stack pointer we need.

```
f0ac9608/16X
0xf0ac9608:    1              0              0              0
               3              1              f015cd94       f016ffac
               fc61607c       80             fc6ca580       1
               19f8309        fc61607c       f0ac9668       f00ee640
f00ee640/i
stubs_common_code+0x6c:       jmpl    %g1, %o7
f0ac9668/16X
0xf0ac9668:    0              f0ac9858       f016b068       fc61607c
               0              f015cd9c       fffffffe0      1424d5e8
               fc61607c       80             fc6ca580       1
               19f8309        fc61607c       f0ac9760       fc606ca0
fc606ca0/i
semctl+0x664:  call    acct + 0x54
f0ac9760/16X
0xf0ac9760:    404000c7       f008534c       fc607824       2
               fc0af000       f027bd44       0              f016ffac
               f0ac9e94       f0ac9920       f0ac9e94       1
               fc607800       fc6ca580       f0ac9858       fc607a14
fc607a14/i
semsys+0x40:   call    semctl
f0ac9858/16X
0xf0ac9858:    404000c0       fc6079d0       f016b068       1a
               0              0              fc03c4c0       fc03c4c0
               f0ac9e94       f0ac9920       0              0
               0              fc607b04       f0ac98b8       f0070898
f0070898/i
syscall+0x3e4: jmpl    %g1, %o7
f0ac98b8/16X
0xf0ac98b8:    88             1              f01567ac       0
               fc0af000       35             f0ac9994       f0ac99e0
               f0160dec       f0ac9eb4       0              f0ac9e90
               fffffffc       ffffffff       f0ac9938       f0041aa0
f0041aa0/i
_sys_rtt+0x4d8: call    syscall
f0ac9938/16X
0xf0ac9938:    40900082       ef76b254       ef76b258       20
               88             4              7              f0ac9938
               35             0              8d03           1
               8              0              effff138       ef790f04
ef790f04/i

data address not found
```

The stack traceback shows that a system call was made that resulted in a call to the *semsys()* routine.

Did you notice that the **$c** output did not match the stack traceback output? When looking at system crashes that resulted from a trap, it is important to remember to use the stack pointer in the trap's register. Otherwise, you may not get an accurate picture of the most recent activity.

The ipcaccess() routine

More than one loadable module in the Solaris 2.3 system has a routine named *ipcaccess()*. However, looking at the stack traceback output, we can see that we were coming up through the semaphore code, specifically the *semsys()* and *semctl()* routines. Let's confirm that there's an *ipcaccess()* routine or symbol in the semaphore module.

```
Hiya...   cd /kernel/sys
Hiya...   ls
c2audit     inst_sync  msgsys     nfs        semsys     shmsys
Hiya...   nm semsys | grep ipcaccess
[47]    |          0|         0|NOTY |GLOB |0     |UNDEF |ipcaccess
Hiya...
```

That looks like a "yes."

Loading the semsys module with modload

Next, let's see what the *ipcaccess()* routine *should* have looked like. To be able to examine *ipcaccess()* on a live system, we have to first make sure the module **/kernel/sys/semsys** is already loaded. If it is not, then we must load it.

You must be root to load a module into the kernel.

```
Hiya...   modinfo | grep semsys
Hiya...   su
Password:
# modload /kernel/sys/semsys
# modinfo | grep semsys
 80 fc5b8000  1b0c  53   1  semsys (System V semaphore facility)
# adb -k /dev/ksyms /dev/mem
physmem 1e05
ipcaccess/10i
ipcaccess:
```

```
ipcaccess:     save    %sp, -0x60, %sp
               sethi   %hi(0xf015cc00), %15
               or      %15, 0x294, %15              ! ipcaccess_info
               ld      [%15 + 0x10], %11
               tst     %11
               be,a    ipcaccess + 0x3c
               restore
               ld      [%15 + 0xc], %11
               ld      [%15], %10
               cmp     %11, %10
$q
#
```

As a reminder, here are the first 10 instructions of the *ipcaccess()* routine from the customer's system crash dump.

```
ipcaccess:     save    %sp, -0x60, %sp
               ld      [%i2 + 0x4], %o0
               orcc    %g0, %o0, %g0
               bne,a   ipcaccess + 0x1c
               ld      [%i0], %o2
               ba      ipcaccess + 0x7c
               unimp   0x0
               cmp     %o0, %o2
               be,a    ipcaccess + 0x6c
               ld      [%i0 + 0x10], %i0
```

Well, that's a surprise! The routines are not the same! How can that be?

Remember to use the same OS!

Following a hunch (in other words, a fellow OS support engineer said, "And what OS are you running? Try using a SPARCstation 10 system instead!"), we moved the analysis work over to a lab system called "sun4m-23," a SPARCstation 10 running Solaris 2.3 FCS. Here is what we found.

```
sun4m-23...  modinfo | grep semsys
 60 fc2dc000 1b0c  53   1  semsys (System V semaphore facility)
sun4m-23...  su
Password:
# adb -k /dev/ksyms /dev/mem
physmem 1e15
ipcaccess/10i
```

```
ipcaccess:
ipcaccess:       save      %sp, -0x60, %sp
                 ld        [%i2 + 0x4], %o0
                 orcc      %g0, %o0, %g0
                 bne,a     ipcaccess + 0x1c
                 ld        [%i0], %o2
                 ba        ipcaccess + 0x7c
                 clr       %i1
                 cmp       %o0, %o2
                 be,a      ipcaccess + 0x6c
                 ld        [%i0 + 0x10], %i0
$q
#
```

Ah, that's much better! But why was there a difference between the two systems in the first place?

What we failed to remember was that the SS20 running Solaris 2.3 being used to analyze the SS10 crash was *actually* running a special version of Solaris 2.3 known as Hardware Release 5/94. 5/94 was specifically generated and released to support the newer members of the Sun family of hardware, which included the SPARCstation 20. While the kernel architecture was the same, thus allowing for analysis of SS10 crashes, some of the software on 5/94 had been enhanced, such as the **semsys** module, making comparison at the assembly instruction level unfeasible.

To be on the safe side, we redid the analysis on a SS10 running Solaris 2.3 FCS. The results were the same as those given on the SS20, with the exception of the code in **semsys**.

So, it appears that the customer's **semsys** *ipcaccess()* routine was corrupt. How was that possible? Let's explore the possibilities.

Is it a hardware failure?

Two possible scenarios come to mind. The first involves the hardware. It is possible that the instruction was set to zero via a hardware error during the loading of the module into memory. However, if the system were suffering from hardware problems, even rare flukes, we would expect to see a rash of problems develop with the system. We would also hope to see a less "clean" failure. Seeing a zero where the instruction should be is not comforting. Had we lost a single bit of the instruction, it would look more like a hardware failure. Had a larger section of code been corrupted, it would be easier to declare it a hardware problem. There is one other possibility, though...

We noted in our analysis that the CPU module was a 50 MHz model. On rare occasions, we saw a timing problem with these chips, one that was readily fixed by a simple patch to the kernel. The patch set kernel variable *enable_sm_wa* to 1. Let's see if that patch had been made to the customer's system.

```
Hiya...  adb -k unix.0 vmcore.0
physmem 3e15
enable_sm_wa/X
enable_sm_wa:
enable_sm_wa:    1
$q
Hiya...
```

Obviously, this customer is well informed and had already installed the fix. The hardware failure theory is getting weaker.

Another interesting piece of data that we have picked up from the analysis is that the system has been up and running for two days. From talking to the customer, it sounds as if they use the semaphore code all of the time, so it is probably safe to assume that the **semsys** module had been loaded and in use for quite some time, in terms of computer time. Is there a way to confirm this?

In the **/usr/include/sys/modctl.h** file, we find that a count is maintained, showing how many times a module has been loaded. However, if the module has been loaded since boot time and was never unloaded, a count of 1 would be perfectly acceptable. Therefore, using the load count won't be of help to us.

Also, digging through **modctl.h**, we find that the time a module is loaded is not recorded anywhere. But, even if it was, that wouldn't prove that the module had been used successfully prior to the time of the crash.

So, we have no way of proving or disproving the hardware theory at this point, other than to wait for another crash and see if it's similar.

How about a software problem?

The other possibility, (yes, you knew it was coming), is that *another program* placed a big fat zero into the *ipcaccess()* routine. Modules are loaded into memory with writable pages! Yes, a program running in kernel mode can write onto another module's pages, changing its instructions and data.

Diving through the SunSolve databases, there are (so far) no recorded instances of modules merrily stomping on other modules the way we have seen in this crash dump. That leaves us the following options.

1. Search every thread that was running to see if it had *very recently* written a zero into *ipcaccess+18*. Sounds like a good idea, but how would we do this without becoming very old in the process? We will come back to this idea in a few minutes.

2. We could query **nm** and see if any of the values for the symbols happens to be that of the address of *ipcaccess+18*. A long shot, at best.

3. We notify the programmer who wrote the custom device driver, letting him know everything we found in the crash dump, so that he can decide if maybe his new driver stomped on the **semsys** module.

4. We put the latest and greatest fixes to **semsys** onto the customer's system and hope that he never sees another crash like this one. Sure, it's a shotgun approach, but if he's using the semaphore code, we might as well help him avoid any other known bugs in the code. (Proactive support is a good thing!)

Option 1 sounds too much like looking for a needle in a haystack. But, if we had the energy to wander through all of the threads, we would probably try to locate the threads running the unknown custom drivers first. At the very least, we could look for a store instruction that writes to *ipcaccess+18*. While we will reject this option (in favor of option 3), we do have another trick up our sleeve, which we will try shortly.

Option 3 takes care of option 1. The programmer will be doing the same thing, and he knows the code to the driver we are most worried about.

Option 4 has been done, with the customer fully aware of the analysis, our findings, and our concerns about his system. He knows it will crash again someday unless the root cause is located.

Using nm to query symbol values

Option 2 is a shot in the dark, but it doesn't take long, so let's try it anyway.

The **nm** command provides us with the decimal values of the symbols. We will ask **nm** if the address of *ipcaccess+18* was stored in a symbol anywhere.

Comments are being added for educational purposes.

```
Hiya...   adb -k unix.0 vmcore.0
physmem 3e15
ipcaccess+18/X                          (Just making sure this is the right place)
ipcaccess+0x18:  0
.=X                                     (Get the address of ipcaccess+18)
                 fc69d458
.=D                                     (We need the address in decimal for nm)
                 -60173224              (As expected, adb gives us a negative value)
```

```
$q
Hiya...  bc                             (Use bc to translate it instead)
ib=16                                   (Set input base to base 16, hexidecimal)
fc69d458
syntax error on line 2, teletype        (Oops! bc hates uppercase)
FC69D458
4234794072
quit
Hiya...  nm unix.0 | grep 4234794072    (No exact matches found)
Hiya...
```

It was worth a try. However, if we had found a match, what would we have done with it? We would have to establish what the symbol does for a living, whether 0xfc69d458 is a valid value for it, and how it is used by other routines.

If, for example, it was something nice and straightforward, such as the address of a certain counter, we would then have to find out who set up the address and why. That would have presented us with yet another difficult or impossible puzzle to unravel, especially without access to the source code.

adb's search command at work

There is another trick that might be worth trying. We can ask **adb** to search for a value. We'll demonstrate this by searching for a known value first, then for the address of the clobbered instruction. We start our searches at *scb*, which is where we find the first page of the kernel.

```
Hiya...  adb -k unix.0 vmcore.0
physmem 3e15
rootdir/X
rootdir:                                (The pointer to the root directory's vnode)
rootdir:        fc190208
scb/L fc190208                          (Starting at scb—the system control block—locate value fc190208)
p0+0x2d0                                (A match was found here, which we can confirm)
./X
p0+0x2d0:       fc190208
+/L fc190208                            (Advance adb pointer and continue search)
rootdir                                 (Another match)
./X
rootdir:
rootdir:        fc190208
                                        (Press Return to advance adb pointer)
clock_lock:
clock_lock:     0
./L fc190208                            (Continue search from here)
```

```
clock_lock                    (No more matches were found, so we stayed here)
ipcaccess+18/X
ipcaccess+0x18: 0               (We want to search for or locate any memory)
.=X                             (location that contains the address of the)
                 fc69d458       (clobbered ipcaccess instruction.)
scb/L fc69d458
scb
$q
Hiya...
```

As we can see from this session, nowhere within the kernel was the address of the clobbered instruction, *ipcaccess+18*, stored as a variable.

Masked searches within adb

Staying with this train of thought, the only other possibility is that the address of *ipcaccess+18* was built by a `sethi` / `store` combination of instructions. To search for the `sethi` instruction, which sets a register value to contain the high-order 22 bits of value 0xfc69d458, we would need to know the actual instruction operation code (opcode) of the command to search for. And, since there are 32 registers available to the `sethi` instruction, we would need to search 32 combinations of opcodes at that!

Fortunately, the **L** command within **adb** happens to have a mask feature. Using it, we can tell **adb** to search for anything that matches some of the value we specify, instead of the whole value.

The first thing we need to know, in order to search for a specific instruction, is the actual opcode. For this type of information, you'll usually need to refer to the chip manual, in our case, the SPARC Version 8 Reference Manual. Alternatively, you could try to disassemble several `sethi` instructions until you figure out the opcode.

Here is the `sethi` opcode layout.

Nib 0	Nib 1	Nib 2	Nib 3	Nib 4	Nib 5	Nib 6	Nib 7
0 1	dest register	1 0 0	22 bits to store in destination register				

Figure 31-1 sethi opcode layout

When we place the high-order 22 bits of the address fc69d458 into this layout, the last six nibbles will contain 3f1a75.

The destination register is the unknown quantity. Any one of 32 registers could be specified in the `sethi` instruction we seek. Therefore, during our search, we want to mask for everything except the destination register field.

The bits we want to match exactly during the search must be masked with a 1 bit. To match perfectly on all bits, our mask would be ffffffff (the default if no mask is specified). We want to match on all but the five destination register bits; therefore, our mask will be c1ffffff.

Let's return to **adb** and try the search command using a mask. First, we will search for something we know exists. Digging around, we found that the *panic_setup()* routine contained a cluster of `sethi` instructions, so we will use it for our example.

```
setup_panic+18,a/X4-i
setup_panic+0x18:           113c060d      sethi   %hi(0xf0183400), %o0
              7ffffe2c      call    mutex_enter
              901222e0      or      %o0, 0x2e0, %o0
              173c0549      sethi   %hi(0xf0152400), %o3
              d602e264      ld      [%o3 + 0x264], %o3        ! panicstr
              8090000b      orcc    %g0, %o3, %g0
              22800007      be,a    setup_panic + 0x4c
              1f3c0556      sethi   %hi(0xf0155800), %o7
              193c0549      sethi   %hi(0xf0152400), %o4
              1b3c05a2      sethi   %hi(0xf0168800), %o5

setup_panic/L 013c0556 c1ffffff
setup_panic+0x34
./i
setup_panic+0x34:           sethi   %hi(0xf0155800), %o7
+/L 013c0556 c1ffffff
mlsetup+0x70
./i
mlsetup+0x70:   sethi   %hi(0xf0155800), %o1

scb/L 013f1a75 c1ffffff
scb
```

During our practice search, we matched on two variations of the `sethi` instruction. Each referenced a different destination register. Sadly, the search for the high-order 22 bits of the address of the *ipcaccess()* routine didn't result in any matches. Still, the effort was a good one!

Conclusion

Since this was a customer's actual crash dump, we had to contact the customer with our findings. Depending on the customer and his understanding of what we were faced with, the conversation could have been uncomfortable at best because we really didn't have the problem figured out.

The tail end of the telephone conversation went something like this:

> "So, let me see if I get this right. You're telling me that either we have a hardware problem or we have a software problem?" the customer wisely summed up the news.

> "Yes, that's what we believe."

> "And, if I understand you correctly, you're telling me that my system will crash again?" he further asked.

> "Um, yeah, that's our feeling."

The customer laughed!

He understood exactly what we had found and appreciated what we were faced with. And, thanks to our analysis, he was now armed with enough information to go back to his device-driver writers and ask for their assistance.

He was also now up to date with Solaris 2 issues and fixes to discovered bugs, especially in the **semsys** module.

It's been over a year since we've heard from this customer about this system. His hardware is fine, and we suspect his new device drivers are coming along nicely.

31

Hanging Instead of Swapping 32 ≡

Let's examine a system hang. This is a SunOS 4.1.2 (Solaris 1.0.1) sun4c machine that was "not responding to the keyboard." The user at the console, using the window system, had the system freeze up on him. It did respond to the L1-A sequence, so he killed it.

Initial information

To start, verify a few things. We can be sure this is a crash dump taken from a hang by looking at the panic message that was printed on the console: "panic: zero" means it was forced by someone via the keyboard (either with an L1-A sequence or a Break). We should also verify that it is a 4.1.2 release kernel.

```
zatch 11: strings vmunix.2|grep SunOS
SunOS Release 4.1.2 (WRANGLER) #2: Thu Aug 20 18:52:38 CDT 1992

zatch 12: adb -k vmunix.2 vmcore.2
*panicstr/s
_va_cache_valid+0x367:     zero
^D
```

The address associated with this string is generally not significant; all we are interested in here is the actual string that was printed. **adb** will try to locate the closest global symbol next to the address we are printing out and use that as the symbolic address to display. In this case, the string is probably in quotes in the middle of some code, so it doesn't really have a name associated with it. **adb** does a "best guess," but we don't really care.

Process status

Now that we've seen that the core dump appears to match the circumstances, we can continue and look at things with some confidence. Since this is a hang, one of the first steps should be to look at the processes on the machine and see if any are stuck.

343

With Solaris 1 systems, we can use the **ps** command to look at a core file, then check for processes in a "D" state ("disk-wait"). If the system is locked up due to a lack of resources or some sort of deadlock, the D-state processes are likely candidates.

Some of the processes in the following **ps** and **adb traceall** output have been deleted for space reasons, so this listing is a little short. Yours may well look a lot longer, especially if the system was busy at the time.

```
zatch 13: ps -axk vmunix.2 vmcore.2
PID TT STAT   TIME COMMAND
   0 ?  D      8:03 swapper
   1 ?  I      4:59 /sbin/init -
   2 ?  D      0:20 pagedaemon
  55 ?  RW     2:46 portmap
  60 ?  IW     0:00 keyserv
  69 ?  I      1:13 in.routed
  72 ?  I      0:03 (biod)
  73 ?  I      0:03 (biod)
  74 ?  I      0:03 (biod)
  75 ?  I      0:03 (biod)
  86 ?  RW     0:01 syslogd
  98 ?  RW     0:08 /usr/lib/sendmail -bd -q1h
 104 ?  IW     0:01 rpc.mountd -n
 106 ?  I      0:00 (nfsd)
 107 ?  I      0:00 (nfsd)
 108 ?  I      0:00 (nfsd)
 109 ?  IW     0:01 rarpd -a
 110 ?  IW     0:00 rarpd -a
 111 ?  I      0:00 (nfsd)
 113 ?  I      0:00 (nfsd)
 114 ?  I      0:00 (nfsd)
 115 ?  I      0:00 (nfsd)
 116 ?  I      0:00 (nfsd)
 117 ?  IW     0:00 rpc.bootparamd
 120 ?  IW     0:00 rpc.statd
 122 ?  IW     0:00 rpc.lockd
 128 ?  RW    18:25 automount -m -f /etc/auto.master
 132 ?  D    532:35 update
 135 ?  RW     0:02 cron
 141 ?  RW     0:54 inetd
 145 ?  IW     0:00 /usr/lib/lpd
5346 co IW     0:00 -csh (csh)
5357 co IW     0:00 sh /home/sat/.openwin
5358 co IW     0:00 /bin/sh /usr/openwin/bin/openwin -dev /dev/fb
5362 co IW     0:00 /usr/openwin/bin/xinit -- /usr/openwin/bin/xnews :0
5363 co D     67:05 /usr/openwin/bin/xnews :0 -dev /dev/fb
5370 co IW     0:00 sh /home/sat/.xinitrc
5382 co IW     0:04 mwm -multiscreen -display :0.0 :0.1 :0.2
5385 co IW     0:00 calctool -display :0.1 -title CALC -scale medium
```

```
 5387 co IW    0:00 sv_xv_sel_svc
 5388 co IW    0:00 vkbd -nopopup
 5389 co IW    0:00 dsdm
 5391 co IW    0:00 calctool -display :0.2 -title CALC -scale medium
 5393 co IW    0:00 calctool -display :0.0 -title CALC -scale medium
 5394 co IW    0:00 xterm -C -name SystemConsole -title System Console -sb
 5408 co IW    1:36 xterm -sb -font -misc-*-medium-r-normal-*-15-120-*-*-*-*-*
  148 ?  IW    0:00 - std.9600 ttya (getty)
 5398 ?  IW    0:00 -sh (csh)
 5409 ?  IW    0:00 -sh (csh)
27804 ?  RW    0:00 sleep 30
 4434 ?  R     0:25 gendis second
 4435 ?  I     0:30 recdis second
 4436 ?  R     0:53 gendis first
 4437 ?  I     1:04 recdis first
 5436 ?  IW    0:00 csh go
 5438 ?  IW    0:00 /bin/csh go
 5440 ?  I     3:19 ranger/trcque go.out
 5487 ?  IW    0:30 /bin/sh ps_repeat -p mwm -d 30
 5489 ?  R     0:02 wsini
 5497 ?  IW    0:00 wprntfhost .0
 5498 ?  IW    0:00 wprntfhost .1
 5499 ?  IW    0:00 wprntfhost .2
 5500 ?  R     0:04 csupv primary FICC_PRIMARY_MMF
 5502 ?  RW    0:01 resync
 5503 ?  Z     0:00 <defunct>
 5504 ?  R     0:01 icon32
 5505 ?  R     0:05 colorhost .0
 5507 ?  R     0:05 colorhost .1
 5508 ?  R     0:05 colorhost .2
 5513 ?  IW    0:00 wprntfhost .1
 5514 ?  IW    0:00 wprntfhost .2
 5515 ?  IW    0:00 wprntfhost .0
 5516 ?  IW    0:00 colorhost .0
 5517 ?  IW    0:00 colorhost .2
 5518 ?  I     0:30 colorhost .0
 5519 ?  I     0:33 colorhost .2
 5520 ?  IW    0:00 colorhost .1
 5521 ?  I     0:33 colorhost .1
 5522 ?  I    27:11 keys .0
 5523 ?  R     0:06 navwin .0
 5524 ?  D    23:48 crtout .0 -sync
 5525 ?  R     0:05 navwin .1
 5526 ?  R     0:14 crtout .1 -sync
 5527 ?  R     0:05 navwin .2
 5528 ?  R     0:14 crtout .2 -sync
 5529 ?  D     0:14 taskmon
27805 ?  RW    0:00 sleep 30
27859 ?  D     0:00 play -v 25 dialtone.au
27863 ?  D     0:00 <exiting>
```

Let's note a few things about this **ps** output.

First of all, there are a few processes in D state, but not a lot. However, one of them is OpenWindows, which might account for the console freezing up. We also have the swapper and pagedaemon in D state. Although this is fairly normal, it may be worth looking at the stack traceback to see why they are stopped.

There is nothing at all in DW state, which could mean that the system froze up, and before it had a chance to swap everything out, the alert user at the console decided to kill the system and get a crash. It might also mean that the freeze was related to swapping, and nothing *could* get swapped in or out.

There are also quite a few processes in R or RW state. These are *runnable* programs. The relatively high number makes it look like the system was fairly active at the time of the freeze. However, we have no way of knowing how long those programs were in this state. If a program is waiting, say, for input from the network and the machine crashes, the network does not stop. Even though the panic function is writing out the contents of memory onto disk, a chunk of data may arrive from the Ethernet and cause a process to be "awakened," or put back on the run queue. Interrupts are not disabled, so some of these runnable processes may have become runnable during the time the system was trying to shut itself down.

We should also note that this is obviously a networked system, as we have four **biod** processes running (so this is an NFS server) and eight **nfsd**s running (so this is an NFS client). None of these are in IW state or D state, which means that the network has been fairly busy because all the processes were active recently, and none of them seem to be stuck. To be sure, though, we should check the stack traces for these.

Stack tracebacks for every process

Now let's get a stack traceback for each of the processes on the system to see what they were doing. This is very long output, so we will look at it in smaller chunks. (Some of the output has been deleted for brevity.)

```
zatch: adb -k vmunix.2 vmcore.2
$<traceall
        pid 0
sw_bad(?)
_swtch(0x11901ae3,0xf8180c60,0xf814fc00,0x0,0x3,0x0) + 80
_sleep(0xf8180c60,0xa,0x165e000,0x0,0xa,0xf826e34c) + 1a0
_ufs_getpage(0xfd84c2d0,0x165d000,0x1000,0x0,0xf814edc0,0x1000) + b4
_ufs_l_getpage(0xfd84c2d0,0x165d000,0x1000,0x0,0xf814edc0,0x1000) + c4
_segu_softload(0xfd803678,0xf84a5000,0x1,0x5b,0x1,0x1c7000) + b4
_segu_fault(0xfd803678,0xf84a5000,0x4000,0x2,0x5b,0xfd8069f4) + 104
_swapin(0xf827182c,0x166,0x0,0xfffffffe,0x4000,0x2) + 50
```

```
_sched(0xf8184e70,0xf827182c,0xf8184e40,0x1f,0x2,0x4) + 33c
_main(0x114000e7,0xffffffff,0x2a9b6f81,0xfffe,0xf814f000,0xf826e34c) + 374
```

Timeout! This looks a bit unusual. We can't tell everything from the stack traceback without code to look at, but we can notice a few things. Reading from the bottom up, it looks like process 0, **swapper**, was doing a swap-in. Going up a couple of lines (the *segu* functions refer to the U-area for a process), we see two *getpage* functions that start with *ufs*, which refers to the UNIX File System. This means we were trying to swap from a regular file system, not a raw partition.

To continue:

```
        pid 1
sw_bad(?)
_swtch(0x11800aa5,0xf8180cb0,0xf814fc00,0x0,0x3,0xf8272ef0) + 80
_sleep(0xf8180cb0,0x1e,0xf826e63c,0x0,0x1e,0xf826e408) + 1a0
_wait4(0xf826e63c,0x1,0xf815b640,0xf826e408,0xf8272ef0,0xf8272ef0) + 4a0
_syscall(0xf82e1000) + 3b4
```

According to the **ps** output, process 1, **init**, was in an I state. In other words, **init** was waiting for I/O. The entry point into the system (the last line of the stack traceback) is *syscall()*, which is normally the only way a user process can get into the kernel. The next line up usually identifies the system call that was made—in this case, *wait4()*, a derivative of *wait()* (to stop until a child process changes state). The third, second, and first lines are *sleep()*, *swtch()*, and *sw_bad()*. The third, *sleep()*, is the function in the kernel that gives up control and allows a context switch to some other process. The next function is the actual context switcher, *swtch()*. The top line is an assembly language label (the address does not start with an underscore, which the Solaris 1, bundled C compiler automatically adds to any C function name), so although it looks alarming, it's not significant. It's down in very low-level code in the context switch procedure.

```
        pid 2
sw_bad(?)
_swtch(0x11901ae4,0xf82713c4,0x114010e4,0x0,0x3,0xf82b31ac) + 80
_sleep(0xf8180ce0,0x1,0x154,0xa00,0x1,0xf826e4c4) + 1a0
_pageout(?)
_yield_child(0xf8184c00,0x1,0x1,0xf82a8374,0xf82cd1c4,0x0) + cc
        pid 128
        pid 55
        pid 5408
        pid 60
data address not found
```

```
            pid 5346
data address not found
```

Here we have a bunch of "blanks"— nothing gets printed. If you'll refer back to the **ps** output, these are all in IW or RW state, meaning that they have been swapped out. No stack traceback information is available in memory for these particular processes.

```
            pid 69
sw_bad(?)
_swtch(0x11800aa7,0xf8272798,0x114000a7,0x0,0x3,0x118000a6) + 80
_sleep(0xf8180c10,0x1a,0x400000,0xa00,0x1a,0xf826e92c) + 1a0
_select(0xffbfffff,0x88001,0xf8303fe0,0x0,0xf8303fe0,0xf8304000) + 4cc
_syscall(0xf8304000) + 3b4
```

This type of process (pid 69) is another common sight. A lot of processes which wait for I/O use the *select()* system call, which will alert them when one or more file descriptors have data available.

```
            pid 72
sw_bad(?)
_swtch(0x11800ae0,0xf826eaa4,0xf814fc00,0x0,0x3,0xf82d92bc) + 80
_sleep(0xf8180d70,0x1a,0xf8189c00,0x0,0x1a,0xf826e9e8) + 1a0
_async_daemon(0xfd8a85c4,0xfd8a85b8,0xf815b640,0xf815bb40,0xf8309000,0xf815bb40)
    + 260
_syscall(0xf8309000) + 3b4
```

This process (72) belongs to one of the **biod** processes. It's in the system call, *async_daemon()*, and is sleeping, probably waiting for a network request. All the **biod**s look the same.

```
sw_bad(?)
_swtch(0x11800ae2,0xf826f664,0xf814fc00,0x0,0x3,0xf8027c60) + 80
_sleep(0xf8180c78,0x1a,0xfd844af8,0x100,0x1a,0xf826efc8) + 1a0
_sbwait(0xff64ab38,0xfd8dc688,0x826,0x0,0xffffffff,0x2) + 14
_svc_run(0xfd844af8,0x186a3,0x2,0xf8027d94,0x0,0x110010e7) + 28
_nfs_svc(0xf8330fe0,0x4d8,0xf815b640,0xf815bb18,0xf8331000,0xf815bb18) + 260
_syscall(0xf8331000) + 3b4
```

And here we have an NFS daemon. These all look the same.

Next, we see one of the processes (pid 132) in D state.

```
        pid 132
sw_bad(?)
_swtch(0x11901ae6,0xf8180cd0,0xf814fc00,0x0,0x3,0xf8280c64) + 80
_sleep(0xf8180cd0,0x1,0xf814fc00,0x800,0x1,0xf826f898) + 1a0
_page_cv_wait(0xf82bec8c,0x114010e0,0xf814fc00,0x0,0x1,0x1) + 14
_page_wait(0xf82bec8c,0xf82a4bfc,0x0,0x0,0x16d7000,0xfd84c2d0) + a4
_pvn_getdirty(0xf82bec8c,0xf8326c0c,0x0,0x0,0x16d7000,0xfd84c2d0) + e4
_pvn_vplist_dirty(0xfd84c2d0,0x0,0x0,0x0,0xf8298b2c,0xf82bec8c) + 110
_ufs_putpage(0xfd84c2d0,0xfd84c2c8,0x0,0x0,0x0,0xf826f898) + 350
_ufs_l_putpage(0xfd84c2d0,0x0,0x0,0x0,0x0,0x0) + 30
_syncip(0xfd84c2c8,0x0,0x0,0x2,0x1101,0x0) + 124
_update(0xf8187130,0x104e,0xfd84c2c8,0xfd8a5eb8,0x0,0xfd84c2c8) + 2f0
_ufs_sync(0x0,0xf815dca0,0xf81663c0,0xf8185090,0xf815dca0,0xfd852b98) + 4
_sync(0xf8326fe0,0x120,0xf815b640,0xf815b760,0xf8327000,0xf815dc60) + 3c
_syscall(0xf8327000) + 3b4
```

Process 132 is **update**. The normal function of **update** is to do a sync every 30 seconds. This crash appears to have caught **update** in the middle of one of its sync operations. The system call is *sync()*, and it seems to be going through UFS operations (putting a page out, in this case), and waiting for some sort of resource to be freed in the pageout code. This may be abnormal, or may not. Let's go on and see what other processes there are.

```
        pid 5525
sw_bad(?)
_swtch(0x11801aa7,0xf8271190,0x114010a7,0x0,0x3,0x9a) + 80
_sleep(0xf8180c10,0x1a,0x64,0xa00,0x1a,0xf826fff0) + 1a0
_select(0xffbfffff,0x20088001,0xf847ffe0,0xf7fff1d0,0xf847fdd0,0xf8480000) + 4cc
_syscall(0xf8480000) + 3b4
```

Process 5525, is one of the ones marked in the **ps** output as runnable. It was in a *select* system call, which means that if the system were still up this process would have been continued with the *select*, returning an indication that input was available. This change of state could have been done at any time.

```
        pid 5363
sw_bad(?)
_swtch(0x11901ae7,0xf827124c,0xf814fc00,0x0,0x3,0xf8188c00) + 80
_sleep(0xf8180c60,0xa,0xe7000,0x0,0xa,0xf827068c) + 1a0
_ufs_getpage(0xfd84c2d0,0xe6000,0x1000,0xf838fdbc,0xf838fd58,0x1000) + b4
_ufs_l_getpage(0xfd84c2d0,0xe6000,0x1000,0xf838fdbc,0xf838fd58,0x1000) + c4
_anon_getpage(0x0,0xf838fdbc,0xf838fd58,0x1000,0xfd8487c8,0x324000) + 170
_segvn_faultpage(0xfd8487c8,0x324000,0x64000,0xfd9093c0,0x0,0xf838fdec) + 148
_segvn_fault(0xfd8487c8,0x1000,0x0,0x0,0x324000,0xfd84c9e0) + 5d4
```

```
_as_fault(0x324000,0xfd8487c8,0x1000,0x0,0x1,0x324000) + c0
_pagefault(0x324144,0x0,0x1,0x0,0xf827068c,0xf8188c00) + 1f0
_trap(0x10009) + 5dc
```

Process 5363 is another D-state process. According to the **ps** output, this process is running **/usr/openwin/bin/xnews**, part of OpenWindows. This process entered the kernel through a trap — a page fault. Note that this stack trace goes through *anon_getpage()*, which is used to get anonymous memory. This is usually another name for swap space, and the next routines are going through UFS code again. Hmmm. This is starting to look like a trend.

```
        pid 5524
sw_bad(?)
_swtch(0x11901ae1,0xf826e34c,0xf814fc00,0x0,0x3,0xf8188c00) + 80
_sleep(0xf8180c60,0xa,0x13ec000,0x0,0xa,0xf8270804) + 1a0
_ufs_getpage(0xfd84c2d0,0x13eb000,0x1000,0xf847adbc,0xf847ad58,0x1000) + b4
_ufs_1_getpage(0xfd84c2d0,0x13eb000,0x1000,0xf847adbc,0xf847ad58,0x1000) + c4
_anon_getpage(0x0,0xf847adbc,0xf847ad58,0x1000,0xfd8b2298,0x1f1000) + 170
_segvn_faultpage(0xfd8b2298,0x1f1000,0x45000,0xfd8e70b4,0x0,0xf847adec) + 148
_segvn_fault(0xfd8b2298,0x1000,0x0,0x0,0x1f1000,0xfd84a550) + 5d4
_as_fault(0x1f1000,0xfd8b2298,0x1000,0x0,0x1,0x1f1000) + c0
_pagefault(0x1f14b8,0x0,0x1,0x0,0xf8270804,0xf8188c00) + 1f0
_trap(0x10009) + 5dc
```

Another page fault. Another reference to anonymous memory that goes into the UFS routines and blocks.

```
        pid 5529
sw_bad(?)
_swtch(0x11900ae2,0xf8270804,0xf814fc00,0x0,0x3,0xf8188c00) + 80
_sleep(0xf8180c60,0xa,0x8b9000,0x0,0xa,0xf827124c) + 1a0
_ufs_getpage(0xfd84c2d0,0x8b8000,0x1000,0xf8493dbc,0xf8493d58,0x1000) + b4
_ufs_1_getpage(0xfd84c2d0,0x8b8000,0x1000,0xf8493dbc,0xf8493d58,0x1000) + c4
_anon_getpage(0x0,0xf8493dbc,0xf8493d58,0x1000,0xfd8b32c0,0xe000) + 170
_segvn_faultpage(0xfd8b32c0,0xe000,0x2000,0xfd908548,0x0,0xf8493dec) + 148
_segvn_fault(0xfd8b32c0,0x1000,0x0,0x0,0xe000,0xfd8b5b28) + 5d4
_as_fault(0xe000,0xfd8b32c0,0x1000,0x0,0x1,0xe000) + c0
_pagefault(0xeca4,0x0,0x1,0x0,0xf827124c,0xf8188c00) + 1f0
_trap(0x10009) + 5dc
```

Yes, it looks like we're on to something. Another identical sequence in process 5529.

```
sw_bad(?)
_swtch(0x11900ae7,0xf826e4c4,0xf814fc00,0x0,0x3,0xfd8c7288) + 80
_sleep(0xf8180ce0,0x1,0xfd803698,0x800,0x1,0xf82713c4) + 1a0
_page_cv_wait(0xf82bfccc,0x114000e1,0xf814fc00,0x0,0x258e0be,0x2) + 14
_page_wait(0xf82bfccc,0x1651000,0x2,0x0,0x1651000,0xfd84c2d0) + a4
_anon_decref(0xfd8803b0,0xf84acb38,0xfd8803b0,0x0,0x0,0xf82bfccc) + 54
_anon_free(0xfd925620,0x3,0x0,0x3,0x0,0x4) + 2c
_segvn_free(0xfd8c6db8,0xfd925620,0x0,0xf81804d8,0xfd8c7288,0xfd8b37bc) + 100
_seg_free(0xfd8c6db8,0xf8219060,0xff847000,0x3,0xff847000,0xf81801f0) + 80
_segvn_unmap(0xfd8c6db8,0xff843000,0x4000,0xfd805c80,0xff847000,0xfd8c7288)+ 9c
_as_unmap(0xf81801f0,0xfd8c6db8,0xfd803698,0xff847000,0x4000,0xff843000)+b8
_args_free(0x0,0x20088001,0xf84ad000,0xf8267624,0xf84ad000,0xff843000) + 20
_execve(0xff843000,0x0,0xf7fffffa,0xffffffff,0xfffffffc,0xffffffff) + a5c
_au_execve(0xf84acfe0,0x1d8,0xf815b640,0xf815b818,0xf84ad000,0x0) + 20
_syscall(0xf84ad000) + 3b4
```

This trace appears to be a system call to start up a new process, an *exec()*. As a part of the *exec()* call, normally the system deletes the current process space and overlays it with a new image. We appear to be going through *args_free()*, which sounds a lot like it's releasing argument space, then passing through *anon_free()* (swap space again) on the way to a *page_wait()* and a *sleep()*.

The next two traces are not unusual; they are often seen in stack tracebacks: *sigpause()* indicates a process which is waiting for a signal (often an alarm clock). Process 4435 is doing a *read()* system call, which goes through *soreceive()*. This is socket code, network related.

```
        pid 5500
sw_bad(?)
_swtch(0x11800aa3,0xf826fb88,0xf814fc00,0x0,0x3,0x2f) + 80
_sleep(0xf8180bb0,0x28,0xf8272274,0x0,0x28,0xf8272274) + 1a0
_sigpause(0xf841bfe0,0x378,0xf815b640,0xf815b9b8,0xf841c000,0xf815b9b8) + 4c
_syscall(0xf841c000) + 3b4
        pid 4435
sw_bad(?)
_swtch(0x11800ae3,0xf826ed94,0xf814fc00,0x0,0x3,0x35) + 80
_sleep(0xf8180bb8,0x1a,0x48,0x100,0x1a,0xf82724a8) + 1a0
_sbwait(0xff65d838,0x3,0x0,0x0,0x1,0xc) + 14
_soreceive(0xff65d80c,0x0,0xf8407ea4,0x0,0x4000,0x1000) + 28c
_soo_rw(0xf82660d0,0xf80609a8,0xf8407ea4,0xf8407ec0,0x1,0xf8407ea4) + 30
_rwuio(0xf82660d0,0xf8407ea4,0xf8407eb8,0xc,0xc,0xf8407ea4) + 2b0
_read(0xf8407fe0,0x18,0xf815b640,0xf815b658,0xf8408000,0xf815b658) + 34
_syscall(0xf8408000) + 3b4
```

With the next trace, we're back to another stopped process, pid 27863. If you look at the **ps** output, this belongs to a process called **<exiting>**. In other words, it's trying to go away. This involves releasing all its memory, as we can see it is going through *relvm()* and *anon_free()* on its way to *sleep()*.

```
        pid 27863
sw_bad(?)
_swtch(0x11901ae3,0xf8272c00,0xf814fc00,0x0,0x3,0x0) + 80
_sleep(0xf0100c78,0x1,0x0,0x800,0x1,0xf8272ef0) + 1a0
_page_cv_wait(0xf82b932c,0x114010e5,0xf814fc00,0x0,0x258e0d6,0x1) + 14
_page_wait(0xf82b932c,0x1714000,0x1,0x0,0x1714000,0xfd84c2d0) + a4
_anon_decref(0xfd8809c8,0x11001ae7,0xfd8809c8,0x0,0xf81970d0,0xf82b932c) + 54
_anon_free(0xfd925638,0x1,0x0,0x3,0x0,0x2) + 2c
_segvn_free(0xfd8ce4d0,0xfd925638,0x0,0xfd8ab6b8,0xfd8d74c8,0xfd8a8ab4) + 100
_seg_free(0xfd8ce4d0,0xffffffff,0x12,0x2e8,0xf7795d44,0xfd8c20c0) + 80
_as_free(0xfd8c20c0,0x1000,0xfd8c20c0,0x0,0xf810521c,0x0) + 1c
_relvm(0xf8272ef0,0xf8272ef0,0x0,0x114010a3,0xf8280cf4,0x0) + 2c
_exit(0xff67ff80,0x270,0xf7803860,0xf8272ef0,0xf7795eb8,0x80) + a8
_rexit(0xf84b1fe0,0x8,0xf815b640,0xf815b648,0xf84b2000,0xf815b648) + 18
_syscall(0xf84b2000) + 3b4
```

The fact that we have several processes apparently stuck while trying to access swap seems to be significant. As a final check, let's examine the stack traceback of the process that was running at the time of the halt and see if the system was perhaps stuck in some kernel loop. This is also a good example of how a stack traceback looks for a system that has been manually stopped.

First, the heading is displayed. We will be seeing eight local registers (%l0 through %l7) followed by eight input registers (%i0 through %i7).

```
<sp$<stacktrace
            l0          l1          l2          l3
            l4          l5          l6          l7
            i0          i1          i2          i3
            i4          i5          i6          i7
```

Following this output, each stack frame is printed twice. Note that the address on the left side is the same twice in a row.

```
intstack+0x2ba8:              f826fb88      f8182378      f8421000
                    63        f8052420      63            f8148ba8
                    63        f8173367      f8173367      0
                    0         0             0             f8148c08
                    f81200f8
intstack+0x2ba8:              0xf826fb88    _panic_regs   0xf8421000
                    0x63      _panic+0x6c   0x63          intstack+0x2ba8
                    0x63      _va_cache_valid+0x367  _va_cache_valid+0x367
                    0         0             0             0
                    intstack+0x2c08             _vx_handler+0x50
```

These top stack frames are all on the interrupt stack (*instack*) and are up in the PROM code.

```
intstack+0x2c08:              114036c4      ffe96300      ffe96304
                    f8005f28  a             f8005c00      28
                    f8148be0  ffefb6c8      f3            0
                    0         0             f8172ff8      f8148c88
                    ffe9d2bc
intstack+0x2c08:              0x114036c4    0xffe96300    0xffe96304
                    level10   0xa           int_rtt       0x28
                    intstack+0x2be0 0xffefb6c8  0xf3       0
                    0         0             _mon_clock14_vec+0x10
                    intstack+0x2c88 0xffe9d2bc


intstack+0x2c88:              ffea0d24      5             ffe94f08
                    ffef0040  f81200a8      ffeaee58      ffefefc8
                    ffefebdc  ffea7b14      119006c6      f814fc00
                    1         0             f8280a54      f8148ce8
                    f814343c
intstack+0x2c88:              0xffea0d24    5             0xffe94f08
                    0xffef0040  _vx_handler  0xffeaee58   0xffefefc8
                    0xffefebdc  0xffea7b14   0x119006c6   intu+0x47c
                    1         0             0xf8280a54    intstack+0x2ce8
                    _prom_enter_mon+0xc
```

The return address for this next frame (the last value printed, or %i7) is *kbdinput()* —looks like a keyboard input function.

intstack+0x2ce8:		119006c6	f810b670	f810b674
	f8005f28	a	f8005c00	28
	f8148ca0	0	f8128410	4d
	13	13	f8172c00	f8148d48
	f8128378			
intstack+0x2cc8:		0x119006c6	_usec_delay+0x14	
	_usec_delay+0x18		level10	0xa
	int_rtt	0x28	intstack+0x2ca00	
	_kbdinput+0x608	0x4d	0x13	0x13
	_monthsec	intstack+0x2d48		_kbdinput+0x570
intstack+0x2d48:		f8181c00	f8181c00	f804734c
	80	0	fd83b920	f8175afc
	fd83b920	f8175afc	4d	4d
	0	11f33d	1	f8148dc0
	f8127dc8			
intstack+0x2d48:		_strevent+0xe38	_strevent+0xe38	_xdballoc+4
	0x80	0	0xfd83b920	_keyindex_s4
	0xfd83b920	_keyindex_s4	0x4d	0x4d
	0	0x11f33d	1	intstack+0x2dc0
	_kbdrput+0x168			

The following frame returns to *zsa_process()*. The ZS (Zilog Serial) chip is the hardware that handles the input characters from the keyboard.

intstack+0x2dc0:		13	0	72
	1	0	f8189400	0
	1	fd818f68	fd8195e0	0
	fd83b900	fd8195e0	118006e0	f8148e20
	f812ebac			
intstack+0x2dc0:	0x13	0	0x72	
	1	0	_intrcnt+0xc0	0
	1	0xfd818f68	0xfd8195e0	0
	0xfd83b900	0xfd8195e0	0x118006e0	intstack+0x2e20
	_zsa_process+0x228			
intstack+0x2e20:		1	fd818f69	3f7a0
	4d	6ce	fd817050	fd801920
	1	fd8018d0	1	fd8195e0
	fd801b70	1	0	f8148e80
	f812e8e4			
intstack+0x2e20:		1	0xfd818f69	0x3f7a0
	0x4d	0x6ce	0xfd817050	0xfd801920
	1	0xfd8018d0	1	0xfd8195e0
	0xfd801b70	1	0	intstack+0x2e80
	_zspoll+0x58			

Keyboard input is actually interpreted on every clock tick, as evidenced by the next two return addresses in the next two frames.

```
intstack+0x2e80:                  1              885            4
                  bc              14             c              f8189000
                  14              0              0              f814fc00
                  110001e2        0              fd8018d0       f8148ee0
                  f803c658
intstack+0x2e80:                  1              0x885          4
                  0xbc            0x14           0xc            _ktextseg+8
                  0x14            0              0              intu+0x47c
                  0x110001e2      0              0xfd8018d0     intstack+0x2ee0
                  _softclock+0x80

intstack+0x2ee0:                  f8180400       20             f8180400
                  20              80000000       40             0
                  a               114000c5       f812e88c       0
                  0               114001e3       f8280c64       f8148f40
                  f803c4dc
intstack+0x2ee0:                  _rtable+0xa0   0x20           _rtable+0xa0
                  0x20            0x80000000     0x4            0
                  0xa             0x114000c5     _zspoll        0
                  0               0x114001e3     0xf8280c64     intstack+0x2f40
                  _hardclock+0x564
```

The return address in the next frame is to an assembly language function, *level10()*, corresponding to the actual interrupt handler for the clock tick.

```
intstack+0x2f40:                  f8177ab0       2710           57e40
                  57e40           f4240          f8189400       0
                  1               f810b938       114000c5       f7662914
                  1               f7662914       f8280c64       f8148fa0
                  f8005f80
intstack+0x2f40:                  _time          0x2710         0x57e40
                  0x57e40         0xf4240        _intrcnt+0xc0  0
                  1               _idle+0x34     0x114000c5     0xf7662914
                  1               0xf7662914     0xf8280c64     intstack+0x2fa0
                  level10+0x58
```

This next frame is the first one that gets put on the interrupt stack.

```
intstack+0x2fa0:            11400ac5    f810b938    f810b93c
                 f8005f28    a           f8005c00    28
                 f8420cf8    11800aa6    3e28        0
                 0           0           38          f8420da0
                 f8043c88
intstack+0x2fa0:            0x11400ac5  _idle+0x34  _idle+0x38
                 level10     0xa         int_rtt     0x28
                 0xf8420cf8  0x11800aa6  0x3e28      0
                 0           0           0x38        0xf8420da0
                 _setsigvec+0x1c8
```

The return address for the next frame is in *sleep()*, on the regular stack. It looks like this process was giving up the CPU, if it was, in fact, active at all.

```
0xf8420da0:      118000a6    0           0           100
                 f8421000    0           ffffdfff    0
                 11800aa7    f82720fc    f814fc00    0
                 3           1b          f8420e00    f8045c6c

0xf8420da0:      0x118000a6  0           0           0x100
                 0xf8421000  0           0xffffdfff  0
                 0x11800aa7  0xf82720fc  intu+0x47c  0
                 3           0x1b        0xf8420e00  _sleep+0x1a0

0xf8420e00:      3d          f8177400    f8180bb0    0
                 1           f8421000    60d27       0
                 f8180bb0    28          f826fb88    0
                 28          f826fb88    f8420e60    f8043dc4

0xf8420e00:      0x3d        _utsname+0x38  _slpque   0
                 1           0xf8421000  0x60d27     0
                 _slpque     0x28        0xf826fb88  0
                 0x28        0xf826fb88  0xf8420e60  _sigpause+0x4c

0xf8420e60:      0           fffefeff    f8421000    f826fb88
                 0           f826fb88    0           f76e2d14
                 f8420fe0    378         f815b640    f815b9b8
                 f8421000    f815b9b8    f8420ec0    f8124410

0xf8420e60:      0           0xfffefeff  0xf8421000  0xf826fb88
                 0           0xf826fb88  0           0xf76e2d14
                 0xf8420fe0  0x378       _sysent     _sysent+0x378
                 0xf8421000  _sysent+0x378  0xf8420ec0  _syscall+0x3b4
```

```
0xf8420ec0:    f8421000      f8421000      f826fb88      f815b9b8
               f8421000      f826fb88      0             f76e721c
               f8421000      f8420fb4      f8420fe0      f8421000
               f8421000      f8420fb4      f8420f58      f8005a54

0xf8420ec0:    0xf8421000    0xf8421000    0xf826fb88    _sysent+0x378
               0xf8421000    0xf826fb88    0             xf76e721c
               0xf8421000    0xf8420fb4    0xf8420fe0    0xf8421000
               0xf8421000    0xf8420fb4    0xf8420f58    syscall+8

0xf8420f58:    11400082f     76e2894       f76e2898      20
               80            4             7             f8420f58
               0             f7fff380      0             0
               f774f788      0             f7fff2f8      f76f965c

0xf8420f58:    0x11400082    0xf76e2894    0xf76e2898    0x20
               0x80          4             7             0xf8420f58
               0             0xf7fff380    0             0
               0xf774f788    0             0xf7fff2f8    0xf76f965c
```

The next frame and those following appear to be user-level stack frames. Note that the stack address is now in user space, and the return address is quite small—a valid user code address, but certainly not an address in kernel space.

```
0xf7fff2f8:    ffffdfff      f76629cc      3             c
               1             fd801c4c      ff003000      f774c05c
               0             0             f7662914      0
               f7662914      0             f7fff390      29a4

0xf7fff2f8:    0xffffdfff    0xf76629cc    3             0xc
               1             0xfd801c4c    0xff003000    0xf774c05c
               0             0             0xf7662914    0
               0xf7662914    0             0xf7fff390    0x29a4

0xf7fff390:    82bac         1             2             1
               f75e0000      f766572c      1             f800
               f75e0000      82914         f7662914      f800
               f7662914      14            f7fff430      22b4

0xf7fff390:    0x82bac       1             2             1
               0xf75e0000    0xf766572c    1             0xf800
               0xf75e0000    0x82914       0xf7662914    0xf800
               0xf7662914    0x14          0xf7fff430    0x22b

0xf7fff430:    11400080      f773a0d8      f773a0dc      0
```

	4	4	7	f8420f58
	3	f7fff4f4	f7fff504	c000
	0	0	f7fff490	2064
0xf7fff430:	0x11400080	0xf773a0d8	0xf773a0dc	0
	4	4	7	0xf8420f58
	3	0xf7fff4f4	0xf7fff504	0xc000
	0	0	0xf7fff490	0x2064
0xf7fff490:	0	0	0	0
	0	0	0	0
	0	0	0	0
	0	0	0	0
0xf7fff490:	0	0	0	0
	0	0	0	0
	0	0	0	0
	0	0	0	0

And finally the stack runs out with no more data on it.

Take a look at the frame that was the first one on the interrupt stack. This should be a trap frame, or a special frame used for traps (including system calls) and interrupts. It contains the address of the instruction that was interrupted in register %l1, the second number in the frame. Examining that frame, you see:

intstack+0x2fa0:	0x11400ac5	_idle+0x34	_idle+0x38

The actual address, which indicates where the CPU was executing when the clock ticked, appears to be in the kernel function called *idle()*. This is not exactly an indication that the system was working very hard. Thus, it appears that even though there are a number of runnable processes in the **ps** output, at the moment of the L1-A keystroke, nothing was actually happening. This implies that the D-state processes are in fact locked up, waiting for a resource that isn't available.

All the blocked processes were waiting for anonymous (swap) memory, which appeared to be related to or obtained from UFS disk blocks. One feature of Solaris is the ability to define a swap file, or a regular UNIX file, that can be used as additional swap space. It seems that the problem this system encountered is related to this feature.

Resolution

Subsequent core dumps from the same system showed identical situations. Processes were blocked, waiting for a UNIX swap file to become available. Eliminating the use of a UNIX swap file made the problem go away.

A bug was filed (bug number 1108860), although the problem does not seem to have shown up in SunOS 4.1.3 (Solaris 1.1) and later releases.

Panic'ed Pipes

The following crash dump was generated on a Sun-4 system running SunOS 4.1.3. The customer who submitted it to us for analysis reported that the system had not had problems in the past. Indeed, it was only when one of the users started writing his own programs that the crashes began.

Always get initial information

Let's jump right into **adb** to get some initial information. Data that we use in subsequent **adb** commands is underlined for visibility.

```
Hiya on s4-413...  adb -k vmunix.0 vmcore.0
physmem 3ffd
hostname/s
_hostname:
_hostname:       server01
*boottime=Y
                 1994 Aug 11 10:52:19
*time=Y
                 1994 Aug 12 11:32:37
*panicstr/s
_sizestr+0x89:  Memory address alignment
$c
_panic(0xf8120eb1,0xf86e8cbc,0xffffffff,0x30,0x7c375,0xf7fffdf0) + 6c
_trap(0x7,0xf86e8cbc,0xffffffff,0x30,0x0,0x0) + 2a0
st_have_window(?)
_uiomove(0x0,0x0,0x1000,0x2,0x1002,0x2) + 98
_fifo_rdwr(0xfceaccb0,0xf86e8eac,0x0,0xfceb2525,0x2,0x0) + 5ac
_vno_rw(0xf835bac8,0x1,0xf86e8eac,0x1000,0xfceaccb4,0x0) + a4
_rwuio(0xf835bac8,0xf86e8eac,0xf86e8ea4,0x1000,0x1000,0xf86e8eac) + 2b0
_write(0xf86e8fe0,0x20,0xf8114ad0,0xf8114af0,0xf86e9000,0xf8114af0) + 34
_syscall(0xf86e9000) + 3b4
0xf86e8cbc$<regs
0xf86e8cbc:      psr              pc               npc
                 114000c1         f806f28c         f806f290
0xf86e8cc8:      y                g1               g2               g3
                 0                f8000000         c30022fd         fce07c90
0xf86e8cd8:      g4               g5               g6               g7
                 c                f86e9000         f812d000         f812d000
```

```
      0xf86e8ce8:      o0              o1              o2              o3
                       c00022fd        f8064c10        0               c00022fd
      0xf86e8cf8:      o4              o5              o6              o7
                       ff84a000        0               f86e8d08        f76a2000
      f806f28c/i
      _fifo_rdwr+0x5ec:               ld      [%i3], %i3
```

The failed instruction, `ld [%i3], %i3`, generated a memory alignment error.

Walking the stack by hand

Since we trap'ed instead of panic'ed, it is a good idea to manually walk through the stack to get a more accurate picture of the stack traceback. Doing this one time will allow us to use the **adb $c** command with an understanding of how accurate its output is. Let's walk the stack, starting at register %o6, as seen in the *regs* structure shown above.

```
      f86e8d08/16X
      0xf86e8d08:      2               1000            ffef            fffe
                       5004            1a              1a              0
                       fceaccb0        f86e8eac        0               fceb2525
                       2               0               f86e8d68        f80618ec
      f80618ec/i
      _vno_rw+0xa4:    jmpl    %g1, %o7
      f86e8d68/16X
      0xf86e8d68:      f7743a14        7fffffff        f80ca554        f7745ae4
                       f7748bec        f7745df0        f774429c        19d1
                       f835bac8        1               f86e8eac        1000
                       fceaccb4        0               f86e8dc8        f804cb20
      f804cb20/i
      _rwuio+0x2b0:    jmpl    %g1, %o7
      f86e8dc8/16X
      0xf86e8dc8:      f835bac8        f81170b0        0               f86e8eac
                       f835bac8        102             1000            f835bac8
                       f835bac8        f86e8eac        f86e8ea4        1000
                       1000            f86e8eac        f86e8e40        f804bab4
      ... and so on ...
```

We could continue walking the stack, but we've already accomplished what we needed to. We have confirmed that the **$c** output we are interested in starts with *fifo_rdwr()*. The reference to *uiomove()* is actually a lingering, historical frame on the stack, and tells us that *uiomove()* was the most recent routine called by *fifo_rdwr()*.

From both the stack traceback and the manual stack traceback, we can see that when *fifo_rdwr()* was called, register %i3 contained 0xfceb2525. This value does not represent a full-word address, not even a half-word address. 0xfceb2525 only represents a byte address. The instruction used in the *fifo_rdwr()* routine was a full word load instruction, ld, so the value in %i3 is suspicious at best.

Note – Unfortunately, it is possible that the *fifo_rdwr()* routine may have used register %i3 as a local register *after it finished reading its contents as a calling parameter*, thus modifying %i3, thus affecting the stack traceback information that we see in the postmortem files.

Let's check the assembly code of *fifo_rdwr()* to see whether %i3 has been modified since entering the routine.

Examining assembly code: *fifo_rdwr()*

While still in **adb**, we start off searching for any instruction that has %i3 as the destination register. In this example, we are examining 16 instructions (10 hex) at a time.

```
fifo_rdwr,10/ia
 _fifo_rdwr:
 _fifo_rdwr:                 save    %sp, -0x60, %sp
 _fifo_rdwr+4:               ld      [%i1 + 0x10], %l1
 _fifo_rdwr+8:               ld      [%i1 + 0x8], %o0
 _fifo_rdwr+0xc:             clr     %l7
 _fifo_rdwr+0x10:            orcc    %g0, %o0, %g0
 _fifo_rdwr+0x14:            be,a    _fifo_rdwr + 0x30
 _fifo_rdwr+0x18:            ld      [%i0 + 0x24], %i0
 _fifo_rdwr+0x1c:            ld      [%i1 + 0x8], %o1
 _fifo_rdwr+0x20:            sethi   %hi(0xf8117800), %o0
 _fifo_rdwr+0x24:            call    _printf
 _fifo_rdwr+0x28:            or      %o0, 0x378, %o0
 _fifo_rdwr+0x2c:            ld      [%i0 + 0x24], %i0
 _fifo_rdwr+0x30:            lduh    [%i0 + 0x34], %o1
 _fifo_rdwr+0x34:            andcc   %o1, 0x1, %g0
 _fifo_rdwr+0x38:            be,a    _fifo_rdwr + 0xb4
 _fifo_rdwr+0x3c:            sethi   %hi(0xf811fc00), %l0
 _fifo_rdwr+0x40:
+,10/ia
 _fifo_rdwr+0x40:            sethi   %hi(0xf811fc00), %o2
 _fifo_rdwr+0x44:            ld      [%o2 + 0x48], %o2    ! -0x7ee03b8
 _fifo_rdwr+0x48:            orcc    %g0, %o2, %g0
 _fifo_rdwr+0x4c:            be,a    _fifo_rdwr + 0x64
 _fifo_rdwr+0x50:            sethi   %hi(0xf811cc00), %o4
 _fifo_rdwr+0x54:            sethi   %hi(0xf8112800), %o3
 _fifo_rdwr+0x58:            ld      [%o3 + 0x31c], %o3   ! -0x7eed4e4
```

```
_fifo_rdwr+0x5c:        ba      _fifo_rdwr + 0x6c
_fifo_rdwr+0x60:        mov     %o3, %i5
_fifo_rdwr+0x64:        ld      [%o4 + 0x98], %o4
_fifo_rdwr+0x68:        mov     %o4, %i5
_fifo_rdwr+0x6c:        ld      [%i0 + 0x5c], %o5
_fifo_rdwr+0x70:        cmp     %o5, %i5
_fifo_rdwr+0x74:        be,a    _fifo_rdwr + 0xb4
_fifo_rdwr+0x78:        sethi   %hi(0xf811fc00), %l0
_fifo_rdwr+0x7c:        lduh    [%i0 + 0x34], %o7
_fifo_rdwr+0x80:
```

... and so on ...

Sure enough, fairly deep into the routine, we see that %i3 is indeed modified under various circumstances.

```
+,10/ia
_fifo_rdwr+0x4c0:       call    .mul
_fifo_rdwr+0x4c4:       ld      [%o1 + 0x258], %o1
_fifo_rdwr+0x4c8:       ldsh    [%i0 + 0x80], %o1
_fifo_rdwr+0x4cc:       sub     %o0, %o1, %o0
_fifo_rdwr+0x4d0:       cmp     %o0, %i5
_fifo_rdwr+0x4d4:       bgeu,a  _fifo_rdwr + 0x540
_fifo_rdwr+0x4d8:       ld      [%i0 + 0x64], %i3      <<---- Here
_fifo_rdwr+0x4dc:       call    _fifo_bufalloc
_fifo_rdwr+0x4e0:       mov     %i0, %o0
_fifo_rdwr+0x4e4:       mov     %o0, %i2
_fifo_rdwr+0x4e8:       orcc    %g0, %i2, %g0
_fifo_rdwr+0x4ec:       be,a    _fifo_rdwr + 0x15c
_fifo_rdwr+0x4f0:       ld      [%i1 + 0x10], %i5
_fifo_rdwr+0x4f4:       st      %g0, [%i2]
_fifo_rdwr+0x4f8:       ld      [%i0 + 0x64], %o3
_fifo_rdwr+0x4fc:       orcc    %g0, %o3, %g0
_fifo_rdwr+0x500:
+,10/ia
_fifo_rdwr+0x500:       bne,a   _fifo_rdwr + 0x510
_fifo_rdwr+0x504:       ld      [%i0 + 0x68], %o4
_fifo_rdwr+0x508:       ba      _fifo_rdwr + 0x514
_fifo_rdwr+0x50c:       st      %i2, [%i0 + 0x64]
_fifo_rdwr+0x510:       st      %i2, [%o4]
_fifo_rdwr+0x514:       st      %i2, [%i0 + 0x68]
_fifo_rdwr+0x518:       ldsh    [%i0 + 0x86], %o0
_fifo_rdwr+0x51c:       sethi   %hi(0xf812b400), %o1
_fifo_rdwr+0x520:       call    .mul
_fifo_rdwr+0x524:       ld      [%o1 + 0x258], %o1
_fifo_rdwr+0x528:       ldsh    [%i0 + 0x80], %o1
_fifo_rdwr+0x52c:       sub     %o0, %o1, %o0
_fifo_rdwr+0x530:       cmp     %o0, %i5
```

```
_fifo_rdwr+0x534:        blu      _fifo_rdwr + 0x4dc
_fifo_rdwr+0x538:        nop
_fifo_rdwr+0x53c:        ld       [%i0 + 0x64], %i3        <<---- and here
_fifo_rdwr+0x540:
+,10/ia
_fifo_rdwr+0x540:        ldsh     [%i0 + 0x80], %i2
_fifo_rdwr+0x544:        sethi    %hi(0xf812b400), %o7
_fifo_rdwr+0x548:        ld       [%o7 + 0x258], %o7       ! -0x7ed49a8
_fifo_rdwr+0x54c:        cmp      %i2, %o7
_fifo_rdwr+0x550:        bl,a     _fifo_rdwr + 0x57c
_fifo_rdwr+0x554:        orcc     %g0, %i5, %g0
_fifo_rdwr+0x558:        ld       [%i3], %i3               <<---- and here
_fifo_rdwr+0x55c:        sethi    %hi(0xf812b400), %o0
_fifo_rdwr+0x560:        ld       [%o0 + 0x258], %i0
_fifo_rdwr+0x564:        ld       [%o0 + 0x258], %o0
_fifo_rdwr+0x568:        sub      %i2, %i0, %i2
_fifo_rdwr+0x56c:        cmp      %i2, %o0
_fifo_rdwr+0x570:        bge,a    _fifo_rdwr + 0x55c
_fifo_rdwr+0x574:        ld       [%i3], %i3               <<---- and here
_fifo_rdwr+0x578:        orcc     %g0, %i5, %g0
_fifo_rdwr+0x57c:        be,a     _fifo_rdwr + 0x5fc
_fifo_rdwr+0x580:
+,10/ia
_fifo_rdwr+0x580:        mov      0x42, %o1
_fifo_rdwr+0x584:        sethi    %hi(0xf812b400), %o0
_fifo_rdwr+0x588:        ld       [%o0 + 0x258], %o0       ! -0x7ed49a8
_fifo_rdwr+0x58c:        sub      %o0, %i2, %i4
_fifo_rdwr+0x590:        cmp      %i5, %i4
_fifo_rdwr+0x594:        bgeu,a   _fifo_rdwr + 0x5a4
_fifo_rdwr+0x598:        mov      %i1, %o3
_fifo_rdwr+0x59c:        mov      %i5, %i4
_fifo_rdwr+0x5a0:        mov      %i1, %o3
_fifo_rdwr+0x5a4:        mov      0x1, %o2
_fifo_rdwr+0x5a8:        mov      %i4, %o1
_fifo_rdwr+0x5ac:        call     _uiomove                <<---- Remember this?
_fifo_rdwr+0x5b0:        add      %i3, %i2, %o0
_fifo_rdwr+0x5b4:        mov      %o0, %l7
_fifo_rdwr+0x5b8:        orcc     %g0, %l7, %g0
_fifo_rdwr+0x5bc:        bne,a    _fifo_rdwr + 0xa88
_fifo_rdwr+0x5c0:
+,10/ia
_fifo_rdwr+0x5c0:        ld       [%i0 + 0x60], %o5
_fifo_rdwr+0x5c4:        ld       [%i0 + 0x78], %o2
_fifo_rdwr+0x5c8:        sll      %i4, 0x10, %o3
_fifo_rdwr+0x5cc:        add      %o2, %i4, %o2
_fifo_rdwr+0x5d0:        st       %o2, [%i0 + 0x78]
_fifo_rdwr+0x5d4:        ldsh     [%i0 + 0x80], %o4
_fifo_rdwr+0x5d8:        sra      %o3, 0x10, %o3
_fifo_rdwr+0x5dc:        add      %o4, %o3, %o4
_fifo_rdwr+0x5e0:        sub      %i5, %i4, %i5
```

```
_fifo_rdwr+0x5e4:        orcc    %g0, %i5, %g0
_fifo_rdwr+0x5e8:        sth     %o4, [%i0 + 0x80]
_fifo_rdwr+0x5ec:        ld      [%i3], %i3              <<---- Panic!
_fifo_rdwr+0x5f0:        bne     _fifo_rdwr + 0x584
_fifo_rdwr+0x5f4:        clr     %i2
_fifo_rdwr+0x5f8:        mov     0x42, %o1
_fifo_rdwr+0x5fc:        call    _smark
_fifo_rdwr+0x600:
```

The modifications to register %i3 are surrounded by code that performs a lot of branches and jumps, as some programs do, instead of simply executing in fairly consecutive order. So, at this point, we have to ask ourselves "Do we want to try to walk through this code to figure out what %i3 should have contained when we reached *fifo_rdwr+0x5ec*?" (If you answered "Yes," you might want to consider finding some new hobbies.)

Instead, let's try a different approach. Let's see if the values passed to the routines appear to be good ones.

Calling parameters

What should have been forwarded to *fifo_rdwr()*? Referring to the source code, we see that the calling parameters are: *vp, uiop, rw, ioflag,* and *cred*. A *vp* refers to a *vnode* pointer, or a pointer to a *vnode* structure. Unfortunately, register %i0 conditionally gets modified early on at either *fifo_rdwr+0x18* or *fifo_rdwr+0x2c*, so we don't have the original *vnode* pointer with which to work.

Note – If you don't have access to source, refer to the 4.1.3 function list which you'll find on the Panic! CD-ROM.

Let's back up a bit instead.

The routine that called *fifo_rdwr()* was *vno_rw()*. Its calling parameters are *fp, rw,* and *uiop*. *Fp* refers to a file pointer, or in other words, a pointer to a *file* structure. To find out what a *file* structure looks like, we refer to the SunOS 4.1.3 **/usr/include/sys/file.h** header file, a portion of which is shown below.

```
/*
 * Descriptor table entry.
 * One for each kernel object.
 */
struct   file {
         int     f_flag;            /* see below */
         short   f_type;            /* descriptor type */
```

```
        short   f_count;        /* reference count */
        short   f_msgcount;     /* references from message queue */
        struct  fileops {
                int     (*fo_rw)();
                int     (*fo_ioctl)();
                int     (*fo_select)();
                int     (*fo_close)();
        } *f_ops;
      caddr_t f_data;          /* ptr to file specific struct (vnode/socket) */
off_t   f_offset;
        struct  ucred *f_cred;   /* credentials of user who opened file */
};

struct  file *file, *fileNFILE;
```

Now, back in **adb**, we will use the **file** macro to see if the first calling parameter to *vno_rw()* appears to be valid.

```
$c
_panic(0xf8120eb1,0xf86e8cbc,0xffffffff,0x30,0x7c375,0xf7fffdf0) + 6c
_trap(0x7,0xf86e8cbc,0xffffffff,0x30,0x0,0x0) + 2a0
st_have_window(?)
_uiomove(0x0,0x0,0x1000,0x2,0x1002,0x2) + 98
_fifo_rdwr(0xfceaccb0,0xf86e8eac,0x0,0xfceb2525,0x2,0x0) + 5ac
_vno_rw(0xf835bac8,0x1,0xf86e8eac,0x1000,0xfceaccb4,0x0) + a4
_rwuio(0xf835bac8,0xf86e8eac,0xf86e8ea4,0x1000,0x1000,0xf86e8eac) + 2b0
_write(0xf86e8fe0,0x20,0xf8114ad0,0xf8114af0,0xf86e9000,0xf8114af0) + 34
_syscall(0xf86e9000)$ + 3b4
0xf835bac8$<file
0xf835bac8:     flag            type    count   msgcount
                102             1       3       0
                vnode           offset          cred
                fceaccb4        0               ff1c1514
```

Well, that's encouraging. When compared with the definition of the *file* structure as described in **file.h**, the %i0 value appears to be a valid pointer to a *file* structure.

Next question: Does the *file* structure appear to point to a valid *vnode* structure? Let's see. First, let's look at the *vnode* structure, as described in **/usr/include/sys/vnode.h**.

```
/*
 * vnode types. VNON means no type.
 */
enum vtype      { VNON, VREG, VDIR, VBLK, VCHR, VLNK, VSOCK, VBAD, VFIFO };
```

```
struct vnode {
        u_short         v_flag;                 /* vnode flags (see below) */
        u_short         v_count;                /* reference count */
        u_short         v_shlockc;              /* count of shared locks */
        u_short         v_exlockc;              /* count of exclusive locks */
        struct vfs      *v_vfsmountedhere;      /* ptr to vfs mounted here */
        struct vnodeops *v_op;                  /* vnode operations */
        union {
                struct socket   *v_Socket;      /* unix ipc */
                struct stdata   *v_Stream;      /* stream */
                struct page     *v_Pages;       /* vnode pages list */
        } v_s;
        struct vfs      *v_vfsp;                /* ptr to vfs we are in */
        enum vtype      v_type;                 /* vnode type */
        dev_t           v_rdev;                 /* device (VCHR, VBLK) */
        long            *v_filocks;             /* File/Record locks ... */
        caddr_t         v_data;                 /* private data for fs */
};
```

And now, let's return to our **adb** session and see if we can have a valid *vnode* pointer.

```
fceaccb4$<vnode
0xfceaccb4:     flag    refct   shlockc exlockc
                2       2       0       1
0xfceaccbc:     vfsmnt          vop             pages           vfsp
                0               f8117b00        0               fce05fc8
0xfceacccc:     type            rdev            data
                8               0       0       fceaccb0
f8117b00/P
_fifo_vnodeops:
_fifo_vnodeops: _fifo_open
```

Yes, it looks like a good *vnode* structure, and it references the fifo file system operation routine *fifo_open*, which tells us we are dealing with a fifo. The vnode type of 8 confirms this observation.

Examining assembly code: vno_rw()

If we examine the assembly instructions of *vno_rw()*, we see that it does pass the valid vnode pointer to *fifo_rdwr()*.

```
vno_rw,10/ia
 _vno_rw:
 _vno_rw:               save    %sp, -0x60, %sp
```

```
_vno_rw+4:      ld      [%i0 + 0x10], %i4        <--- Load vp into %i4
_vno_rw+8:      cmp     %i1, 0x1
_vno_rw+0xc:    bne,a   _vno_rw + 0x30
_vno_rw+0x10:   ld      [%i2 + 0x10], %i3
_vno_rw+0x14:   call    _isrofile               <--- Is vp pointing to read-only file?
_vno_rw+0x18:   mov     %i4, %o0                 <--- Copy vp into %o0 during call delay
_vno_rw+0x1c:   orcc    %g0, %o0, %g0
_vno_rw+0x20:   be,a    _vno_rw + 0x30          <--- Read write, branch to 30
_vno_rw+0x24:   ld      [%i2 + 0x10], %i3
_vno_rw+0x28:   ba      _vno_rw + 0xf4          <--- Read-only, branch to return
_vno_rw+0x2c:   mov     0x1e, %i5
_vno_rw+0x30:   ld      [%i4 + 0x18], %o0       <--- Using %o0 as a local register
_vno_rw+0x34:   clr     %i5                          now. Watch how it is used
_vno_rw+0x38:   cmp     %o0, 0x1                     but is reset to the vp just
_vno_rw+0x3c:   bne,a   _vno_rw + 0x4c              as we jump into a vnode
_vno_rw+0x40:                                        operations routine later on.
+,10/ia
_vno_rw+0x40:   ld      [%i0], %o1
_vno_rw+0x44:   mov     0x1, %i5
_vno_rw+0x48:   ld      [%i0], %o1
_vno_rw+0x4c:   andcc   %o1, 0x8, %g0
_vno_rw+0x50:   be,a    _vno_rw + 0x60
_vno_rw+0x54:   ld      [%i0], %o2
_vno_rw+0x58:   or      %i5, 0x2, %i5
_vno_rw+0x5c:   ld      [%i0], %o2
_vno_rw+0x60:   sethi   %hi(0x2000), %o3
_vno_rw+0x64:   andcc   %o2, %o3, %g0
_vno_rw+0x68:   be,a    _vno_rw + 0x78
_vno_rw+0x6c:   ld      [%i0], %o4
_vno_rw+0x70:   or      %i5, 0x4, %i5
_vno_rw+0x74:   ld      [%i0], %o4
_vno_rw+0x78:   sethi   %hi(0x1000), %o5
_vno_rw+0x7c:   andcc   %o4, %o5, %g0
_vno_rw+0x80:
+,10/ia
_vno_rw+0x80:   be,a    _vno_rw + 0x90
_vno_rw+0x84:   ld      [%i4 + 0xc], %g1        <--- This area of code is using a table
_vno_rw+0x88:   or      %i5, 0x10, %i5              of file system operations to figure
_vno_rw+0x8c:   ld      [%i4 + 0xc], %g1           out where we want to jump, based
_vno_rw+0x90:   mov     %i5, %o3                   on our file system type. The final
_vno_rw+0x94:   ld      [%g1 + 0x8], %g1          address is in %g1.
_vno_rw+0x98:   ld      [%i0 + 0x18], %o4      <--- Start preparing calling parameters.
_vno_rw+0x9c:   mov     %i1, %o2
_vno_rw+0xa0:   mov     %i2, %o1
_vno_rw+0xa4:   jmpl    %g1, %o7               <--- Jump into fifo_rdwr, moving vp
_vno_rw+0xa8:   mov     %i4, %o0              <--- into %o1 during the jmpl delay.
_vno_rw+0xac:   mov     %o0, %i5
_vno_rw+0xb0:   orcc    %g0, %i5, %g0
_vno_rw+0xb4:   bne     _vno_rw + 0xf4
_vno_rw+0xb8:   nop
```

```
_vno_rw+0xbc:      ld        [%i0], %10
_vno_rw+0xc0:
+,10/ia
_vno_rw+0xc0:      andcc     %10, 0x8, %g0
_vno_rw+0xc4:      bne,a     _vno_rw + 0xe0
_vno_rw+0xc8:      ld        [%i2 + 0x10], %14
_vno_rw+0xcc:      ld        [%i4 + 0x18], %i4
_vno_rw+0xd0:      cmp       %i4, 0x8
_vno_rw+0xd4:      bne,a     _vno_rw + 0xf4
_vno_rw+0xd8:      clr       %i5
_vno_rw+0xdc:      ld        [%i2 + 0x10], %14
_vno_rw+0xe0:      ld        [%i2 + 0x8], %i2
_vno_rw+0xe4:      sub       %i3, %14, %14
_vno_rw+0xe8:      sub       %i2, %14, %14
_vno_rw+0xec:      st        %14, [%i0 + 0x14]
_vno_rw+0xf0:      clr       %i5
_vno_rw+0xf4:      ret
_vno_rw+0xf8:      restore   %g0, %i5, %o0
_vno_ioctl:
_vno_ioctl:        save      %sp, -0xb8, %sp
_vno_ioctl+4:
```

So far, it appears that a good *vnode* pointer was given to *fifo_rdwr()*. What about the other calling parameters? Since *vno_rw()* is a somewhat short and rather easy-to-follow routine, we can also check the parameters without going through too much pain. Refer to the assembly code above.

```
$c
_panic(0xf8120eb1,0xf86e8cbc,0xffffffff,0x30,0x7c375,0xf7fffdf0) + 6c
_trap(0x7,0xf86e8cbc,0xffffffff,0x30,0x0,0x0) + 2a0
st_have_window(?)
_uiomove(0x0,0x0,0x1000,0x2,0x1002,0x2) + 98
_fifo_rdwr(0xfceaccb0,0xf86e8eac,0x0,0xfceb2525,0x2,0x0) + 5ac
_vno_rw(0xf835bac8,0x1,0xf86e8eac,0x1000,0xfceaccb4,0x0) + a4
_rwuio(0xf835bac8,0xf86e8eac,0xf86e8ea4,0x1000,0x1000,0xf86e8eac) + 2b0
_write(0xf86e8fe0,0x20,0xf8114ad0,0xf8114af0,0xf86e9000,0xf8114af0) + 34
_syscall(0xf86e9000) + 3b4
0xf835bac8+18/X
0xf835bae0:        ff1c1514     <---- See vno_rw+0x98. %o4 points to a credentials structure.
ff1c1514$<ucred
0xff1c1514:        ref       uid       gid
                   5         0         1
0xff1c1520:        groups
                   0                   -1             -1             -1
                   -1                  -1             -1             -1
0xff1c151c:        ruid      rgid
                   0         1
```

```
0xf86e8eac$<uio              <---- See vno_rw+0xa0. %o1 contains a uio pointer.
0xf86e8eac:    iovcnt            offset         seg    resid
               1                 4096           0      0
0xf86e8ea4:    base   7630            len   0
7630/X
0x7630:        ff8
```

As we can see, when *vno_rw()* called *fifo_rdwr()*, three apparently valid pointers were sent as parameters *vp*, *uiop*, and *cred*. The other two parameters, *rw* and *ioflag*, are both small values. *Ioflag* was created on-the-fly by *vno_rw()* and *rw* was simply forwarded.

We can safely assume things were going along well until we were executing the *fifo_rdwr()* routine. But, where exactly did things go wrong? Since *fifo_rdwr()* is a long routine, without source code this question is not easily answered.

Don't work too hard! Use SunSolve!

Instead of trying to debug UNIX internals code without the proper tools (Source!), let's jump into research mode to see if this is a known problem. Yes, we hear a few of you mumbling "It's about time!", but think of all that you learned.

Using Sun's SunSolve program, let's search the bugs and patches databases for the following keywords:

- fifo_rdwr
- vno_rw
- alignment
- 4.1.3

Picking search keywords is sometimes an art of its own, so let's explain why we chose the keywords we did. The first two are from the stack traceback. Alignment is a good word to use to search for memory alignment panics. Specifying the operating system will help eliminate non-4.1.3 bug reports. The results in this search: Bug 1050077.

Bug 1050077 reports a problem with the following stack traceback shown as an example.

```
physmem bf3
_panic(0xf81514e9,0xf825acbc,0x0,0x0,0xf825b,0xf7fffc78) + 6c
_trap(0x7,0xf825acbc,0x0,0x0,0x0,0x0) + 184
fixfault(?)
_uiomove(0x0,0x0,0x1000,0x2,0x1002,0x2) + 50
_fifo_rdwr(0xff0b3600,0xf825aeac,0x0,0xff0d5757,0x2,0x0) + 5ac
_vno_rw(0xf81b39e0,0x1,0xf825aeac,0x1000,0xff0b3604,0x0) + a4
_rwuio(0xf81b39e0,0xf825aeac,0xf825aea4,0x1000,0x1000,0xf825aeac) + 2b0
```

```
_write(0xf825afe0,0x20,0xf813af88,0xf813afa8,0xf825b000,0xf813afa8) + 34
_syscall(0xf825b000) + 3b4
```

Interesting, isn't it? You couldn't ask for a much nicer match!

Next, we search the patch database for bug 1050077 and get a match on patch number 100347. The patch description reads as follows:

"Problem Description: Under a heavy load, writing to a named pipe (fifo) can cause a kernel panic, if one doesn't have the definition in fifo.h set up correctly. Specifically, the definition for FIFOBUF must be greater than FIFOBSZ. Otherwise, you end up using a union instead of a structure, and the union pointer gets overwritten."

Resolution

The customer who submitted this system crash dump to us installed patch 101347 and tried unsuccessfully to crash his system. Needless to say, the system stayed up despite his efforts, and he was quite pleased with the results.

A Sleeping Dragon   34 ≡

The crash dump we are about to explore was submitted to us by a customer who was experiencing unexplained system hangs on his Sun SPARCcenter 2000, what we at Sun often affectionately refer to as a "Dragon."

The history of this particular Dragon was commendably blemish free. Installation went without a hitch, bringing it on line into production mode went quite smoothly, and aside from a few tuning issues, no trouble had been reported. Things were going well, until...

...new software was brought on line and the Dragon started experiencing hangs.

Since this is a sun4d system running Solaris 2.3, we will use another Dragon running the same OS to do our analysis. As the customer asked to not have his company name used in this book, nor the name of the third party software, we will be modifying some of the output to comply with his wishes.

This is a fun crash dump that we think you'll enjoy! Let's begin!

Initial information

It's always good practice to get initial information. How long was the system up? In the case of a multiple CPU system, how many CPUs are on line and what where they doing? We will use some of the macros we wrote earlier.

```
Hiya on p4d-2000a... cp $HOME/adb/mymacros/* .
Hiya on p4d-2000a... adb -k unix.0 vmcore.0
physmem fd87
$<initial-info

                Initial Dump Information
                ========================
utsname+0x101:  dragon          Hostname

                1994 Aug 30 09:08:12        Time of boot
time:
time:           1994 Sep  1 14:30:48       Time of crash
$<msgbuf
msgbuf:
```

```
msgbuf:                 magic           size            bufx            bufr
                        8724786         1fe8            16a             0
msgbuf+0x10:    Y\
panic[cpu0]/thread=0xe18b1ec0: zero
                syncing file systems...panic[cpu0]/thread=0xe18d8ec0: panic sync
                  timeout
                12081 static and sysmap kernel pages
                  176 dynamic kernel data pages
                  565 kernel-pageable pages
                    0 segkmap kernel pages
                    0 segvn kernel pages
                    0 current user process pages
                12822 total pages (12822 chunks)

                dumping to vp f584c804, offse
*panicstr/s
cpr_info+0x13c4:                        zero
$<proconcpu
ncpus:
ncpus:          Number of CPUS:  4

cpu0+8:         e18d8ec0                Thread address
0xe18d8f60:     e00ee110                Proc address
p0+0x260:       sched

                Next CPU...
tcl_endptopen+0x50b0:                   e18f1ec0        Thread address
0xe18f1f60:     e00ee110                Proc address
p0+0x260:       sched
                This CPU was idle

                Next CPU...
tcl_endptopen+0x3cb0:                   e1914ec0        Thread address
0xe1914f60:     e00ee110                Proc address
p0+0x260:       sched
                This CPU was idle

                Next CPU...
tcl_endptopen+0x38b0:                   e1937ec0        Thread address
0xe1937f60:     e00ee110                Proc address
p0+0x260:       sched
                This CPU was idle
```

Based on what we see so far, the system was up for over two days when it was manually forced to panic. The "panic: zero" tells us this.

Walking the stack by hand

We also see that three of the four CPUs were idle. The fourth was handling the panic. Let's confirm this via **adb**. This is a particularly interesting example, because the first thing we notice is that the **$c** output below is short. Occasionally, the **$c** output of **adb** will come up a bit short. If it doesn't look as if a system call or interrupt is at the bottom of the stack traceback, be suspicious! To make sure we aren't missing anything exciting, we walked the stack by hand, just to be on the safe side.

```
$c
complete_panic(0x0,0xe18cfd1c,0xe18b1ec0,0xe18b1ec0,0xe18b1ee4,0xe00fdd28) + d0
do_panic(?) + 20
vcmn_err(0xe00dc000,0xe18cfd1c,0xe18cfd1c,0x73,0x73,0x3)
cmn_err(0x3,0xe00dc000,0x0,0x0,0x0,0x0) + 1c


e18d8ec0$<thread      <--- Using the thread address from the non-idle CPU structure seen earlier
adb
0xe18d8ec0:
                link            stk             stksize
                0               e18d8e60        1ec0
0xe18d8ecc:
                bound           affcnt          bind_cpu
                e00fd240        0               -1
0xe18d8ed4:
                flag            procflag        schedflag       state
                9               0               11              4
0xe18d8ee0:     pri             epri            pc              sp
                169             0               e000ffe8        e18d8cc8
0xe18d8eec:     wchan0          wchan           cid             clfuncs


                .... remainder of thread output omitted ....


e18d8cc8/16X
0xe18d8cc8:     0               f               0               d
                1               e00d1800        e00fd240        1
                e00e7400        1               e00d1c00        e00fd240
                0               e00e7400        e18d8d30        e000fbf0
e000fbf0/i
do_panic+0x20:  call     complete_panic
e18d8d30/16X
0xe18d8d30:     f               37              f               0
                f5659000        e00e7710        4               e010166c
                e00e0054        e18d8e38        e00e7400        f
                c               0               e18d8d90        e000fbc0
e000fbc0/i
panic+0x1c:     call     do_panic
e18d8d90/16X
0xe18d8d90:     f               1               f               4
```

A Sleeping Dragon

```
                   1                  e00e7710          4                 e010166c
                   e00e0054           e00dc000          12534f0           62
                   1                  0                 e18d8df0          e003f3f4
e003f3f4/i
clock+0x58:     call      panic
e18d8df0/16X
0xe18d8df0:        e00fa024           1                 e00d1c00          4
                   a                  5                 2                 4
                   0                  4                 fff01080          ffefefc8
                   ffffffff           64                e18d8c60          e000666c
e000666c/i
L14_front_end+0x2c8:                  call      clock
e18d8e60/16X
0xe18d8e60:        41401fc2           f54c93f8          f54c93fc          e00fd240
                   a                  a9                e18d8ec0          e18cf7e0
                   8                  f54b4400          fff01080          ffefefc8
                   2                  8                 e18cf888          f54c93e4
f54c93e4/i
md_daemon+0x14: call      md_get_status
e18cf888/16X
0xe18cf888:        414019c3           e0009944          e0009948          e00fd240
                   a                  e18b1ec0          e18d8ec0          f54b4518
                   1                  f54b4518          c58f6ff           f54b4538
                   f54b4528           0                 e18cf8e8          f54debfc
f54debfc/i
md_stripe_strategy+0x23c:             call      md_daemon
e18cf8e8/16X
0xe18cf8e8:        f68127e8           1                 f56f4e00          f5a9cadc
                   f5a9cb04           f5a9caf8          0                 f6832c00
                   4d746              0                 0                 0
                   8                  f68127e8          e18cf960          e003ba6c
e003ba6c/i
bwrite+0x8c:    call      bdev_strategy
e18cf960/16X
0xe18cf960:        11eb39             71b8c             f5499f84          3
                   a                  e18b1ec0          e18d8ec0          e18cf918
                   f68127e8           0                 c0b               ffefefc8
                   80a                e00fd240          e18cf9c0          e003c3d8
e003c3d8/i
bflush+0x19c:   call      bwrite
e18cf9c0/16X
0xe18cf9c0:        f5704b30           f5705148          f5705148          f5704b30
                   c0b                28f               e00fd0ac          2000
                   ffffffff           0                 0                 f6812848
                   f6105f68           f68127e8          e18cfa20          f5499e94
f5499e94/i
ufs_update+0x20c:                     call      bflush
e18cfa20/16X
0xe18cfa20:        414019c7           d8                f681ca00          0
                   f54a5c6c           1                 0                 f5490308
```

```
                12              f5aca600        f681cad8        f5aca62c
                f5b10000        0               e18cfa88        f549cb20
f549cb20/i
ufs_sync+0x1c:  call    ufs_update
e18cfa88/16X
0xe18cfa88:     0               7007ee          e00e9d90        2
                0               8               e00fdd84        e00fdd84
                0               0               f54ad500        f5490308
                f549cb04        e00fdd86        e18cfae8        e0093630
e0093630/i
sync+0x54:      jmpl    %o4, %o7
e18cfae8/16X
0xe18cfae8:     e00fa024        e00e6c00        e000ff98        f5408000
                10              80a             200             e00e7518
                e00e4fa4        0               e00fdd84        e00d6d00
                2               20              e18cfb48        e009421c
e009421c/i
vfs_syncall+0x58:               call    sync
e18cfb48/16X
0xe18cfb48:     410019c2        e002bd94        e001009c        e00fd240
                a               e00e4c00        e00e4c00        4
                e00e4fc4        e00e4fbc        ffffffec        410010e3
                41001ce3        0               e18cfba8        e00100a8
e00100a8/i
complete_panic+0x190:           call    vfs_syncall
e18cfba8/16X
0xe18cfba8:     c               1               e00d2000        9
                1               e00d2000        e00fd240        0
                0               e18cfd1c        e18b1ec0        e18b1ec0
                e18b1ee4        e00fdd28        e18cfc10        e000fbf0
e000fbf0/i
do_panic+0x20:  call    complete_panic
e18cfc10/16X
0xe18cfc10:     41401cc4        e00401cc        7a              7a
                7a              ffef0000        7               418010e6
                e00dc000        e18cfd1c        e18cfd1c        73
                73              3               e18cfc70        e00401bc
e00401bc/i
cmn_err+0x1c:   call    vcmn_err
e18cfc70/16X
0xe18cfc70:     73              0               63              63
                63              63              63              63
                3               e00dc000        0               0
                0               0               e18cfcd0        e0011220
e0011220/i
vx_handler+0xa4:                call    cmn_err
e18cfcd0/16X
0xe18cfcd0:     41801dc6        ffd8d898        1               e00d1c00
                ffef0000        0               f0120000        0
                ffed4440        7               e00041e0        0
```

```
                e00d2010        e00d2008        e18cfd50        ffd56178
ffd56178/i

data address not found
e18cfd50/16X
0xe18cfd50:     ffd5d0e0        0               ffd48d8c        ffef0000
                e001117c        ffd7ecf0        ffefefc8        ffefebdc
                2               ffd418a0        b               e00d1fb6
                0               1               e18cfdb0        e0037878
e0037878/i
prom_enter_mon+0x60:            jmpl    %o1, %o7
e18cfdb0/16X
0xe18cfdb0:     60              e0006758        f               10
                1               e00e7710        1               e010166c
                2e0000          6b              2e0000          4
                1               6b              e18cfe10        e0010860
e0010860/i
debug_enter+0x100:              call    prom_enter_mon
e18cfe10/16X
0xe18cfe10:     10              e0029dd8        e00d30c8        e00fa084
                e00fd240        0               4               0
                0               0               44              0
                740000          740002          e18cfe80        e0010744
e0010744/i
abort_sequence_enter+0x18:      call    debug_enter
e18cfe80/16X
0xe18cfe80:     740000          44              0               10
                e0000000        1               0               80
                0               1               44              1
                0               f576205c        e18cfee0        f5760a94
f5760a94/i
zs_high_intr+0xc4:              jmpl    %g1, %o7
e18cfee0/16X
0xe18cfee0:     f5762460        e00b1800        0               e00f7000
                0               2               1               e00d1993
                f543861c        2               3               c
                e00fd240        f5762000        e18cff40        e000cdd8
e000cdd8/i
slow_intr+0x9c: jmpl    %i1, %o7
e18cff40/16X
0xe18cff40:     410001c4        e00e6c00        e00458b4        e00fd240
                a               e18b1ec0        e18d8ec0        e00e7518
                c               f57609d0        e00e6f14        0
                0               0               e18cffa0        e000637c
e000637c/i
_level1+0xa0:   call    slow_intr
e18cffa0/16X
0xe18cffa0:     41400cc5        e0044258        e004425c        e000637c
                c               414000c5        1               e18b1d58
                1b              0               0               ffffffff
```

```
                0            e00fd240        e18b1e00        e0044294
e0044294/i
idle+0xcc:      call    disp_getwork
e18b1e00/16X
0xe18b1e00:     41000ac2     e0006754        e00fd240        e00ee110
                e00fd280     0               e00fd28c        e00fd28d
                e00fd240     0               e00fd244        e00fd35c
                0            0               c18b1e60        e000a0c8
e000a0c8/i
thread_start+4: jmpl    %i7, %o7
e18b1e60/16X
0xe18b1e60:     0            0               0               0
                0            0               0               0
                0            0               0               0
                0            0               0               e00441c8
e00441c8/i
idle:
idle:           save    %sp, -0x60, %sp
```

What did we learn by doing this manual stack traceback? Something quite important actually! The first CPU was also idle when the panic was forced. Basically, this Dragon was quietly snoozing until someone walked up to its console and woke it up.

Using the threadlist macro

To find out what the Dragon was dreaming about, we need to look at *all* of the threads. We do this via the **adb** macro **threadlist** on Solaris 2 systems. On Solaris 1 systems, we use the **traceall** macro.

Note – Threadlist and **traceall** output can be thousands of lines long on heavily used servers. You might want to consider sending the **adb** output to a file. Also, you'll discover that it actually takes **adb** quite a while to do all of this thread tracing for you. This **threadlist** took over six minutes to run. So, yes, this is a good time to get coffee!

Here is the command we used to collect the thread information.

```
Hiya on p4d-2000a...  time adb -k unix.0 vmcore.0 > allthreads
$<threadlist
$q

real      6:23.0
user      1:31.8
```

```
sys       4:46.6
Hiya on p4d-2000a...
```

While some of you might be curious to see the whole **threadlist** output, we think it best to keep the output shown here a bit limited. First, we'll show you a few of what appear to be boring threads, examples of what we are *initially* ignoring....

```
                    thread_id e18dbec0     <--- Thread quietly awaiting a certain condition
?(?) + dffff7a8
cv_wait(0xe00fd1c8,0xe00fd1c8,0x0,0x10000,0x0,0x0)
background(0x0,0xfffffffe,0x10000,0xf5f3e488,0x0,0xe00fd1c8) + e8

                    thread_id e18e1ec0
?(?) + dffff7a8
cv_wait(0xe01023f0,0xe01023f0,0xc70f6ff,0x1,0x3,0xf5437100)
qwriter_outer_thread(0x0,0xf5437100,0xe00fdbc4,0x0,0xe01023f0,0x0) + 74

                    thread_id e18eaec0     <--- Problem with $c output  (We'll get back to this)
?() + dffff7a8
data address not found

                    thread_id e18f1ec0     <--- A CPU being awakened for the panic
?(?) + dffff7a8
poll_obp_mbox(0xffeef001,0xfc,0x1,0x4,0xe00ee098,0xfc)
level14_handler(0xe18f1d54) + 4
L14_front_end(?) + 68
flush_windows(0x414000e0)
resume(?) + 4
disp_getwork(0xf571d800,0x0,0x0,0xffffffff,0x0,0xf571c000)
idle(0xf571d800,0x0,0xf571d804,0xf571d91c,0x1,0x0) + cc

                    thread_id f572ee00
?(?) + dffff7a8
biowait(0xf60950f0,0x0,0x0,0xf64604d0,0xf68ed3ec,0xf60950f0)

                    thread_id f63f0e00     <--- Thread quietly awaiting a signal
?(?) + dffff7a8
cv_wait_sig(0x0,0xf628a558,0x1,0xf623f000,0xe1d5b9e0,0xf63f0e00)
strwaitq(0xf628a500,0xf5fad746,0x400,0xf5fad700,0xe1d5b7a4,0x2) + 234
strread(0x0,0xf628a558,0xf628a510,0xe1d5b828,0x0,0x600000) + 14c
rw(0x400,0xe1d5b920,0x1,0x0,0xe00d626c,0xf5d9c804) + 1e4
syscall(0xe00de9f0) + 3d8
```

Here are the more interesting threads. The underlined data shows what the trained eye takes notice of.

```
                 thread_id e18c9ec0
?(?) + dffff7a8
mutex_enter(0xe00ecb34,0xe00ecb3a,0xe00ecb34,0xb36940ff,0xf5a98ffb,f5a98fe0)
polltime(0xf6263000,0x0,0xc64f6ff,0xb36940ff,0x124c054,0xf571d800) + 8
callout_execute(0xe00fe5d0,e00fe9e0,0x124c054,80000000,f59da8fc,a0f67454) + 8c
realtime_timein(0xe00fe5d0,0x0,0x100,0x410000e0,0x41000de0,0x0) + 14
softint(0xe003e2d0,0xe00eaea0,0x0,0x0,0x0,0xe00eb1c4) + 8c
softlevel1(0x0,0xc6c76ff,0xe00d7088,0x1,0x41000de2,0xe00eb1c4) + 4
soft_pseudo_intr(0xe00d709c,0x0,0xe00a337c,0x0,0x0,0x1) + 44
cpu_intr(0x1,0x1f00606,0xe1d1c9e0,0xe000ce30,0xe00ae708,0x0) + 70
_level1(0xe00fd240,0x0,0xe0000000,0x0,0x4b,0x100)

                 thread_id e18d8ec0
?(0xe00e7400,0x1,0xe00d1c00,0xe00fd240,0x0,0xe00e7400) + dffff7a8
do_panic(0xe00e0054,0xe18d8e38,0xe00e7400,0xf,0xc,0x0) + 20
panic(0xe00e0054,0xe00dc000,0x12534f0,0x62,0x1,0x0) + 1c
clock(0x0) + 58

                 thread_id e1bd8ec0
?(?) + dffff7a8
mutex_enter(0xe00ecb34,0xe00ecb3a,0xe00ecb34,0xb36940ff,0xf5a98ffb,0xf5a98fe0)
pollwakeup(0xf5c3ad40,0x41,0xe00ec800,0xe00ecb34,0x0,0xe0102248) + 3c
strrput(0xf6acd700,0x0,0xdec76ff,0xf5c3ad00,0x1,0xf5c3ad58) + 320
putnext(0xf5c3aa00,0xf6acd700,0xf5c3ad00,0x1ff00,0xe007acd8,0xf5c3aaa8) + 134

                 thread_id f5ab7400
?(?) + dffff7a8
mutex_enter(0xe00ecb34,0xe00ecb3a,0xe00ecb34,0xb36940ff,0xf5a98ffb,0xf5a98fe0)
pollwakeup(0xf6acea40,0x41,0xe00ec800,0xe00ecb34,0x0,0xe0102248) + 3c
putback(0xf6acea58,0xf6acea58,0xf69e6600,0x0,0xe1ef8808,0x0) + 98

                 thread_id f5a3ce00
?(?) + dffff7a8
mutex_enter(0xe00ecb34,0xe00ecb3a,0xe00ecb34,0xb36940ff,0xf5a98ffb,0xf5a98fe0)
cv_wait_sig_swap(0x0,0xe00ecb34,0x1,0xf5d2f800,0xe1b9a9e0,0xf5a3ce00) + 170
poll(0x1,0xf6b7738c,0xf6a9edf8,0x0,0x0,0xffffffff) + 54c
syscall(0xe00de9f0) + 3d8

                 thread_id f6756000
?(?) + dffff7a8
mutex_enter(0xe00ecb34,0xe00ecb3a,0xe00ecb34,0xb36940ff,0xf5a98ffb,0xf5a98fe0)
poll(0xf66b21b0,0xe1c47920,0x0,0x0,0x1,0x0) + 208
syscall(0xe00de9f0) + 3d8

                 thread_id f57a1c00
?(?) + dffff7a8
```

```
mutex_enter(0xe00ecb34,0xe00ecb3a,0xe00ecb34,0xb36940ff,0xf5a98ffb,0xf5a98fe0)
pollwakeup(0xf63e1d40,0x41,0xe00ec800,0xe00ecb34,0x0,0xe0102248) + 3c
strrput(0xf6b7ba80,0x0,0xabd0e0ff,0xf63e1d00,0xe1b88808,0xf63e1d58) + 320
putnext(0xf63e1800,0xf6b7ba80,0xf63e1d00,0x1ff00,0xe007acd8,0xf63e18a8) + 134


                    thread_id e1b6bec0
?(?) + dffff7a8
mutex_enter(0xe00ecb34,0xe00ecb3a,0xe00ecb34,0xb36940ff,0xf5a98ffb,0xf5a98fe0)
pollwakeup(0xf6098b40,0x41,0xe00ec800,0xe00ecb34,0x0,0xe0102248) + 3c
strrput(0xf66df700,0x0,0xdb5f6ff,0xf6098b00,0x0,0xf6098b58) + 320
```

Looking at this trimmed output, we see seven calls to *mutex_enter()*. This routine is called with one parameter, the pointer to a mutual exclusive lock. What is surprising is that each of the seven threads is calling *mutex_enter()* with the same *mutex* pointer, 0xe00ecb34.

Examining mutex locks

Using **adb**, let's find out more about this *mutex* that seven threads are waiting to use.

```
0xe00ecb34$<mutex
poll_lock:
poll_lock:         owner
                   f66d2800
poll_lock:
poll_lock:         lock      type      waiters
                   ff        0         fe02
```

This *mutex* structure, *poll_lock*, is currently owned by thread f66d2800. What is that thread and what is it doing? Let's find out, looking in the **allthreads** file we created.

```
                thread_id f66d2800
?() + dffff7a8
data address not found
```

That output looks a bit suspicious. Since the **threadlist** macro calls **$c**, we may not have gotten all of the information we need. Let's walk this thread's stack by hand. Better yet, let's write our own macros to walk a stack for us, given a stack pointer. Here are a set a macros designed to do the job.

strace *macro*

```
.="Easy to read stack traceback"n
.,.$<strace.nxt
```

strace.nxt *macro*

```
.>f
.=2n
*(<f+0t60)/i
.="First 6 arguments..."n
(<f+20)/6Xn
(<f+38)/"Next stack --> "Xn
*(<f+0t56),.$<strace.nxt
```

On Solaris 2.3, the *thread* structure maintains the stack pointer at *thread+0x28*. Remember to always check the header file, **/usr/include/sys/thread.h**, to verify the offsets. Using this, let's look at the stack for thread f66d2800 which is holding the *mutex* that seven other threads are waiting to access.

```
*(f66d2800+28)$<strace
                  Easy to read stack traceback

abc_readit+0x90:             call     mutex_enter
                  First 6 arguments...
0xe1ed1718:      f6080f4c        f6080f52        f6080f4c        c8676ff
                  f5a98e7b        f5a98e60
0xe1ed1730:      Next stack --> e1ed1758

abc_pollit+0xd8:             call     abc_readit
                  First 6 arguments...
0xe1ed1778:      2a5d            4               b36940ff        40
                  c8              0
0xe1ed1790:      Next stack --> e1ed17c8

poll+0x348:      jmpl    %g1, %o7
                  First 6 arguments...
0xe1ed17e8:      1b80000         40              0               f67911d6
                  40              f5fdd2f4
0xe1ed1800:      Next stack --> e1ed1830

syscall+0x3d8:   jmpl    %g1, %o7
```

```
                    First 6 arguments...
0xe1ed1850:         40              f67e6160        f67911d0        0
                    f5d43d94        f67f2e00
0xe1ed1868:         Next stack --> e1ed18b8

_sys_rtt+0x4d4: call    syscall
                    First 6 arguments...
0xe1ed18d8:         e00de9f0        e1ed1eb4        0               e1ed1e90
                    fffffffc        ffffffff
0xe1ed18f0:         Next stack --> e1ed1938

data address not found
```

Fascinating! Thread f66d2800 is trying to access a *mutex* lock. Let's find out more about that lock.

```
f6080f4c$<mutex
0xf6080f4c:         owner
                    190cec0
0xf6080f4c:         lock    type    waiters
                    ff      0       e602
```

The owner of this unnamed *mutex* is actually thread e190cec0.

Note – The **mutex** macro on Solaris 2.3 prefixes an "f" to owner addresses when appropriate, but not the "e." Read the macro and see if you can figure out why!

Next, let's find out what thread e190cec0 is doing. This time, we'll just look at the top of it's stack, then at the whole stack if we feel it's necessary.

```
*(e190cec0+28)/16X
0xe190cab8:         f66d2800        e00fd240        e00de794        e0000000
                    e0000000        ffffffe0        f5fbbcf4        f5fbbcf9
                    f5fbbcf4        f5fbbcfa        f5fbbcf4        b00760ff
                    f5a98edb        f5a98ec0        e190cb18        f5fd6008
f5fd6008/i
abc_alloc+0x54:     call    mutex_enter
```

Oh my! Another call to *mutex_enter()*. We'll keep going. At this point, you should be able to follow what we are doing.

```
f5fbbcf4$<mutex
0xf5fbbcf4:     owner
                f600ec00
0xf5fbbcf4:     lock      type      waiters
                ff        0         ec02
*(f600ec00+28)/16X
0xe1d1c368:     e1937ec0      e00fd240      e00de794      e0000000
                e0000000      ffffffe0      f5fde918      f5fde91d
                f5fde918      f5fde91e      f5fde918      b36940ff
                f5a98e9b      f5a98e80      e1d1c3c8      f5fd9cd0
f5fd9cd0/i
abc_opensocket+0x40c:                call      mutex_enter
f5fde918$<mutex
abc_top_mutex:
abc_top_mutex:  owner
                f66d2800
abc_top_mutex:
abc_top_mutex:  lock      type      waiters
                ff        0         e802
```

Does the thread address f66d2800 look familiar to you? That's the same thread that owns the *poll_lock mutex* that seven threads are waiting to use.

We've seen the stack tracebacks of all but one of the threads, e190cec0, which are waiting for mutex locks to become available. Checking e190cec0 in the **allthreads** file, we again see the "data address not found," so we might want to consider checking out the other threads that failed to be traced.

Data address not found? Dig deeper!

Using the **allthreads** file as a reference, we will manually display the top stack of the "missing" threads. This is hard, manual labor, but is sometimes worth it.

Of the 43 missing threads, all but five were in a *cvwait()* routine (or a variation of same), waiting for a condition variable to be met before continuing with execution. We've already seen three of them.

Here are the other two threads that were not in *cvwait()*.

```
*(e18d2ec0+28)/16X
0xe18d2c40:     e1937ec0        e00fd240        e00de794        e0000000
                e0000000        ffffffe0        f5fde910        f5fde915
                f5fde910        f5fde916        f5fde910        b36940ff
                f5a98ebb        f5a98ea0        e18d2ca0        f5fd1334
f5fd1334/i
abc_doit+0x14:      call    mutex_enter


*(f6226e00+28)/16X
0xe1eb36d0:     e1937ec0        e00fd240        e00de794        e0000000
                e0000000        ffffffe0        f5490308        f549030d
                f5490308        f549030e        f5490308        ab9770ff
                f5a98f3b        f5a98f20        e1eb3730        f5499ca0
f5499ca0/i
ufs_update+0x18:            call    mutex_enter
```

Very interesting! Two more calls to *mutex_enter()*! Let's find out which *mutex* locks these two threads are trying to access.

```
f5fde910$<mutex
abc_last_mutex:
abc_last_mutex: owner
                f66d2800
abc_last_mutex:
abc_last_mutex: lock    type    waiters
                ff      0       ea02

f5490308$<mutex
0xf5490308:     owner
                f572ee00
0xf5490308:     lock    type    waiters
                ff      0       f202
```

We've not seen thread f572ee00 before, but thread f66d2800 certainly is familiar to us!

Additional analysis tools

Partway through the analysis of this system, it became apparent that this crash dump was going to present a bit of a puzzle. Sensing this, we resorted to a little-known trade secret among the kernel gurus. Yes, we grabbed a pad of paper and a pencil and started recording what we were finding.

The initial result is the table below.

Thread	Mutex	Symbol Name	Owner
e18c9ec0	e00ecb34	poll_lock	f66d2800
e1bd8ec0	e00ecb34	poll_lock	f66d2800
f5ab7400	e00ecb34	poll_lock	f66d2800
f5a3ce00	e00ecb34	poll_lock	f66d2800
f6756000	e00ecb34	poll_lock	f66d2800
f57a1c00	e00ecb34	poll_lock	f66d2800
e1b6bec0	e00ecb34	poll_lock	f66d2800
f66d2800	f6080f4c	(none)	e190cec0
e190cec0	f5fbbcf4	(none)	f600ec00
f600ec00	f5fde918	abc_top_mutex	f66d2800
e18d2ec0	f5fde910	abc_last_mutex	f66d2800
f6226e00	f5490308	(none)	f572ee00

After we stared at this for a few minutes, it seemed that this Dragon was stuck in what is called a "deadlock condition" or "deadlock chain." To confirm this, we went right back to the pad of paper and started drawing lines and circles, tracking the dependencies. In other words, we needed to see which processes were waiting for which locks which were owned by which processes which were waiting for which locks, and so on.

In the end, it turns out that the deadlock involved only three of the processes shown in the table, as drawn here. However, the nine other processes were "hung," waiting around for the deadlock to be resolved.

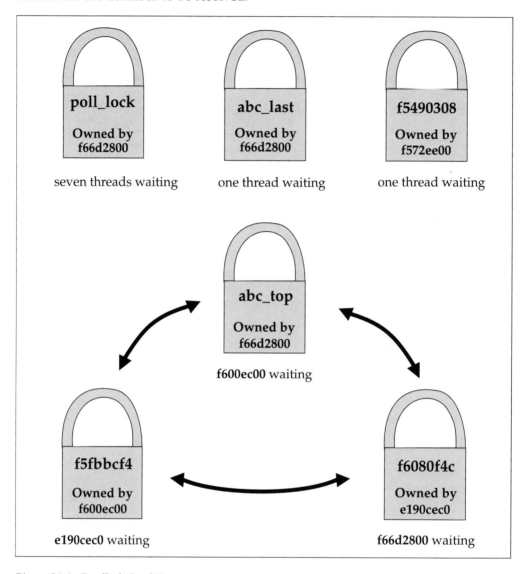

Figure 34-1 Deadlock Condition

How this deadlock condition was created is anyone's guess. If the system administrator was patient, would the deadlock eventually be resolved? The answer is to that question is "No," thus the name *deadlock*.

Which processes were waiting for locks?

We've found a deadlock situation involving 12 threads. On a system that may be running hundreds of threads, this doesn't necessarily cause a system to be hung. It just hangs those 12 threads. What we have to ask now is this: "Did the deadlock involve processes that gave the system a "hung" feeling from the end-users' point of view?"

To find that out, we will check which processes were involved. Using offsets into the *thread* structure and the *proc* structure, we will take advantage of **adb**'s ability to use pointers to pull the commands for the 12 threads involved.

```
*(e18c9ec0+a0)+260/s
p0+0x260:       sched
*(e1bd8ec0+a0)+260/s
p0+0x260:       sched
*(f5ab7400+a0)+260/s
0xf620ca60:     /bin/sh /local/bin/abc.sh dragon
*(f5a3ce00+a0)+260/s
0xf5d2fa60:     /usr/lib/lpsched
*(f6756000+a0)+260/s
0xf66b2260:     abc_job.x -s multiprocessor -g gateway1,gateway2,gateway3
*(f57a1c00+a0)+260/s
modlexec+0x7f3c:            /usr/lib/saf/sac -t 300
*(e1b6bec0+a0)+260/s
p0+0x260:       sched
*(e18d2ec0+a0)+260/s
p0+0x260:       sched
*(f6226e00+a0)+260/s
0xf5ae1260:     abc_daemon -e /export/dragon/abc_files

                  The next three are the deadlocked processes
*(e190cec0+a0)+260/s
p0+0x260:       sched
*(f600ec00+a0)+260/s
0xf626e260:     abc_printer
*(f66d2800+a0)+260/s
0xf5d43a60:     abc_job.x -s multiprocessor -g gateway1,gateway2,gateway3
```

The processes involved in the "hang" included a lot of third-party software. Also, it was surprising to see the kernel involved (always shown as command **sched**) so many times. So, on a hunch, we decided to dig a bit more.

Loadable kernel modules

We decided to look at the *modules* table in the kernel to see which modules were loaded in the system. Sure enough, after we reviewed the nearly 1200 lines of output, it appeared we were dealing with a system that not only had a third-party application, but also involved a fair number of third-party kernel modules!

Here is a tiny snippet of the output, just so you can see what it looks like. Here we see two of the entries in the *modules* table. To view the information, we used the **modules** macro.

```
Hiya on clem...   adb -k unix.0 vmcore.0
physmem fd87
$<modules                                       (Severely trimmed output)
fdvfs+0x6bdc:   module          'abc_watch'
fdvfs+0x4adc:   file            '/usr/kernel/drv/abc_watch'
fdvfs+0x485c:   next            prev            id              mp
                f5b1ee40        f59b8340        67              f5b1e700
fdvfs+0x486c:   thread          modinfo         linkage
                0               0               f5bafa64
fdvfs+0x4878:   filename        module name
                f59b8740        f59ba840
fdvfs+0x4880:   busy            stub hold       state
                0               0               d0000000
fdvfs+0x488c:   requisites      dependents      loadcnt
                f59b8a80        0               1


0xf5f33640:     module          'abc_streams'
0xf5cff5f0:     file            'strmod/abc_streams'
pckt_bufcall_lock+0x6acc:       next            prev            id              mp
                f5f33780        f5f5d740        76              f5cdff00
pckt_bufcall_lock+0x6adc:       thread          modinfo         linkage
                0               0               f5f75624
pckt_bufcall_lock+0x6ae8:       filename        module name
                f5cff5f0        f5f33640
pckt_bufcall_lock+0x6af0:       busy            stub hold       state
                0               0               c0000000
pckt_bufcall_lock+0x6afc:       requisites      dependents      loadcnt
                f5f3f560        0               1
```

Yes, from this, it was safe to say that the "abc" application had customized the kernel via the use of loadable modules!

Conclusion

We called the owner of the Dragon and let him know what we had found. We explained the deadlock condition to him. Since we didn't know anything about the processes involved, we asked if these were critical processes that could render the whole system useless. Sure enough, they were!

We prepared a full report for the customer. He then forwarded this to the software vendor who was designing and writing their application.

A month later, we checked in with the customer again, just to see how things were going. Sure enough, they agreed that the hang was caused by the new software, and the problem was being addressed by the programmers.

At the beginning of this case history, we clearly pointed out that problems didn't start on the Dragon until new software was installed. However, that may have just been a coincidence. Performing an analysis of the system crash dump, we were able to confirm that the new software was causing problems and to discover why the Dragon had fallen asleep on the job.

34

Once Is Not Enough

When we talked about the **savecore** program in Chapter 3, we said that sometimes it is quite helpful to have more than one crash from a system. This case history provides an excellent example of this advice.

A city council in England suddenly started experiencing frequent crashes on one of their Sun SPARCstations. Once they enabled **savecore**, they kept it enabled. Thus, they were able to send us several system crash dumps. Together, we will look at two of them.

The first captured crash

The first crash was not captured, because the **savecore** program had not been enabled. After the system rebooted, the customer called Sun's United Kingdom Answer Centre for assistance. He was advised how to use **savecore** and was told what to do should the system crash again.

Later that day, the system panic'ed. The system crash dump files were immediately forwarded to the UKAC engineer.

Always get initial information

Let's look at the first crash dump, collecting initial information.

```
Hiya...  strings vmcore.0 |more
SunOS Release 4.1.3_U1 (cityboy) #1: Thu May 19 11:49:57 BST 1994
Copyright (c) 1983-1993, Sun Microsystems, Inc.
Data fault
/dev/mouse
/dev/mouse
BAD TRAP
PROTOCOM_Z_VIP_Spid 218, `clock':
Data fault
kernel read fault at addr=0x160, pme=0x0
SunOS Release 4.1.3_U1 (cityboy) #1: Thu May 19 11:49:57 BST 1994
Copyright (c) 1983-1993, Sun Microsystems, Inc.
mem = 24576K (0x1800000)
avail mem = 22339584
```

```
Ethernet address = 8:0:20:1f:d9:aa
cpu = SUNW,Sun 4/40
zs0 at obio 0xf1000000 pri 12
zs1 at obio 0xf0000000 pri 12

... and so on ...
```

Based on what we found in the **strings** output, we will use a sun4c system running
SunOS 4.1.3_U1 to do the analysis. We also now know that we're going to see a "bad
trap: data fault" in this crash.

```
Hiya on p4c-50a...  adb -k vmunix.0 vmcore.0
physmem 17a9
hostname/s
_hostname:
_hostname:      cityboy
*boottime=Y
                1994 Oct 25 09:53:49
*time=Y
                1994 Oct 25 10:26:46
$c
_panic(0xf81443e3,0xf82b3bf4,0x160,0x80,0xf82b4,0xf7fff7e8) + 6c
_trap(0x9,0xf82b3bf4,0x160,0x80,0x1,0x0) + 184
callhatfault(0x0,0x1,0xff00a3e8,0x4,0xf76dfa10,0xfce2f658) + 34
_vno_select(?)
_swtch(0x800ae5,0xf81f5948,0x4000e5,0x0,0x3,0x2) + 30
_sleep(0xf814c810,0x1a,0x29,0xa00,0x1a,0xf81f5ac0) + 1a0
_select(0xffbfffff,0x20008001,0xf82b4380,0xf76dfa10,0xf82b3d70,0xf82b4000) + 4cc
_indir(0xf82b4000,0x5d,0xf8131010,0x14,0xf82b4394,0xf82b3ff8) + 1d4
_syscall(0xf82b4000) + 3b4
$<msgbuf
0xf8002000:     magic           size            bufx            bufr
                63062           1ff0            1200            d8d
0xf8002d9d:     BAD TRAP
                pid 218, `clock': Data fault
                kernel read fault at addr=0x160, pme=0x0
                Sync Error Reg 80<INVALID>
                pc=0xf80e5d64, sp=0xf82b3c40, psr=0x4000c3, context=0x5
                g1-g7: 0, 0, ffffffff, 0, f82b4000, f8148000, f8148000
                Begin traceback... sp = f82b3c40
    (Trimmed output )
```

A trap occurred

The system didn't panic due to a software condition. Instead, it panic'ed due to a "bad trap: data fault." The hardware detected a condition that should not have occurred while trying to access memory.

Using the second argument to the *trap()* call, we dump out the trap registers and look further into the trap.

```
0xf82b3bf4$<regs
0xf82b3bf4:     psr             pc              npc
                4000c3          f80e5d64        f80e5d68
0xf82b3c00:     y               g1              g2              g3
                c800000         0               0               ffffffff
0xf82b3c10:     g4              g5              g6              g7
                0               f82b4000        f8148000        f8148000
0xf82b3c20:     o0              o1              o2              o3
                f814c708        2               1               0
0xf82b3c30:     o4              o5              o6              o7
                182             f82b3c60        f82b3c40        a
f80e5d64/i          <--- Instruction being executed
_idle:
_idle:          sethi    %hi(0xf8148000), %g1
f80e5d68/i          <--- Instruction next in the pipeline
_idle+4:        ld       [%g1 + 0x160], %g1       ! -0x7eb7ea0
f82b3c40$c          <--- Get stack traceback starting at the stack pointer
?(?)
_swtch(0x800ae5,0xf81f5948,0x4000e5,0x0,0x3,0x2) + 4034
_sleep(0xf814c810,0x1a,0x29,0xa00,0x1a,0xf81f5ac0) + 1a0
_select(0xffbfffff,0x20008001,0xf82b4380,0xf76dfa10,0xf82b3d70,0xf82b4000) + 4cc
_indir(0xf82b4000,0x5d,0xf8131010,0x14,0xf82b4394,0xf82b3ff8) + 1d4
_syscall(0xf82b4000) + 3b4
```

Did you notice that the **regs** macro output and the *msgbuf* ring buffer both contained the stack pointer and the program counter?

The sethi instruction

The failed instruction, `sethi`, is the first instruction in the *idle()* routine, a routine called thousands, maybe millions, of times per day. To have it crash there seems unlikely. But what is more unlikely is for the `sethi` instruction to cause a trap, especially a data fault, which is caused by illegal attempts to access memory.

The `sethi` instruction does not access memory. Instead, it loads a 22-bit value into a register. So, the trap type and the instruction (according to the PC) do not match.

Examining nPC

If we look again at the trap error messages, we see that the failure is reported as being due to a "kernel read fault at addr=0x160." The `sethi` instruction had nothing to do with address 0x160.

At this point, it is a good idea to look at the next instruction in the pipeline. Maybe, somehow, the *trap()* routine just didn't report the correct PC. Let's look at nPC now.

```
f80e5d68/i          <--- Instruction next in the pipeline
_idle+4:       ld      [%g1 + 0x160], %g1       ! -0x7eb7ea0
```

That's a bit better. However, in the previous instruction, we had set %g1 to contain the high-order 22 bits of the value 0xf8148000. Therefore, this load instruction should have been trying to read address f8148160, not address 160.

Something went wrong!

The `sethi` instruction never completed its job. Had it done so, %g1 would contain a valid address. At this point, we can only assume that the system had suffered some sort of hiccup.

The second captured crash

When looking at a collection of related crashes, you hope to find a pattern. In the case of "cityboy," we found a very definite pattern.

Initial information

Even though this is a crash from the same customer, it's a good idea to make sure that it's definitely from the same system. More than once we've puzzled over a crash that didn't match the others, only to find that it was from a different system, but the customer was hoping you might look at it anyway.

Also, it sometimes helps to know how long the system was up before it went down. What is the crash frequency? Is there a recognizable pattern in the crash times? Is the crash frequency increasing? As you can probably imagine, there's a lot that you can deduce from the uptime and crash times.

Here's what we found.

```
Hiya on p4c-75a...  adb -k vmunix.1 vmcore.1
physmem 17a9
hostname/s
_hostname:
_hostname:      cityboy
*boottime=Y
                1994 Oct 25 10:43:51
*time=Y
                1994 Oct 26 04:20:12
$c
_panic(0xf81443e3,0xf82f4bf4,0x338,0x80,0xf82f5,0xf7fff9a0) + 6c
_trap(0x9,0xf82f4bf4,0x338,0x80,0x1,0x0) + 184
callhatfault(?)
_splx(0x100,0x1001e3,0xf8127c00,0xf81f6ae8,0xb80b0,0x0) + 34
_soo_select(?)
_swtch(0x800ae4,0xf81f644c,0x4000e4,0x0,0x3,0xa7) + 15c
_sleep(0xf814c810,0x1a,0x29,0xa00,0x1a,0xf81f6ae8) + 1a0
_select(0xffbfffff,0x20088001,0xf82f5380,0xb80b0,0xf82f4d70,0xf82f5000) + 4cc
_indir(0xf82f5000,0x5d,0xf8131010,0x14,0xf82f5394,0xf82f4ff8) + 1d4
_syscall(0xf82f5000) + 3b4
$<msgbuf
0xf8002000:     magic           size           bufx           bufr
                63062           1ff0           1d7e           1917
0xf8003927:     BAD TRAP
                pid 752, `event_manager': Data fault
                kernel read fault at addr=0x338, pme=0x0
                Sync Error Reg 80<INVALID>
                pc=0xf80e5dc0, sp=0xf82f4c40, psr=0x4000c2, context=0x2
                g1-g7: 0, 0, ffffffff, 0, f82f5000, f8148000, f8148000
                Begin traceback... sp = f82f4c40
(Trimmed output )
```

The system suffered another data fault, this time while trying to read the contents of location 0x338.

Collecting trap information

So, again, we need to look at the trap registers to find the failed instruction.

```
0xf82f4bf4$<regs
0xf82f4bf4:     psr             pc             npc
                4000c2          f80e5dc0       f80e5dc4
0xf82f4c00:     y               g1             g2             g3
                19000000        0              0              ffffffff
```

```
0xf82f4c10:      g4                g5                g6                g7
                 0                 f82f5000          f8148000          f8148000
0xf82f4c20:      o0                o1                o2                o3
                 8000              0                 0                 fce31880
0xf82f4c30:      o4                o5                o6                o7
                 0                 f8047e68          f82f4c40          f8089c00
f80e5dc0/i
_idle+0x5c:      orcc    %g0, %g1, %g0
```

The trap is reported as having occurred during the ORing of two registers. And, again, we are in the *idle()* routine. At 4 a.m., that's not surprising!

The orcc instruction

Like the `sethi` instruction we saw in the first crash, the `orcc` instruction does not attempt to access memory. Therefore, a data fault is not a trap we would expect to see generated by this instruction.

Once again, the fault that occurred and the instruction that was referenced by the PC do not match.

Examining nPC

Let's take a look at the next instruction in the pipeline. It's possible that we have another case of the nPC referencing the failing instruction. Let's look forward a few instructions.

```
f80e5dc4/3i
_idle+0x60:      be      _idle
                 nop
                 call    _runqueues
```

Well, that's not what we expected, is it? Maybe the problem occurred *before* the reported PC. Let's go back a few instructions.

```
idle+50,4/ia
_idle+0x50:      stba    %g0, [%g2] 0x2
_idle+0x54:      sethi   %hi(0xf8147800), %g1
_idle+0x58:      ldub    [%g1 + 0x338], %g1          ! -0x7eb84c8
_idle+0x5c:      orcc    %g0, %g1, %g0
_idle+0x60:
```

Well, this is very interesting! The instruction executed just prior to the reported PC was a "load unsigned byte" instruction, `ldub`. We were trying to read a byte from the memory location whose address was stored in `%g1`. According to the code shown above, `%g1` should have contained address 0xf8147b38 (0xf8147800 + 0x338). However, according to the trap registers and the trap error messages, we actually tried to read memory location 0x338.

The other crashes

As we examined the other crashes the customer sent in, we saw a definite pattern emerge. Each crash dump showed the following characteristics:

- The PC according to *trap()* was always off by at least one instruction.
- The failing instruction always involved an "incomplete" memory address.
- The failing instruction was using `%g1`.
- The failures were not limited to the *idle()* routine.

Also, the frequency of the problems was increasing. The customer's system was in trouble!

The solution

The pattern didn't include any software commonalities. We weren't always running a certain program or exercising a certain driver. The system was just up and dying, both when being used and when sitting idle. This pointed more to a hardware fault.

The UKAC engineer who worked on this problem quickly ordered up a new CPU for the system. It was installed that day. The system didn't crash again after that.

Conclusion

Hardware problems don't always exhibit themselves in obvious ways. Sometimes the failing component will only cause faults under certain environmental conditions. Other times, it may take a certain electrical load to push the hardware over the edge.

If the hardware is acting up and staying up only some of the time, you'll probably want more than one crash dump to be sure. Once is not enough.

Life Without A Root Directory 36 ≡

In Chapter 5, we showed you how to intentionally crash your own system. Now let's analyze the system crash dump files that were generated by the panic.

Get initial information

First, let's take a look at the **strings** output.

```
Hiya...  strings vmcore.0 | more
Generic_101318-45
Data fault
P+
PRLR
v@ (
X,DD
XBAD TRAP: type=9 rp=f05d04c4 addr=3 mmu_fsr=3a6 rw=2
fm_flb: Data fault
kernel write fault at addr=0x3, pme=0x0
MMU sfsr=3a6: Invalid Address on supv data store at level 3
pid=496, pc=0xf0048918, sp=0xf05d0510, psr=0x404000c7, context=408
g1-g7: 0, 0, ffffff00, 0, f05d09e0, 1, fc45c600
Begin traceback... sp = f05d0510
Called from f009e214, fp=f05d0680, args=f05d06e4 0 f05d06ec 0 0 fc01dd14
Called from f00e4790, fp=f05d06f0, args=0 0 1 0 f05d07f4 0
Called from f00e14c4, fp=f05d0848, args=3cad8 0 3 b40 f05d08ac 0
Called from f007095c, fp=f05d08b8, args=3cad8 3 b48 f05d0920 3cad8 f0156628
Called from f0041aa0, fp=f05d0938, args=f0160f3c f05d0eb4 0 f05d0e90 ffffffffc
   ffffffff
Called from ef75de2c, fp=efffea08, args=3cad8 2 efffeb48 1 0 f016b620
End traceback...
panic: Data fault
                { We quit out of more at this point }
Hiya...
```

The system panic'ed due to a data fault, a bad trap type number 9. The output shown above is the same as the messages that appeared on the system console during the panic.

Since this was our experimental crash, we already know which system it came from and which OS was running. For this panic, the authors used a Sun SPARCstation 20 running Solaris 2.3. So, using the same system, let's jump into **adb** and start examining the crash dump. Items of particular interest are underlined.

```
Hiya...  adb -k unix.0 vmcore.0
physmem 1e05
$c
complete_panic(0xf0049460,0xf05d03ac,0xf05d0238,0x3,0x0,0x1) + 10c
do_panic(?) + 1c
vcmn_err(0xf015f7a8,0xf05d03ac,0xf05d03ac,0x3cad8,0x2,0x3)
cmn_err(0x3,0xf015f7a8,0x0,0x18,0x18,0xf0152400) + 1c
die(0x9,0xf05d04c4,0x3,0x3a6,0x2,0xf015f7a8) + 78
trap(0x9,0xf05d04c4,0xf01822d8,0x3a6,0x2,0x0) + 598
fault(?) + 84
mutex_enter(0x0,0xd,0x64,0x1,0xd,0xf05d06ec)
lookuppn(0xf05d06e4,0x0,0xf05d06ec,0x0,0x0,0xfc01dd14) + 148
lookupname(0x0,0x0,0x1,0x0,0xf05d07f4,0x0) + 28
vn_open(0x3cad8,0x0,0x3,0xb40,0xf05d08ac,0x0) + a4
copen(0x3cad8,0x3,0xb48,0xf05d0920,0x3cad8,0xf0156628) + 70
syscall(0xf0160f3c) + 3e4
0xf05d04c4$<regs
0xf05d04c4:     psr               pc                npc
               404000c7          f0048918          f004891c
0xf05d04d0:     y                 g1                g2                g3
               20000000          0                 0                 ffffff00
0xf05d04e0:     g4                g5                g6                g7
               0                 f05d09e0          1                 fc45c600
0xf05d04f0:     o0                o1                o2                o3
               0                 d                 64                1
0xf05d0500:     o4                o5                o6                o7
               d                 f05d06ec          f05d0510          f009e378
f0048918/i
mutex_enter+4:  ldstub   [%o0 + 0x3], %g6
```

First, we get the stack traceback, and using the second parameter to the trap routine, we collect the trap registers. In the trap registers, we find the contents of the PC and the actual instruction that caused the trap and panic.

The instruction that failed, ldstub, is a very special SPARC instruction because it can read and write to memory atomically. In other words, the ldstub instruction cannot be interrupted during its work. ldstub reads an unsigned byte from memory into a register, then writes all ones (hexadecimal 0xff) to that byte of memory.

Specifically, the ldstub instruction that triggered the trap was trying to work with the memory location represented by [%o0 + 0x3]. Since %o0 contained 0 according to the output from the **regs** macro, the ldstub instruction was trying to access location 0x3.

The first page of memory is always off limits. Attempts to read or write to page zero result in data faults. In this case, we were trying to write to the page. If you look back at the messages, you will see that this was well reported in the diagnostic output from the *trap()* routine.

Invoking mutex_enter()

Looking at the PC, we saw that the failing instruction is at location *mutex_enter+0x4*. So, we had just entered the *mutex_enter()* routine.

mutex_enter() is invoked whenever a mutex (mutually exclusive) lock is needed. The mutex locks protect data structures from being used by more than one thread at a time. (Of course, this only works if everyone agrees to use the locking mechanism and to follow the rules that go with it.)

Whenever *mutex_enter()* is invoked, it is called with a pointer to a *mutex* structure. Once in *mutex_enter()*, the mutex is tested to see if it is already in use. If it is not, the requesting thread gets the mutex and the address of the thread (aka "the owner") is stored in the *mutex* structure. There's a good explanation of this in **/usr/include/sys/mutex.h**, should you want to learn more.

In this crash, we see that *mutex_enter()* was called with an incoming parameter of zero. This null pointer is obviously incorrect, as a valid memory address was expected.

So, we've found the reason that the system panic'ed — illegal access to page zero caused by a null pointer argument in the call to *mutex_enter()*. Now we need to find out why this happened in the first place.

What process was involved?

It may prove helpful to find out what process was involved at the time of the trap. Let's find out what was running. To do this, we look at the *cpu* structures (there is only one on this system, so this is quick and easy), get the running *thread*, offset into the associated process (*proc*) structure, and pull the command line.

```
$<cpus
cpus:
cpus:        id          flags          thread        idle_t
             0           1b             fc45c600      f03c1ec0
cpus+0x10:   lwp         callo          fpu
             f05d09e0    0              f05e8d18
cpus+0x1c:   next        prev           next on       prev on
             f017caa0    f017caa0       0             0
cpus+0x2c:   lock   npri queue          limit         actmap
```

	0	110	fc00a000	fc00a528	fc03b460
cpus+0x3c:	maxrunpri	max unb pri	nrunnable		
	-1	-1	0		
cpus+0x4c:	runrun kprnrn	chsnlevel		dispthread	thread lock
	0 0	0		fc45c600	0
cpus+0x58:	intr_stack	on_intr		intr_thread	intr_actv
	f03dffa0	0		f03dcec0	0
cpus+0x68:	base_spl				
	0				

```
fc45c600+a0/X
0xfc45c6a0:    fc44f800
fc44f800+260/s
tmp_mdevmap+0x5c88:
               /apps/dist/share/framemaker,v4.0/bin/sunxm.s5.sparc/fm_flb
```

From this, we see that a FrameMaker® program was running at the time. This is surprising and a bit humorous to the authors, as when we crashed the system on purpose, we firmly believed it crashed due to an **ls /** command we had executed. But that's not what the evidence shows!

Let's find out what the **fm_flb** program was trying to accomplish when it caused the system to crash.

Going back through time

We need to go back through time, reviewing the history for this thread. To do this, we need the stack traceback. As a reminder, here it is.

```
$c
complete_panic(0xf0049460,0xf05d03ac,0xf05d0238,0x3,0x0,0x1) + 10c
do_panic(?) + 1c
vcmn_err(0xf015f7a8,0xf05d03ac,0xf05d03ac,0x3cad8,0x2,0x3)
cmn_err(0x3,0xf015f7a8,0x0,0x18,0x18,0xf0152400) + 1c
die(0x9,0xf05d04c4,0x3,0x3a6,0x2,0xf015f7a8) + 78
trap(0x9,0xf05d04c4,0xf01822d8,0x3a6,0x2,0x0) + 598
fault(?) + 84
mutex_enter(0x0,0xd,0x64,0x1,0xd,0xf05d06ec)
lookuppn(0xf05d06e4,0x0,0xf05d06ec,0x0,0x0,0xfc01dd14) + 148
lookupname(0x0,0x0,0x1,0x0,0xf05d07f4,0x0) + 28
vn_open(0x3cad8,0x0,0x3,0xb40,0xf05d08ac,0x0) + a4
copen(0x3cad8,0x3,0xb48,0xf05d0920,0x3cad8,0xf0156628) + 70
syscall(0xf0160f3c) + 3e4
```

From this, we see that **fm_flb** made a system call, requesting to open or create a file. *copen()* is a common routine used to open and create files. It calls *vn_open()* to open the associated vnode. *vn_open()* calls *lookupname()*, which collects the pathname of the file to open. *lookupname()* calls *lookuppn()*, which walks each component of the pathname, finally reaching the final component.

The arguments to each of these routines, per the source, are as follows.

```
copen       (fname, filemode, createmode, rvp)
vn_open     (pnamep, seg, filemode, createmode, vpp, crwhy)
lookupname  (fnamep, seg, followlink, dirvpp, compvpp)
lookuppn    (pnp, followlink, dirvpp, compvpp)
```

From this, we can guess at what most of the arguments might be. The letter p used at the end of a variable name usually means "pointer." Sometimes, as done here, you'll see double p's, which usually means "pointer to a pointer." So, *vpp* is actually a pointer to a vnode pointer, and *compvpp* is the pointer to the vnode pointer for the final component of the pathname.

As you can tell, you really need the source code at this point. However, let's see what we can do without it.

What's still useful in the stack traceback?

Looking at the stack traceback and the expected arguments as shown above, it becomes fairly obvious that the first argument in the call *lookupname()* is not a pointer to a filename. So, there are two questions that need to be asked.

1. Is *fnamep* used only upon return from *lookupname()* and thus could be useless at the time the crash occurred?

2. Was the value of %i0, which was stored in the frame, overwritten after it was used?

The lookupname() routine

Let's look at the assembly code for *lookupname()* and see if we can answer the questions.

```
lookupname,12/ia
lookupname:      save     %sp, -0x70, %sp
lookupname+4:    add      %fp, -0xc, %o2
lookupname+8:    mov      %i1, %o1
```

```
lookupname+0xc: call     pn_get
lookupname+0x10:                mov      %i0, %o0
lookupname+0x14:                orcc     %g0, %o0, %i0
lookupname+0x18:                bne      lookupname + 0x3c
lookupname+0x1c:                mov      %i4, %o3
lookupname+0x20:                mov      %i3, %o2
lookupname+0x24:                mov      %i2, %o1
lookupname+0x28:                call     lookuppn
lookupname+0x2c:                add      %fp, -0xc, %o0
lookupname+0x30:                mov      %o0, %i0
lookupname+0x34:                call     pn_free
lookupname+0x38:                add      %fp, -0xc, %o0
lookupname+0x3c:                ret
lookupname+0x40:                restore
lookuppn:         save    %sp, -0x170, %sp
lookuppn+4:
```

Right at the start, the *lookupname()* routine calls *pn_get()*. Upon returning, we OR the contents of %o0 with %g0 and store the result in %i0, thus overwriting the first argument to *lookupname()*.

Since we are ORing %o0 with the **/dev/null** of registers, %g0, placing the results in %i0, we are really copying the contents of %o0 to %i0. However, because it's an orcc instruction, condition bits are being set in the Processor Status Register, PSR. These bits are tested by the next instruction, bne, branch if not equal. In effect, this code tests to see if %o0 is equal to zero. If not, we exit *lookupname()* immediately.

What does this sequence suggest? It suggests that *pn_get()* sends back a return code of zero or non-zero to the caller.

The pn_get() routine

What did the call to *pn_get()* do? If for no other reason than pure curiosity, we should take a look at it. Here it is.

```
pn_get,20/ia
pn_get:           save    %sp, -0x60, %sp
pn_get+4:         call    pn_alloc
pn_get+8:         mov     %i2, %o0
pn_get+0xc:       orcc    %g0, %i1, %g0
pn_get+0x10:      bne     pn_get + 0x30
pn_get+0x14:      mov     0x400, %o2
pn_get+0x18:      mov     %i0, %o0
pn_get+0x1c:      ld      [%i2 + 0x4], %o1
```

```
pn_get+0x20:      call      copyinstr
pn_get+0x24:      add       %i2, 0x8, %o3
pn_get+0x28:      ba        pn_get + 0x44
pn_get+0x2c:      ld        [%i2 + 0x8], %l6
pn_get+0x30:      mov       %i0, %o0
pn_get+0x34:      ld        [%i2 + 0x4], %o1
pn_get+0x38:      call      copystr
pn_get+0x3c:      add       %i2, 0x8, %o3
pn_get+0x40:      ld        [%i2 + 0x8], %l6
pn_get+0x44:      orcc      %g0, %o0, %i0
pn_get+0x48:      sub       %l6, 0x1, %l6
pn_get+0x4c:      be        pn_get + 0x5c
pn_get+0x50:      st        %l6, [%i2 + 0x8]
pn_get+0x54:      call      pn_free
pn_get+0x58:      mov       %i2, %o0
pn_get+0x5c:      ret
pn_get+0x60:      restore
pn_set:           save      %sp, -0x60, %sp
```

(output trimmed)

The *pn_get()* routine, based on the value of input register %i1, calls either *copyinstr()* or *copystr()*. The copy routines copy a string from a source to a destination. One is used for copying from user space to kernel space, the other works solely within kernel space.

The argument in %i1 is listed as *seg*. What might this be? Well, this wouldn't be an easy one to guess at, so we'll tell you. It is an enumerated flag that shows what segment is being referenced. Look in **/usr/include/sys/uio.h**, and you'll find:

```
/*
 * Segment flag values.
 */
typedef enum uio_seg { UIO_USERSPACE, UIO_SYSSPACE, UIO_USERISPACE } uio_seg_t;
```

So, knowing this, we can see that if %i1 is zero (*seg* is set to UIO_USERSPACE), then we call *copyinstr()*. Otherwise, we use *copystr()* to copy the string.

When *pn_get()* has completed the copy, it modifies %i0. If we were to follow this further, we would find that the copy routines also modify the calling parameters.

The call to *pn_get()* in *lookupname()* is nearly immediately followed by a call to *lookuppn()*, so let's find out what it does next.

The lookuppn() routine

The *lookuppn()* routine, according to the stack traceback, does appear to have a valid memory address as the first argument. This is listed as being a *pnp*, a pointer to a *pn*, probably a pathname. Let's see what we find there and if it looks valid.

We will be looking at address 0xf05d06e4, the value of the first calling parameter to *lookuppn()*, as seen in the $c output we got earlier.

```
0xf05d06e4/X
0xf05d06e4:        fc26a000
fc26a000/X
ledmadelay+0x404:                       2f646576
./s
ledmadelay+0x404:                       /dev/ticotsord
```

The value 2f646576 looked like it was possibly an ASCII value, so we redisplayed at it as a string. Sure enough, we now have the name of the file that **fm_flb** was trying to open!

Now, we get to a trouble spot. According to $c, we called *mutex_enter()* from location *lookuppn+0x148*. That's fairly deep down into the program, making variable-chasing a lot of work.

Let's look at some of the assembly code first.

```
lookuppn,20/ia
lookuppn:         save    %sp, -0x170, %sp
lookuppn+4:       st      %i2, [%fp + 0x4c]
lookuppn+8:       sethi   %hi(0xf0165400), %o0
lookuppn+0xc:     st      %i3, [%fp + 0x50]
lookuppn+0x10:    add     %o0, 0x264, %l2
lookuppn+0x14:    ldsh    [%g7 + 0x1a], %o3
lookuppn+0x18:    sethi   %hi(0xf00f1400), %o1
lookuppn+0x1c:    add     %o3, 0x1, %o3
lookuppn+0x20:    sth     %o3, [%g7 + 0x1a]
lookuppn+0x24:    ld      [%g7 + 0x58], %o5
lookuppn+0x28:    add     %o1, 0x370, %l5
lookuppn+0x2c:    ld      [%o5 + 0xf4], %o0
lookuppn+0x30:    add     %o0, 0x1, %o0
lookuppn+0x34:    st      %o0, [%o5 + 0xf4]
lookuppn+0x38:    ldsh    [%g7 + 0x1a], %o2
lookuppn+0x3c:    sub     %o2, 0x1, %o2
lookuppn+0x40:    sll     %o2, 0x10, %o2
lookuppn+0x44:    sra     %o2, 0x10, %o2
```

```
lookuppn+0x48:   sth     %o2, [%g7 + 0x1a]
lookuppn+0x4c:   orcc    %g0, %o2, %g0
lookuppn+0x50:   bne,a   lookuppn + 0x78
lookuppn+0x54:   ld      [%fp + 0x4c], %l1
lookuppn+0x58:   ld      [%g7 + 0x58], %o0
lookuppn+0x5c:   ldsb    [%o0 + 0x4d], %o0
lookuppn+0x60:   orcc    %g0, %o0, %g0
lookuppn+0x64:   be,a    lookuppn + 0x78
lookuppn+0x68:   ld      [%fp + 0x4c], %l1
lookuppn+0x6c:   call    kpreempt
lookuppn+0x70:   clr     %o0
lookuppn+0x74:   ld      [%fp + 0x4c], %l1
lookuppn+0x78:   clr     %i4
lookuppn+0x7c:   orcc    %g0, %l1, %g0
lookuppn+0x80:
+,20
lookuppn+0x80:   be      lookuppn + 0x90
lookuppn+0x84:   clr     %l4
lookuppn+0x88:   ba      lookuppn + 0x94
lookuppn+0x8c:   mov     0x1, %l7
lookuppn+0x90:   clr     %l7
lookuppn+0x94:   ld      [%g7 + 0xa0], %i5
lookuppn+0x98:   ld      [%i5 + 0x2d0], %i5
lookuppn+0x9c:   call    mutex_enter
lookuppn+0xa0:   mov     %i5, %o0
lookuppn+0xa4:   ld      [%i5 + 0xc], %o1
lookuppn+0xa8:   mov     %i5, %o0
lookuppn+0xac:   add     %o1, 0x1, %o1
lookuppn+0xb0:   call    mutex_exit
lookuppn+0xb4:   st      %o1, [%i5 + 0xc]
lookuppn+0xb8:   cmp     %i1, 0x1
lookuppn+0xbc:   bne,a   lookuppn + 0xc8
lookuppn+0xc0:   clr     %o2
lookuppn+0xc4:   mov     0x1, %o2
lookuppn+0xc8:   ld      [%fp + 0x50], %l0
lookuppn+0xcc:   add     %i0, 0x8, %i2
lookuppn+0xd0:   add     %i0, 0x4, %l3
lookuppn+0xd4:   clr     %i3
lookuppn+0xd8:   mov     %o2, %l6
lookuppn+0xdc:   ld      [%i2], %o5
lookuppn+0xe0:   orcc    %g0, %o5, %g0
lookuppn+0xe4:   bne,a   lookuppn + 0xf4
lookuppn+0xe8:   ld      [%i2], %o7
lookuppn+0xec:   ba      lookuppn + 0x684
lookuppn+0xf0:   mov     0x2, %i1
lookuppn+0xf4:   orcc    %g0, %o7, %g0
```

```
lookuppn+0xf8:    be,a     lookuppn + 0x108
lookuppn+0xfc:    clr      %i1
lookuppn+0x100:
+,20
lookuppn+0x100:   ld       [%l3], %i1
lookuppn+0x104:   ldsb     [%i1], %i1
lookuppn+0x108:   cmp      %i1, 0x2f
lookuppn+0x10c:   bne,a    lookuppn + 0x184
lookuppn+0x110:   sethi    %hi(0xf0181800), %o1
lookuppn+0x114:   call     vn_rele
lookuppn+0x118:   mov      %i5, %o0
lookuppn+0x11c:   call     pn_skipslash
lookuppn+0x120:   mov      %i0, %o0
lookuppn+0x124:   ld       [%g7 + 0xa0], %o0
lookuppn+0x128:   ld       [%o0 + 0x2d4], %o0
lookuppn+0x12c:   orcc     %g0, %o0, %g0
lookuppn+0x130:   be,a     lookuppn + 0x144
lookuppn+0x134:   sethi    %hi(0xf0178c00), %i1
lookuppn+0x138:   ld       [%g7 + 0xa0], %i1        ! vph_mutex + 0x7f4c
lookuppn+0x13c:   ba       lookuppn + 0x148
lookuppn+0x140:   ld       [%i1 + 0x2d4], %i1
lookuppn+0x144:   ld       [%i1 + 0x1d0], %i1
lookuppn+0x148:   call     mutex_enter
lookuppn+0x14c:   mov      %i1, %o0
lookuppn+0x150:   ld       [%i1 + 0xc], %o7
lookuppn+0x154:   mov      %i1, %o0
lookuppn+0x158:   add      %o7, 0x1, %o7
lookuppn+0x15c:   st       %o7, [%i1 + 0xc]
lookuppn+0x160:   call     mutex_exit
lookuppn+0x164:   mov      %i1, %i5
lookuppn+0x168:   sethi    %hi(0xf0181800), %o0
lookuppn+0x16c:   ld       [%o0 + 0xe8], %o0       ! audit_active
lookuppn+0x170:   orcc     %g0, %o0, %g0
lookuppn+0x174:   be       lookuppn + 0x1a0
lookuppn+0x178:   mov      0x1, %o1
lookuppn+0x17c:   ba       lookuppn + 0x198
lookuppn+0x180:
```

We can take two approaches at this point.

1. Start at the beginning, working toward the failure point.

2. Start at the failure point, working back toward the beginning.

Working with source code, it's fairly easy to take the first approach. However, without source, we are making educated guesses about what the code might be doing. We may get it right, or we may end up way off track. Without source code, it is probably best to start at the point of failure and work backwards, which we will do shortly.

The magic of %g7 in Solaris 2.3 & 2.4

The user program, **fm_flb**, made a system call to open **/dev/ticotsord**. System calls are actually software traps (one of the good traps as compared to bad traps), and it is the system call software trap that brought us into kernel mode.

On this particular hardware with this particular OS, since we trapped, %g7 has special meaning. %g7 contains the address of the thread that trapped.

Note – At this point, the trap code is down deep in the guts of the UNIX system. The source code involved is **locore.s**, which is pure assembly code. From vendor to vendor, release to release, architecture to architecture, do not expect to see or count on register %g7 being used in the same manner. For Sun's Solaris 2.3 and 2.4 on SPARC architectures, the trap software in **locore.s** does use %g7 this way.

In *lookuppn()*, %g7 is used a lot. To help find the source of the panic, we are going to make use of %g7. First, let's take another quick look at the area of code we are going to closely examine.

```
lookuppn+0x124: ld      [%g7 + 0xa0], %o0
lookuppn+0x128: ld      [%o0 + 0x2d4], %o0
lookuppn+0x12c: orcc    %g0, %o0, %g0
lookuppn+0x130: be,a    lookuppn + 0x144
lookuppn+0x134: sethi   %hi(0xf0178c00), %i1
lookuppn+0x138: ld      [%g7 + 0xa0], %i1      ! vph_mutex + 0x7f4c
lookuppn+0x13c: ba      lookuppn + 0x148
lookuppn+0x140: ld      [%i1 + 0x2d4], %i1
lookuppn+0x144: ld      [%i1 + 0x1d0], %i1
lookuppn+0x148: call    mutex_enter
lookuppn+0x14c: mov     %i1, %o0
```

As you'll recall, it is the calling parameter to *mutex_enter()* that caused trouble. So, we need to see if we can figure out what happens to %o0, as this is where we will find the source of the trouble.

At *lookuppn+x0124*, we set %o0 to the address of the *proc* structure for the running thread. Using that, we set %o0 again to the contents of the *proc* structure + 0x24d. We will call this *keyvalue*. If you have the time and patience, you might try to figure out what variable is stored at offset 0x24d in the *proc* structure, although that isn't really so important at this stage. You will find that it is variable *u_rdir*, which is part of the *u* or *user* structure within the *proc* structure. Refer to **/usr/include/sys/user.h** and **/usr/include/sys/proc.h** for full details.

According to the *lookuppn()* code, if *keyvalue* is zero, we branch to *lookuppn+0x144*. The delay instruction, `sethi`, and the `ld` instruction at *lookuppn+0x144* work together to put the value 0xf0178dd0 into `%i1`. We then call *mutex_enter()*, copying 0xf0178dd0 into the output register as we go.

If *keyvalue* is non-zero, we skip the `sethi` instruction. We *do not* execute the `sethi` in the delay slot by virtue of the `, a` annul flag in the `be` instruction. The annul bit says that the `sethi` instruction is executed *only* when we branch. We execute the instructions at offsets 0x138, 0x13c, and 0x140. In effect, we are reloading *keyvalue* (the process's *u_rdir* value), this time putting it into register `%i1`. We call *mutex_enter()* next, copying the value over to `%o0`. (Yes, this is a bit redundant, but that's what the compiler came up with for final executable code.)

Now, let's see which path was taken by the *lookuppn()* routine. First, we have to find out what *u_rdir* is set to.

```
$c
complete_panic(0xf0049460,0xf05d03ac,0xf05d0238,0x3,0x0,0x1) + 10c
do_panic(?) + 1c
vcmn_err(0xf015f7a8,0xf05d03ac,0xf05d03ac,0x3cad8,0x2,0x3)
cmn_err(0x3,0xf015f7a8,0x0,0x18,0x18,0xf0152400) + 1c
die(0x9,0xf05d04c4,0x3,0x3a6,0x2,0xf015f7a8) + 78
trap(0x9,0xf05d04c4,0xf01822d8,0x3a6,0x2,0x0) + 598
fault(?) + 84
mutex_enter(0x0,0xd,0x64,0x1,0xd,0xf05d06ec)
lookuppn(0xf05d06e4,0x0,0xf05d06ec,0x0,0x0,0xfc01dd14) + 148
lookupname(0x0,0x0,0x1,0x0,0xf05d07f4,0x0) + 28
vn_open(0x3cad8,0x0,0x3,0xb40,0xf05d08ac,0x0) + a4
copen(0x3cad8,0x3,0xb48,0xf05d0920,0x3cad8,0xf0156628) + 70
syscall(0xf0160f3c) + 3e4
0xf05d04c4$<regs
0xf05d04c4:     psr         pc          npc
                404000c7    f0048918    f004891c
0xf05d04d0:     y           g1          g2          g3
                20000000    0           0           ffffff00
0xf05d04e0:     g4          g5          g6          g7
                0           f05d09e0    1           fc45c600
0xf05d04f0:     o0          o1          o2          o3
                0           d           64          1
0xf05d0500:     o4          o5          o6          o7
                d           f05d06ec    f05d0510    f009e378
fc45c600+a0/X
0xfc45c6a0:     fc44f800
```

```
fc44f800+2d4/X
tmp_mdevmap+0x5cfc:              0
```

It appears that *u_rdir* is set to zero. Therefore, *lookuppn()* would have used the other value instead as the argument to *mutex_enter()*. Let's go look at it now.

```
f0178dd0/X
rootdir:
rootdir:         0
```

Aha! We've found our problem at last! The *rootdir* variable was set to zero. What should have been there? According to **/usr/include/sys/systm.h**, *rootdir* is a pointer to the vnode of the root directory.

Why was FrameMaker involved?

Some of you might still be wondering how the FrameMaker **fm_flb** was involved in this crash. After all, the authors specifically changed *rootdir* to zero and then ran the UNIX **ls -l** command.

Actually, any command that needed a file (or device, as in the case of **fm_flb** needing **/dev/ticotsord**) would have triggered the crash in the same way. Sure, from our point of view, it sure felt like we had beat the other processes to the punch, but that just wasn't the case. And the proof is in the system crash dump files!

Disk Woes in the Wee Hours

Instead of a customer system, this case history involves one of the systems in the Sun UK offices. The system is one of the older Sun-4/400 servers, one of the first SPARC-based systems Sun manufactured.

At one time, the system, Zen, was heavily used as a home file system server for several different departments as well as a disk server for several diskless systems. Now, its work load is much lighter.

Between July 25th and October 2nd, Zen experienced four system crashes. Let's take a look at them.

Get initial information

Since we have four crashes, the approach we will take this time is to gather some initial information from each crash dump and see if we are going to be working with one type of problem or more.

```
Hiya on zen...   cd /var/crash/zen
Hiya on zen...   ls -l
total 45777
-rw-rw-rw-  1 root            3 Oct  2 03:26 bounds
-rw-r--r--  1 root     10248192 Jul 25  1994 vmcore.11
-rw-r--r--  1 root     10436608 Aug 10 08:43 vmcore.12
-rw-r--r--  1 root      9052160 Sep 26 07:49 vmcore.13
-rw-r--r--  1 root      9732096 Oct  2 03:26 vmcore.14
-rw-r--r--  1 root      1832133 Jul 25  1994 vmunix.11
-rw-r--r--  1 root      1832133 Aug 10 08:43 vmunix.12
-rw-r--r--  1 root      1832133 Sep 26 07:49 vmunix.13
-rw-r--r--  1 root      1832133 Oct  2 03:26 vmunix.14
Hiya on zen...
```

The first thing we can assume, based on the time stamps on the crash dump files, is that the problem doesn't appear to occur on a regular basis.

Let's look at the crash 11.

```
Hiya on zen...   adb -k vmunix.11 vmcore.11
physmem 1ff8
hostname/s
_hostname:
_hostname:      zen
*boottime=Y
                1994 May 31 11:13:37
*time=Y
                1994 Jul 23 03:31:14
$c
_panic(0xf8174abb,0xf817e784,0xf817e798,0x283,0xa000,0xf84c6b98) + 6c
_assfail(0xf817e784,0xf817e798,0x283,0xfcfdbdb0,0x1,0xf83817a8) + 3c
_pvn_vplist_dirty(0xfcfdbdb0,0x0,0x0,0xf83817a8,0xf8359758,0xfcfdbdb0) + 250
_ufs_putpage(0xfcfdbdb0,0xfcfdbda8,0x0,0x0,0x0,0xf82f43d8) + 33c
_ufs_l_putpage(0xfcfdbdb0,0x0,0x0,0x0,0x0,0x0) + 30
_syncip(0xfcfdbda8,0x0,0x0,0x7,0x1101,0x0) + 124
_update(0xf81a7900,0x104e,0xfcfdbda8,0xfcf1e808,0x0,0xfcfdbda8) + 2f0
_ufs_sync(0x0,0xf8175ac8,0xf817d820,0xf81a5c48,0xf8175ac8,0xfce792c4) + 4
_sync(0xf84c6fe0,0x120,0xf8173468,0xf8173588,0xf84c7000,0xf8175a88) + 3c
_syscall(0xf84c7000) + 3b4
*panicstr/s
_prtmsgbuflines+0x87:           assertion failed
$<msgbuf
0xf8002000:     magic           size            bufx            bufr
                63062           1bf0            af5             8e5
0xf80028f5:     id010e: block 134678(134678 abs): read: Uncorrectable Data Check
                assertion failed: pp->p_vnode == NULL, file: ../../vm/vm_pvn.c,
                line: 643
                panic: assertion failed
                syncing file systems... done
                00353 low-memory static kernel pages
                00558 additional static and sysmap kernel pages
                00000 dynamic kernel data pages
                00223 additional user structure pages
                00000 segmap kernel pages
                00000 segvn kernel pages
                00002 current user process pages
                00112 user stack pages
                01248 total pages (1248 chunks)

                dumping to vp fce25f4c, offset 239514
$q
Hiya on zen...
```

The system had been up nearly two months before crashing.

Notice the panic messages in the message buffer. These are a good example of verbose panic messages that include information about where to find the call to *panic()* in the source code. They may be useless to some of us, but to those with the source code, they are a helpful aid in problem diagnosis.

Let's look at crash 12.

```
Hiya on zen...   adb -k vmunix.12 vmcore.12
physmem 1ff8
hostname/s
_hostname:
_hostname:       zen
*boottime=Y
                 1994 Jul 25 08:07:30
*time=Y
                 1994 Aug 10 03:23:05
$c
_panic(0xf8174abb,0xf817e784,0xf817e798,0x283,0xa000,0xf84ccb98) + 6c
_assfail(0xf817e784,0xf817e798,0x283,0xfd0cd5a8,0x1,0xf8385088) + 3c
_pvn_vplist_dirty(0xfd0cd5a8,0x0,0x0,0xf8385088,0xf8386b40,0xfd0cd5a8) + 250
_ufs_putpage(0xfd0cd5a8,0xfd0cd5a0,0x0,0x0,0x0,0xf82f607c) + 33c
_ufs_l_putpage(0xfd0cd5a8,0x0,0x0,0x0,0x0,0x0) + 30
_syncip(0xfd0cd5a0,0x0,0x0,0x4e,0x1101,0x0) + 124
_update(0xf81a7900,0x104e,0xfd0cd5a0,0xfcfaf218,0x0,0xfd0cd5a0) + 2f0
_ufs_sync(0x0,0xf8175ac8,0xf817d820,0xf81a5c48,0xf8175ac8,0xfcea1d44) + 4
_sync(0xf84ccfe0,0x120,0xf8173468,0xf8173588,0xf84cd000,0xf8175a88) + 3c
_syscall(0xf84cd000) + 3b4
*panicstr/s
_prtmsgbuflines+0x87:            assertion failed
$<msgbuf
0xf8002000:    magic       size        bufx        bufr
               63062       1bf0        241         31
0xf8002041:    id010e: block 134678(134678 abs): read: Uncorrectable Data Check
               assertion failed: pp->p_vnode == NULL, file: ../../vm/vm_pvn.c,
               line: 643
               panic: assertion failed
               syncing file systems... done    (Remainder of output trimmed)
```

We see that this is very much the same as crash 11.

Take a look at crash 11's crash time and crash 12's boot time. What does this tell us? The system was probably unable to reboot itself successfully without operator intervention. It appears that Zen was down until someone came into the office on Monday morning, July 25th.

So, we now have two crashes. Both involve id010e. What is id010e? That is one of the IPI disk drives. Both crashes specifically report problems with block 134678 of id010e.

What will crash 13 tell us? Let's see.

```
Hiya on zen...   adb -k vmunix.13 vmcore.13
physmem 1ff8
hostname/s
_hostname:
_hostname:      zen
*boottime/Y

data address not found
*boottime=Y
                1994 Sep  7 11:58:24
*time=Y
                1994 Sep 26 03:21:01
$c
_panic(0xf8174abb,0xf817e784,0xf817e798,0x283,0xa000,0xf84c6b98) + 6c
_assfail(0xf817e784,0xf817e798,0x283,0xfce7af78,0x1,0xf8355bf8) + 3c
_pvn_vplist_dirty(0xfce7af78,0x0,0x0,0xf8355bf8,0xf8355c20,0xfce7af78) + 250
_ufs_putpage(0xfce7af78,0xfce7af70,0x0,0x0,0x0,0xf82f5b58) + 33c
_ufs_l_putpage(0xfce7af78,0x0,0x0,0x0,0x0,0x0) + 30
_syncip(0xfce7af70,0x0,0x0,0x7,0x1101,0x0) + 124
_update(0xf81a7900,0x104e,0xfce7af70,0xfcf9c6a8,0x0,0xfce7af70) + 2f0
_ufs_sync(0x0,0xf8175ac8,0xf817d820,0xf81a5c48,0xf8175ac8,0xfceb206c) + 4
_sync(0xf84c6fe0,0x120,0xf8173468,0xf8173588,0xf84c7000,0xf8175a88) + 3c
_syscall(0xf84c7000) + 3b4
$<msgbuf
0xf8002000:     magic           size            bufx            bufr
                63062           1bf0            297             87
0xf8002097:     id010e: block 134678(134678 abs): read: Uncorrectable Data Check
                assertion failed: pp->p_vnode == NULL, file: ../../vm/vm_pvn.c,
                line: 643
                panic: assertion failed            (Remainder of output trimmed)
```

This certainly looks like the other crashes. Another problem with block 134678 on drive id010e.

Sure! By now you're screaming "Fix the disk!" However, with Zen being a semi-retired system, you have to remember that no one may be taking much notice of the crashes.

By the way, did you notice the boot time on this crash? Did you compare it to the time of the last crash? What was the system doing between August 10th and September 7th? Chances are **savecore** had been disabled, then re-enabled. Or, maybe the system was actually **shutdown** for one reason or another: backups, hardware maintenance, or maybe even system relocation.

Finally, let's take a look at the 14th crash. Want to guess what we're going to see there?

```
Hiya on zen...  adb -k vmunix.14 vmcore.14
physmem 1ff8
*boottime=Y
                1994 Sep 26 03:21:50
*time=Y
                1994 Oct  2 03:24:47
$c
_panic(0xf8174abb,0xf817e784,0xf817e798,0x283,0xa000,0xf84deb98) + 6c
_assfail(0xf817e784,0xf817e798,0x283,0xfce4a2a8,0x1,0xf834a500) + 3c
_pvn_vplist_dirty(0xfce4a2a8,0x0,0x0,0xf834a500,0xf8381e88,0xfce4a2a8) + 250
_ufs_putpage(0xfce4a2a8,0xfce4a2a0,0x0,0x0,0x0,0xf82f5fc0) + 33c
_ufs_1_putpage(0xfce4a2a8,0x0,0x0,0x0,0x0,0x0) + 30
_syncip(0xfce4a2a0,0x0,0x0,0x7,0x1101,0x0) + 124
_update(0xf81a7900,0x104e,0xfce4a2a0,0xfce779d8,0x0,0xfce4a2a0) + 2f0
_ufs_sync(0x0,0xf8175ac8,0xf817d820,0xf81a5c48,0xf8175ac8,0xfce71dbc) + 4
_sync(0xf84defe0,0x120,0xf8173468,0xf8173588,0xf84df000,0xf8175a88) + 3c
_syscall(0xf84df000) + 3b4
$<msgbuf
0xf8002000:     magic           size            bufx            bufr
                63062           1bf0            1b7d            196d
0xf800397d:     id010e: block 134678 (134678 abs): read: Uncorrectable Data Check
                assertion failed: pp->p_vnode == NULL, file: ../../vm/vm_pvn.c,
                line: 643
                panic: assertion failed        (Remainder of output trimmed)
```

No surprises there.

Look for patterns

When analyzing a series of UNIX system crash dumps from one machine, we look for patterns. These four crash dumps all certainly have a strong similarity (in fact are as nearly identical as crashes can get). The most obvious similarity is the failure to access block 134678 on disk id010e. However, there is another very strong similarity. Did you notice it?

Look at the crash times. All four crashes occurred between 3:21 and 3:31 in the morning. They occurred on four different days of the week: Saturday, Wednesday, Monday, and Sunday. What does that make you think about?

Good old **cron** jobs, of course. A quick run of **ps** on any of the crash dumps reveals that the following command was being run at the time.

```
find / -name .nfs* -mtime +7 -exec rm -f {} ; -o -fstype nfs -prune
```

Another interesting note is that the system seems to have had trouble rebooting on at least two occasions. Look again at the time stamps on the crash dump files themselves. As you know, **savecore** creates the postmortem files during the execution of **/etc/rc.local**, in other words, when the system is nearing completion of the boot-up process.

It appears that crashes 12 and 13 didn't get saved until someone came into the office.

Inodes & vnodes

We know that a block on id010e is in trouble. But, we have not yet confirmed that that alone is the reason for the crashes. (Though, yes, it's a pretty safe bet.)

Before we declare id010e in need of attention from hardware support, let's look more closely at the stack tracebacks we've been getting from the dumps.

First, the routines involved:

```
assfail (a, f, 1)
pvn_vplist_dirty (vp, off, flags)
ufs_putpage (vp, off, len, flags, cred)
ufs_1_putpage (vp, off, len, flags, cred)
syncip (ip, flags, waitfor)
update ()
ufs_sync (vfsp)
```

The calling parameters listed as *vp* are vnode pointers. The parameter *ip* is a pointer to an *inode* structure.

The stack traceback shows that the process that crashed was performing a file system sync. The recently updated inodes were being written back to disk. This process is done inode by inode. The *syncip()* routine is called by *update()* for each inode that needs to be sync'ed, in other words, updated on the disk.

Before we try to establish which inode *syncip()* was working with, take a moment to look at the definition of an inode, as described in **/usr/include/ufs/inode.h.**

```
struct   inode {
         struct   inode *i_chain[2];      /* must be first */
         struct   vnode i_vnode;   /* vnode associated with this inode */
         struct   vnode *i_devvp; /* vnode for block I/O */
         u_short i_flag;
         dev_t    i_dev;              /* device where inode resides */
         ino_t    i_number;          /* i number, 1-to-1 with device address */
         off_t    i_diroff;          /* offset in dir, where we found last entry */
         struct   fs *i_fs;          /* file sys associated with this inode */
         struct   dquot *i_dquot;    /* quota structure controlling this file */
         long     i_owner;           /* proc index of process locking inode */
         long     i_count;           /* number of inode locks for i_owner */
         union {
            daddr_t if_nextr;        /* next byte read offset (read-ahead) */
struct   socket *is_socket;
         } i_un;
         struct   {
                  struct inode   *if_freef;        /* free list forward */
                  struct inode   **if_freeb;       /* free list back */
         } i_fr;
         struct   icommon {
                  u_short ic_mode;          /*  0: mode and type of file */
                  short   ic_nlink;         /*  2: number of links to file */
                  uid_t   ic_uid;           /*  4: owner's user id */
                  gid_t   ic_gid;           /*  6: owner's group id */
                  quad    ic_size;          /*  8: number of bytes in file */
#ifdef   KERNEL
                  struct timeval ic_atime; /* 16: time last accessed */
                  struct timeval ic_mtime; /* 24: time last modified */
                  struct timeval ic_ctime; /* 32: last time inode changed */
#else
                  time_t  ic_atime;         /* 16: time last accessed */
                  long    ic_atspare;
                  time_t  ic_mtime;         /* 24: time last modified */
                  long    ic_mtspare;
                  time_t  ic_ctime;         /* 32: last time inode changed */
                  long    ic_ctspare;
#endif
                  daddr_t ic_db[NDADDR];    /* 40: disk block addresses */
                  daddr_t ic_ib[NIADDR];    /* 88: indirect blocks */
                  long    ic_flags;         /* 100: status, currently unused */
                  long    ic_blocks;        /* 104: blocks actually held */
                  long    ic_gen;           /* 108: generation number */
                  /*
                   * XXX - the disk spares were used to avoid changing
                   * the size of the incore inode in a minor release.
```

```
                        * Fix for 5.0 release.
                        * Also remove the code in iget, iupdat that clears them.
                        */
                    long    ic_delaylen;    /* 112: delayed writes, units=bytes */
                    long    ic_delayoff;    /* 116: where we started delaying */
                    long    ic_nextrio;     /* 120: where to start the next clust */
                    long    ic_writes;      /* 124: number of outstanding writes */
            } i_ic;
    };
```

The interesting thing about UFS inodes is that the *vnode* structure is built into the *inode* structure. Therefore, let's also look at the *vnode* structure, as described in **/usr/include/sys/vnode.h.**

```
    enum vtype      { VNON, VREG, VDIR, VBLK, VCHR, VLNK, VSOCK, VBAD, VFIFO };

    struct vnode {
            u_short             v_flag;                 /* vnode flags (see below) */
            u_short             v_count;                /* reference count */
            u_short             v_shlockc;              /* count of shared locks */
            u_short             v_exlockc;              /* count of exclusive locks */
            struct vfs          *v_vfsmountedhere;      /* ptr to vfs mounted here */
            struct vnodeops     *v_op;                  /* vnode operations */
            union {
                    struct socket   *v_Socket;          /* unix ipc */
                    struct stdata   *v_Stream;          /* stream */
                    struct page     *v_Pages;           /* vnode pages list */
            } v_s;
            struct vfs          *v_vfsp;                /* ptr to vfs we are in */
            enum vtype          v_type;                 /* vnode type */
            dev_t               v_rdev;                 /* device (VCHR, VBLK) */
            long                *v_filocks;             /* File/Record locks ... */
            caddr_t             v_data;                 /* private data for fs */
    };
```

Okay, we are now ready to go take a look at the inode in question in the crashes. We will also establish what process was actually running at the time of the crash.

Crash 11: A closer look

We will start with the stack traceback and print out the inode involved. Using the owner field of the *inode* structure (the process currently handling the inode, not the user who owns the inode), we will find out what process is at work. We will confirm the process by looking at the variable *masterprocp*, which is a pointer to the current running process.

```
Hiya on zen...  adb -k vmunix.11 vmcore.11
physmem 1ff8
$c
_panic(0xf8174abb,0xf817e784,0xf817e798,0x283,0xa000,0xf84c6b98) + 6c
_assfail(0xf817e784,0xf817e798,0x283,0xfcfdbdb0,0x1,0xf83817a8) + 3c
_pvn_vplist_dirty(0xfcfdbdb0,0x0,0x0,0xf83817a8,0xf8359758,0xfcfdbdb0) + 250
_ufs_putpage(0xfcfdbdb0,0xfcfdbda8,0x0,0x0,0x0,0xf82f43d8) + 33c
_ufs_1_putpage(0xfcfdbdb0,0x0,0x0,0x0,0x0,0x0) + 30
_syncip(0xfcfdbda8,0x0,0x0,0x7,0x1101,0x0) + 124
_update(0xf81a7900,0x104e,0xfcfdbda8,0xfcf1e808,0x0,0xfcfdbda8) + 2f0
_ufs_sync(0x0,0xf8175ac8,0xf817d820,0xf81a5c48,0xf8175ac8,0xfce792c4) + 4
_sync(0xf84c6fe0,0x120,0xf8173468,0xf8173588,0xf84c7000,0xf8175a88) + 3c
_syscall(0xf84c7000) + 3b4
0xfcfdbda8$<inode
0xfcfdbda8:     forw            back
               fcfdbbe8        f81a7900
0xfcfdbdb0:     flag     refct  shlockc exlockc
               0        8       0       0
0xfcfdbdb8:     vfsmnt          vop              pages            vfsp
               0               f817d8b8         f83723c0         fce4f658
0xfcfdbdc8:     type            rdev             data
               2               01       0250    fcfdbda8
0xfcfdbdd8:     devvp           flag     maj    min      ino
               fce51b94        111      026    0204     28682
0xfcfdbde8:     fs              dquot            owner            count
               fde66000        0                f82f43d8         2
0xfcfdbdf8:     nextr           freef            freeb
               24576           0                0
0xfcfdbe04:     delayoff        delaylen         nextrio          writes
               0               0                c000             0
0xfcfdbe04:     mode     links  uid      gid     size
               040700   2       1889     17      162816
0xfcfdbe14:     atime 1994 Jul 23 03:31:08
               mtime 1994 May 26 12:03:15
               ctime 1994 May 26 12:03:15
0xfcfdbe28:     addresses
0xfcfdbe2c:     101a8           10300            10458            10638
               10708           10860            109b8            10b10
               10ca0           10dc0            10f18            110f0
               1e4f8           0                0
0xfcfdbe68:     flags           blocks           gen
               0               336              1967826125
*time=Y
               1994 Jul 23 03:31:14
f82f43d8$<proc
0xf82f43d8:     link            rlink            nxt              prev
```

```
                    f8198b90         0                f82f4260         f82f5aa4
0xf82f43e8:         as               segu             stack            uarea
                    fce6c6e8         f84c4000         f84c6f58         f84c7000
0xf82f43f8:         upri     pri     cpu      stat    time     nice
                    071      01      037      03      06       024
0xf82f43fe:         slp      cursig  sig
                    0        0       0
0xf82f4404:         mask             ignore           catch
                    2000             300001           2000
0xf82f4410:         flag             uid      suid    pgrp
                    80001            0        0       52
0xf82f441c:         pid      ppid    xstat    ticks
                    186      1       0        10
0xf82f4424:         cred             ru               tsize
                    fce12780         0                0
                                                     (Output trimmed)
!ps axk vmunix.11 vmcore.11 | grep 186
   186 ?  R   586:57 update
!
f84c7000$<u
0xf84c7000:         pc               sp               psr              uwm
                    f80532d0         f84c6af0         11900ae2         0
0xf84c7010:
0xf84c7358:         flags
                    80000000
0xf84c7364:         procp            ar0              comm
                    f82f43d8         f84c6fb4         update^@^@^@^@
0xf84c7380:         arg0             arg1             arg2
                    f7fffff3         f7fffff0         0
0xf84c73a0:         uap              qsave                             error
                    f84c6fe0         f80e918c         f84c6ec0         0
0xf84c73ac:         rv1              rv2              eosys
                    0                0                0
0xf84c73c0:         signal
                    0                1                0                0
                    0                0                0                0
                    0                0                0                0
                                                     (Output trimmed)
masterprocp/X
_masterprocp:
_masterprocp:       f82f43d8
```

The **update** program was trying to update (sync) inode 28682 on the device with major and minor numbers of 026 and 204.

Checking quickly, let's make sure that the macro we used, **/usr/lib/adb/inode**, isn't reporting the major and minor numbers as octal values.

```
Hiya on zen...  cd /usr/lib/adb
Hiya on zen...  more inode
./"forw"16t"back"n2X
+$<<vnode
+/"devvp"16t"flag"8t"maj"8t"min"8t"ino"nXx2bD4+
+/"fs"16t"dquot"16t"owner"16t"count"n4X
+/"nextr"16t"freef"16t"freeb"nD2X
+$<<dino
.,<9-1$<inode
Hiya on zen...
```

Good thing we checked! So the reported major/minor of 26/204 is really, in decimal, major 22 and minor 132. What device is that on Zen?

```
Hiya on zen...  cd /dev
Hiya on zen...  ls -l | grep " 132 "
brw-r-----  1 root      22, 132 Dec  9  1992 id010e
crw-r-----  1 root      72, 132 Jan 12 12:15 rid010e
crw-r-----  1 root      17, 132 Dec  9  1992 rsd16e
brw-r-----  1 root       7, 132 Dec  9  1992 sd16e
Hiya on zen...
```

What caused a change to inode 28682 which required it to be updated to the disk at nearly 3 a.m.? The **find** command! **find** looks at each inode. By nature of UFS, referencing an inode for any reason results in updating the inode's "last access time" field. Thus, the inode is "dirty." In other words, the inode is modified and needs to be updated on disk. Compare the last access time in the *inode* structure and the crash time. They are within seconds of each other.

As you can see, running a **find** command on a UNIX system actually results in a lot of disk activity.

Let's whip through the other crashes and see if the same inode and process are at work.

Crash 12: A closer look

Here's the information we found in crash 12.

```
Hiya on zen...  adb -k vmunix.12 vmcore.12
physmem 1ff8
$c
_panic(0xf8174abb,0xf817e784,0xf817e798,0x283,0xa000,0xf84ccb98) + 6c
_assfail(0xf817e784,0xf817e798,0x283,0xfd0cd5a8,0x1,0xf8385088) + 3c
_pvn_vplist_dirty(0xfd0cd5a8,0x0,0x0,0xf8385088,0xf8386b40,0xfd0cd5a8) + 250
_ufs_putpage(0xfd0cd5a8,0xfd0cd5a0,0x0,0x0,0x0,0xf82f607c) + 33c
_ufs_1_putpage(0xfd0cd5a8,0x0,0x0,0x0,0x0,0x0) + 30
_syncip(0xfd0cd5a0,0x0,0x0,0x4e,0x1101,0x0) + 124
_update(0xf81a7900,0x104e,0xfd0cd5a0,0xfcfaf218,0x0,0xfd0cd5a0) + 2f0
_ufs_sync(0x0,0xf8175ac8,0xf817d820,0xf81a5c48,0xf8175ac8,0xfcea1d44) + 4
_sync(0xf84ccfe0,0x120,0xf8173468,0xf8173588,0xf84cd000,0xf8175a88) + 3c
_syscall(0xf84cd000) + 3b4
0xfd0cd5a0$<inode
0xfd0cd5a0:     forw            back
               fce4bcc8        f81a7900
0xfd0cd5a8:     flag    refct   shlockc exlockc
               0       79      0       0
0xfd0cd5b0:     vfsmnt          vop             pages           vfsp
               0               f817d8b8        f8386a00        fce47c98
0xfd0cd5c0:     type            rdev            data
               2               01      0250    fd0cd5a0
0xfd0cd5d0:     devvp           flag    maj     min     ino
               fce5149c        111     026     0204    28682
0xfd0cd5e0:     fs              dquot           owner           count
               fde5c000        0               f82f607c        2
0xfd0cd5f0:     nextr           freef           freeb
               24576           0               0
0xfd0cd5fc:     delayoff        delaylen        nextrio         writes
               0               0               c000            0
0xfd0cd5fc:     mode    links   uid     gid     size
               040700  2       1889    17      162816
0xfd0cd60c:     atime 1994 Aug 10 03:22:58
               mtime 1994 May 26 12:03:15
               ctime 1994 May 26 12:03:15
0xfd0cd620:     addresses
0xfd0cd624:     101a8           10300           10458           10638
               10708           10860           109b8           10b10
               10ca0           10dc0           10f18           110f0
               1e4f8           0               0
0xfd0cd660:     flags           blocks          gen
               0               336             1967826125
*time=Y
               1994 Aug 10 03:23:05
masterprocp/X
```

```
_masterprocp:
_masterprocp:     f82f607c

f82f607c$<proc
0xf82f607c:     link            rlink           nxt             prev
                f8198b90        0               f82f5e48        f82f5fc8
0xf82f608c:     as              segu            stack           uarea
                fcea29f8        f84ca000        f84ccf58        f84cd000
0xf82f609c:     upri    pri     cpu     stat    time    nice
                071     01      036     03      05      024
0xf82f60a2:     slp     cursig  sig
                0       0       0
0xf82f60a8:     mask            ignore          catch
                2000            300001          2000
0xf82f60b4:     flag            uid     suid    pgrp
                80001           0       0       45
0xf82f60c0:     pid     ppid    xstat   ticks
                198     1       0       20
                                            (Output trimmed)
!ps axk vmunix.12 vmcore.12 | grep 198
  198 ?   R    163:51 update
!
$q
Hiya on zen...
```

Same inode. Same device. Same process. Same scenario where the inode had just been accessed seconds prior to the panic, most likely by the **find** command.

Crashes 13 & 14: A closer look

Yes, both of these crashes tell the same story that the first two tell. Each crashed within a few seconds of inode 28682 being accessed, thus requiring that the inode be updated on disk.

We are now quite sure that disk id010e had a hardware problem of some sort. It appeared that the problem was isolated to a small area; however, not knowing how much of the disk was actually in use, that really isn't a safe statement to make.

Resolution

The best course of action for a problem like that which Zen encountered is obvious. The disk should receive medical attention as soon as possible!

Shortly after crash 14, Zen received the attention it needed. Zen hasn't had a similar crash since.

SPARC: The Gory Details

When working with the postmortem remains of a system, it helps to have a good understanding of the anatomy of the system in question. The more you know about the involved processor and its native instruction set, the easier your work will be.

In this section, we talk about the SPARC processor. For further information, we highly recommend the reference we used, *The SPARC Architecture Manual, Version 8* from SPARC International.

All CPUs are similar

Even if your system doesn't have a SPARC processor inside it, you'll learn something about your own processor while reading this chapter. How is that? Just as all automobile engines have similarities, so do all computer processors.

Some processors consist of dozens of large printed circuit boards, whereas other processors reside on a chip you can hold on the end of your fingertip. Yet, even the largest of processors and the tiniest have components in common, such as registers used for manipulating data and arithmetic units that perform math.

Let's take a look at the SPARC processor now.

The SPARC processor

In very simple terms, the SPARC processor is logically divided into three major components, as illustrated below.

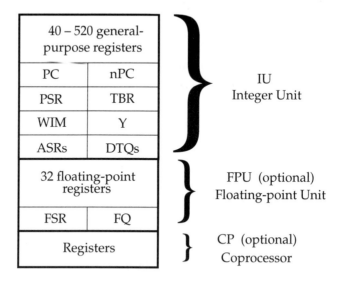

Figure A-1   SPARC processor

Integer Unit (IU)

The Integer Unit is really the heart of the SPARC processor; the central processing unit, if you prefer. The IU controls the overall operation of the processor. It loads and controls the execution of program instructions, calculates memory addresses, and has an arithmetic and logic unit (ALU).

The IU also owns the registers we will be referencing most often during system crash dump analysis, as well as a few we may never use. All of the IU registers are 32 bits wide. Let's discuss each of them.

General-purpose registers

According to the SPARC Version 8 specification, there may be anywhere from 40 to 520 general-purpose registers. These are also referred to as working data registers. These are the registers used to transfer data between memory and the processor or to hold results of operations performed in the IU.

SPARC general-purpose registers are viewed in groups or clusters known as windows. We'll be discussing the concept of windows a little later in this appendix. Another discussion, in more detail, can be found in Chapter 17, "Stacks."

PC — Program Counter

The Program Counter contains the address of the instruction currently being executed by the integer unit.

nPC — next Program Counter

As its name suggests, the nPC contains the address of the next instruction expected to be executed by the IU.

When a delayed control transfer instruction is executed, nPC will point to the target of the instruction. This might not mean much to you right now, but it will as soon as we start talking, in Appendix B, about the different instructions available on the SPARC processor.

PSR — Processor Status Register

The PSR contains useful information regarding, as the name implies, the status of the processor. Let's look at the Processor Status Register bit by bit. We point out the nibble boundaries because you'll be looking at this register in hexadecimal, and each hex digit represents one nibble (half a byte)

Nib 0	Nib 1	Nib 2	Nib 3	Nib 4		Nib 5		Nib 6		Nib 7
impl	*vers*	*icc*	reserved	E C	E F	PIL	S	P S	E T	CWP
31:28	27:24	23:20	19:14	13	12	11:8	7	6	5	4:0

Figure A-2   Process Status Register bits

The *impl* and *vers* fields, implementation and version, are hardwired by the processor manufacture to identify the processor chip and its revision level.

The *icc* field, Integer Condition Codes, is used by the arithmetic logic unit to record conditions caused by the arithmetic and logic instructions whose names end in **cc**. There are four bits in the *icc* field, one for each of the following conditions:

- Bit 23   Condition n, <u>n</u>egative result occurred
- Bit 22   Condition z, result was <u>z</u>ero
- Bit 21   Condition v, o<u>v</u>erflow occurred
- Bit 20   Condition c, bit 31 was <u>c</u>arried or borrowed

The EC and EF fields, Enable Coprocessor and Enable Floating-point unit, are set accordingly when these optional pieces of hardware are available for use. If a unit is not enabled and an instruction tries to access the unit, a trap will occur.

The PIL field of the Processor Status Register identifies the Processor Interrupt Level above which the processor will accept an interrupt. Interrupt level 15 is the highest possible interrupt on this architecture; thus, only 4 bits are needed for the PIL field.

The S field is set to 1 when the processor is running in Supervisor mode, 0 when running in user mode. In user mode, certain privileged instructions cannot be executed. The S bit can only be set by the hardware and is set whenever a trap occurs. Once the bit set, the operating system clears it when Supervisor mode is no longer needed. Essentially, this is done on return to a user program.

The PS field contains the value of the S bit at the time of the most recent trap — the previous S bit. Examining this flag will allow the kernel to identify when a trap was issued from a user program or from kernel code.

The ET field of the Processor Status Register is set to 1 when Traps are Enabled. When set to 0, traps are ignored.

The CWP field is the Current Window Pointer and identifies which register window is in use. This SPARC implementation allows up to 32 register windows, numbered 0 to 31, thus, only 5 bits are needed for the CWP.

TBR — Trap Base Register

The TBR contains three fields that, when concatenated, become a valid memory address pointing to where control is transferred when a trap occurs. The TBR is diagrammed below.

Nib 0	Nib 1	Nib 2	Nib 3	Nib 4	Nib 5	Nib 6	Nib 7
TBA					tt		zero
31:12					11:4		3:0

Figure A-3   Trap Base Register bits

Here's a rare example of when TBA does not mean "To Be Announced." The TBA field contains the Trap Base Address. This will be the most significant 20 bits of the trap vector table address.

The 8-bit-wide tt, or trap type field, is written by the hardware when a trap occurs. It provides the offset into the trap vector table.

Bits 3:0 are zero. This means that the TBR will always represent hexadecimal memory addresses that end in 0 (addresses that are on 4-word boundaries).

WIM — Window Invalid Mask

The 32-bit WIM register contains a bit for each possible window in the SPARC Version 8 implementation. The low-order bit represents window 0. The high-order bit represents window 31. One bit is normally set and marks the point at which a window overflow or underflow would occur. This could result in destruction of the register contents if not correctly handled, so a trap is issued if an instruction would result in making this window available for use.

The WIM register is used in conjunction with the CWP (Current Window Pointer) during window shifts. We will be discussing this use in more detail later on.

Y — Multiply/Divide Register

32-bit by 32-bit multiplication can result in up to 64-bit results. The most significant 32 bits are stored in the Y register. The Y register is also used during division and holds the most significant word of the dividend.

The Version 7 architecture, which had no full multiply or divide, used this register as temporary storage for individual "steps" in a multiplication or division sequence.

ASRs — Ancillary Status Registers (optional)

The SPARC Version 8 Specification allows for up to 31 additional registers. Ancillary registers 1 through 15 are reserved for future use. ASRs 16 through 31 can be used as desired by each implementation.

The Solaris operating systems assume that no ASRs are available for use.

DTQs - Deferred-Trap Queues (optional)

According to the SPARC Version 8 Specification, an implementation may contain zero or more deferred-trap queues on the processor. These queues would be used to implement resumable deferred-traps caused by the Integer Unit.

The Solaris operating systems assume that no DTQs are available for use.

Floating-Point Unit (FPU)

The Floating-Point Unit is an optional part of the SPARC processor. As its name suggests, the FPU handles all floating-point operations and arithmetic. Like the Integer Unit, the FPU has a set of working data registers, a control and status register, and an optional deferred-trap queue.

Floating-point instructions and data formats, as defined by the SPARC Version 8 Specification, conform to the ANSI/IEEE Standard 754-1985. However, the SPARC specification doesn't require that *all* aspects of the ANSI/IEEE standard be implemented in the SPARC hardware. In cases where the hardware implementation does not meet the ANSI/IEEE standard, an exception trap may be generated and the operating system software performs the necessary work instead.

Since the Floating-Point Unit is optional, the operating system must be able to completely and properly provide the user with precisely the exact results that the FPU would have provided, as according to the ANSI/IEEE standard. The user needn't worry about whether an FPU exists on his system. When an FPU is available, the Integer Unit will just pass all the floating-point instructions over to it for execution. This means the FPU will be operating in parallel with the IU.

If the FPU doesn't exist in a SPARC processor, or if the enable floating-point EF bit in the PSR is set to 0 and a floating-point instruction is executed, an *fp_disabled* trap will occur. Again, in this case, the operating system intervenes and performs the floating-point operation via software instead of via hardware.

As you can probably imagine, performing all floating-point operations on an FPU instead of via software can make a huge performance difference. FPU performance is often measured in units of megaflops, or millions of floating-point operations per second.

FPU F Registers

The FPU has thirty-two 32-bit floating-point working data registers, known as *f* registers. The f registers can be used to represent 32 single-precision, 16 double-precision, or 8 quad-precision floating-point values at a given time, or combinations of these. Unlike the windowed IU general purpose registers, all 32 f registers can be accessed by a routine at any time.

Floating-point State Register

Like the IU, the FPU has a status and control register. We won't be using this register very often during system crash dump analysis, so we will only introduce you to it. For complete technical information about the FSR and the contents of some of its fields, refer to both the SPARC Version 8 Specification and the ANSI/IEEE Standard 754-1985, preferably on nights when you can't sleep. The register fields and their bit assignments are diagrammed below.

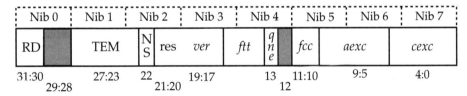

Figure A-4   FPU status and control register

The RD field selects the "rounding direction" for floating-point results.

Bits 29, 28, and 12 are currently undefined in the SPARC Version 8 Specification.

The TEM field contains the Trap Enable Mask. Each bit represents a different exception type that may be generated by floating-point operations. If the bit is set, the exception will generate a trap. We will list the possible exceptions shortly.

The NS bit, when set, allows the FPU to produce nonstandard results, that is, results that may not meet the ANSI/IEEE Standard 765-1985.

Bits 21 and 20 are reserved for future use.

The *ver* field contains the FPU implementation version number.

The *ftt* field is used to identify floating-point exception trap types.

The *qne* bit is set if there is an optional floating-point deferred-trap queue (FQ) and it is not empty.

The *fcc* field is the FPU's equivalent to the IU's *icc* field in the PSR. The two bits are used to represent different floating-point relationships, which are recorded when working with two floating-point values. They are as follows:

Table A-1   FPU fcc bits

fcc bits	Relationship Between Two Floating-point Values	
00	$f_1 = f_2$	Values were equal
01	$f_1 < f_2$	f1 less than f2
10	$f_1 > f_2$	f1 greater than f2
11	$f_1 ? f_2$	f1 and f2 are unordered

The *aexc* and *cexc* fields are used to record the accumulated exceptions and the current exceptions generated by floating-point operations. The five bits of each of these fields correspond to the five bits of the TEM field. Starting with the high-order bit, they are:

- NV — Invalid operation
- OF — Overflow
- UF — Underflow
- DZ — Divide by zero
- NX — Rounded result differs from exact correct result

Floating-point deferred-trap queue (FQ)

Like the Integer Unit, the Floating-Point Unit can optionally be implemented to include a floating-point deferred-trap queue. If a deferred-trap queue does not exist on the FPU, the FSR *qne* bit will be set to 0. The contents and operations of the FQ are completely implementation dependent.

Coprocessor (CP)

The SPARC Version 8 Specification allows for a second processing unit, which is referred to as a coprocessor. Its design and use are implementation dependent.

The Solaris operating systems assume that no coprocessor unit is present.

Windows & use of SPARC registers

Now that you have an idea of the SPARC processor hardware, let's return to the Integer Unit to talk more about register windows. The concept of windowing is quite important when we discuss stacks, frame, and stack trace backs.

As you know, SPARC processors that comply with the SPARC Version 8 architecture specification can have anywhere between 40 to 520 general-purpose, 32-bit registers. At any one time, however, a routine can only access 32 of these registers, 24 of which are clustered into what is referred to as a "window." The other 8 registers, always the same 8 and referred to as "global registers," are visible at all times.

With up to 520 general-purpose registers available on a SPARC processor, a window provides the executing routine a limited "view" of the hardware's full set of registers, to put it simply.

Note – From this point on, when we use the word "register," we will be referring to a general-purpose register. When we need to refer to another register, such as a floating-point register, we will refer to it with a specific name.

When a `save` instruction is executed, the window, or limited view of the full set of registers, shifts to a new, adjacent window. Traps cause the same action. When a `restore` instruction is executed, the view of the registers shifts back to the former window. The interesting detail about these window shifts is that the new view overlaps the old view by eight registers. We'll get back to this in a moment.

The 24 general-purpose registers within a register window view may be addressed in SPARC assembly language as registers `%r8` through `r31`. However, they are more commonly referred to by other names, as shown below.

Table A-2 SPARC general purpose registers

Window Register Address	r Register Address	Description of Registers
g0 – g7	r0 – r7	Global registers. Always available to all routines.
o0 – o7	r8 – r13	Output registers. New window's input registers.
l0 – l7	r14 – r23	Local registers. Unique to each procedure.
i0 – i7	r24 – r32	Input registers. Old window's output registers.

As hinted at in the chart above, the input and output registers, or i and o registers, are the ones that overlap from window to window. The local, or l registers, are unique to each window. Together, the i, o, and l registers make up the 24-register window view.

Registers `r0` through `r7` are actually outside the register window. However, since they are available to all procedures, in addition to the 24 i, o, and l window registers, they are assigned window register address names. These 8 global registers are referred to as g0 through g7.

In closing

The SPARC processor, as described in *The SPARC Architecture Manual, Version 8*, is the recommended description and standard by which SPARC Version 8 processor chips should be manufactured. To learn the exact details and additional enhancements of your specific SPARC processor, read the hardware specification for that chip.

Now that you've gotten an idea of what the SPARC processor looks like, you are better armed to learn about the SPARC instruction set, which follows.

SPARC Instruction Set

Now that you have a feel for the SPARC processor hardware, let's talk about the native instruction set and software language of the SPARC processor. In this section we'll cover most of the instructions in some detail; however, we'll refer you to *The SPARC Architecture Manual, Version 8* from SPARC International as the definitive reference.

Instruction set summary

The SPARC instruction set consists of 69 instructions. Each instruction takes exactly 32 bits. The complete set is often described as having six basic categories, as follows:

1. Memory access instructions

2. Arithmetic / logical / shift instructions

3. Control transfer instructions

4. State register instructions

5. Floating-point unit instructions

6. Coprocessor instructions

We will cover each of these categories in detail.

Operation codes & instruction formats

When discussing a processor's native language, we sometimes talk about the individual operation codes (opcodes) of each instruction. This discussion often involves learning the specific bit-by-bit organization of the instructions, or instruction formats.

The SPARC processor uses three basic instruction formats for the complete instruction set. As a software analyst examining system crash dumps, it is rare indeed that you will ever need to look at the raw instructions of a program in hexadecimal, because **kadb** and **adb** will be converting the values into assembly language for you. This process is referred to as "disassembling." Should you want to explore this extremely detailed aspect of the instruction set, please refer to *The SPARC Architecture Manual, Version 8*.

The SPARC assembly language instructions, with which we will be working, and the SPARC opcodes are usually the same. We will point out the few cases where they differ.

Assembly language syntax

When looking at SPARC assembly language via **adb**, we will see **adb**'s disassembled interpretation of the opcodes it finds. In very simple terms, the general syntax of assembly instructions we will see are as follows:

```
label:  instruction  source  destination

        instruction  label
```

As we discuss each category of instruction, we will show the syntax of the instructions and some examples of assembly language code.

Instruction syntax

Throughout the rest of this chapter, while discussing the individual instructions in the SPARC instruction set and their syntax, we will use the following conventions. These are the same conventions you will find in *The SPARC Architecture Manual, Version 8*.

Registers

When we refer to *reg* in the instruction syntax, we are referring to any Integer Unit, general-purpose register name. It may be any one of the following:

- %r0 through %r31   General-purpose registers
- %g0 through %g7   Globals   (aka %r0 through %r7)
- %o0 through %o7   Out registers   (aka %r8 through %r15)
- %l0 through %l7   Local registers   (aka %r16 through %r24)
- %i0 through %i7   In registers   (aka %r25 through %r31)
- %fp   Frame pointer   (aka %i6 and %r30)
- %sp   Stack pointer   (aka %o6 and %r14)

When we refer to *sreg* and *dreg* in the instruction syntax, one general-purpose register is the source register and the other is a destination register.

Note – In SPARC assembly language, the percent sign, %, must be used in front of all register names.

The symbols *freg* and *creg* will be used in instruction syntax to represent any floating-point processor and coprocessor register names.

- %f0 through %f31   The floating-point registers
- %c0 through %c31   Possible coprocessor registers

When we refer to *sfreg* and *dfreg* in the instruction syntax, one floating-point register is the source register and the other is a destination register.

Special symbol names

The following special symbols are used in SPARC assembly language. You'll recognize most of these from the chapter about the SPARC processor. We will discuss the last two, %hi and %lo, later on in this chapter.

- %psr   Processor state register
- %fsr   Floating-point state register
- %csr   Coprocessor state register
- %wim   Window invalid mask register
- %tbr   Trap base register
- %y   Multiply / divide register
- %fq   Floating-point queue
- %cq   Coprocessor queue
- %hi   Unary operator that extracts the high 22 bits of its operand
- %lo   Unary operator that extracts the low 10 bits of its operand

Operand values

SPARC instructions use operands that may include the following symbols.

- *simm13*   A signed immediate constant that can be represented in 13 bits.
- *const22*   A constant that can be represented in 22 bits.
- *as*   An alternate address space identifier (0 to 255)
- *value*   An unspecified, integer value

Register values

When discussing instructions that access memory, we will use [*address*] in the instruction syntax to represent any of the following methods of deriving a memory address.

- *reg*   Address = Contents of register (address is stored in register)
- *simm13*   Address = Signed 13-bit immediate value or offset
- *reg +/- simm13*   Address = Contents of register plus or minus an offset value
- *reg1 + reg2*   Address = Value of one register + value of a second register

Some instructions only use register values (the above methods, which don't involve use of a *simm13* offset value). When discussing those instructions, we will use [*regaddr*] in the instruction syntax instead of [*address*].

For instructions that can only use *either* one register *or* a signed 13-bit immediate value to represent an address or other value, we will use `reg_or_imm` in the instruction syntax.

When talking about the trap instructions, we will use `sw_trap_num` in the instruction syntax to represent software trap numbers, which may be any value from 0 to 127.

Labels

When discussing instructions that branch or jump, we will use `label` to represent a location within the routine. Labels in SPARC assembler may consist of alphanumeric characters (a–z, A–Z, 0–9), underscores (_), dollar signs ($), and periods (.). The first letter of a label cannot be a decimal digit (0-9). When examining disassembled code (from **adb**), labels used by branch instructions will usually be shown as a variable (routine name) plus an offset value.

Note that the 4.x bundled C compiler automatically prefaced C variable and function names with an underscore (_). This convention allows you to identify assembly code labels, which are normally not defined with a leading underscore unless they are to be callable from C-language functions. This convention was discarded with the ANSI C compilers.

Memory access instructions

Unlike some other instruction sets, the SPARC Version 8 instruction set never embeds memory addresses into the instructions. Thus, no instructions can directly modify the contents of memory. Instead, all data manipulation is performed in the SPARC general purpose registers.

Two basic memory access operations can be performed on SPARC systems. These are "load" and "store" or, in other words, "read from memory" and "write to memory." There are several variations of these two operations which handle different data sizes.

Using load instructions, data is read in from memory and stored into a register. Once in a register, the data can be manipulated as needed. Using store instructions, the modified data is written back to memory.

Load instructions

The load instruction is used to read a value stored in memory, placing the data into a register when it can then be manipulated. Here are six commonly used load instructions:

Table B-1   SPARC load instructions

Instruction Syntax	Operation
ld [*address*], *reg*	Read word from memory (address) and load into register
ldd [*address*], *reg*	Read double word and load into register and next register
ldsb [*address*], *reg*	Read signed byte from memory and load into register
ldsh [*address*], *reg*	Read signed half-word and load into register
ldub [*address*], *reg*	Read unsigned byte and load into register
lduh [*address*], *reg*	Read unsigned half-word and load into register

Now let's look at a couple of examples. The instruction below reads the word of data stored at the memory address indicated by input register %i0 and loads it into output register %o1.

```
ld [%i0], %o1
```

The next example reads an unsigned byte of data from memory, loading it into output register %o3. The memory address where the byte is read is the contents of input register %i4 plus hexadecimal 8. In a case like this, the value in %i4 may often be the pointer to a structure. The offset of 8 points to the most significant byte of the third word in the structure, the 9th byte.

```
ldub [%i4 + 0x8], %o3
```

The example below reads a double word (two words) from memory and loads the data into two registers starting with register %l4. So, if %i3 contains address 0xfea603b0, this load instruction will read memory location 0xfea603b0 and 0xfea603b4, loading the data into registers %l4 and %l5, respectively.

```
ldd [%i3], %l4
```

Loading from alternate address space

Each of the six load instructions shown above also has a variation that says to load the information from an alternate address space, such as the control registers for the Memory Management Unit. Each SPARC implementation may offer different alternate addressable registers that can be accessed via the load alternate address space instructions. During system crash dump analysis, odds are very good you will not run into these instructions, since they are not generated by the compiler, but we'll show them just in case you do encounter them. Here they are.

Table B-2   Load instructions from alternate address space

Instruction Syntax	Operation
lda [*reg*]*asi, reg*	Load word from alternate space
ldda [*reg*]*asi, reg*	Load double word from alternate space
ldsba [*reg*]*asi, reg*	Load signed byte from alternate space
ldsha [*reg*]*asi, reg*	Load signed half-word from alternate space
lduba [*reg*]*asi, reg*	Load unsigned byte from alternate space
lduha [*reg*]*asi, reg*	Load unsigned half-word from alternate space

Loading from the floating-point unit & coprocessor

The next six load instructions are specifically for the optional floating-point unit and the optional coprocessor. While in assembly language they appear to be instructions we've seen earlier, the actual opcodes differ.

Table B-3   Load instructions for optional FPU

Opcode	Instruction Syntax	Operation
LDF	ld [*address*], *freg*	Load word from memory into *freg*
LDDF	ldd [*address*], *freg*	Load double word from memory into *freg*
LDFSR	ld [*address*], %fsr	Load word into floating-point state reg
LDC	ld [*address*], *creg*	Load word from memory into *creg*
LDDC	ldd [*address*], *creg*	Load double word from memory into *creg*
LDCSR	ld [*address*], %csr	Load word into coprocessor state register

Store instructions

If you feel comfortable with the various load instructions, the store instructions will be a piece of cake. After data in a register has been manipulated, we use the store instruction to write the data to a specified memory location.

There are four basic store operations and four alternate address space variations of them. They are as follows:

Table B-4   SPARC store instructions

Instruction Syntax	Operation
stb *reg*, [*address*]	Store least significant byte to memory (aka stub and stsb)
sth *reg*, [*address*]	Store least significant half-word (aka stuh and stsh)
st *reg*, [*address*]	Store word to memory

Table B-4   SPARC store instructions   (Continued)

Instruction Syntax	Operation
`std reg, [address]`	Store double word to memory
`stba reg, [regaddr]asi`	Store byte to alternate space (aka `stuba` and `stsba`)
`stha reg, [address]asi`	Store half-word to alternate space (aka `stuha` and `stsha`)
`sta reg, [address]asi`	Store word to alternate space
`stda reg, [address]asi`	Store double word to alternate space

Let's take a look at a couple of examples of store instructions. The one below stores the contents of input register `%i3` into the memory location whose address is in local register `%l6`.

```
st %i3, [%l6]
```

The next example stores the least significant byte in register `%i0` into the 2nd byte of the word whose address is contained in register `%l5`.

```
stb %i0, [%l5 + 1]
```

Storing from the floating-point unit & coprocessor

Of course, we also have additional store instructions that are used in conjunction with the optional floating-point processor and optional coprocessor. As with the load instructions, these instructions differ a bit between assembly language and the actual SPARC opcode.

Table B-5   SPARC additional store instructions

Opcode	Instruction Syntax	Operation
STF	`st freg, [address]`	Store word in *freg* to memory
STDF	`std freg, [address]`	Store double word in *freg* to memory
STFSR	`st %fsr, [address]`	Store `%fsr` to memory
STDFQ	`st %fq, [address]`	Store double `%fq` to memory
STC	`st creg, [address]`	Store word in *creg* to memory
STDC	`std creg, [address]`	Store double word in *creg* to memory
STCSR	`st %csr, [address]`	Store `%csr` to memory
STDQC	`std %cq, [address]`	Store double `%cq` to memory

Atomic memory access instructions

Two instructions in the SPARC instruction set and two alternate address space variations of them can perform a read from memory *and* a write to memory atomically.

What do we mean by atomically? The instruction cannot be interrupted during its execution; the read and the write happen in the same breath. In a multiprocessor system, two or more processors executing the instructions addressing the same byte simultaneously are guaranteed to execute them in an undefined, but serial order.

Here are the instructions:

Table B-6 SPARC atomic energy access instructions

Instruction Syntax	Operation
ldstub [address], reg	Atomic load-store unsigned byte
ldstuba [regaddr]asi, reg	Atomic load store unsigned byte into alternate space
swap [address], reg	Swap register with memory
swapa [regaddr]asi, reg	Swap register with alternate space memory

The ldstub instructions read an unsigned byte from memory into a register, then write all ones (hexadecimal 0xff) to that byte of memory. The swap instructions interchange the contents of a memory location with the contents of a register.

In general terms, both of these instructions, since they involve a lot of work, usually take longer to execute than others. However, when integrity of the data being manipulated is critical and timing is everything, these atomic instructions are invaluable. For example, it is the ldstub instruction that provides SPARC systems the ability to have safe, predictable locking mechanisms.

Note – Instruction execution times differ with each SPARC implementation. Refer to the specific processor's technical manual for timing data.

Possible traps during memory access instructions

The memory access instructions generate the most traps. With the exception of the floating-point and coprocessor trap conditions, the traps shown below will cause a user program to terminate, dumping core. When these conditions are detected during execution of kernel code, it is considered catastrophic, and the system will immediately panic with a "bad trap."

Table B-7 SPARC trap conditions and causes

Trap Condition	How The Condition Is Caused
Illegal instruction	The operation code of the instruction being executed did not represent a valid instruction.
Privileged instruction	The processor is not in privileged mode and the instruction being executed is a privileged instruction. Alternate address space instructions, stdfq and stdcq are all privileged instructions and will cause this when PSR bit S is 0.

Table B-7   SPARC trap conditions and causes   (Continued)

Trap Condition	How The Condition Is Caused
Memory address not aligned	A double word, full word or half-word instruction is trying to access memory that is not double word, full word or half-word aligned. Byte instructions cannot cause this condition.
Data access exception	Failure to access the data due to a condition such as the page of memory being marked as invalid or write-protected.
Data access error	The instruction failed to complete access of the data due to a condition such as a data cache parity error or an uncorrectable ECC memory error.
Data store error	The instruction failed to complete storage of the data due to a condition such as a bus parity error.
FP / CP disabled	Attempt to access the floating-point processor (or coprocessor) that is not present or while PSR EF (or EC) bit is set to 0.
FP / CP exception	A floating-point (or coprocessor) instruction generated an exception.

When analyzing a system crash dump caused by a "bad trap," you'll usually find that a load or store instruction caused the crash.

Arithmetic / logical / shift instructions

Using the memory access instructions, we can move data between the processor's registers and memory. Now let's discuss the instructions used to manipulate the data once it is loaded into the registers. This set of register-based instructions is used to:

- Perform integer math
- Perform logical operations (AND, OR, exclusive OR, etc.)
- Shift or rotate data
- Save and restore windows

The syntax we will see most often used in this set of instructions follows:

```
instruction  sreg, reg_or_imm, dreg
```

In this syntax, `sreg` and `reg_or_imm` are the source operands and `dreg` is the destination register where the result of the instruction is stored. Most often, `sreg` contains the data to be manipulated, and `reg_or_imm` is the value used in conjunction with the data to generate the final result. `reg_or_imm` can be either another register or a signed 13-bit value.

Let's look at an example:

```
add %g2, 1, %g2
```

This example instruction's source register, *sreg*, is register %g2. The *reg_or_imm* is simply a value of 1. The contents of %g2 and the value of 1 are added together. The result is stored in the destination register, *dreg*, register %g2.

Note – The *sreg*, *reg_or_imm* and *dreg* values in arithmetic / logical / shift instructions may reference the same registers.

Integer arithmetic

Okay, let's start off with the most commonly used arithmetic instructions:

Table B-8   SPARC arithmetic instructions

Instruction Syntax	Operation
add *sreg, reg_or_imm, dreg*	Add the contents of *sreg* to the value represented by *reg_or_imm* and store result in *dreg*
addcc *sreg, reg_or_imm, dreg*	Add and modify the PSR *icc* fields
addx *sreg, reg_or_imm, dreg*	Add and add in *icc* carry bit
addxcc *sreg, reg_or_imm, dreg*	Add, add in carry bit and modify *icc* fields
sub *sreg, reg_or_imm, dreg*	Subtract the value represented by *reg_or_imm* from the contents of *sreg* and store result in *dreg*
subcc *sreg, reg_or_imm, dreg*	Subtract and modify the PSR *icc* fields
subx *sreg, reg_or_imm, dreg*	Subtract and subtract *icc* carry bit
subxcc *sreg, reg_or_imm, dreg*	Subtract, subtract carry bit and modify *icc* fields
umul *sreg, reg_or_imm, dreg*	Unsigned integer multiply
smul *sreg, reg_or_imm, dreg*	Signed integer multiply
umulcc *sreg, reg_or_imm, dreg*	Unsigned multiply and modify PSR *icc* fields
smulcc *sreg, reg_or_imm, dreg*	Signed multiply and modify *icc* fields
udiv *sreg, reg_or_imm, dreg*	Unsigned integer divide
sdiv *sreg, reg_or_imm, dreg*	Signed integer divide
udivcc *sreg, reg_or_imm, dreg*	Unsigned divide and modify PSR *icc* fields
sdivcc *sreg, reg_or_imm, dreg*	Signed divide and modify *icc* fields

We've already seen one example of these instructions. What do you think this next example instruction does?

```
sub %g4, %13, %g4
```

In programming terms, this might be expressed as:

```
%g4 = %g4 - %13
```

The contents of local register %13 is subtracted from the contents of global register %g4 and the result is stored back into %g4. Here's another instruction.

```
addxcc %10, 20, %11
```

This instruction adds the contents of %10 and 20. It also adds in the PSR *icc* carry bit, which is either 0 or 1. The result is stored in %11. Meanwhile, any integer condition codes occurring during the addition are recorded in the PSR *icc* fields. For example, if the result of the addition was negative, the *icc* negative bit would be set.

The next set of integer arithmetic instructions are not used often and are unlikely to appear during the course of system crash dump analysis.

Table B-9   SPARC integer arithmetic instructions

Instruction Syntax	Operation
taddcc *sreg, reg_or_imm, dreg*	Tagged add and modify the PSR *icc* fields
taddcctv *sreg, reg_or_imm, dreg*	Tagged add, modify *icc* fields and trap on overflow
tsubcc *sreg, reg_or_imm, dreg*	Tagged subtract and modify *icc* fields
tsubcctv *sreg, reg_or_imm, dreg*	Tagged sub, modify *icc* fields and trap on overflow

Tagged arithmetic operations assume tagged-format data where the least significant two bits of the operands have special meaning. Languages such as LISP and Smalltalk use tagged arithmetic for dynamically typed data.

The tagged arithmetic instructions `taddcctv` and `tsubcctv` can cause tag overflow traps that would be handled by the operating system. These traps would not cause the system to panic and crash.

Logical instructions

The logical instructions perform bitwise operations. The general syntax used is the same as the integer arithmetic instructions:

```
instruction  sreg, reg_or_imm, dreg
```

Here are the instructions.

Table B-10 SPARC logical instructions

Instruction Syntax	Operation
and *sreg, reg_or_imm, dreg*	Bitwise AND
andcc *sreg, reg_or_imm, dreg*	AND and modify PSR *icc* fields
andn *sreg, reg_or_imm, dreg*	AND NOT
andncc *sreg, reg_or_imm, dreg*	AND NOT and modify PSR *icc* fields

Table B-10 SPARC logical instructions

Instruction Syntax	Operation
or *sreg, reg_or_imm, dreg*	Bitwise inclusive OR
orcc *sreg, reg_or_imm, dreg*	Inclusive OR & modify PSR *icc* fields
orn *sreg, reg_or_imm, dreg*	Inclusive OR NOT
orncc *sreg, reg_or_imm, dreg*	Inclusive OR NOT and modify PSR *icc* fields
xor *sreg, reg_or_imm, dreg*	Bitwise exclusive OR
xorcc *sreg, reg_or_imm, dreg*	Exclusive OR and modify PSR *icc* fields
xnor *sreg, reg_or_imm, dreg*	Exclusive NOR (Exclusive OR NOT)
xnorcc *sreg, reg_or_imm, dreg*	Exclusive NOR and modify PSR *icc* fields

Let's try a few examples. Given that %g4 contains 0x055, what would register %12 contain after each of the following instructions?

and %10, 73, %12	Answer: 51
or %10, 73, %12	Answer: 77
xor %10, 73, %12	Answer: 26
xnor %10, 73, %12	Answer: ffff ffd6

If you aren't clear about how these answers were reached, you might want to talk to a programmer or refer to a good programming book.

None of the logical instructions generate traps.

Shift instructions

The shift instructions use the same general syntax we've seen in the integer arithmetic and logical instructions.

```
instruction  sreg, reg_or_imm, dreg
```

The shift instructions shift the value in *sreg* left or right by a certain number of bit positions, as represented by *reg_or_imm*, and place the result in *dreg*. As the shift occurs, bits that drop off the end of the working register are lost. The PSR *icc* fields are not modified by the shift instructions.

There are no true "rotate" instructions in the SPARC instruction set. However, if a rotate is needed, the clever assembly language programmer can use the addcc instruction and the PSR *icc* overflow bit to his advantage.

Here are the three shift instructions:

Table B-11 SPARC shift instructions

Instruction Syntax	Operation
sll *sreg, reg_or_imm, dreg*	Shift left logical
srl *sreg, reg_or_imm, dreg*	Shift right logical
sra *sreg, reg_or_imm, dreg*	Shift right arithmetic

The logical shifts replace the vacated bits with zeroes. The arithmetic shift replaces the vacated bits with the most significant bit of the value in *sreg*.

Here is an example of a shift instruction.

```
sll %l7, 2, %l7
```

If the contents of %l7 started as 0x04, the result after shifting left two positions would be 0x10.

Note – In effect, each shift left by 1 is the same as multiplying by 2. Shift rights are like divides. This is good to remember as, on some SPARC implementations, the integer multiply and divide instructions take longer to execute than the shift instructions.

The shift instructions do not generate traps.

Miscellaneous arithmetic / logical / shift instructions

There are only a few miscellaneous instructions in the arithmetic / logical /shift set of SPARC instructions. Unlike the others, these instructions have differing syntaxes.

The sethi instruction is usually used in conjunction with a second command, such as a load. Let's look at an example.

```
sethi %hi(0xf0155000), %o3
ld [%o3 + 0x2a0], %l2
```

The sethi instruction sets the high-order 22 bits of output register %o3 to the high-order 22 bits of the value 0xf0155000. The load instruction then reads the value stored in memory location [%o3 + 0x2a0] (which calculates to 0xf01552a0) into local register %l2.

Why was this method used to read the value at memory location f01552a0? If you remember, due to the 32-bit width restriction of SPARC instructions, it is not possible to say "put 0xf01552a0 into %o3." If we add up the number of opcode bits used to identify the put instruction, the 32 bits of the value 0xf01552a0 and the bits needed to point to %o3, we would have an instruction that is well over 32 bits in width.

The sethi instruction only contains the high-order 22 bits of the value 0xf01552a0 (thus, f0155000). The load instruction can include an offset of 13 bits in the [*address*] field, more than is needed to construct a valid memory address.

The nop instruction is actually a variation of the sethi instruction, as shown below.

```
sethi 0, %g0
```

Register %g0 is rather like the **/dev/null** of registers. Reading %g0 always results in zero. Writing to %g0 has no effect.

The nop instruction is actually executed, but it makes no modifications to the registers or memory. nops are used when timing delays are required. There are actually many different instructions which could serve equally well as a nop. The compiler uses sethi. **adb** should recognize other varieties and display them as nop.

The mulscc instruction is a very busy little instruction that conditionally shifts a value, conditionally performs addition and updates the *icc* fields. You will see the mulscc instruction used on systems that do not have the integer multiply and divide instructions implemented in the hardware.

save and restore instructions are used to manipulate the register windows.

In the set of miscellaneous arithmetic / logical / shift instructions, only the save and restore instructions can generate traps. The save instruction can cause a "window overflow" trap and the restore can cause a "window underflow" trap. Neither of these traps will cause the system to crash. Instead, the kernel kicks in and does some special window handling. We discuss windows in more detail in Chapter 17, "Stacks."

Control transfer instructions

We talked a little bit about control transfer instructions in Chapter 16 on the SPARC assembly language, specifically regarding the delay instruction. Now let's talk about them in more detail.

Control transfer instructions perform the following tasks:

- Test and branch based on the values of the PSR *icc* fields (integer condition codes)
- Test and branch based on the values of the floating-point unit's condition codes
- Test and branch based on the values of the coprocessor unit's condition codes
- Unconditional branches
- Test and trap based on the values of the PSR *icc* fields
- Orderly return from a trap

We will start with the test and branch or conditional branch instructions. They all have the same general instruction format, as shown here:

```
instruction{,a} label
```

`{,a}` represents an option that each conditional branch instruction offers and refers to the annul bit. If `,a` is appended to the instruction, the annul bit is set. We will talk about the annul bit again later on.

Branch on integer condition codes instructions

The next table shows the conditional test and branch instructions for the integer unit. The third column shows which conditions the PSR *icc* bits must satisfy in order for the branch to be taken. As a reminder, the *icc* bits are:

- Condition N, **n**egative result occurred
- Condition Z, result was **z**ero
- Condition V, **o**verflow occurred
- Condition C, bit 31 was **c**arried or borrowed

Here are the branch on integer condition codes instructions:

Table B-12 Branch on integer condition codes instructions

Instruction Syntax	Operation	*icc* Test
`ba{,a}` *label*	Branch always to *label*	
`bn{,a}` *label*	Branch never to *label*	
`bne{,a}` *label*	Branch on not equal	not Z
`be{,a}` *label*	Branch on equal	Z
`bg{,a}` *label*	Branch on greater	not (Z or (N xor V))
`ble{,a}` *label*	Branch on less or equal	Z or (N xor V)
`bge{,a}` *label*	Branch on greater or equal	not (N xor V)
`bl{,a}` *label*	Branch on less	N xor V
`bgu{,a}` *label*	Branch on greater unsigned	not (C or Z)
`bleu{,a}` *label*	Branch on less or equal unsigned	C or Z
`bcc{,a}` *label*	Branch on carry clear (greater or equal unsigned)	not C
`bcs{,a}` *label*	Branch on carry set (less unsigned)	C
`bpos{,a}` *label*	Branch on positive	not N
`bneg{,a}` *label*	Branch on negative	N
`bvc{,a}` *label*	Branch on overflow clear	not V
`bvs{,a}` *label*	Branch on overflow set	V

Here is a snippet of assembly code that demonstrates how a branch instruction might be used.

```
main+0x34:      ld      [%14 - 0x8], %10
main+0x38:      subcc   %10, 0x6, %g0
main+0x3c:      bne     main + 0x5c
main+0x40:      nop
main+0x44:      ld      [%fp - 0x8], %10
```

A value is read in from memory and placed into local register %10.

Using the "subtract & modify *icc*" instruction, we subtract 6 from the value in %10. No result is stored because the *dreg* or destination register is the **/dev/null** of registers, %g0; however, the *icc* bits are modified as appropriate.

Using the "branch on not equal" instruction, we test the setting of the Z bit. If it is set to 1, the values were equal; the value in memory was a 6. If the Z bit is clear, the values were not equal and we jump to location *main+0x5c*.

While doing the branch, the delay instruction, nop, gets executed.

If the branch is *not* taken, we still execute the nop instruction and then continue to the following load instruction at location *main+0x44*.

The branch on integer condition codes instructions do not generate traps.

Branch on FPU condition codes instructions

The *fcc* field of the floating-point status register, %fsr, is updated by the floating-point compare instructions. The branch on floating-point condition codes instructions test the *fcc* field and branches accordingly. As a reminder, here are the *fcc* codes.

fcc bits	Code	Relationship Between Two Floating Point Values	
00	E	$freg_1 = freg_2$	Values were equal
01	L	$freg_1 < freg_2$	$freg_1$ less than $freg_2$
10	G	$freg_1 > freg_2$	$freg_1$ greater than $freg_2$
11	U	$freg_1 ? freg_2$	$freg_1$ and $freg_2$ are unordered

If a floating-point unit exists, the following branch instructions can be executed:

Table B-13 Branch instructions, FPU

Instruction Syntax	Operation	*fcc* Test
`fba{,a} label`	Branch always to *label*	
`fbn{,a} label`	Branch never to *label*	
`fbu{,a} label`	Branch on unordered	U
`fbg{,a} label`	Branch on greater	G
`fbug{,a} label`	Branch on unordered or greater	G or U
`fbl{,a} label`	Branch on less	L
`fbul{,a} label`	Branch on unordered or less	L or U
`fblg{,a} label`	Branch on less or greater	L or G
`fbne{,a} label`	Branch on not equal	L or G or U
`fbe{,a} label`	Branch on equal	E
`fbue{,a} label`	Branch on unordered or equal	E or U
`fbge{,a} label`	Branch on greater or equal	E or G
`fbuge{,a} label`	Branch on unordered, greater, or equal (not less)	E or G or U
`fble{,a} label`	Branch on less or equal	E or L
`fbule{,a} label`	Branch on unordered, less, or equal (not greater)	E or L or U
`fbo{,a} label`	Branch on ordered	E or L or G

These commands can generate *fp disabled* and *fp exception* traps, neither of which should cause panics. When one of these traps does occur, the operating system, not the hardware, is responsible for performing the floating-point operation.

Branch on coprocessor condition codes instructions

When this book was being written, there were no SPARC processor implementations that had yet incorporated a coprocessor. Even so, *The SPARC Architecture Manual, Version 8* does define recommended instructions specific to the coprocessor.

The branch on coprocessor condition codes instructions assume there are two bits in the coprocessor status register that are used to represent conditions. The possible values for these two bits are: 0, 1, 2, and 3.

Here are the branch on coprocessor condition codes instructions.

Table B-14 Branch on coprocessor condition codes

Instruction Syntax	Operation Based on *ccc*
`cba{,a} label`	Branch always to *label*
`cbn{,a} label`	Branch never to *label*
`cb3{,a} label`	Branch on 3

Table B-14 Branch on coprocessor condition codes

Instruction Syntax	Operation Based on *ccc*
cb2{,a} *label*	Branch on 2
cb23{,a} *label*	Branch on 2 or 3
cb1{,a} *label*	Branch on 1
cb13{,a} *label*	Branch on 1 or 3
cb12{,a} *label*	Branch on 1 or 2
cb123{,a} *label*	Branch on 1 or 2 or 3
cb0{,a} *label*	Branch on 0
cb03{,a} *label*	Branch on 0 or 3
cb02{,a} *label*	Branch on 0 or 2
cb023{,a} *label*	Branch on 0 or 2 or 3
cb01{,a} *label*	Branch on 0 or 1
cb013{,a} *label*	Branch on 0 or 1 or 3
cb012{,a} *label*	Branch on 0 or 1 or 2

Like the floating-point unit branch instructions, these instructions can cause coprocessor disabled and coprocessor exception traps. Both of these traps should not cause system panics and should instead cause the operating system to intervene and perform the required task.

The annul bit

The delayed transfer control instructions that we've seen all have an optional annul flag or bit which can be specified in the instruction by appending , a to the instruction opcode. When set, the annul bit says to execute the delay instruction only if we take the branch. If we don't take the branch, a set annul bit annuls or nullifies the execution of the delay instruction; the delay instruction is not executed.

Here is the same snippet of assembly code we used earlier to demonstrate how a branch instruction might be used. This time, the bne instruction has been changed to bne,a.

```
main+0x34:    ld      [%14 - 0x8], %10
main+0x38:    subcc   %10, 0x6, %g0
main+0x3c:    bne,a   main + 0x5c
main+0x40:    nop
main+0x44:    ld      [%fp - 0x8], %10
```

This time, if the value in %l0 is not equal to 6, we will jump to *main+0x5c* while executing the nop instruction. Conversely, if the value in %l0 is equal to 6, we will skip the delay instruction all together and move on to the load instruction. Usually the delay instruction consists of something that does real work, instead of a nop. Unoptimized compiler output will often contain nop instructions.

For the "branch always" and "branch never" instructions, the delay instruction is executed if the annul bit is not set, and it is not executed when the annul bit is set.

Unconditional branches

Two instructions perform unconditional branches. They are:

Table B-15 Unconditional branch instructions

Instruction Syntax	Operation
call *label*	Save PC in %o7 and branch to *label*
jmpl *address, reg*	Save PC in *reg* and branch to *address*

The call instruction transfers control to an address relative to the current PC, whereas the jump and link, jmpl, instruction performs a register-indirect control transfer.

The call instruction places the current value of the Program Counter into register %o7, whereas the jmpl instruction allows the programmer to specify in which register to store the PC.

The call instruction does not generate any traps.

The jmpl instruction generates a "memory address not aligned" trap when *address* is not word aligned.

Trap on integer condition codes instructions

We talk about traps in detail in another chapter. For now, let's just say that normally a trap is any condition in the hardware that shouldn't have occurred. Generalizing, we could say when an instruction is executing, if something goes wrong, the instruction gets stuck or trapped and can't finish its job. When this happens, the hardware suddenly switches to "Plan B," records the current Program Counter and jumps to a special trap handler. The operating system gets involved and may decide to panic, kill the offending program, or simply provide assistance to the hardware via software routines.

The SPARC processor offers the programmer a way to *force* a trap condition. Using the PSR *icc* field, a routine can test the condition codes and based on the results, force a trap. When the trap is "taken," the hardware still switches to "Plan B," records the PC, and jumps into the trap handler, specifically to the section set aside for software trap number specified as *sw_trap_num*. This is the way a user program actually issues a system call— by trapping into the kernel with a specific code.

Here are the trap on integer condition codes instructions. You'll see that they are quite similar to the branch on *icc* instructions.

Table B-16 Trap on integer condition codes instructions

Instruction Syntax	Operation	*icc* Test
`ta` *sw_trap_num*	Trap always	
`tn` *sw_trap_num*	Trap never	
`tne` *sw_trap_num* `(aka tnz)`	Trap on not equal	not Z
`te` *sw_trap_num* `(aka tnz)`	Trap on equal	Z
`tg` *sw_trap_num*	Trap on greater	not (Z or (N xor V))
`tle` *sw_trap_num*	Trap on less or equal	Z or (N xor V)
`tge` *sw_trap_num*	Trap on greater or equal	not (N xor V)
`tl` *sw_trap_num*	Trap on less	N xor V
`tgu` *sw_trap_num*	Trap on greater unsigned	not (C or Z)
`tleu` *sw_trap_num*	Trap on less or equal unsigned	C or Z
`tcc` *sw_trap_num* `(aka tgeu)`	Trap on carry 0 (> or = unsigned)	not C
`tcs` *sw_trap_num* `(aka tlu)`	Trap on carry 1 (<unsigned)	C
`tpos` *sw_trap_num*	Trap on positive	not N
`tneg` *sw_trap_num*	Trap on negative	N
`tvc` *sw_trap_num*	Trap on overflow clear	not V
`tvs` *sw_trap_num*	Trap on overflow set	V

The trap on integer condition codes instructions *never* execute the delay instruction.

These instructions all generate a *trap instruction* trap.

Orderly return from a trap

After a trap condition is handled by the operating system and everyone is happy again, instruction execution returns to the previously scheduled program that had caused the condition. The instruction, `rett` or return from a trap, does this control transfer.

Instruction Syntax	Operation
`rett` *address*	Return from trap, returning to *address*

Under various conditions, `rett` can cause any of the following traps.

Table B-17 rett traps

Trap Condition	How The Condition Is Caused
Illegal instruction	The bit-by-bit operation code of the instruction being executed did not represent a valid instruction.
Privileged instruction	The processor is not in privileged mode and the instruction being executed is a privileged instruction. Alternate address space instructions, `stdfq` and `stdcq` are all privileged instructions and will cause this condition when PSR bit S is 0.
Memory address not aligned	A double word, full word or half-word instruction is trying to access memory that is not double-word-, full-word- or half-word-aligned. Byte instructions can not cause this condition.
Window underflow	Register window management needed.

`rett` is a privileged instruction.

State register instructions

As we saw earlier in Appendix A on the SPARC processor, there are several special registers. To read and write to those registers, we use the following instructions.

Table B-18 State register instructions

Opcode	Instruction Syntax	Operation
RDY	rd %y, *dreg*	Read contents of %y and place into a register
RDASR	rd *asr_reg*, *dreg*	Read an ancillary state register into *dreg*
RDPSR	rd %psr, *dreg*	Read contents of %psr into *dreg*
RDWIM	rd %wim, *dreg*	Read contents of %wim into *dreg*
RDTBR	rd %tbr, *dreg*	Read contents of %tbr into *dreg*
WRY	wr *sreg*, *reg_or_imm*, %y	**xor** the values of *sreg* and *reg_or_imm* and write result into %y
WRASR	wr *sreg*, *reg_or_imm*, *asr_reg*	**xor** the values of *sreg* and *reg_or_imm* and write result into an ancillary state register
WRPSR	wr *sreg*, *reg_or_imm*, %psr	**xor** the values of *sreg* and *reg_or_imm* and write result into %psr
WRWIM	wr *sreg*, *reg_or_imm*, %wim	**xor** the values of *sreg* and *reg_or_imm* and write result into %wim
WRTBR	wr *sreg*, *reg_or_imm*, %tbr	**xor** the values of *sreg* and *reg_or_imm* and write result into %tbr

The write instructions are delayed-write instructions. This means that the changes to the register may not be completed until up to three instructions later! When you encounter write instructions while looking at your running kernel or a system crash dump, you will note that they are usually followed by three nop instructions. This programming practice guarantees that the new value has been written to the specified register before the program moves on to the next task.

All but the instructions that address register %y are privileged and therefore are capable of generating *privileged instruction* traps. Also, these instructions can generate *illegal instruction* traps under certain conditions.

Miscellaneous state register instructions

The other three SPARC instructions in the state register category are:

Table B-19 Miscellaneous SPARC instructions

Instruction Syntax	Operation
unimp	Unimplemented
stbar	Store barrier
flush *address*	Flush

The unimp instruction is an unimplemented instruction that, when executed, will generate an *illegal instruction* trap.

The stbar instruction forces all pending stores and atomic load-stores to complete prior to moving on to subsequent stores and atomic load-stores. The stbar instruction does not generate any traps.

The flush instruction forces all pending memory access instructions involving the specified address to complete before subsequent accesses are attempted.

The stbar and flush instructions are made available for memory management implementations that use memory caches, thus not guaranteeing instant modification of memory.

Floating-point unit instructions

The floating-point instructions perform several operations, including:

* Floating-point arithmetic
* Floating-point value conversions
* Floating-point value comparisons

We will see that the floating-point instructions follow three general syntax rules:

```
instruction freg₁, freg₂

instruction sfreg, dfreg

instruction sfreg₁, sfreg₂, dfreg
```

Floating-point arithmetic instructions

Here are the arithmetic instructions.

Table B-20 SPARC floating-point arithmetic instructions

Instruction Syntax	Operation
fsqrts *sfreg, dfreg*	Put square root of single word in *sfreg* into *dfreg*
fsqrtd *sfreg, dfreg*	Square root, double word
fsqrtq *sfreg, dfreg*	Square root, quad word
fadds *sfreg₁, sfreg₂, dfreg*	Add single words *sfreg1* and *sfreg2*, put result in *dfreg*
faddd *sfreg₁, sfreg₂, dfreg*	Add double words
faddq *sfreg₁, sfreg₂, dfreg*	Add quad words
fsubs *sfreg₁, sfreg₂, dfreg*	Subtract single word *sfreg2* from *sfreg1*, put result in *dfreg*
fsubd *sfreg₁, sfreg₂, dfreg*	Subtract double words
fsubq *sfreg₁, sfreg₂, dfreg*	Subtract quad words
fdivs *sfreg₁, sfreg₂, dfreg*	Divide single word *sfreg1* by *sfreg2*, result in *dfreg*
fdivd *sfreg₁, sfreg₂, dfreg*	Divide double words, result in *dfreg*
fdivq *sfreg₁, sfreg₂, dfreg*	Divide quad words, result in *dfreg*
fmuls *sfreg₁, sfreg₂, dfreg*	Multiply single words, single word result in *dfreg*
fmuld *sfreg₁, sfreg₂, dfreg*	Multiply double words, double word result
fmulq *sfreg₁, sfreg₂, dfreg*	Multiply quad words, quad word result
fsmuld *sfreg₁, sfreg₂, dfreg*	Multiply single words, double word result
fsmulq *sfreg₁, sfreg₂, dfreg*	Multiply double words, quad word result

Floating-point value conversions

When working with floating-point values, it is often necessary to convert the values to integer values, or from integer back to floating-point. There are also times when a conversions from one floating-point precision to another are needed. The following instructions perform all of the floating-point value conversions:

Table B-21 Floating-point value conversion instructions

Instruction Syntax	Operation
`fitos sfreg, dfreg`	Convert integer value in `sfreg` to single word, result in `dfreg`
`fitod sfreg, dfreg`	Convert integer value `sfreg` to double word `dfreg`
`fitoq sfreg, dfreg`	Convert integer value `sfreg` to double word `dfreg`
`fstoi sfreg, dfreg`	Convert single word in `sfreg` to integer value, result in `dfreg`
`fdtoi sfreg, dfreg`	Convert double word `sfreg` to integer value `dfreg`
`fqtoi sfreg, dfreg`	Convert quad word `sfreg` to integer value `dfreg`
`fstod sfreg, dfreg`	Convert single word in `sfreg` to double word, result in `dfreg`
`fstoq sfreg, dfreg`	Convert single word `sfreg` to quad word `dfreg`
`fdtos sfreg, dfreg`	Convert double word `sfreg` to single word `dfreg`
`fdtoq sfreg, dfreg`	Convert double word `sfreg` to quad word `dfreg`
`fqtos sfreg, dfreg`	Convert quad word `sfreg` to single word `dfreg`
`fqtod sfreg, dfreg`	Convert quad word `sfreg` to double word `dfreg`

Floating-point value comparisons

Earlier, we saw that the floating-point unit has a set of condition code bits and that there are a set of branch on floating-point conditions codes instructions. What we have not yet seen is how the *fcc* bits get modified.

As a reminder, the comparison instructions set the *fcc* bits, as shown below.

fcc bits	Code	Relationship Between Two Floating-Point Values	
00	E	$freg_1 = freg_2$	Values were equal
01	L	$freg_1 < freg_2$	$freg_1$ less than $freg_2$
10	G	$freg_1 > freg_2$	$freg_1$ greater than $freg_2$
11	U	$freg_1 ? freg_2$	$freg_1$ and $freg_2$ are unordered

Here are the floating-point value comparison instructions.

Table B-22 Floating-point value comparison instructions

Instruction Syntax	Operation
`fcmps freg_1, freg_2`	Compare single words
`fcmpd freg_1, freg_2`	Compare double words
`fcmpq freg_1, freg_2`	Compare quad words

Table B-22 Floating-point value comparison instructions

Instruction Syntax	Operation
fcmpes $freg_1$, $freg_2$	Compare single words and cause an fp exception if unordered
fcmped $freg_1$, $freg_2$	Compare double words and cause exception if unordered
fcmpeq $freg_1$, $freg_2$	Compare quad words and cause exception if unordered

Miscellaneous floating-point instructions

There are three miscellaneous floating-point instructions, as follows:

Table B-23 Miscellaneous floating-point instructions

Instruction Syntax	Operation
fmovs sfreg, dfreg	Copy sfreg into dfreg
fnegs sfreg, dfreg	Copy sfreg into dfreg with the sign bit complemented (reversed)
fabss sfreg, dfreg	Copy sfreg into dfreg with the sign bit cleared

The floating-point instructions can generate *fp exception* and *fp disabled* traps, all of which must result in the operating system processing the requested instruction via software, such as floating-point library routines.

Coprocessor instructions

Each SPARC Version 8 implementation that utilizes the optional coprocessor unit must define its own instructions. However, there are two instruction opcodes reserved for coprocessor instructions:

Table B-24 Instruction opcodes reserved for coprocessor instructions

Opcode	Recommended Instruction Syntax
COop1	cpop1 opc, $screg_1$, $screg_2$, dcreg
COop2	cpop2 opc, $screg_1$, $screg_2$, dcreg

opc would represent the specific operation, two source registers screg1 and screg2 could be specified, and of course, there would be a destination register, dcreg. All of the registers would reside on the coprocessor.

The coprocessor instructions can generate *cp exception* and *cp disabled* traps.

B

Synthetic instructions

At this point, we've covered every instruction in the SPARC Version 8 instruction set. However, during system crash dump analysis, you may run into several additional SPARC instructions that are referred to as synthetic instructions. These instructions may be provided in a SPARC assembler for the convenience of assembly language programmers. They tend to be more suitable, some have easier-to-remember instruction names, and the syntax is often slimmed down. As you read the table, you'll see what we mean:

Table B-25 Common SPARC synthetic instructions

Synthetic Instruction	Actual Instruction	Description
`jmp address`	`jmpl address, %g0`	Jump
`call address`	`jmpl address, %o7`	Call a subroutine
`tst reg`	`orcc %g0, reg, %g0`	Test
`ret`	`jmpl %i7+8, %g0`	Return from subroutine
`restore`	`restore %g0, %g0, %g0`	Trivial restore
`save`	`save %g0, %g0, %g0`	Trivial save
`set value, reg`	`sethi %hi (value), reg`	*When (value&0x1ffff)==0*
	`OR or %g0, value, reg`	*When (-4096<=value<=4095)*
	`OR sethi %hi (value),   reg`	*Otherwise. Warning: Do not use*
	`or reg, %lo (value),   reg`	*set as a delay instruction.*
`not sreg, dreg`	`xnor sreg, %g0, dreg`	One's complement
`not reg`	`xnor reg, %g0, reg`	One's complement
`neg sreg, dreg`	`sub %g0, reg, reg`	Two's complement
`neg reg`	`sub %g0, reg, reg`	Two's complement
`inc reg`	`add reg, 1, reg`	Increment by 1
`inc const13, reg`	`add reg, const13, reg`	Increment by *const13*
`inccc reg`	`addcc reg, 1, reg`	Increment by 1 and set ICC
`inccc const13, reg`	`addcc reg, const13, reg`	Increment by *const13* and set ICC
`dec reg`	`sub reg, 1, reg`	Decrement by 1
`dec const13, reg`	`sub reg, const13, reg`	Decrement by *const13*
`deccc reg`	`subcc reg, 1, reg`	Decrement by 1 and set ICC
`deccc const13, reg`	`subcc reg, const13, reg`	Decrement by *const13* and set ICC
`btst reg_or_imm, reg`	`andcc reg, reg_or_imm, %g0`	Bit test
`bset reg_or_imm, reg`	`or reg, reg_or_imm, reg`	Bit set
`bclr reg_or_imm, reg`	`andn reg, reg_or_imm, reg`	Bit clear
`btog reg_or_imm, reg`	`xor reg, reg_or_imm, reg`	Bit toggle
`clr reg`	`or %g0, %g0, reg`	Clear (zero) register
`clrb [address]`	`stb %g0, [address]`	Clear byte
`clrh [address]`	`sth %g0, [address]`	Clear half-word
`clr [address]`	`st %g0, [address]`	Clear word

Table B-25 Common SPARC synthetic instructions (Continued)

Synthetic Instruction	Actual Instruction	Description
mov *reg_or_imm*, *reg*	or %g0, *reg_or_imm*, *reg*	Move value into register
mov %y, *reg*	rd %y, *reg*	Move %y into reg (Variations exist for %asm, %psr, %wim, %tbr)
mov *reg_or_imm*, %y	wr %g0, *reg_or_imm*, %y	Move reg into %y (Variations exist for %asm, %psr, %wim, %tbr)

Always keep an instruction set reference handy!

When working with system crash dumps, you will be working with code that was most likely originally written in C. In the best of scenarios, you'll have access to the source code, but even then, it is assembly language that you will see when using **adb**, not C. Therefore, it is important to feel comfortable with the native language of the processor on which you're working.

We don't expect anyone to learn assembly language overnight! However, we know from our own experience that it's always very helpful to have a assembly language reference handy for those times when you do need to remember the instruction set. If your own system is not a SPARC Version 8 processor and you haven't done so already, get your hands on some sort of assembly language instruction set cheatsheet and keep it handy! Write your own, if you have to. During system crash dump analysis, you are going to need it.

≡ *B*

Index

Index

Panic! System Crash Dump Analysis

LICENSE AGREEMENT AND LIMITED WARRANTY

READ THE FOLLOWING TERMS AND CONDITIONS CAREFULLY BEFORE OPENING THIS DISK PACKAGE. THIS LEGAL DOCUMENT IS AN AGREEMENT BETWEEN YOU AND PRENTICE-HALL, INC. (THE "COMPANY"). BY OPENING THIS SEALED DISK PACKAGE, YOU ARE AGREEING TO BE BOUND BY THESE TERMS AND CONDITIONS. IF YOU DO NOT AGREE WITH THESE TERMS AND CONDITIONS, DO NOT OPEN THE DISK PACKAGE. PROMPTLY RETURN THE UNOPENED DISK PACKAGE AND ALL ACCOMPANYING ITEMS TO THE PLACE YOU OBTAINED THEM FOR A FULL REFUND OF ANY SUMS YOU HAVE PAID.

1.   **GRANT OF LICENSE:** In consideration of your payment of the license fee, which is part of the price you paid for this product, and your agreement to abide by the terms and conditions of this Agreement, the Company grants to you a nonexclusive right to use and display the copy of the enclosed software program (hereinafter the "SOFTWARE") on a single computer (i.e., with a single CPU) at a single location so long as you comply with the terms of this Agreement. The Company reserves all rights not expressly granted to you under this Agreement.

2.   **OWNERSHIP OF SOFTWARE:** You own only the magnetic or physical media (the enclosed disks) on which the SOFTWARE is recorded or fixed, but the Company retains all the rights, title, and ownership to the SOFTWARE recorded on the original disk copy(ies) and all subsequent copies of the SOFTWARE, regardless of the form or media on which the original or other copies may exist. This license is not a sale of the original SOFTWARE or any copy to you.

3.   **COPY RESTRICTIONS:** This SOFTWARE and the accompanying printed materials and user manual (the "Documentation") are the subject of copyright. You may not copy the Documentation or the SOFTWARE, except that you may make a single copy of the SOFTWARE for backup or archival purposes only. You may be held legally responsible for any copying or copyright infringement which is caused or encouraged by your failure to abide by the terms of this restriction.

4.   **USE RESTRICTIONS:** You may not network the SOFTWARE or otherwise use it on more than one computer or computer terminal at the same time. You may physically transfer the SOFTWARE from one computer to another provided that the SOFTWARE is used on only one computer at a time. You may not distribute copies of the SOFTWARE or Documentation to others. You may not reverse engineer, disassemble, decompile, modify, adapt, translate, or create derivative works based on the SOFTWARE or the Documentation without the prior written consent of the Company.

5.   **TRANSFER RESTRICTIONS:** The enclosed SOFTWARE is licensed only to you and may not be transferred to any one else without the prior written consent of the Company. Any unauthorized transfer of the SOFTWARE shall result in the immediate termination of this Agreement.

6.   **TERMINATION:** This license is effective until terminated. This license will terminate automatically without notice from the Company and become null and void if you fail to comply with any provisions or limitations of this license. Upon termination, you shall destroy the Documentation and all copies of the SOFTWARE. All provisions of this Agreement as to warranties, limitation of liability, remedies or damages, and our ownership rights shall survive termination.

7.   **MISCELLANEOUS:** This Agreement shall be construed in accordance with the laws of the United States of America and the State of New York and shall benefit the Company, its affiliates, and assignees.

8.   **LIMITED WARRANTY AND DISCLAIMER OF WARRANTY:** The Company warrants that the SOFTWARE, when properly used in accordance with the Documentation, will operate in substantial conformity with the description of the SOFTWARE set forth in the Documentation. The Company does not warrant that the SOFTWARE will meet your requirements or that the operation of the SOFTWARE will be uninterrupted or error-free. The Company warrants that the media on which the SOFTWARE is delivered shall be free from defects in materials and workmanship under normal use for a period of thirty (30) days from the date of your purchase. Your only remedy and

the Company's only obligation under these limited warranties is, at the Company's option, return of the warranted item for a refund of any amounts paid by you or replacement of the item. Any replacement of SOFTWARE or media under the warranties shall not extend the original warranty period. The limited warranty set forth above shall not apply to any SOFTWARE which the Company determines in good faith has been subject to misuse, neglect, improper installation, repair, alteration, or damage by you. EXCEPT FOR THE EXPRESSED WARRANTIES SET FORTH ABOVE, THE COMPANY DISCLAIMS ALL WARRANTIES, EXPRESS OR IMPLIED, INCLUDING WITH-OUT LIMITATION, THE IMPLIED WARRANTIES OF MERCHANTABILITY AND FITNESS FOR A PARTIC-ULAR PURPOSE. EXCEPT FOR THE EXPRESS WARRANTY SET FORTH ABOVE, THE COMPANY DOES NOT WARRANT, GUARANTEE, OR MAKE ANY REPRESENTATION REGARDING THE USE OR THE RESULTS OF THE USE OF THE SOFTWARE IN TERMS OF ITS CORRECTNESS, ACCURACY, RELIABIL-ITY, CURRENTNESS, OR OTHERWISE.

IN NO EVENT, SHALL THE COMPANY OR ITS EMPLOYEES, AGENTS, SUPPLIERS, OR CON-TRACTORS BE LIABLE FOR ANY INCIDENTAL, INDIRECT, SPECIAL, OR CONSEQUENTIAL DAMAGES ARISING OUT OF OR IN CONNECTION WITH THE LICENSE GRANTED UNDER THIS AGREEMENT, OR FOR LOSS OF USE, LOSS OF DATA, LOSS OF INCOME OR PROFIT, OR OTHER LOSSES, SUSTAINED AS A RESULT OF INJURY TO ANY PERSON, OR LOSS OF OR DAMAGE TO PROPERTY, OR CLAIMS OF THIRD PARTIES, EVEN IF THE COMPANY OR AN AUTHORIZED REPRESENTATIVE OF THE COMPANY HAS BEEN ADVISED OF THE POSSIBILITY OF SUCH DAMAGES. IN NO EVENT SHALL LIABILITY OF THE COMPANY FOR DAMAGES WITH RESPECT TO THE SOFTWARE EXCEED THE AMOUNTS ACTU-ALLY PAID BY YOU, IF ANY, FOR THE SOFTWARE.

SOME JURISDICTIONS DO NOT ALLOW THE LIMITATION OF IMPLIED WARRANTIES OR LIABILITY FOR INCIDENTAL, INDIRECT, SPECIAL, OR CONSEQUENTIAL DAMAGES, SO THE ABOVE LIMITATIONS MAY NOT ALWAYS APPLY. THE WARRANTIES IN THIS AGREEMENT GIVE YOU SPE-CIFIC LEGAL RIGHTS AND YOU MAY ALSO HAVE OTHER RIGHTS WHICH VARY IN ACCORDANCE WITH LOCAL LAW.

ACKNOWLEDGMENT

YOU ACKNOWLEDGE THAT YOU HAVE READ THIS AGREEMENT, UNDERSTAND IT, AND AGREE TO BE BOUND BY ITS TERMS AND CONDITIONS. YOU ALSO AGREE THAT THIS AGREEMENT IS THE COMPLETE AND EXCLUSIVE STATEMENT OF THE AGREEMENT BETWEEN YOU AND THE COMPANY AND SUPERSEDES ALL PROPOSALS OR PRIOR AGREEMENTS, ORAL, OR WRITTEN, AND ANY OTHER COMMUNICATIONS BETWEEN YOU AND THE COMPANY OR ANY REPRESENTATIVE OF THE COMPANY RELATING TO THE SUBJECT MATTER OF THIS AGREEMENT.

Should you have any questions concerning this Agreement or if you wish to contact the Company for any reason, please contact in writing at the address below.

Robin Short
Prentice Hall PTR
One Lake Street
Upper Saddle River, New Jersey 07458